HC441 POL

The Political Economy of

SOUTH-EAST ASIA

Markets, power and contestation

THIRD EDITION

Heat w/ hairdryer to erase this ink

Edited by
Garry Rodan,
Kevin Hewison and
Richard Robison

WITHDRAWN
FROM STOCK
QMUL LIBRARY

OXFORD
UNIVERSITY PRESS

253 Normanby Road, South Melbourne, Victoria 3205, Australia

Oxford University Press is a department of the University of Oxford.
It furthers the University's objective of excellence in research, scholarship, and education by publishing worldwide in

Oxford New York

Auckland Cape Town Dar es Salaam Hong Kong Karachi
Kuala Lumpur Madrid Melbourne Mexico City Nairobi
New Delhi Shanghai Taipei Toronto

With offices in

Argentina Austria Brazil Chile Czech Republic France Greece
Guatemala Hungary Italy Japan Poland Portugal Singapore
South Korea Switzerland Thailand Turkey Ukraine Vietnam

OXFORD is a trade mark of Oxford University Press
in the UK and in certain other countries

Copyright © Garry Rodan, Kevin Hewison and Richard Robison 2006
First published 1997
Reprinted 1998, 1999
Second edition published 2001
Reprinted 2002
Third edition published 2006

This book is copyright. Apart from any fair dealing for the purposes of private study, research, criticism or review as permitted under the Copyright Act, no part may be reproduced, stored in a retrieval system, or transmitted, in any form or by any means, electronic, mechanical, photocopying, recording or otherwise without prior written permission. Enquiries to be made to Oxford University Press.

Copying for educational purposes

Where copies of part or the whole of the book are made under Part VB of the Copyright Act, the law requires that prescribed procedures be followed. For information, contact the Copyright Agency Limited.

National Library of Australia
Cataloguing-in-Publication data:

The political economy of South-East Asia : markets, power and contestation.

3rd ed.
Bibliography.
Includes index.
ISBN 9 78019551 7583.

1. Globalisation. 2. Southeast Asia—Economic conditions. 3. Southeast Asia—Economic policy. 4. Southeast Asia—Politics and government. 5. Southeast Asia—Foreign economic relations. I. Rodan, Garry, 1955–. II. Hewson, Kevin J. III Robison, Richard, 1943-.
330.959053

Typeset by Mason Design
Printed in Hong Kong by Sheck Wah Tong Printing Press Ltd

CONTENTS

TABLES AND FIGURES

TABLES

FIGURES

CONTRIBUTORS

Mark Beeson is Senior Lecturer in the School of Political Science and International Studies at the University of Queensland, Brisbane, Australia

Melanie Beresford is Associate Professor and Associate Dean of Research in the Division of Economic and Financial Studies at Macquarie University, Sydney, Australia

Shaun Breslin is Professor of Politics and International Studies and Associate Fellow, Centre for the Study of Globalisation and Regionalisation, University of Warwick, Coventry, United Kingdom

Frederic C. Deyo is Professor of Sociology and Director of Undergraduate Studies at State University of New York, Binghamton, USA and Honorary Professor, Centre for Development Studies, University of Auckland, Auckland, New Zealand

Jim Glassman is Assistant Professor in the Department of Geography, University of British Columbia, Vancouver, Canada

Khoo Boo Teik is Associate Professor in the School of Social Sciences, Universiti Sains Malaysia, Penang, Malaysia

Vedi R Hadiz is Associate Professor in the Department of Sociology at National University of Singapore, Singapore

Kevin Hewison is Director of the Carolina Asia Center and Professor in the Department of Asian Studies at University of North Carolina at Chapel Hill, USA

Jane Hutchison is Lecturer in the Politics and International Studies Program and a Fellow of the Asia Research Centre, Murdoch University, Perth, Australia

Kanishka Jayasuriya is Principal Senior Research Fellow at the Asia Research Centre, Murdoch University, Perth, Australia

Richard Robison is Professor of Political Economy at the Institute of Social Studies, The Hague, Netherlands

Garry Rodan is Director of the Asia Research Centre and Professor of Politics and International Studies, Murdoch University, Perth, Australia

Andrew Rosser is Research Fellow at the Institute of Development Studies at the University of Sussex, Brighton, United Kingdom

PREFACE

This is the third edition of *The Political Economy of Southeast Asia.* As do the previous two, this edition addresses an important phase in the ever-changing social, political, and economic landscape of South-East Asia and seeks to explain the larger meaning of the dynamics involved in terms of the latest comparative theoretical debates about change and conflict. In 1996, as we completed the first edition of *The Political Economy of South-East Asia*, many of the countries of the region were undergoing remarkable transformations, spurred on by a decade-long economic boom. Enthusiasm for an Asian development approach was at its peak and the region was hailed as a model for other developing countries. Some of the political rulers within the region even proclaimed the end of liberal orthodoxies and the triumph of an Asian model of development.

How rapidly things changed. By the time of the second edition in 2001, the region was embroiled in turmoil and conflict. Following the 1997–98 economic crisis, the political and economic elites that had long dominated in the region faced considerable challenges. Powerful business groups, for example, that had formerly flourished on the basis of rising investment flows and ever-larger access to global financial markets now found themselves scrambling to protect their assets from creditors and to hold off bankruptcy. Several of the region's governments also found themselves under siege. Political volatility in Thailand saw a government fall soon after the economic crisis hit. At the same time, there developed a groundswell of popular opposition to the neoliberal reforms sponsored by international financial institutions. In Malaysia, the crisis precipitated a major rift within the ruling coalition. This manifested itself not only in competing economic policy ideas, but also in a remarkable resurgence of political opposition and activism. In Indonesia, in addition to the demise of the long-standing New Order regime, the whole framework of economic and corporate power upon which it had rested was thrown into disarray.

By 2005, with the writing of the third edition, contestation over political and economic power entered a new phase. While the immediate problems of economic recovery, political reorganisation, and stabilisation of business and investment were, to varying degrees, ameliorated, new questions arose. What kinds of regimes would emerge from the new political and economic dynamics at work in the region? Would this involve qualitatively new amalgams of political and economic power or merely refinements and reconsolidations of existing ones? And how would new regimes contrast with established liberal political and economic regimes elsewhere? The chapters in the new edition take seriously the task of analysing contestion over the shape and control of markets and political power ensuing from this dynamic process. It is the premise of this volume that the continuing conflict over the complexion of economic and political regimes is driven by dynamic and competing coalitions of interest. In identifying and analysing these forces and conflicts, the chapters in this volume examine their national and international dimensions.

In Singapore, for example, we see unprecedented critical international scrutiny of the opaque practices of government-linked companies. Elements of the international business community have focused attention on the impediments domestic regulatory regimes pose for open markets, some of which the Singapore government has moved to accommodate. By contrast, in Thailand, international demands for regulatory reform were met by opposition, led by domestic capitalists. Weakened by the economic crisis, these capitalists successfully entered the political arena to oppose and moderate the pace of change.

These examples highlight a broader feature of post-economic crisis responses. International pressures for change are mediated by domestic forces and coalitions, resulting in varied responses in each country in the region. This applies to both political and economic regimes. Indeed, far from there being a uniform—if incremental—shift towards economic and political liberalism, we continue to see a range of directions that deviate from the historical experience of advanced capitalist countries.

As shown in a number of this edition's chapters, the mediation of the domestic and international has recently been influenced by the new geopolitical realities that have followed the events of 11 September 2001 and the resultant 'war on terror'. In particular, as was the case in the Cold War period, there is new scope for authoritarian leaders to exploit security concerns to bolster or preserve constraints on political opposition and civil society. This is one element in the lastest phase of contestation associated with the attempt to further embed capitalist market systems in the region.

The important point is that the precise form of markets is politically constructed. In the region, we thus see attempts by competing interests and coalitions to harness the power of the state to ensure their protection and advancement through market systems. The third edition recognises the dynamism of the international and domestic contexts. It attempts to reflect on and evaluate the various conflicts that emerged following the economic crisis and assesses how these conflicts have since matured, been resolved, or been exacerbated.

The previous volume asked whether the crisis had signalled the end of Asian models of political and economic organisation and confirmed the inevitability of a convergence towards liberal markets and democracy. Would Asian capitalisms inevitably come to resemble Anglo-American capitalisms and were South-East Asian institutions incapable of coping with the crisis? This volume considers the proposition that the advance of market capitalism may, indeed, be forged within varying and often illiberal amalgams of political and economic institutions. These range from the highly effective amalgam of markets and authoritarian politics in Singapore, to the populist social contracts that underpin a more centralised form of parliamentary rule in Thailand, and the ongoing struggle in the Philippines between the tendencies of centralised populism, manifested in the Estrada presidency and the more entrenched clientelist oligarchy represented by mainstream politics.

We are forced to ask whether Malaysia is, indeed, making a transition from the tightening grip of political and business oligarchies that were consolidated under Mahathir to a more liberal regime under Badawi and whether Singapore's amalgam of state and market capitalism is sustainable. In Indonesia we must consider the apparent paradox of a reorganisation of many of the old political and economic relationships within new institutions of markets and parliaments. We must ask how the social contracts of Thaksin are embedded and whether they are sustainable. These questions and interests lead to other important considerations, one being theoretical and the other being connected to the changing framework of global power within which the region now operates.

Theoretically, we must consider how the various models of authoritarianism, or democracies based on populism, social contracts, and clientelism that have emerged can be reconciled with market economies and the changing global order within which they are now located. Are these a last ditch stand by various rent-seeking or predatory interests against rational individuals or state technopols who seek the sorts of common welfare benefits found in markets? Or do they represent the triumph of much broader coalitions of illiberal interest who have harnessed the market to their ends? Does change and reform emerge from policy and institutional fixes that isolate and neutralise predatory interests or from the formation of powerful liberal coalitions able to capture the state? Lurking under all of this is the issue of whether markets really do go together with liberal politics in all situations or are regimes of technomanagerial authority or populist social contracts able to provide more effective synergies?

In the complex dynamics that are critical to the future of the region, we see nationalism, money politics, and constitutions playing roles. So, too, do international organisations, big business, foreign investors, small farmers, workers, and a range of intellectuals and non-governmental organisations.

The vocabularies of openness, rules, good governance, and transparency compete with the language of money, influence, collusion, corruption, and nepotism. These discourses reflect wider political and economic competition; one of the defining features of the current situation is related to the way larger changes in global power are influencing the region.

One of the new global influences came in the form of a push for increased neoliberal reform, transparency, and good governance reinforced by the position of the International Monetary Fund (IMF) as the financier of recovery in some countries and the new leverage given to international investors and banks as many countries sought to attract new capital in an atmosphere of suspicion and doubt. Calls for democracy and the development of civil society had became stronger, coinciding with neoliberal strategies for reform and development in the economic sphere. Yet criticisms of the IMF's approach to reform saw calls for a new international financial architecture that extended beyond South-East Asia. The response of the international financial institutions and Anglo-American capitalisms saw the development of a post-Washington Consensus that reoriented the agendas of many development organisations around the issues of institution-building, good governance, participation, and transparency. The political implications of many of these issues have been especially noticeable in Indonesia and Thailand, but have not been insignificant in the other countries of the region.

A central question is, therefore, how can this apparent strengthening of neoliberal power be reconciled with the seeming consolidation of various illiberal amalgams of state and markets in the regions? On the one hand, we explore the idea that neoliberalism itself may be more ambivalent about democracy than supposed and that global investors may be less wary of illiberal regimes, providing they are stable and predictable. At another level, we address some developments that may be either consolidating or diminishing American ascendancy and thereby influencing the strength of the neoliberal push. One factor is, of course, the new importance of terrorism as an issue. We ask whether terrorism forces the US to consider its strategic interests over liberal market principles, offering new opportunities to various illiberal regimes within the American economic umbrella. Another factor is the prospect of regional cooperation in which China potentially plays a leading role. To what extent is this a realistic model for the future, offering new opportunities to illiberal state-market amalgams and to what extent is this offset by the spread of international institutions such as the World Trade Organization (WTO) or the proliferation of bilateral trade agreements between the US and the countries of the region?

THE CHAPTERS

The importance of these issues and the reassessment they have caused mean that the present collection has undergone such extensive revisions as to be essentially new. In the chapters of this volume, we begin with an analysis of the different political economy approaches to understanding the relationship between markets and politics in South-East Asia: neoclassical political economy, historical institutionalism, and social conflict theory. The neoclassical theorists' abstract and technical conception of markets is distinguished from the historical institutionalist notion of markets as social institutions with an historical basis. The depiction of markets and the institutions that define them as the product of wider and system-level processes of social and political conflict contrasts social conflict theory with both these approaches. Garry Rodan, Kevin Hewison, and Richard Robison adopt this third approach in a critical evaluation of the competing explanations that the three approaches offer for the various phases in South-East Asian development. As the chapter's title indicates, for these authors, the recurring dynamic shaping the establishment, development, and nature of market systems in the region has involved the exercise of power and contestation over its use.

In the subsequent chapters of this volume, we begin with a series of country studies to examine processes of development in detail. This is followed by more thematic and comparative studies examining such issues as the implications of US foreign policy and the war on terrorism, economic liberalisation in the wake of the Asian crisis, labour–state relations, the significance of international financial institutions, and the relationship between China's development and the political economy of South-East Asia. Careful readers will detect that the contributions to this book evidence a degree of theoretical heterodoxy. Although all authors reject the orthodox economic approach, it is notable that they all take seriously the insights of the historical institutionalists. However, there is also a generalised critique of this approach along the lines set out above. Each of the contributors looks to place considerable emphasis on the social, political, and economic forces at work—and conflicts therein—in explaining boom, bust, recovery, and the geopolitics of the war on terror.

Jane Hutchison explains in chapter 2 that political crises and disappointing economic performance in the Philippines—as evident in sustained, widespread poverty and inequality—are often explained by weak state capacities arising from the particularistic demands of a wealthy elite on key institutions. However, she also points out that this historical institutionalist approach can obscure other important aspects of social and political contestation arising from capitalist development and the restoration of formal democracy in the late 1980s. To the degree that historical institutionalists stress the continuities in patronage politics, they can miss some important changes in the nature and sources of elite power with globalisation that underline the elite's capacity to survive and prosper in a more liberal market environment. The restoration of formal democracy is often said to have reproduced the institutional conditions for continued elite dominance, but as well it has stimulated the activism of an array of marginalised interests and sectors in civil society. Hutchison argues that while these forces are opposed to the elite, it is clear that they are not always united in their engagements with the state. The people power that overthrew the authoritarian Marcos regime in 1986 has more lately revealed political frictions between the poor and middle class, most obviously over the ousting of President Joseph Estrada and the attempted consolidation of his successor, Gloria Macapagal Aroyo, thereafter. In this environment, it is argued, the US-led war on terror will likely consolidate the weak state by strengthening the hand of forces resistant to institutional and political reforms to curb corruption and human rights abuses and to enhance processes of more representative politics.

In chapter 3, Kevin Hewison underlines the periodic nature of crisis. He argues that Thailand's capitalist development has been punctuated by crises that herald the emergence of new accumulation regimes. However, the 1997–98 crisis was especially significant as it precipitated a new phase of social competition and conflict. First, pressure for intensified neoliberal reform in the teeth of an acute recession severely compounded the problems for the poorest sections of the Thai population, and brought with it the potential for considerable social conflict. Second, a broad-based social movement emerged to oppose the IMF's prescriptions. Third, domestic business recognised the threat neoliberal reform posed to their interests and responded vigorously. It was out of this context that the Thai Rak Thai (TRT) Party was established in 1998 and triumphed at the 2001 polls. In effect, argues Hewison, through the TRT under the leadership of local business tycoon Thaksin Shinawatra, the restructured domestic capitalist class has taken direct control of the state for the first time in Thailand's history. Hitherto fractious domestic interests coalesced around Thaksin with the aim of restoring their competitiveness in the face of foreign challenges. The TRT embarked on a populist electoral platform to woo rural voters with assorted programs that were a nationalist trade-off or new social contract. The party of big domestic business promised increased social protection and economic opportunities for the relatively poor majority of the population in return for electoral support and the opportunity to recover, free from immediate neoliberal demands for further liberalisation. In other words, domestic business has used state power to regain its strength. This protection means that it is now in a better position as competition returns and further economic restructuring is possible.

In their analysis of Indonesia in chapter 4, Richard Robision and Vedi Hadiz also draw attention to the particular nature of contemporary conflict associated with capitalism. Although precipitated by panic and speculation in global capital markets, the dramatic unravelling of Indonesia's economic and political regimes after 1997, they argue, is rooted in a specific pathology of power and interest. The very predatory arrangements that made rapid economic growth possible, and constituted the cement of a seemingly invulnerable power structure, were also the seeds of its destruction, producing huge private-sector debt and overinvestment. The crisis was a watershed because it fractured the alliances underpinning the regime. In the struggle to carve out new economic regimes, a cohesive coalition that will drive a coherent reform agenda is yet to take shape. In particular, despite active encouragement by the IMF and the World Bank, there has been no effective coalition mobilised behind a neoliberal project. Moreover, old politico–business alliances have also proven adept at maintaining their ascendancy within new institutional frameworks. Established power relations have been reproduced through a new system of parties, parliaments, and elections, ensuring that interests that were central to the New Order remain influential. Indeed, far from these institutions transforming Indonesia inexorably towards a fully-fledged liberal democracy, entrenched interests have politically reorganised themselves to effectively pre-empt any serious challenge to the underlying nature of state power from which they benefit.

Against the background of rising expectations in recent years of a reduced economic role for the state in Singapore, Garry Rodan submits in chapter 5 a different view. He emphasises the continuing centrality of the state in Singapore's economic development, but argues that the precise form of this role is very definitely in transition. This is tied to a new phase in capital accumulation that entails a fuller official embrace of internationalisation and promotion of the so-called knowledge economy—a direction that has gathered momentum since the Asian crisis struck. In the process, the state is instituting corporate governance reforms and opening up more of the domestic economy to foreign competition. Crucially, Rodan locates the economic and political interests of the People's Action Party (PAP) as integral to this direction. Indeed, he points to new tensions in the PAP's attempt to reconcile state capitalism with neoliberal globalisation as Singapore's economic governance regimes come in for growing critical scrutiny by elements of international capital. Rodan also draws out the various conflicts arising from the economic restructuring process, including rising material inequalities and reforms to increase labour market flexibility—and their political implications.

Khoo Boo Teik's analysis of Malaysia in chapter 6 demonstrates how extensive state economic intervention has been intricately related to a political agenda of social engineering, and one that has given expression at various times to open conflict. Khoo rejects the popular portrayal of conflict as fundamentally ethnic and argues, instead, that such tensions 'encompass class conflicts, the emergence of Malay capital, rise and decline of bureaucratic interests, politicisation of business, aggrandisement of powerful conglomerates, and promotion of economic nationalism'. Yet if the contemporary Malaysian political economy is essentially characterised by a continuing power structure divided among the interests of the state, foreign capital, and domestic capital, Khoo nevertheless discerns important changes afoot. The freedom of manoeuvre by the state is being curtailed to some extent as the importance of foreign direct investment declines relative to that of mobile global finance and speculative capital. Bumiputera commercial and industrial conglomerates have also emerged alongside traditional ethnic Chinese capital.

The dynamic relations among these three centres of power will chart Malaysia's future.

In chapter 7, Melanie Beresford's focus is on Vietnam—a case of transition from a planned to a market economy, which formally began with Doi Moi (Renovation) in 1986. This is a transition born out of coalitions between the political leaders and interests standing to benefit from the reforms. However, the trajectory of the Vietnamese political economy is unlikely to see a wholesale shift towards a conventional capitalist economy. Rather, state business interests will remain a powerful brake on the establishment of an economy that is founded primarily on private property. Concern within the party and bureaucracy about the potential for private capital interests to develop a power base for opposition parties acts as another moderating influence.

Jim Glassman begins the series of thematic and comparative chapters with his analysis of US foreign policy and the war on terrorism in South-East Asia in chapter 8. He argues that the concept of imperialism is not without utility here, although he emphasises that 'it has to be interpreted in ways that allow for the recognition of both social conflicts within states and transnational collaboration between different elites across state boundaries'. It is proposed that forms of imperialism change in accordance with the uneven development of capitalism and in the post-Cold War context of South-East Asia this has meant that Asian elites are less likely today to accommodate US projects that are not clearly perceived to be in their own interests. According to Glassman, the war on terrorism not only provides the impetus for more concerted US military and security interests in the region, but it also provides opportunities for South-East Asian elites 'to repackage—and gain leverage in—a variety of domestic struggles'. This Glassman illustrates via analyses of the Philippines, Indonesia, and Thailand, where, in different ways and with different emphases, elites have harnessed the US-led war on terrorism to obstruct forces for democratic change and other challenges to elite power.

Extending the theme of US hegemony and its significance for South-East Asia, in chapter 9 Mark Beeson takes up the specific issue of the influence of international financial institutions (IFIs), notably the World Bank and the International Monetary Fund. IFIs, Beeson contends, have 'frequently acted as an extension of US foreign policy', the contemporary expression of which is their endeavour to promote governance regimes and policies in South-East Asia along neoliberal capitalist lines. In examining the different phases of IFI influence on the region's development, Beeson acknowledges points by Glassman and others in this volume about the various domestic factors mediating external influences. However, he emphasises that the 'US is no longer as prepared as it once was to ignore political practices of which it does not approve, and neither are the IFIs'. This is occurring in a context of increasing worldwide critical scrutiny of the role of IFIs, as well as a South-East Asian context of growing interest in developing independent regional institutional infrastructure to manage the structural pressures of globalisation more effectively. Yet, for Beeson, 'the influence of some form of augmented Washington consensus looks likely to continue'.

Kanishka Jayasuriya and Andrew Rosser analyse the differential progress towards economic liberalisation after the Asian crisis in Malaysia, Singapore, Thailand, and Indonesia in chapter 10. They argue that these variances are a function of contrasting domestic political and social variables, institutional capacities, and the extent to which the crisis has shifted the balance of power among coalitions of interest. The strong resonances across these countries' development strategies during the boom years, characterised by interventionist states, have diminished since the crisis. According to Jayasuriya and Rosser, the pattern of reform in Thailand has entailed two phases. In the immediate post-crisis period, when the Democrats were in power, there was a full embrace of neoliberal reform. Subsequently, though, a nationalist and populist agenda has prevailed that has diluted but not completely replaced neoliberal reform programs. By contrast, little economic reform liberalisation at all has materialised in Indonesia. Meanwhile, an official nationalist backlash has been evident in Malaysia as has a policy of offensive adjustment, rather than wholesale winding back of state intervention. In Singapore, selective economic liberalisation has been accompanied by new institutional frameworks of economic governance, a development that is related to emerging tensions and contradictions within and between various state apparatuses. Crucially, Jayasuriya and Rosser emphasise that the differential responses of states in the region to the pressures of neoliberal globalisation are not simply reflective of dynamics in relations between interests, coalitions, and groups on the one hand, and the state on the other. Rather, it is the relocation of power within the state that is at work. In other words, it is only by understanding transformations in the complex relationships embodied in the state that we can explain the varying trajectories of economic reform in South-East Asia.

In chapter 11, Frederic Deyo investigates the implications for labour of sustained industrialisation in South-East Asia. Deyo identifies the growing global influence of neoliberal ideas and the adoption of more flexible post-Fordist production systems as crucial dynamics. The net effect of these has been to limit the capacity of enlarged working classes to significantly enhance their political and organisational strength. Instead, elite strategies of industrial management are being consolidated—a pattern not fundamentally altered by the effects of the Asian economic crisis. Deyo argues that it is precisely the continued exclusion of the popular sector from politics that fosters a measure of tolerance by elites for parliamentary institutions. The price of this is, however, potential political instability in the long term, which might even include hostility from within the masses towards democratic institutions that are perceived as mechanisms of exclusion by the elites.

Production is also Shaun Breslin's focus in the final chapter with his analysis of the changing relationship between China and South-East Asia. In particular, Breslin emphasises that regional economic relations with China are conditioned by the way in which elements of the Chinese economy have been inserted into transnational, commodity-driven production networks. This approach departs significantly from purely bilateral understandings of international economic relations emanating from realist theory, steering attention instead towards consideration of how individual national economies, bilateral relations, and global forces influence regional production structures. Seen in this way, closer economic relations between China and South-East Asia are not simply a product of the rise of China. In addition to challenging such influential realist orthodoxy, Breslin also refutes culturalist interpretations that place fundamental emphasis on Chinese ethnic affinities in analysing China's development implications for the region.

Garry Rodan
Kevin Hewison
Richard Robison
September 2005

ACKNOWLEDGMENTS

The editors are most grateful to all the contributors for the quality of their involvement in this volume. Thanks also to Tamara Dent of the Asia Research Centre, Murdoch University, for her expertise in the production of the manuscript, and to Lucy McLoughlin of Oxford University Press for her strong support throughout all stages of the manuscript's preparation.

ABBREVIATIONS

ADB	Asian Development Bank
AEM	Asian economic model
AFP	Armed forces of the Philippines
AFTA	ASEAN Free Trade Agreement
AMP	Association of Muslim Professionals
APEC	Asia–Pacific Economic Cooperation
ASB	Amanah Saham Bumiputera
ASEAN	Association of South-East Asian Nations
ASG	Abu Sayyaf group
ASN	Amanah Saham Nasional
BI	Bank Indonesia (see also BLBI)
BLBI	Bantuan Likwiditi Bank Indonesia (see also BI)
BN	Barisan Nasional
BNM	Bank Negara Malaysia
BOI	Board of Investment
BPK	Supreme Audit Agency
BPKP	State Comptroller of Finance and Development
BPPC	Badan Penyangga dan Pemasaran Cengkeh
BS	Barisan Sosialis
C&W	Cable and Wireless
CAR	capital adequacy ratio
CBU	completely built up
CCP	Chinese Communist Party
CDRAC	Corporate Debt Restructuring Advisory Committee
CDRC	Corporate Debt Restructuring Committee
CEO	chief executive officer
CFB	Chinese Family Business
CFR	Council on Foreign Relations

CIA	Central Intelligence Agency
COLT	Commercial Offshore Loan Team
CPF	Central Provident Fund
CPP	Communist Party of the Philippines
CSI	Coalition of Service Industries
DAP	Democratic Action Party
DBS	Development Bank of Singapore
DFI	direct foreign investment
DRV	Democratic Republic of Vietnam
EAEC	East Asian Economic Caucus
EDAS	Economic Development Assistance Scheme
EDB	Economic Development Board
EOI	export-oriented industrialisation
EPZ	export processing zone
ERC	Economic Review Committee
FDI	foreign direct investment
FTA	free trade agreement
FYP	five-year plan(s)
GAM	Gerakan Aceh Merdeka
GATT	General Agreement on Tarriffs and Trade
GDP	gross domestic product
GIC	Government of Singapore Investment Corporation
GLC	government-linked company
GNP	gross national product
GSP	generalised system of preferences
HDB	Housing Development Board
HICOM	Heavy Industries Corporation of Malaysia
IAC	International Advisory Council
IAS	International Accountancy Standards
IBRA	Indonesian Banking Restructuring Agency
IBRD	International Bank for Reconstruction and Development
ICA	Industrial Coordination Act
ICG	International Crisis Group
IDA	Infocom Development Authority
IFI	international financial institutions
ILO	International Labour Organization (or Office)
IMF	International Monetary Fund
INTECH	Initiative for New Technology

IPE	international political economy
IPTN	Industri Pesawat Terbang Nusantara
ISI	import-substitution industrialisation
IT	information technology
JI	Jema'ah Islamiyah
JTC	Jurong Town Corporation
K-Economy	Knowledge-based Economy
KLSE	Kuala Lumpur Stock Exchange
KMT	Kuomintang
LLC	local leased circuits
LLL	legal lending limits
MARA	Majelis Amanah Rakyat
MAS	Monetary Authority of Singapore
MCP	Malay Communist Party
MCA	Malayan Chinese Association
MDAS	Manpower Development Assistance Scheme
MIC	Malayan Indian Congress
MICCI	Malaysian International Chamber of Commerce and Industry
MILF	Moro Islamic Liberation Front
MIT	Massachusetts Institute of Technology
MITI	Ministry of International Trade and Industry
MNC	multinational corporation
MNLF	Moro National Liberation Front
MoF	Ministry of Finance
MSAA	Master Settlement and Acquisition Agreements
NDP	National Development Plan
NEAC	National Economic Action Council
NEP	New Economic Policy
NESDB	National Economic and Social Development Board
NGO	non-government organisation
NIC	newly industrialised (or industrialising) country
NMP	nominated members of parliament
NLF	National Front for the Liberation of Southern Vietnam
NOC	National Operations Council
NOL	Neptune Orient Lines
NPA	New People's Army
NPLs	non-performing loans
NSTB	National Science and Technology Board

NTUC	National Trades Union Congress
NWC	National Wages Council
OCBC	Overseas Chinese Banking Corporation
ODA	official development assistance (or overseas development aid)
OHQ	operational headquarters
PAP	People's Action Party
PAS	Parti Islam SeMalaysia
PERNAS	Perbadanan Nasional
Petronas	Petroliam Nasional
PIEU	Pioneer Industries Employees' Union
PKI	Partai Komunis Indonesia
PLA	People's Liberation Army
PLN	Perusahaan Listrik Negara
PMIP	Pan-Malaysian Islamic Party
PNAC	Project for a New American Century
PNB	Permodalan Nasional Berhad
PRC	People's Republic of China
PSA	Port of Singapore Authority
PSB	Productivity and Standards Board
QFB	qualifying full banking
R&D	research and development
RBF	Regional Business Forum
RIDA	Rural and Industrial Development Authority
RVN	Republic of Vietnam
SARS	severe acute respiratory syndrome
SDP	Singapore Democratic Party
SEDC	state economic development corporation
SET	Stock Exchange of Thailand
SILO	Singapore Industrial Labour Organisation
SingTel	Singapore Telecommunications
SME	small and medium enterprises
SOBSI	Sentral Organisasi Buruh Seluruh Indonesia
SOE	state-owned enterprise
SPSI	Serikat Pekerja Seluruh Indonesia
SPH	Singapore Press Holding
STC	Singapore Technologies Corporation
TFP	total factor productivity
TNC	transnational corporation

TNI	Tentara Nasional Indonesia
TRT	Thai Rak Thai (Thai Love Thai)
TVE	Township and Village Enterprise
UDA	Urban Development Authority
UMNO	United Malays National Organization
UNCTAD	United Nations Conference on Trade and Development
USSFTA	United States–Singapore Free Trade Agreement
VAT	value added tax
WTO	World Trade Organization

1

Theorising Markets in South-East Asia: Power and Contestation

Garry Rodan, Kevin Hewison, and Richard Robison[1]

KEY TOPICS

INTRODUCTION

EXPLANATIONS of South-East Asia's recent development vary widely. This is especially the case for accounts of the processes of boom, bust, and recovery since the mid 1980s. In this chapter, we outline the ways in which different varieties of political economy explain South-East Asia's development. As we show, these approaches acknowledge some sort of relationship between the political and the economic; they all posit a relationship between politics and development. However, assumptions vary considerably about the nature and significance of politics, as well as the underlying dynamics of society and how this shapes the organisation of economic activity. This has profound implications for analysis and leads to dramatic contrasts in their respective assessments and policy prescriptions.

These approaches are, broadly, neoclassical political economy, historical institutional theory, and social conflict theory. Although they are unequally represented in the literature on South-East Asia, each is influential in similar debates on East Asia, Latin America, and/or Europe. We have been selective in developing these approaches for discussion. The point of this exercise is to show how political economy can be brought to bear on the study of South-East Asian development. In the process of this survey, we will argue that social conflict theory is the most illuminating. In the substantive accounts of development in South-East Asia provided in the subsequent chapters, readers will also observe that social conflict theory is a central theoretical influence.

After clarifying their essential features, we will systematically examine how these approaches explain the formative periods of development in South-East Asia, the subsequent economic boom in the region, and, ultimately, the 1997–98 Asian crisis and aftermath. The relative influence in academic and policy circles of each of these different approaches has waxed and waned over time. This can be explained partly by the way in which the course of development appeared to validate or challenge prevailing theory. The degree to which these approaches have resonated or clashed with other powerful ideas and interests is no less important in explaining their impact. These approaches, however, have not always dominated. Modernisation theory and, in turn, dependency theory, were at different times ascendant in the literature on South-East Asia before the mid 1970s. They have resurfaced periodically, plugging into the very debates of concern to political economists. We introduce them below when the economic boom is discussed and thereafter integrate them, where relevant, into the systematic survey of the different ways of accounting for South-East Asian development.

Finally, it should be appreciated that these approaches represent ideal type categories that are convenient and indicative for setting out important theoretical fault lines in political economy debates. Some writers will draw on aspects across these different approaches—not always in a coherent fashion. The value of these categories, however, is in setting out the essential choices for students adopting a political economy approach to the study of the region.

OUTLINING THE APPROACHES

Neoclassical political economy

In neoclassical economic theory, the principal preoccupation is with the functioning of markets. The concept of 'the market' is an abstracted notion that is not concerned with the social relationships that it embodies. The assumption is that markets are naturally and universally efficient mechanisms, driven by their own internal laws and the rational choices of individuals who seek to maximise their gains within them. This results in the most efficient allocation of resources and, in the long run, the greatest wealth for society as a whole. Good public policy is, therefore, that which gives full expression to the free operation of markets. Where this happens, development occurs; where it is obstructed, notably by state intervention, development suffers. It has been on this basis that international organisations such as the World Bank and the International Monetary Fund (IMF) have emphasised development strategies based on economic deregulation, privatisation, and fiscal austerity—the so-called 'Washington Consensus' that operated until the Asian economic crisis (Williamson 1994).

When market principles are extended as policy prescriptions for the general conduct of social life, neoclassical theory translates into neoliberal ideology. Quite often advocacy for free-market reforms consistent with neoclassical economic theory is driven by this general ideological disposition. At such points, the debate goes beyond functional or technical considerations. Neoliberal ideologues have a normative preference for market relations, which means that they think that these relations *should* be the basis of social activity. This is a statement about a preferred set of power relations and institutional forms.

Many neoclassical theorists are perplexed by the refusal of governments to choose the right market-enhancing policies; to the extent that they have an explanation for this, it rests on a particular notion of politics. Politics in this view is seen as a set of external factors hampering the natural functioning of markets. In particular, groups seeking to gain special advantages through the state, so-called rent-seekers, represent a political threat to efficient markets. Good public policy can therefore take one of two forms. First, it involves eliminating the interventions of the state in economic life, or minimising these interventions to a regulatory role. Second, and this is a recent concession made by such theorists in the face of apparent market failures, it means enhancing the capacity of the state to manage markets to insulate rent-seekers and distributional coalitions from a position of influence. In either case, the task of reform is to sweep away politics and entrench a state that provides sufficient regulation to allow the efficient operation of the market. Ironically, then, this approach recognises that a political process, however much otherwise eschewed, is required to remove obstacles to market efficiency. The assumption here is that effecting change is a matter of technical and policy choice. This view has profound implications. In effect, it suggests that democratic or representative politics can be an impediment to good policy development—a position that has, on occasions, been quite explicit from adherents to the neoclassical position, as we will see below.

Two important influences within the neoclassical camp are new institutional economics and public choice theory. New institutional economists argue that individuals create institutions to overcome transaction costs. Development, they maintain, requires solutions to collective problems through general systems of rules and regulation; that is, institutions (North 1981, 1994, 1995). However, expectations that this would take place as rational individuals spontaneously aggregated to solve collective-action dilemmas were not to be realised. Instead, individuals generally preferred to seek their interests in rents. Public choice theorists understood this. They saw the roots of the problem lying in the state. In public choice theory, the political sphere was conceptualised as a marketplace of transactions among individual politicians, officials, and contending interest lobbies. Its product was the appropriation and sale of public policy and public goods in return for political support. The predatory interests of political leaders were seen to lock them frequently into a pattern of rule aimed at keeping contending interests satisfied, ruining the economy in the process (see Bates 1981).[2] At another level, the state itself was seen to have interests in accumulating ever-increasing revenues (Krueger 1974; Lal 1983; Buchanan & Tullock 1962). Such perspectives reinforced the neoclassical theme that there was a struggle between economics and politics.[3] But it also identified the solution as one of constraining the state if predatory behaviour was to be restricted.

However, the weakness of the public choice argument was demonstrated by what followed the collapse of the state in Russia in the late 1980s: chaos, collusion, gangsterism, and widespread market failure. From this point, new institutionalist economists began to look increasingly to the state to enforce rules and regulations to safeguard the operations of the market.

What all neoclassical theorists share, however, is an abstract notion of markets and a belief that they are inherently efficient. Differences centre around the precise way this is best realised. Importantly, there is general agreement that marginalising politics from the policy process will help liberate markets. In that sense, all neoclassical theorists understand development as a technical question of how best to unleash the positive forces of markets. As we will see below, historical institutionalist and social conflict theorists in particular have, in their different ways, challenged this understanding of markets and politics.

Historical institutionalism

New institutionalism emerged as a reaction against both behaviouralist and pluralist approaches. In turn, historical institutionalism is distinguished from rational choice economic institutionalism by its interpretations of rationality and preferences that produce different approaches to markets and politics. Whereas rational choice theorists see constraints on rational political actors and value individual agency, historical institutionalists prefer to see actors' choices, interests, and preferences shaped by collective organisations and institutions that carry their own histories and rules, laws, norms, and ideas. Rather than viewing actors as rational, historical institutionalists tend to see them as self-reflective. Much of their theoretical heritage is in the works of Max Weber (Immergut 1998; Thelen & Steinmo 1992).

For the purposes of this chapter, two broad trends in historical institutionalism—an application that is state-centred and one that is more society-centred—can be identified.[4] Rapid growth in East Asia prompted statist historical institutionalists to emphasise the significance of state capacity for development—public institutions with an organisational form that enabled the making and implementation of effective policy. As we have seen, the importance of institutions was also taken up within the neoclassical camp, but historical institutionalists emphasised that institutional forms are derived from historically evolved pathways.[5] The form of the state resulting from such contrasting histories could generate varied forms of capitalism. In other words, the state-centred historical institutionalists' view is that capitalism can advance within *various* institutional frameworks, of which liberal capitalism is but one. This contrasts with the neoclassical prescriptions for institution-building, cautioning against both the desirability and feasibility of attempts to impose liberal arrangements against the historical grain.

These theorists emphasise that the state (and its institutions) played a pivotal role among late-industrialising countries. This perspective is based on an appreciation of a common structural predicament facing late-industrialising economies, namely the need to amass large concentrations of investment capital and to make strategic inroads into established global markets (Amsden 1989; Johnson 1982; Zysman 1994). Such experiences have involved state officials in crucial, positive roles as developmental elites. In this account, markets are not abstract entities but are largely constructed by developmental elites. They make their calculations, however, within specific historical pathways defined by previous layers of institutions embedded in structures of social power and culture (Johnson 1989; Zysman et al. 1994).

After the earlier emphasis on insulation from vested interests as necessary for development, state-centred historical institutionalists argued that developmental elites needed to forge coalitions with dominant forces in business (Evans 1992, 1995). This was an implicit endorsement of politics. However, they shared the neoclassical theorists' concern about influences that could subvert the institutional rationality of the state. Such influences are best excluded through an 'embedding' of institutional autonomy. Development thus requires that the state adopt a distinctive organisational logic, one that contrasts with the logic of the unfettered market. In this way, national—rather than private, market-oriented—developmental goals can be pursued. So, although markets might be seen as constructions of politics, there are definitely preferred state forms. This often sees the introduction of Weberian notions regarding the potential for elites to transform society and economy, together with a view of the policy processes of developmental states in terms of rational action rather than as reflective of broader and deeper political processes.

Society-centred historical institutionalists agreed, but argued that a focus on the role of one or two institutions in development—state and market—drew attention away from an ensemble of non-state and non-market institutions that played important roles in economic success. These included banks, commercial networks, and business associations (Doner & Ramsey 1997). According to Doner and Hawes (1995:168–9), in South-East Asian economies dynamic private sectors were more significant than states. The state was still important but, whereas East Asia displayed relatively strong developmental states, in South-East Asia private institutions have been strong, with states having been relatively weaker. The more constructivist approach taken by historical institutionalists has been useful. The notion of 'historical pathways' and the abiding interests of the state appear helpful in providing explanations for continuity. By focusing on institutions, historical institutionalists identify a concept that allows for a powerful examination of an intersection where structure and agency meet past and present (Katznelson 1998:196). It is also noticeable that society-centred historical institutionalists have, in attempting to address change, given considerable attention to the political and conflictual construction of interests (Immergut 1998:20–2). State-centred analysts tended to miss or downplay the complexity of interests involved in state-led development strategies, and of the relations between and within state and society that sustain state-led strategies. Society-centred analysts recognise that these are significant, and tend to define institutions as sites that mediate system-level structures (Thelen & Steinmo 1992:10–12).

Despite these advances, historical institutionalism exhibits a number of shortcomings. First, its concentration on intermediate 'variables' means that system-level structures are left unexplained (Katznelson 1998:196). For all of the competition, complexity, and historical contingency involved in the development and progress of institutions, it must be recognised that the interplay of social relations, power, and politics necessarily goes beyond institutions and the positions held in them by particular actors (Immergut 1998:28). Second, historical institutionalism, in focusing on constraints on institutional change ('stickiness'), emphasises order rather than change (see Peters 1999:68–71).[6] When change is examined, these analysts are concerned principally with addressing change within and as a result of institutions. Third, and related, these analysts tend to engage in institutional determinism (Thelen & Steinmo 1992:16). This is clearest in statist approaches, where developmental states are presented as being insulated from interests and political conflict. Further, for all of their emphasis on interests, historical institutionalists seldom address the interests at work in the development of capitalism.

Social conflict theory

According to social conflict theorists, markets and the institutions that define them are forged within wider and system-level processes of social and political conflict (Hewison et al. 1993; Chaudhry 1994, 1997). This approach is thus concerned to delineate the patterns of power that produce particular institutional, political, and social outcomes. It rejects abstract notions of markets, which are seen to mask the power relations that define the economic and political regimes within which they operate, and the social conflicts associated with their establishment and reproduction. Institutions, then, are not just about efficiency. Markets cannot be understood apart from the power relationships and institutions in which they are located. They are not natural. This applies to liberal markets, no less than to state-led or any other market systems.

The point of the analytical exercise, therefore, is not to uncover the magic responsible for market growth. Instead, it is to explain the particular structure of the power and politics accounting for the form and extent of Asian development. So social conflict theorists focus analytical attention on the different *but competing* interests that structure the development, spread, and enforcement of capitalist markets (see Panitch & Leys 1999). This assists in understanding how policy and institutional transformation take place within broader patterns of social and political power. These analysts thus look to system-level conflict when explaining how it is that particular institutions are arranged, maintained, and changed.

Existing regimes therefore cannot be dismantled at will because they embody a specific arrangement of economic, social, and political power. Institutions that might appear dysfunctional for growth and investment often persist because elites are prepared to sacrifice efficiency where their social and political ascendancy is threatened (see Badhan 1989). Equally, however, these dominant forces might embrace 'reforms' that further their control or weaken their opponents in broad struggles over social, political, and economic ascendancy. The point is that these responses relate to wider struggles and alliances. This contrasts with the historical institutional approach in that it seeks to explain change (and resistance to it) and the configuration of power at the system level.

In this approach, institutions might persist, not because of any simple historical momentum, but because they are integral to a specific set of power relations. Elites struggle to preserve existing institutional frameworks even in the face of what neoclassical theorists would regard as increasingly outmoded and inefficient systems, or where the economy is collapsing around them. In Malaysia and Indonesia, for example, there has been resistance to the idea that institutions need to be reformed in the face of economic crisis. This is precisely because of the implications this has for the existing mechanisms for allocating power and dispensing patronage. In other words, the question of power must be placed at the centre of analysis. The more normative, functional, and technical approaches of neoclassical theory and historical institutionalism evaluate institutions in terms of their efficiency in promoting development. Social conflict theorists, in contrast, direct their attention to the forces that structure society and its ensemble of institutions.

Change is therefore not driven by rational individuals, neutralising obstacles to a naturally efficient market. Nor is it forged in global conflicts among contending models of economic organisation. Rather, structural changes such as new technologies, dynamic systems of production, the globalisation of markets, urbanisation, and environmental degradation—all products of an evolving capitalist epoch—represent the focal points of conflict. Struggles and competition over production and economic power, as well as over land, property rights, and civil rights, involve various coalitions of class and state interest across and within national borders.

It is not surprising that South-East Asia's official development strategies have supported markets. Market-friendly policies were adopted not necessarily because politicians, bureaucrats, and technocrats were listening to capitalists or including them in policy-making—sometimes they did—but because structural imperatives required that the state support private enterprise. Policy outcomes are not a measure of the abilities of institutions (state or private) or of the relative insulation of decision-makers. Rather, policy results from competition and conflict over production, profits, wealth, and power. These conflicts are intimately bound to the trajectory of various classes and class fractions. This has seen competition within domestic capital, and between domestic and international capital. The crisis highlights that these struggles or conflicts are sharpest when competitive capitalist interests are restructuring. Only by understanding the nature of globalised corporate battles can policy outcomes be adequately understood.

As we will see in more detail below, this idea of conflict also differs from that within dependency theory that focuses on core–periphery, or North–South, divisions in the global system. Dependency approaches treat conflict associated with capitalism as a problem of national dependency rather than of domestic and international power relations. For social conflict theorists, issues such as exploitation, the nature of economic power and control, the character and power of the state and its relationship to society, must instead be understood as both a domestic *and* external matter (see Brenner 1977; Kay 1975; Miliband 1989).

BEFORE THE BOOM

The approaches mentioned above did not become prominent until the 1970s when many of the East and South-East Asian economies entered a period of rapid growth. Before this, the main theoretical concern was to explain why these economies were seemingly caught in poverty traps. Nevertheless, the antecedents of these contemporary theories can be traced to earlier traditions of intellectual thought. New institutional economics, for example, has affinities with the structural functionalism of Talcott Parsons (1951) and the political order theory of Samuel Huntington (1968). Similarly, many current notions of the global clash between a neoliberal model of Western capitalism and a more interventionist East Asian model owe something to the dependency approaches that emerged in the late 1960s.

Modernisation theory

The first major attempt to explain development in South-East Asia drew heavily on an approach labelled 'modernisation theory'. Theorists asserted that the former colonies could replicate the 'original transition' of Western Europe (see Roxborough 1979:chs 1–2). A variety of modernisation approaches emerged from the different emphases placed on sociological, psychological, and economic factors in the transition (see Hoogvelt 1982:chs 3–4; Larrain 1989:87–98). Modernisation approaches begin by establishing a dichotomy between tradition and modernity, and see an evolutionary movement from the former to the latter. Traditional societies were seen as 'pre-state, pre-rational and pre-industrial' (Higgott et al. 1985:17–18). To modernise, traditional societies needed to adopt the same organisational structures and social and political values of the West. Significantly, this included the adoption of liberal-democratic political arrangements, seen as a natural accompaniment to economic development.

However, the optimism inherent in modernisation theory soon waned as growth languished. It became clear that many of the assumptions about the conditions required for development were not emerging and young democracies were not maturing but being replaced by authoritarianism. It was Huntington (1968) who made the strongest case that modernisation was threatened by political instability. For him, it was not democracy that mattered, but order. While the middle classes remained weak, strong government and political order were required if development was to proceed; democracy could come later, when the middle classes assumed centre stage.

For many South-East Asian governments struggling against political instability, Huntington's ideas provided a handy rationale for the suppression of opposition. This was complemented by policies for economic development, fostered by international agencies, that emphasised the need to maximise growth so that its benefits would eventually trickle down to all levels of society. Growth was to be enhanced through policies attractive to foreign investment, thereby alleviating any shortage of domestic capital (Higgott et al. 1985:24–7). One of the legacies of Huntington's approach was the recognition of institutions and the state as central actors in transforming dysfunctional systems. These elements were revived in the late 1990s as theorists attempted to explain economic crisis in South-East Asia.

Dependency theory

At the time that modernisation theory was being revised to account for the apparent failure of development, dependency theory emerged to challenge it in fundamental ways. Dependency approaches had their origins in Latin America, where economists contested the notion that modernisation could be diffused to poor countries (see Frank 1967, 1969; Larrain 1989:102–10).

André Gunder Frank radically shifted the focus of analysis to various global factors that conditioned development and the nature of political and economic regimes in developing countries. Frank turned modernisation theory on its head, arguing that the development of the already developed countries depended on the *under*development of poor countries. He contended that poor countries, caught in a web of international political and economic relationships, stayed poor because of the exploitative relationship established between them and the already developed countries.

In explaining this, Frank argued that the economic surplus of poor countries was lost precisely because the structures considered important by modernisation theorists—foreign investment through transnational corporations, foreign aid, international loans, and international trade regimes—were the structures responsible for sucking the surplus from underdeveloped countries. Local capitalists and the state act as compradors, providing the links between the developed and underdeveloped economies necessary for surplus extraction. Although Frank's position was refined by a range of theorists (Amin 1974, 1976; Bennett & Sharpe 1985; Cardoso & Faletto 1979; Evans 1979; Gereffi 1982), his primary proposition remained—stunted or incomplete development resulted from decisions taken at corporate headquarters in the advanced capitalist centres.

When it became obvious that many of the economies of South-East Asia were experiencing sustained growth, both the dependency and modernisation approaches were challenged. The fact that authoritarian regimes tended to oversee this growth, and that controlled rather than free markets were involved, were inconsistent with early modernisation theory. But Huntington was not vindicated either. Sometimes rapid development under authoritarian rule took place with the existence of vibrant middle classes. Indeed, as growth consolidated, some Asian leaders even asserted the functional superiority of these arrangements over Western liberalism—a claim that was eventually accompanied by notions of 'Asian values' underpinning such a model. The emergence of countries such as South Korea, Taiwan, Hong Kong, and Singapore as important industrial exporters in the late 1970s delivered a serious blow to dependency theory. Rather than being consigned to perpetual underdevelopment in a global system of exploitation dominated by the advanced industrial centres, these 'peripheral economies' increasingly appeared to be clawing their way to prosperity via substantial export manufacturing. Dependency theorists dismissed this progress unconvincingly as 'dependent' or 'semi-peripheral' development, on the grounds that it lacked the same integrity as earlier industrialisation processes. The fact that growth among the Asian Tigers[7] saw significant gains in material life, health, and welfare was a further defiance of dependency predictions.

As the old approaches faded, the three categories of analysis outlined at the beginning of this chapter began to exert increased influence.

EXPLAINING THE BOOM

Neo-classical accounts

Although dependency theorists could not explain the development of East and South-East Asian capitalism, theorists and policy-makers influenced by neoclassical economics were quick to fill the breach and claim superiority. The success of the Asian Tigers, they argued, reflected the adoption of policies that embraced global market forces. Export orientation was seen as crucial in rapid industrialisation—being regarded as a force for greater competitive discipline and a more efficient manufacturing sector. This was contrasted with production primarily for domestic markets, which was often heavily protected and seen as inefficient (see Krueger 1981). Importantly, the basis of export success was considered to be the exploitation of comparative advantage—concentrating production in areas of relative abundance in land, labour, or capital. Initially, in those economies that were labour-rich and capital-scarce, this meant low-cost, labour-intensive production (Little 1981).

Seen in this way, policy-makers in the Asian Tiger economies had simply chosen technically correct economic policies and the lesson was there for others to emulate. This perspective exerted considerable influence on the World Bank, which exhorted developing countries to follow, for example, the South Korean model. Subsequently, loans—especially for structural adjustment—were often conditional on recipient countries accepting an export-oriented industrialisation (EOI) strategy.

Although neoclassical economists urged the withdrawal of the state from economic activity in Asia to consolidate economic gains (Bauer 1970; Balassa 1971; Krueger 1974; Little et al. 1970), it became difficult to ignore the fact that Asian industrialisation had often been accompanied by state intervention. Neoclassical economists were initially to deny the importance of the state's role, but later redefined it as a market-facilitating role—assisting decisions that would have been made by the market in any case. However, recognition of the importance of the state in economic development did extract concessions from the influential *East Asian Miracle* study (World Bank 1993). Significantly, the serious consideration given to the role of the state had followed Japanese pressure regarding the Bank's free-market prescriptions for all developing countries (Awanohara 1993:79).

The Bank's concessions on the importance of the state were extended in the *World Development Report 1997: The State in a Changing World*. This report made a general case for acknowledging and supporting the role of the state in facilitating globalisation. As the report observed, 'Globalization is a threat to weak or capriciously governed states. But it also opens the way for effective, disciplined states to foster development and economic well-being, and it sharpens the need for efficient international cooperation in pursuit of global collective action' (World Bank 1997:11). It seemed that within the Bank it was realised that a deeper internationalisation of capital was reliant upon the effective regulatory and coordinating capacities of states.

Important as this critical World Bank reflection on its theoretical approach was, we should not exaggerate its significance. It conceded the importance of the state in keeping inflation low, maintaining political and macroeconomic stability, establishing the rule of law, encouraging education, keeping taxes low, promoting trade, and encouraging foreign and local investment. The policy lesson was that governments should ensure that they had policies and institutions in place to support the growth of private investment.

Furthermore, states were acknowledged only to the extent that they were able to rise above politics. Politics remained a dirty word. For example, the Thailand study associated with the *Miracle* report explains that the military coup did 'perform an important function'. The military junta 'assumes broad legislative powers, and ... break[s] the legislative logjam developed in previous elected parliaments' (Christensen et al. 1993:19–20). The former legislature was seen as relatively unproductive 'in making laws, especially when members of parliament are elected'. Almost as an afterthought, it was also noted that bureaucrats were not immune to extra-bureaucratic demands.

The *Miracle* report drew attention to the fact that the state in South-East Asia had been less cohesive in its control and marshalling of economic organisation and strategy than in South Korea, Taiwan, or Japan. Protective trade and investment policies and state ownership were not usually tied into strategic, disciplined, national programs for building export competitiveness. They were often devices for allocating preferential access or bolstering the interests of the state and its officials. Unlike the developmental states of North-East Asia, they were, in the language of neoclassical political economy, more likely to be predatory states led by rent-seeking bureaucrats, rather than far-sighted bureaucrats. Consequently, the neoclassical debate over South-East Asia has tended to be concerned with the transition from predatory and statist economic systems to markets.[8] As we will show, this concern was to be substantially extended with the advent of the Asian crisis.

Apart from opening up competing interpretations over the roles of states and markets, the Asian economic boom witnessed a remarkable comeback by modernisation theory. The argument that economic development set in train dynamics exerting pressures for democratisation was aggressively reasserted. This time the literature was more sophisticated, with greater attention being paid to the factors mediating the influence of economic development on politics—including culture and leadership. Two influential books, by Huntington (1991) and Fukuyama (1992), did much to reignite the idea that the triumph of capitalism paved the way for democracy (see Diamond 1993; Diamond et al. 1989). According to this argument, authoritarian leaders might resist democratisation, but complex social changes accompanying capitalist development render such efforts problematic. The social pluralism resulting from capitalist transformations was exerting mounting and, in many cases, irresistible pressures for political pluralism. The burgeoning middle classes were viewed as the strategic agents of political change. The downfall of authoritarian regimes in South Korea and Taiwan gave rise to a confidence that similar changes could be anticipated in South-East Asia.

Historical institutionalist accounts

There was increased interest in historical institutionalist approaches during the boom, especially when the South-East Asian economic performance was compared with that of East Asia. According to state-centred historical institutionalists, the remarkable feature of Asian industrialisation was the role of the state in orchestrating public and private capital to achieve strategic national economic goals—not, as neoclassical economists conceded, in facilitating markets. Within a framework of complex trade and industry regimes, export strategies and systems of state–business cooperation states could organise corporate juggernauts able to successfully assault global markets (Amsden 1989; Johnson 1982, 1987; Matthews & Ravenhill 1996; Wade 1990; Weiss & Hobson 1995). But this was dependent on 'state capacity' (Weiss 1998). Predictions of an impending Asian Century were accepted within this camp of theorists who depicted these highly organised systems of East Asia as functionally well suited to export-oriented industrialisation.[9]

The idea that authoritarian states could play a positive development role became attractive within the West at a time when growth rates lagged behind some Asian rates. But this was not because of any perception that state-led industry policies were a more efficient means of organising resources and global strategies. Within Western business circles, many looked approvingly at the state's role in sweeping aside 'distributional coalitions' (labour, welfare, and environmental groups) and instituting low tax regimes. These were the aspects of the Asian experience they believed provided broader economic lessons (see *FEER* 18 August 1994:5; 24 November 1994:43–9).

State-centred explanations often assumed that the developmental state was the backbone of economic dynamism in Asia. The problem was that, in South-East Asia, it was only Singapore that seriously fitted this model (Haggard 2000a:136). Despite this, rapid industrialisation certainly did occur in Thailand, Indonesia, Malaysia, and, to a lesser extent, the Philippines. As noted above, society-centred historical institutionalists argued that the focus on the state and the market neglected non-state and non-market institutions. They argued that it was these institutions that had determined much economic success. Focusing on private sector institutions, these analysts argued that such organisations were required to play critical directing roles within the economy (Doner & Ramsey 1997:273). The relationship between business and state was far more problematic in much of South-East Asia under the impact of patronage and cronyism, but business developed its own dynamic institutional arrangements to drive industrialisation. In examining the boom, then, these analysts devoted considerable attention to the development of collective private sector institutions (Anek 1992; Doner 1992; Hutchcroft 1991). The implication was that states and their institutions were important, but that the private sector and its institutions could compensate for relatively weak states.

Social conflict accounts

Within the social conflict perspective, rapid industrialisation was not to be understood in terms of the triumph of 'good' policy or competent technocrats, the triumph of developmental elites over self-interested rent-seekers, or, necessarily, in the ability of business to develop its own institutions. Instead, institutions, elites, and technocrats are seen to operate within a broader power structure where the influence of vested economic and political interests is definitive. Growth in South-East Asia occurred across a range of countries, each with different resource endowments exhibiting a variety of political regimes. But what was common was a compatibility between political regimes and associated interests on the one hand and the prevailing structures of capital accumulation on the other.

In particular, the boom decade from the mid 1980s was facilitated by the emergence of regimes that altered the nature of their engagement with global markets. From being exporters of primary commodities, the major South-East Asian economies became export manufacturers. This different engagement with global markets did not necessarily reflect a neoliberal political or policy ascendancy. At one level, the boom was made possible by structural shifts in the global economy and the attendant mobility of international capital. The 1985 Plaza Accord, for example, released a flood of manufacturing investment to the region as Japanese companies sought a new base for low-wage manufacturing. At another level, the engagement was mediated by changes taking place within these countries. In each case, the old hierarchies of power that had been constructed to further commodity trade were reconstituted in the transition to manufacturing and market development.

Hence, a range of social, political, and institutional outcomes accompanied the shift from commodity trade to import-substitution industrialisation (ISI) and, in turn, to EOI and the progressive deregulation of economic life across the region in the 1980s. For example, in Thailand, EOI and deregulation went hand in hand with the transformation of class power as conglomerates in banking and industry were consolidated while the old trading business groups declined. State officials played a significant role in facilitating this process (Hewison 1989). Importantly, however, these transformations were accompanied by political reform that saw the power of state officials harnessed increasingly to private interests. By contrast, deregulation and EOI in Indonesia in the 1980s, partly enforced by the collapse in oil prices, took place in an economy dominated by coalitions of state and private corporate oligarchies. What transpired was a transfer of public monopoly into the hands of private interest. Unlike what occurred in Thailand, economic deregulation in Indonesia was not accompanied by political reform. The system of authoritarian state capitalism was simply harnessed to the needs of burgeoning corporate conglomerates. Short-term international bank credit replaced oil as the driving force in the economy (Robison 1986:387–8). New oligarchies and coalitions were liberated from centralised systems of state capitalism and given free reign to borrow short term to set up enterprises and banks without regulatory scrutiny.[10]

Of course, these alignments of power and interest in the region were doomed. In a post-Cold War world, Western governments and international financial institutions were less constrained by strategic political considerations to prop up conservative and anti-communist forces with aid and loans. At the same time, increased international competition and the need for financial liberalisation to drive further industrialisation required a reconstitution of economic and political power for continued expansion of these economies. Relationships that enabled private projects to receive massive state favours and to accumulate huge private debt were likely to be challenged from both domestic and international sources. However, the nature of that challenge was necessarily different in each of the countries of South-East Asia. The economic crisis has been a significant element in this challenge.

MIRACLES GO BUST

The optimism regarding South-East Asian development evaporated when the region's economies stalled in 1997. With the exception of Singapore, those economies that had opened their financial sectors to global markets—specifically, Thailand, Malaysia, Indonesia, and, to a lesser extent, the Philippines—experienced significant financial and economic collapse. These downturns resulted in social and political pressure. This chapter is not the place to recount the events of the crisis, especially as there are numerous accounts of the onset, contagion, and economic collapse that followed Thailand's devaluation in July 1997 (see, for example, Arndt & Hill 1999; Robison et al. 2000; Roubini et al. 1998). Furthermore, much of this will be taken up for each country in the subsequent chapters of the present volume. Our concern here will be with the debate about the nature and causes of the crisis. However, there are some points we wish to highlight as background.

The initial impact of the crisis was evidenced in the financial sector, where the collapse of currencies caused havoc as borrowers found they had over-extended. Investment dried up and insolvency mushroomed. Some of this translated into social unrest as unemployment rose and inflation soared. Not surprisingly, these economic and social problems soon had their effects in the political sphere. To different degrees, fiscal crisis and growing opposition besieged governments, whose inability to stem the tide of economic decay undermined what had been a central pillar of their political legitimacy.

Intra-elite friction was precipitated or intensified by these economic pressures. In Thailand, Prime Minister Chavalit Yongchaiyudh was forced to resign in the face of his government's failure to come to grips with the economy's downward spiral and its inability to deal with the IMF.[11] In Malaysia, the economic crisis brought leadership questions to a head, as Deputy Prime Minister Anwar Ibrahim's policy prescriptions contrasted with those of Prime Minister Mahathir. More than differences over the extent of state intervention in the economy, the rhetoric of Anwar and his allies declaring the need to unravel crony capitalism was an attack on Mahathir's power base. Anwar's sacking and arrest ensured that the economic crisis became a full-scale political crisis. Most stunning of all developments, however, was that the crisis precipitated the fall of President Soeharto, who had reigned supreme in Indonesia for over three decades.

Turning now to debates regarding the crisis, there are two questions in these debates that will be pursued. First, why did a crisis occur? How was it that such apparently buoyant and vigorous economies as Malaysia, Thailand, and Indonesia suddenly unravelled and, in the latter two cases, found themselves in the hands of the IMF? Second, has the crisis been a fundamental historical watershed, making liberal market systems the model for all economies and, in any case, what is going to determine the future directions of these economies?

Neoclassical accounts

Mainstream neoclassical theorists, particularly those within the IMF, seized on the crisis as validation of their primary arguments concerning the perils of obstructing free markets and the need for governments to embrace markets if development was to be sustained. For IMF head, Michel Camdessus, (quoted in *Asian Wall Street Journal* [*AWSJ*] 13 November 1997:1) the crisis was a 'blessing in disguise'. The influence and power of international organisations such as the IMF, Asian Development Bank, and the World Bank ensured that these views prevailed in policy circles (see Jayasuriya 2000). For beleaguered governments in countries such as Thailand and Indonesia, these institutions represented the only viable source of funds to mitigate the crisis. This gave the institutions unprecedented leverage in domestic policy agendas.

With the crisis, collusive state–business relations became the objects of intense critical attention. Whereas the *Miracle* report grudgingly acknowledged that the state had played a significant development role, the crisis allowed neoclassical analysts to reassert aggressively that state involvement distorted markets. They argued that cosy political arrangements and the absence of adequate accounting standards and transparency distorted 'price signals' and led to a misallocation of resources. This created a 'moral hazard' in which borrowers and lenders of money (especially borrowers) operated in the expectation of government rescue should things go awry (Arndt & Hill 1999; Frankel 1998; Roubini et al. 1998; Wolfe 1998). Market discipline, they argued, was simply not strong enough in these economies, and the task of recovery had to centre on establishing this discipline.[12]

Yet the crisis also led to several challenges to the Washington Consensus that had dominated neoclassical policy strategies for well over two decades—not least from within the neoclassical school itself. It had become clear that, where market deregulation was embraced, there were often negative consequences. This forced neoclassical theorists to become more interested in the political dimensions of markets, and they focused on questions associated with the rise of rent-seekers and how to dispose of them. Successful deregulation required particular sorts of institutions.

The Asian crisis necessarily reinforced the need for far more attention to be given to state capacity—if for no other reason than the need to enforce deregulation and break the power of cronies (see Camdessus 1998). But institution-building is conceived here in elitist terms, for the ideal remains that a band of rational technocrats are able to operate above the constraints of vested interests (Schamis 1999:236). Interestingly, however, differences surfaced between the IMF and the World Bank over the question of regulation and the role of the state. In particular, the Bank's then senior vice-president and chief economist, Joseph Stiglitz (1998, 1999), advocated a role for the state that went beyond refining the capacity to implement deregulation and insulating policy-makers from vested interests. In effect, Stiglitz asked, on behalf of the Bank, why institutions could be successfully transplanted in some instances but not others—an issue of concern to new institutional economists in the 1990s, but which had not been convincingly accounted for.[13]

The World Bank had recognised the importance of social and political processes even before the crisis,[14] motivated by development failures and setbacks in Africa and Eastern Europe. Thus the Bank began a somewhat vague advocacy of 'good governance', acknowledging the social underpinnings of corrupt or weak institutional frameworks (World Bank 1991:6–7). Now, however, Stiglitz and the Bank became more expansive about what this entailed and the reform agenda attached to it. The language of participation, civil society, social capital, and community organisation became prominent as the social basis of sustainable markets was emphasised (see World Bank 1998). It was asserted that the state needed to work in concert with a range of social organisations to cement the social structures, values, and norms supportive of markets.[15] According to Stiglitz (1998:12), 'The hard part of capacity building is the development of organizational/social capital, including the institutions that enable society to function well.' On these grounds, the Bank distinguished itself from the IMF on the question of fiscal austerity. It began to emphasise social safety nets for those who fell through the cracks in liberalising market systems.[16] Of course, this also reflected a concern about the kinds of destabilising events seen in Indonesia and criticisms that World Bank and IMF policies were deepening the crisis there and in Thailand. There was a related worry that such resentment threatened the hegemony of neoliberal ideas.

The direction taken within the Bank situated it squarely within the so-called post-Washington Consensus, which embraces the idea of institution-building and sees it as a primary objective in the development of sustainable market systems in South-East Asia. The above theoretical refinements notwithstanding, this position still has some fundamental problems. First, it retains a functional understanding of social institutions, with the emphasis on the way in which social structures and processes can be harnessed to support market systems by producing social cohesion and a sense of community. Implicit in this is a view that the inherently unequal and conflictual power relations and material outcomes of the market require management. The market is thus not analysed as an expression or outcome of competing interests and differential power, but rather as a system with functional requirements essential to its effective operation—and that includes the containment of conflict. This perpetuates the conception of the market in abstract and apolitical terms, and suggests sanitised notions of civil society. State-sponsored consultation processes in authoritarian states, such as Singapore, for example, could be seen as part of the institutions and social capital that enhance the market.

Second, the building of institutions remains an exercise that is conceived in voluntarist terms. Who builds institutions, states, and social capital? How are values and norms institutionalised throughout society? It is one thing to recognise the importance of these things, quite another to theorise how they come into being. Because markets continue to be understood by neoclassical analysts as abstract entities defined in terms of functional efficiency, the assumption of a universally applicable and technically correct set of arrangements still pervaded their thinking. There is no recognition, therefore, of how power structures and social interests might complicate or facilitate the introduction of the requisite structures and values to which they now refer. It is as if these things can simply be supplied and will thereafter take root and generate the desired outcome.

In short, for all their emphasis on institutions, the idea of politics and conflict as things dysfunctional and threatening to markets survives. At the level of political analysis, this approach remains naive.

Crisis as global conflict: historical institutionalists

Whereas neoclassical analysts concentrated on domestic weakness in explaining the crisis, historical institutionalists have, not unexpectedly, directed their attention to institutional problems.

State-centred historical institutionalists have seen the crisis as a conflict between competing models of capitalism. Indeed, the neoclassical account is seen as an apologia for the liberal, Anglo-American variant of capitalism and an unjustified dismissal of the East Asian developmental state model. Far from conceding that the crisis invalidated arguments about state capacity, statists attributed Asia's economic problems to compromised state capacity due to liberalisation. Furthermore, the question of the functional superiority of the respective models is far from settled, despite the triumphant mood prevalent in the neoclassical camp.

The work of Robert Wade, extrapolating from the South Korea case, has been central to this argument (Wade 1998a, 1998b; Wade & Veneroso 1998). Wade characterised Asian industrial capitalism as a 'high debt model', in which domestic banks were able to mobilise high levels of domestic savings that supported productive investments by private firms. This process was often reinforced and harnessed through government incentives. Although this led to high debt-to-equity ratios, it worked to 'propel the region's fast economic development over several decades' (Wade 1998a:362). However, liberalisation altered the logic of the system. Banks and private companies found that they could borrow cheaply from abroad and, often, then profitably on-lend. Foreign banks and finance companies also entered local markets in search of higher returns. Consequently, 'narrow and short-term interests of shifting coalitions' replaced the government–bank–firm productive investment nexus (Wade 1998a:364). Opening the capital account is also seen to have been instrumental in exposing domestic financial structures to new forces and pressures that were not always so productively oriented—especially given the underdeveloped nature of corporate supervision and governance in the region. According to Wade (1998a:373), fuller integration into international finance markets and the superimposition of a regulatory regime based on Anglo-American prudential norms would exacerbate the problem. From this perspective, recovery necessitated rebuilding institutions consistent with the historical pathways that have accompanied these hitherto successful state-led systems.

Linda Weiss, who locates the cause of the crisis in the vulnerability associated with limited or weakened state capacity, develops a similar theme. The worst-hit crisis economies, she argues, were those in which 'the common denominator is weak or decomposing institutional capacities' (Weiss 1999: 319). For Thailand and Indonesia, this was reflected in their institutional inability to direct investment into productive sectors and accelerate the pace of upgrading skills and technology. In South Korea, it was reflected in a decline in institutional capacity and a reduced ideological consistency for state direction. The result in these countries was declining exports, rising current account deficits, excess productive capacity, increased private foreign indebtedness, and a field day for speculators (Weiss 1999:321–3, 326; Weiss & Hobson 2000).

The vulnerability of economies with limited or diminished regulatory capacity contrasted with the strength of the US's international state power, referred to by state-centred institutionalists as the 'US Treasury–Wall Street–IMF complex'. According to Weiss (1999:332), the US has used the crisis to open markets further, and has played a role in making an 'ordinary crisis' into a 'deep crisis'. The problem is not just that there are external interests involved, but also that the prescriptions coming from these quarters are grounded in assumptions about the universal applicability of a liberal market model.

Far from the crisis signalling 'the death throes of Asian state capitalism', Wade and other statists believe the jury is still out (Wade 1998b:1536). They point out that liberal capitalism in the advanced capitalist countries has its own unresolved and potential critical problems, not the least being the rising social inequalities that accompany neoliberal globalisation. Its long-term political sustainability remains problematic. Moreover, the structural power of international capital notwithstanding, the crisis has engendered an apprehension and reaction on the part of some Asian leaders about the neoliberal model. Wade (1998b:1551) predicts that the Asian model has considerable staying power and might still be influential 'in setting norms for international economic and financial regimes'. Weiss's (1999) conclusion is that the crisis shows that strong states are essential to globalisation—not antithetical to it.

Others are less sanguine. Chung-In Moon and Sang-young Rhyu (2000: 98) conclude that, 'Convergence to Western capitalism is likely to be the fate of the Asian economy. In a sense, Asian capitalism could have been a temporal detour in the longer historical evolution.' From this perspective, the developmental state has been irrevocably damaged. New distributional coalitions have impaired its effective functioning, and the insulation of the state has been breached (Moon & Rhyu 2000:97).

These state-centred historical institutionalists argue that attempts to establish liberal economic institutional change in the region have failed to generate positive results because of their mismatch with historical pathways. In effect, liberal institutions do not fit established Asian institutional pathways. Although this appears to account for post-crisis resistance to change, it does not allow for a disaggregation of the elements of resistance or change. Nor does it direct attention to the forces structuring these elements and sculpting their responses. Change taking place is not a choice between models —whether Asian developmentalist or Anglo-American neoliberal. Rather, change involves complex questions of power, including the structure and capacities of domestic business, its various linkages with the state and other interests and classes, and the relationships between these structures and the changing international economy.

Those historical institutionalists with a greater focus on society make more of the decline of institutional arrangements. Hutchcroft (1999:474), for example, argues that, in Thailand, the boom saw business gradually establish its collective interests over the state. Market liberalisation, with little attention to building appropriate institutions, together with an increasing tendency for politicians to enhance patronage through access to state coffers and policy, set the stage for crisis.

This theme is taken up by Doner and Ramsey (1999) and by Haggard (2000a). Interestingly, their arguments are similar to those of the statists, faulting the region's institutions. However, they extend their critique beyond state capacity to include weak political structures or systems, policy mistakes, lack of transparency, and moral hazard. The basic argument is that the institutional arrangements that created the boom were inappropriate for these economies as they internationalised and opened. Indeed, the crisis has revealed previously hidden weaknesses in these arrangements. Whereas Thailand's commercial banks were once at the forefront of private sector dynamism, resolving collective action problems, they are now identified as too powerful (Doner & Ramsey 1999:175, 183). Haggard (2000a:137) argues that it was through government inaction that these same banks became collusive.

These institutionalists favour technocratic solutions to such problems. Clearly, they see that institutional failures must be put right. Hutchcroft (1999:488) argues that reform in Thailand requires the political ascendancy of conservative urban elites who must capture the state and parliament from unsophisticated and patrimonial 'country bumpkins' (elected politicians). Haggard (2000a:131–2) also identifies Thailand's party system as encouraging patrimonialism, further noting the instability of multi-party coalitions.[17] This patrimonial and non-transparent pattern was also seen in Indonesia and Malaysia. It is noticeable that this society-focused approach tends to emphasise order. Reform, for example, is often seen to involve establishing order, stability, and accountability (Hutchcroft 1999:486–8). Similarly, when discussing private-sector actors, there is a tendency to downplay the competition and conflict among them. Where conflict is discussed, it tends to be in the context of the state and its officials versus the private sector.[18] Among others things, the crisis laid bare the contradictory relationships among the various fractions of capital and indicated that, although the state was responsible for the interests of capital in general, state actors were also cognisant of the relative power and significance of domestic and international capital.

Crisis as global conflict: neodependency

In spite of the theoretical attacks discussed above, some versions of dependency theory had remained influential—especially with non-government organisations (NGOs)—and the Asian crisis prompted its re-emergence. The elements of dependency theory that attracted NGO interest, and which were incorporated into explanations of the crisis, included:

- strong, sometimes moral, critiques of the negative impacts of development
- the power of rich countries (or the North) to exploit, impoverish, and dominate poor countries (the South)
- the need for a radical economic program that emphasises national development (Bello & Rosenfeld 1990; Hart-Landsberg 1991).

Some continued to argue that the wealth of the rich countries was extracted from poor countries, with financial domination being a new colonialism (Lummis n.d.; Khor 2000). When the crisis struck, it seemed to vindicate longstanding criticisms of the dependent nature of South-East Asian development (see Bello et al. 1998).

For these analysts, the crisis was a demonstration of the power of rich countries and the weakness of the South-East Asian nations. The IMF was condemned for deepening the crisis through its blind push for neoliberal reforms. These radicals joined with others in attacking the IMF and the US for taking advantage of the crisis to reassert their influence in the region through reforms demanding a more thoroughgoing liberalisation (see Bello 1998a:15; Bullard et al. 1998:124). Like historical institutionalists, they made much of the so-called Washington conspiracy. This collusion was to enforce policies that reduced damage to developed-country banks and gave firms from the North significant advantages in doing business in the region. These advantages were to be derived from neoliberal reform reproducing institutions and markets that were in 'the image of the US economy' (Bello 1998a:16, 1998b). The triumphalism of various US commentators when the crisis struck apparently confirmed the conspiracy (Bello 2000a).

The IMF reforms were thus seen as enhancing policies that were identified as having caused the crisis in the first place. In response, some radicals argued for a more nationalist approach to development, including reorientating production to domestic markets (Bello et al. 1998:249). This was considered the only way to avoid domination by the North (see Raghaven n.d.). They also asserted that there must be capital controls to prevent the damage caused by the free flow of finance. Such positions were supported by a number of South-East Asian NGOs (see, for example, Hewison 2000a). Malaysia's adoption of capital controls and Mahathir's attacks on globalisation as a Western conspiracy and a new form of colonialism were eagerly taken up by radical analysts and NGOs (Chossudovsky 1998; see also, Nesadurai 2000). Vietnam, yet to engage in the same levels of financial liberalisation, was also used to illustrate that an economy that was not so open did better when the crisis struck (Bello & Mittal 2000).

This approach necessarily directed attention to national responses to the perceived negative impacts of globalisation; it also saw curious political alliances emerge as radicals and NGOs lined up with NGO-unfriendly governments such as Malaysia and a range of US conservatives in opposing the free trade agenda. Bello (2000b), for example, endorsed Mahathir as an 'eloquent ... critic of the [West's] development paradigm'. However, Mahathir (1999) was, in fact, extending the idea that economic liberalism—no less than political liberalism—was antithetical to the 'Asian way'.[19] Bello (2000c) also supported attacks by US conservatives on the IMF and the World Bank.

There is a certain resonance between neodependency and historical institutionalist accounts, particularly in the way that they both laid much of the blame for the crisis at the door of externally promoted deregulation. However, the former did not conceptualise the clash as one between competing models of capitalism; nor was it in adulation of the developmental states championed by historical institutionalists. Rather, they saw South-East Asian economies as having long been in the adverse grip of a system of global capitalism. The crisis was a manifestation of a new phase of that process. Like those that preceded it, this sacrificed the interests of integrated national economies in South-East Asia on the altar of global capitalist exploitation.

Crisis as social conflict

For many social conflict theorists, the Asian crisis represented a specific manifestation of the normal boom–bust nature of capitalism (Hewison 2000b). On this particular occasion, over-capacity in a number of industrial sectors led to a rapid erosion of rates of return; after all, markets for products embodying low-cost labour were not inexhaustible (Bernard 1999; Gill 1999; McNally 1999). The crisis represented an impasse in export-oriented capitalism, necessitating a restructuring of power and state–society relations throughout the region as new accumulation strategies were developed (Bernard 1999:184–90).[20] Competition among capitalists, and competition between labour and capital, were part of this process, reflected in the impacts of financial liberalisation and globalisation on the region (Tabb 1999:1; see also, Tabb 1998). The deregulation of the finance sector, for instance, was seen to serve the interests of various fractions of local and transnational capital in different ways (Bernard 1999:191).

From this perspective, the crisis also exposed the suspect political grounds on which some historical institutionalists have been attracted to the so-called East Asian model—the challenge to free-market forces that it represents (Bernard 1999:201). The class-biased nature of developmental state regimes, overlooked during the boom years by enthusiasts for the model, were harder to ignore once discriminatory measures to stem the crisis were introduced by these states.[21]

One of the puzzles of the economic crisis has been the widely diverging nature of its consequences for the region's political and economic regimes. Despite the trauma and magnitude of IMF-enforced reforms, many of the institutions regarded by neoclassical analysts as sources of the crisis have been resilient.[22] The crisis, then, is critical, precisely to the extent that it makes it possible for entrenched elites to be weakened as a result of the threat to the existing institutional arrangements that previously benefited those elites. It is also important to the extent that it creates opportunities for reformist coalitions to exert greater influence.

In this context, then, crises might well be decisive events, not because of the lessons they bring in terms of the economic costs of intervention or because of the benefits of reform, but for focusing attention on contestation within society. At one level this might be between, on the one hand, entrenched regimes attempting to hold together a political and economic fabric that sustains their interests and, on the other hand, those who would alter these arrangements. A crisis might also demonstrate the contradictions of capitalism and the cyclical nature of its production. Crises are one way in which these contradictions are worked out, and will require economic, political, and institutional restructuring. But even where an economic crisis delivers fatal wounds to existing authoritarian or predatory regimes, their collapse does not guarantee a shift to liberal markets or democratic politics. It might, but it also opens the door to a fresh round of struggles that could lead elsewhere, too.

The social conflicts that are shaping institutional change cannot be understood as efforts to improve functional efficiency in governance or as the strengthening of civil society. They are about how power is distributed in the processes of production, work, and the accumulation of capital and wealth. These are not simply conflicts between enlightened technocrats and rent-seekers or between a progressive bourgeoisie and reactionary predators. Instead, fluid alliances are constructed around a vast array of issues that arise as capitalism spreads and is transformed—over property rights, land title, labour rights, corporate law, environmental protection, and trade and financial regulation. In these conflicts, the bourgeoisie is not a necessary force for political liberalism and democracy within these coalitions; indeed, if it serves their interests, elements of it might well be profoundly illiberal and anti-democratic.

The importance of the crisis is that it has shifted the structural balance of social, state, and transnational power within which these conflicts operate. In Indonesia, for example, the state is no longer able to enforce the highly efficient systems of social control that previously sustained it; nor can it guarantee the centralised organisation of corruption. There has been a flowering of competing organisations, interests, and coalitions. But in the ensuing power deflation, none has yet been able to establish its ascendancy. Corruption and human rights abuses, for example, can no longer be hidden, but neither can they be stopped (Robison & Rosser 2000).

If social conflict drives institutional change, how do we explain the way in which social interest is translated into political power, policy agenda, and institutional change? As we have seen, the relationship between the state and social interest has been a constant problem for both neoclassical and historical institutional theorists. It is no less a problem for theorists who emphasise the importance of social conflict as the primary driver of institutional change.

It is true, as historical institutionalists recognise, that social interest exerts an influence in the form of structural constraints on the choices of state managers. Even the most authoritarian regimes, for example, must ensure that food prices remain under control, not for reasons of social justice, but for concerns about stability. Nevertheless, one of the defining features of the political economy of South-East Asia, with the exception of Singapore, is the highly instrumental nature of capitalist control of state power. The money politics of Thailand and the politics of capitalist oligarchy in the Philippines provide mechanisms by which powerful corporate interests directly capture and appropriate state power. In Malaysia, the distinction between the state and the interests of a tight oligarchy is difficult to draw in a situation where the latter is constructed upon state contracts, credit, and economic concessions (Gomez & Jomo 1999). Perhaps this instrumentalism has been most dramatically illustrated in Indonesia. Despite claims from neoclassical supporters of Indonesia's economic technocrats that the Indonesian government was insulated from vested interests (Bhattacharya & Pangestu 1992; Liddle 1991), this autonomy did not extend much beyond macroeconomic policy. Nowhere was the crude exercise of state power for private interest more blatant than in the construction of patronage networks and corporate interests for the family of President Soeharto. As Soeharto's children plundered the state, it was difficult to distinguish the public and private interest, or to understand the state except in terms of the possession of powerful private oligarchies.

As capitalists renegotiate their competitive arrangements among themselves, locally and internationally, and with labour and other classes, this has necessarily involved the state and its officials. It is both a domestic conflict and a competition between international and national capitals. Hence, the international state—in the form of the international financial institutions—has also been heavily involved, at times mediating, at other times mentoring. This brings together some strange bedfellows. The IMF, for example, seeks to impose a common institutional regime that will remove exclusive arrangements favouring local investors. Middle-class reformers often support these moves because they break down local concentrations of power. Local investors, on the other hand, often attempt to link with nationalists to save the nation from foreign predators and are joined in this call by leftist NGOs. The fundamental point is, however, that the crisis is about reshaping class relations; it is this that social conflict theorists seek to understand.

SOCIAL CONFLICT AND THE WAR ON TERROR

The various contests and tensions between different interests and ideologies exacerbated or generated by the Asian crisis—highlighted in the social conflict approach above—ultimately relate to the fundamental issue of power relations and the shape of economic and political regimes. While the Asian crisis brought some of these conflicts into sharp relief, so too has the so-called war on terror declared by US President George W. Bush in the wake of the attacks of 11 September 2001. The geopolitical shifts associated with the war on terror exert a significant influence over contestation about the shape of regimes in South-East Asia (see Rodan & Hewison 2004).

The new geopolitics has powerful resonances with the Cold War period. In particular, it has created new opportunities for authoritarian practices in South-East Asia. These opportunities not only relate to a strengthening of the repressive powers of the state, which can be used for political rather than security purposes, but also to an environment conducive to ideologies justifying these and other measures hostile to political pluralism. The US's linking of trade access to security is also reminiscent of the US aid, trade, and investment that propped up a range of authoritarian leaders in the region during the Cold War (*FEER* 30 October 2003:17).

Yet, there are limits to the Cold War parallels. The structure of the global political economy has permanently changed from what it was during the Cold War. Consequently, not all forms of authoritarian regime can be reconciled with that structure and the interests embodied in it. Furthermore, the complexion of US neoconservative and business interests represented within the Bush administration is historically specific, complex, and contradictory. This affects both the form of capitalism and the institutions through which it is advanced in the US and abroad.

The early labelling of South-East Asia as the 'second front in the war on terror' (after Afghanistan) reflected the depth of the US government's security concerns in the region after 9/11. This concern was compounded by bombings in Bali and Jakarta in 2002 and 2003, respectively, and the understanding that al Qa'eda is a transnational force. To be sure, there were Islamic groups in the region that were connected with global terrorist networks and al Qa'eda. Jema'ah Islamiyah (JI), for instance, had region-wide networks and training links with organisations in Afghanistan under the Taliban, and early preparation for the September 11 attacks included al Qa'eda meetings in Malaysia (*washingtonpost.com*, 3 February 2002). However, the splintered and local character of these groups has been their predominant feature (International Crisis Group 2005; Wright-Neville 2004). In a climate where US President (Bush 2001) declared that 'You are either with us or with the terrorists', South-East Asian governments have quickly learnt that acting decisively against terrorist threats earns praise from the US and other Western governments, while governments seen to be ineffectual come under pressure.

Ironically, the one country in the region that had made significant strides away from authoritarian rule—Indonesia—was immediately subjected to scrutiny from the US. Having repealed repressive laws allowing detention without trial, now it was condemned for not emulating neighbouring authoritarian governments in Singapore and Malaysia where such laws were being exercised to arrest suspected terrorists (*AWSJ* 11 March 2002:A11). Subsequently, some of the powers of the military and security forces that had diminished with the fall of Soeharto were restored. In turn, the US resumed training of the Indonesian military, the TNI, through the International Military Education and Training program. This support had previously been withdrawn because of extensive human rights violations by the TNI in East Timor. Similarly, authoritarian tendencies in Thailand, under Prime Minister Thaksin Shinawatra, received a fillip when the war on terror was used to justify a string of repressive new laws and when decrees were implemented to bolster state powers (Rodan & Hewison 2004). Meanwhile, in Singapore and Malaysia, the war on terror was drawn upon to rationalise the consolidation and extension of official powers of detention and surveillance, including preemptive measures against cyberterrorism. Opposition campaigns to have Internal Security Acts repealed that began prior to September 11 were also stifled (Rodan 2004a).

In this context, the scope for political persecution under the guise of maintaining security increased across the region. Thus, in Malaysia, for example, members of the main opposition party, Parti Islam SeMalaysia (PAS), were caught up in ISA detentions; these detentions were questioned by domestic human rights groups.[23] Similarly, after Thaksin aligned his government with the US-led war on terror, ethnic Malay Muslims in southern Thailand, where separatist and nationalist movements have enjoyed strong support, faced increasingly ruthless treatment from authorities resulting in more than 550 deaths in 2004 (*BBC News* 25 February 2005).

The linking of trade and security helped elicit increased responsiveness from governments in South-East Asia. At the October 2003 Bangkok Asia Pacific Economic Cooperation (APEC) forum, the US made it clear that countries in Asia delivering security cooperation would receive preferential access to the US market. As then US Trade Representative, Robert Zoellick, explained, the US was ready to extend trade benefits to 'can-do' Asian countries (as quoted in *FEER* 30 October 2003:17). Protracted negotiations towards a bilateral free trade agreement (FTA) between Singapore and the US were expedited and couched in rhetoric about the commitment and importance of Singapore to the US's security objectives (Rodan 2004b). Thailand's initial reluctance to sign up for Washington's war against terror was soon put aside in order to move towards a US–Thailand FTA. Subsequently, and despite initial reservations expressed by majority Muslim nations Indonesia and Malaysia about the linking of trade with security, governments of these South-East Asian countries sought US endorsement for bilateral trade agreements.

Significantly, authoritarianism was no impediment in the dispensation of trade rewards for cooperation in the war on terror. Indeed, the concept of democracy became flexible as the priority turned to security issues. For example, in establishing the Malaysian Trade, Security and Economic Cooperation Caucus, US Member of Congress Pete Sessions declared that the Caucus would inform Congress and government officials 'about the benefits of a cooperative, anti-terrorist, pro-democracy, free trading, and pro-economic growth relationship with the country of Malaysia' (quoted in *ST*, 2 May 2002:2). Subsequently, an *AWSJ* (23–24 July 2004:A7) editorial generously bestowed the virtues of this 'mainly Muslim, but also multireligious and multiethnic' country that 'has burnished its free-market credentials and has a working democracy…' Indeed, Malaysia was described as 'an example to other Islamic nations of progressive Islam'. Apart from over a hundred detentions under the ISA by this time, Malaysian cooperation in the war on terror has included the establishment of a Southeast Asia Regional Center for Counter terrorism (SEARCCT)—an initiative suggested by President Bush—and joint military exercises.

Clearly, US security concerns have been important in mediating conflicts over political regimes in South-East Asia in favour of authoritarianism. Yet this reveals as much about the limits as it does about the extent of US influence. In effect, in pursuing its security interests, the US has had to reconcile itself to the reality that authoritarian elements are either ascendant or resilient in much of the region. For their own reasons, as we have seen, these elements have generally seized on the prosecution of the war on terror, not least out of the desire to contain radical Islam. The cooperation of these elements may be seen as necessary for US security objectives to be realised, but not necessarily as the ideal partners for US foreign policy. But, as US Deputy Defence Secretary Paul Wolfowitz acknowledged, the Cold War had demonstrated the 'importance of leadership and what it consists of: not lecturing and posturing and demanding, but demonstrating that your friends will be protected and taken care of, that your enemies will be punished, and those who refuse to support you will regret having done so' (cited in *New York Times* 17 March 2005:14).

During the Cold War, the US indicated that it could tolerate dictators and gross human rights abuses in South-East Asia. The support for a string of military regimes in Thailand, Marcos in the Philippines, and Soeharto in Indonesia reflected the need for allies in the region. Human rights issues only came into the political calculation when these regimes were well past their use-by dates in terms of international embarrassment over human rights abuses and corruption, to which could be added their clear failure to maintain political and economic stability. In a sense, then, the 2005 resumption of aid to the Indonesian military may be viewed as an admission of the US's inability to curb the military's power and human rights abuses in Indonesia as well as a—perhaps—grudging recognition that friends need support. Similarly, the Thai military's brutal solution to the situation in southern Thailand certainly was not welcomed by US officials. The point is, however, that if the US has, post-Cold War, a preference for 'low intensity democracy' (Gills et al. 1993), it must nevertheless work with those forces most closely aligned with its security agenda.

If post-September 11 geopolitics have worked in favour of authoritarianism in South-East Asia, then there have also been implications for neoliberal economic reform. The shift in US foreign policy priorities towards security, for instance, resulted in a further dilution of the US's commitment to multilateral economic institutions—a major plank of the neoliberal agenda of the 1990s—in favour of bilateral trade agreements (Higgott 2004). Under George W. Bush, the influence of economic neoliberals in the US administration was reduced in favour of those now identified as neoconservatives. These people were generally more nationalistic and suspicious of multilateral institutions of any kind, and argued that US economic power needed the bolster of a harder military edge (Micklethwait & Wooldridge 2004). If, in the 1990s, there was a coalescing of the interests of finance capital based in the northeast of the US with the international economic agenda of neoliberal ideologues within the IMF, the Treasury, and the World Bank (Peet 2003), then, under Bush it has been the interests of businesses that are less internationally oriented and those benefiting from the enhanced military and security agenda that have enjoyed increased support (Briody 2004; Bryce 2004). Indeed, to the extent that the US's invasion of Iraq was motivated by concerns about oil, this appears to be driven more by the desire to cut domestic production costs of national companies than to inflate the profits of multinational oil companies.[24]

Consequently, in South-East Asia the security agenda has provided opportunities for those seeking to deflect pressure for changes to economic regimes. Yet there are limits to this, since there are still powerful economic interests—from outside and inside the region—seeking to advance capital accumulation. Thus, negotiations over the Singapore–US FTA involved critical attention by Americans on the governance and regulation of Singapore's government-linked companies in domestic telecommunications, financial, and other sectors (Rodan 2004b). The Singapore government thus gave ground on some issues, including over the establishment of a competition policy. Arguably, the US negotiators would have pushed harder on such issues had security not become such a pressing concern. At the same time, the structural economic power exerted by US capital should not be overestimated; it remains uneven across the region, which means that the capacity to exert economic leverage in pursuit of strategic political ends is also variable.

Despite this unevenness and the impact of the new security context, political regimes must be able to provide the conditions for sophisticated forms of investment and the requirements of global governance. The successful reproduction of authoritarian rule in Singapore stems in large measure from the responsiveness of authorities to such pressures, yet even here this involves continuing regime modifications (Rodan 2004c). The US is unlikely to support authoritarian regimes that, regardless of their utility for US security objectives, are unable to provide for the requirements of business development.

The war on terror has generated other tensions for South-East Asian regimes. First, the alignments of governments in the region with US actions, such as the Iraq War, have alienated domestic Muslim populations and have the potential to fan a more radical political Islam. Second, bilateral relations between various South-East Asian countries have been complicated, manifestations of which include tension between the Malaysian and Thai governments over the treatment of ethnic Malays in southern Thailand and accusations of Malaysian and Indonesian support for Thai Muslim separatists (*atimes.com* 1 March 2005; *Malaysiakini* 17 November 2004).

Furthermore, as already noted, the US's approach to the war on terror has fostered a diminished commitment to multilateral economic institutions and an acceleration of bilateral FTAs. Despite signing up for FTAs, South-East Asian governments have continued to foster regionalism. Part of the reason for this is the rise of China as a major trading partner and nascent investor in the region (Frost 2004). The prospect of a major regional economic grouping—especially one in which China has been the driving force for integration—from which the US is excluded is a matter of potential friction (*AFR* 25 February 2005:26).[25]

What, in essence, then, do the geopolitics associated with the war on terror mean for the contests in South-East Asia over economic and political regimes and, indeed, for the global political economy in general? Within the social conflict approach, two responses have emerged. First, under George W. Bush, the war on terror is considered to have accentuated a trend towards securitisation of US foreign economic policy. According to Higgott (2004: 425), 'globalization is now seen not simply in neoliberal economic terms, but also through the lenses of the national security agenda of the United States'. In this view, economic globalisation has become a security problem that necessitates a more coercive military role by the US. Second, it is possible to understand the securitisation of globalisation as a new phase of the neoliberal advance (Lafer 2004; Robison 2004). Neoliberal ideologues now face the challenge of forming coalitions with neoconservative political elements and predatory capitalists. Yet, at another level, the new geopolitical framework offers capital expansion defined in terms of 'empire, strategic cartels, and bilateral partnerships' (Robison 2004:408). In this context, there may well be an effective congruence of military and political regulation, and the expansion of market relations.

This perspective has important implications for political trajectories in South-East Asia. In particular, modernising elites that embrace a mixture of market values and social conservatism will continue to find numerous points of material and ideological intersection with interests based inside and outside the region. This leaves the door open for new forms of political regime to develop, forms that may be quite different from traditional authoritarianism, but which nevertheless eschew substantive political pluralism and class-based political organisations challenging market values and the power of capital.

NOTES

1 We gratefully acknowledge the invaluable constructive criticisms on an earlier draft from Mark Beeson, Jane Hutchison, and Kanishka Jayasuriya.

2 Mancur Olson (1982) saw economic growth in democratic political systems strangled by vested interests seeking to share the spoils of growth (distributional coalitions), preventing good policy in the public interest, and diverting scarce resources from productive investment.

3 Approaches influenced by this version of political economy, juxtaposing rational economic technocrats seeking market reforms with self-seeking officials and politicians dealing in rents, corruption, and grandiose schemes, were applied widely to governance in South-East Asia (Christensen & Ammar 1993; Liddle 1992; Soesastro 1989).

4 Thelen and Steinmo (1992:10–11) argue that historical institutionalism is important precisely because it bridges the divide between state-centred and society-centred theories. We contend that these theoretical proclivities, associated with 'systems-level' theories are, in fact, reproduced in 'intermediate-level' historical institutionalist literature.

5 The concept of 'historical pathway' is explained by Zysman (1994:243) thus: 'The particular historical course of each nation's development creates a political economy with a distinctive institutional structure for governing the markets of labour, land, capital, and goods. The institutional structure induces particular kinds of corporate and government behaviour by constraining and laying out a logic to the market and policy-making process that is particular to that political economy.'

6 Immergut (1998:26) contends that historical institutionalists account for change by arguing that institutions are never in equilibrium. However, the literature suggests that there is more attention to explaining persistence rather than change. In any case, pointing to constant change does not amount to an explanation of that change. It is noteworthy that the Asian crisis was a surprise to analysts (Haggard 2000a:130) who focused on institutional stability rather than change. They also failed to assess the changed global and regional context in which institutions operated.

7 A term coined to designate the rapidly growing and industrialising economies of East and South-East Asia.

8 Of course, markets had long existed. In this context, neoclassical theorists were concerned with the development of 'free markets'.

9 Some South-East Asian leaders portrayed 'culture' as an ingredient of the 'Asian model' and pronounced it a political asset. They argued the need for preserving authoritarian political arrangements because, as parts of 'Asian culture', they were essential for economic success (see Robison 1996; Rodan 1996).

10 For social conflict accounts of Malaysia, see Jomo (1988); for Singapore see Rodan (1989).

11 Initial IMF interventions drove these economies into deeper recession.

12 Indeed, *The Economist* (1998), ever the champion of the orthodox neoclassical model, was critical of the IMF's rescue packages—because they protected foreign lenders from the full force of the Asian crisis.

13 In explaining why some countries proved better at constructing efficient institutions, Douglass North (1994:366–7) relied heavily on culture as the factor driving both resistance and innovation, arguing that it was the 'mental models of the actors that will shape choices'.

14 In one report, the World Bank (1991:6–7) insists that, 'While donors and outsiders can contribute resources and ideas to improve governance, for change to be effective, it must be rooted firmly in the societies concerned, and cannot be imposed from outside.'

15 Here, the World Bank drew on the earlier academic research of Putnam (1993) who had argued the importance of civil society—through the trust and networks of support and reciprocity that characterise it—to development.

16 It is worth noting that the bank was a latecomer to social safety nets, via the criticism of agencies such as UNICEF and UNDP, and bitter experiences in Eastern Europe (see Deacon et al. 1997).

17 He does not, however, explain how it is that these same conditions existed for most of the period of the boom after 1985. This example indicates a tendency in historical institutionalist analysis to identify the same institutions with both successes and failures in economic policy and implementation.

18 In this vein, Haggard (2000b:220) contends that, 'Reducing East Asia's vulnerability is therefore not simply a question of changing policies, but of reconsidering the privileged position domestic business has enjoyed during the high growth period, and subjecting business to greater regulatory restraint and accountability.'

19 The idea that democracy posed a threat to the East Asian model of development, long expressed by authoritarian leaders in the region, had academic subscribers (see Wu 1996).

20 Gill (1999) maintains that the problems of over-production were compounded by the unprecedented availability of credit associated with the market liberalisations of the 1990s. High-risk investments in construction and real estate made possible by overseas borrowings added to the vulnerability of these economies.

21 Bernard was taking particular exception to the work of Weiss (1997).

22 Malaysia provided a dramatic model in defying the IMF by imposing capital controls and priming its banks with state funds. Despite the corporate and banking meltdown in Indonesia and the rapid unravelling of the seemingly indestructible Soeharto regime, old interests and power have also proven resilient. Corporate restructuring and bank recapitalisation is bitterly contested. Even in Thailand, where the IMF and further liberalisation were initially welcomed, the vigour of opposition has been surprising.

23 The ruling Barisan Nasional coalition used the arrests to try and discredit PAS, depicting it as violent and dangerous (FEER 11 October 2001). Yet the history of PAS is, arguably, a good example of how political Islam can be channelled via peaceful, constitutional means.

24 It was revealed by Greg Palast in the BBC TV's *Newsnight* program on 17 March that plans were afoot by Pentagon neoconservatives, even before the September 11 attacks, to affect a coup in Iraq. The idea was to privatise state oil companies and undermine the OPEC cartel through massive production increases. However, this plan was opposed by executives of US multinational oil companies who sought to preserve high oil prices (BBC News 17 March 2005).

25 It cannot be forgotten that, prior to 11 September 2001, the US identified China as its major military competitor in the region and foresaw increased economic competition from that nation.

REFERENCES

Amin, Samir (1974) *Accumulation on a World Scale*, New York: Monthly Review Press.

——(1976) *Unequal Development*, New York: Monthly Review Press.

Amsden, Alice (1989) *Asia's Next Giant: South Korea and Late Industrialization*, New York: Oxford University Press.

Anek Laothamatas (1992) *Business Associations and the New Political Economy of Thailand: From Bureaucratic Polity to Liberal Corporatism*, Boulder: Westview Press.

Arndt, Heinz W. and Hal Hill (eds) (1999) *Southeast Asia's Economic Crisis: Origins, Lessons, and the Way Forward*, Sydney: Allen & Unwin.

Awanohara, Susumu (1993) 'The magnificent eight', *FEER*, 22 July:79–80.

Badhan, Pranab (1989) 'The New Institutional Economics and Development Theory: A Brief Critical Assessment', *World Development*, 17(9):1389–95.

Balassa, Bela (1971) 'Trade policies in developing countries', *American Economic Review, Papers and Proceedings*, 61:168–87.

Bates, Robert (1981) *Markets and States in Tropical Africa*, Berkeley: University of California Press.

Bauer, Peter T. (1970) *Dissent on Development*, London: Weidenfeld and Nicholson.

Bello, Walden (1998a) 'The Rise and Fall of South-East Asia's Economy', *The Ecologist*, 28(1):9–17.

——(1998b) 'Testimony of Walden Bello before Banking Oversight Subcommittee, Banking and Financial Services Committee', US House of Representatives, <www.igc.org/dgap/walden.html>.

——(2000a) 'Davos 2000: Global Conspiracy or Capitalist Circus?', *Focus on Trade*, 45 (February).

——(2000b) 'UNCTAD X: An Opportunity Lost?', *Focus on Trade*, 46 (March).

——(2000c) 'Meltzer Report on Bretton Woods Twins Builds a Case for Abolition But Hesitates', *Focus on Trade*, 48 (April).

——and Anuradha Mittal (2000) 'Dangerous Liaisons: Progressives, the Right, and the Anti-China Trade Campaign', *Focus on Trade*, 50 (May).

——and Stephanie Rosenfeld (1990) *Dragons in Distress: Asia's Miracle Economies in Crisis*, San Francisco: Institute for Food and Development Policy.

——,Shea Cunningham and Li Kheng Poh (1998) *A Siamese Tragedy: Development and Disintegration in Modern Thailand*, London: Zed Books.

Bennett, Douglas C. and Kenneth E. Sharp (1985) 'The Worldwide Automobile Industry and its Implications', in Richard S. Newfarmer (ed.) *Profits, Progress and Poverty: Case Studies of International Industries in Latin America*, Notre Dame: Notre Dame University Press, pp. 193–226.

Bernard, Mitchell (1999) 'East Asia's Tumbling Dominoes: Financial Crises and the Myth of the Regional Model', in Leo Panitch and Colin Leys (eds) *The Socialist Register 1999: Global Capitalism Versus Democracy*, Woodbridge: The Merlin Press, pp. 178–208.

Bhattacharya, Amarendra and Mari Pangestu (1992) 'Indonesian Development Transformation Since 1965 and the Role of Public Policy', World Bank Workshop on the Role of Government and East Asian Success, East–West Center, Hawai'i, 19–21 November.

Brenner, Robert (1977) 'The origins of capitalist development: a critique of neo-Smithian Marxism', *New Left Review*, 104:25–93.

Briody, Dan (2004) *The Halliburton Agenda: The Politics of Oil and Money*, Hoboken: Wiley.

Bryce, Robert (2004) *Cronies: Oil, the Bushes, and the Rise of Texas, America's Superstate*, New York: Public Affairs.

Buchanan, James M. and Tullock, Gordon (1962) *The Calculus of Consent*, Anne Arbor: University of Michigan Press.

Bullard, Nicola, Walden Bello and Kamal Malhotra (1998) 'Taming the Tigers: The IMF and the Asian Crisis', in K. S. Jomo (ed.) *Tigers in Trouble. Financial Governance, Liberalisation and Crises in East Asia*, London: Zed Books, pp. 85–136.

Bush, George W. (2001) 'Address to a Joint session of Congress and the American People', United States Capitol, Washington, DC, 20 September, <www.whitehouse.gov/news/releases/2001/09/20010920-8.html>.

Camdessus, Michel (1998) 'The IMF and Good Governance', address at Transparency International, Paris, 21 January, <www.imf.org/external/np/speeches/1998/012198.htm>.

Cardoso, Fernando Henrique and Enzo Faletto (1979) *Dependency and Development in Latin America*, Berkeley: University of California Press.

Chaudhry, Kiren Aziz (1994) 'Economic liberalization and the lineages of the rentier state', *Comparative Politics*, 27(1):1–25.

——(1997) *The Price of Wealth: Economic Institutions in the Middle East*, Ithaca and London: Cornell University Press.

Chossudovsky, Michel (1998) 'Financial Warfare Triggers Global Economic Crisis', *Third World Network*, <www.twnside.org.sg/title/trig-cn.htm>.

Christensen, Scott and Ammar Siamwalla (1993) 'Beyond Patronage: Tasks for the Thai State', paper presented at Thailand Development Research Institute 1993 Year-End Conference, 10–11 December, Jomtien.

Christensen, Scott, David Dollar, Ammar Siamwalla and Pakorn Vichyanond (1993) *The Lessons of East Asia, Thailand: The Institutional and Political Underpinnings of Growth*, Washington, DC: World Bank.

Deacon, Bob, Michelle Hulse and Paul Stubbs (1997) *Global Social Policy. International Organisations and the Future of Welfare*, London: Sage Publications.

Diamond, Larry (ed.) (1993) *Political Culture and Democracy in Developing Countries*, Boulder: Lynne Rienner Publishers.

——,Juan J. Linz and Seymour Martin Lipset (eds) (1989) *Democracy in Developing Countries, Volume Three, Asia*, Boulder: Lynne Rienner Publishers.

Doner, Richard (1992) 'Limits of state strength: toward an institutional view of economic development', *World Politics*, 44(3):398–431.

Doner, Richard F. and Ansil Ramsey (1997) 'Competitive Clientelism and Economic Governance: The Case of Thailand', in Sylvia Maxfield and Ben Ross Schneider (eds) *Business and the State in Developing Countries*, Ithaca: Cornell University Press, pp. 237–76.

——(1999) 'Thailand: From Economic Miracle to Economic Crisis', in Karl D. Jackson (ed.) *Asian Contagion. The Causes and Consequences of a Financial Crisis*, Boulder: Westview Press, pp. 171–207.

Doner, Richard F. and Gary Hawes (1995) 'The Political Economy of Growth in Southeast and Northeast Asia', in Manochehr Dorraj (ed.) *The Changing Political Economy of the Third World*, Boulder: Lynne Rienner Publishers, pp. 145–85.

Economist (1998) 'Risk in penance-free rescue', 10 January, p. 13.

Evans, Peter (1979) *Dependent Development: The Alliance of Multinational, State, and Local Capital in Brazil*, Princeton: Princeton University Press.

——(1992) 'The state as problem and solution: predation, embedded autonomy and structural change', in Stephan R. Haggard and Robert Kaufman (eds) *The Politics of Economic Adjustment*, Princeton: Princeton University Press, pp. 139–81.

——(1995) *Embedded Autonomy: States and Industrial Transformation*, Princeton: Princeton University Press.

Frank, André Gunder (1967) *Capitalism and Underdevelopment in Latin America*, New York: Monthly Review Press.

——(1969) *Latin America: Underdevelopment or Revolution*, New York: Monthly Review Press.

Frankel, Jeffrey A. (1998) 'The Asian Model, The Miracle, The Crisis and the Fund', paper delivered at US International Trade Commission, April, <www.stern.nyu.edu/~nroubini/asia/AsiaHomepage.html>.

Frost, Stephen (2004) 'Chinese outward direct investment in Southeast Asia: how big are the flows and what does it mean for the region?', *Pacific Review*, 17(3): 323–40.

Fukuyama, Francis (1992) *The End of History and the Last Man*, New York: Avon Books.

Gereffi, Gary (1982) *The Pharmaceutical Industry and Dependency in the Third World*, Princeton: Princeton University Press.

Gill, Stephen (1999) 'The Geopolitics of the Asian Crisis', *Monthly Review*, 50(10):1–9.

Gills, Barry, Joel Rocamora and Richard Wilson (eds)(1993) *Low Intensity Democracy: Political Power in the New World Order*, London: Pluto Press.

Gomez, James and K. S. Jomo (1999) *Malaysia's Political Economy: Politics, Patronage and Profits*, Cambridge: Cambridge University Press.

Haggard, Stephan (2000a) 'The Politics of the Asian Financial Crisis', *Journal of Democracy*, 11(2):130–44.

——(2000b) *The Political Economy of the Asian Financial Crisis*, Washington, DC: Institute for International Economics.

Hart-Landsberg, Martin (1991) 'Dragons in Distress: Asia's Miracle Economies in Crisis', *Monthly Review*, 43(4):57–63.

Hewison, Kevin (1989) *Bankers and Bureaucrats: Capital and the Role of the State in Thailand*, New Haven: Yale University Southeast Asia Monographs Series.

——(2000a) 'Resisting Globalization: A Study of Localism in Thailand', *Pacific Review*, 13(2): 279–96.

——(2000b) 'Thailand's Capitalism Before and After the Economic Crisis', in Richard Robison et al. (eds) *Politics and Markets in the Wake of the Asian Crisis*, London: Routledge, pp. 192–211.

——, Richard Robison and Garry Rodan (eds) (1993) *Southeast Asia in the 1990s: Authoritarianism, Democracy and Capitalism*, Sydney: Allen & Unwin.

Higgott, Richard (2004) 'After Neo-liberal Globalization: The 'Securitization' of U.S. Foreign Economic Policy in East Asia', *Critical Asian Studies*, 37(3): 425–44.

——et al. (1985) 'Theories of development and underdevelopment: implications for the study of Southeast Asia', in Richard Higgott and Richard Robison (eds) *Southeast Asia: Essays in the Political Economy of Structural Change*, London: Routledge and Kegan Paul, pp. 16–61.

Hoogvelt, Ankie M. M. (1982) *The Third World in Global Development*, London: Macmillan.

Huntington, Samuel P. (1968) *Political Order in Changing Societies*, New Haven: Yale University Press.

——(1991) *The Third Wave: Democratization in the Late Twentieth Century*, Norman: University of Oklahoma Press.

Hutchcroft, Paul D. (1991) 'Oligarchs and cronies in the Philippine state: the politics of patrimonial plunder', *World Politics*, 43:414–50.

——(1999) 'After the Fall: Prospects for Political and Institutional Reform in Post-Crisis Thailand and the Philippines', *Government and Opposition*, 33(4):473–97.

Immergut, Ellen M. (1998) 'The Theoretical Core of the New Institutionalism', *Politics & Society*, 26(1):5–34.

International Crisis Group (2005) *Recycling Militants in Indonesia: Darul Islam and the Australian Embassy Bombing*, Asia Report No. 92, Singapore/Brussels: International Crisis Group, 22 February.

Jayasuriya, Kanishka (2000) 'See Through a Glass, Darkly: Models of the Asian Currency Crisis of 1997–98', in Holger Henke and Ian Boxill (eds) *The End of the 'Asian Model'?*, Amsterdam and Philadelphia: Hohn Benjamins, pp. 141–61.

Johnson, Chalmers (1982) *MITI and the Japanese Miracle: The Growth of Industrial Policy, 1925–1975*, Stanford: Stanford University Press.

——(1987) 'Political Institutions and Economic Performance: A Comparative Analysis of the Government–Business Relationship in Japan, South Korea and Taiwan', in Frederic C. Deyo (ed.) *The Political Economy of the New Asian Industrialism*, Ithaca: Cornell University Press, pp. 136–64.

——, Laura Tyson and John Zysman (eds) (1989) *Politics and Productivity: The Real Story of Why Japan Works*, Cambridge: Ballinger.

Jomo, K. S. (1988) *A Question of Class: Capital, the State, and Uneven Development in Malaya*, New York: Monthly Review Press.

Katznelson, Ira (1998) 'The Doleful Dance of Politics and Policy: Can Historical Institutionalism Make a Difference?', *American Political Science Review*, 92(1):191–7.

Kay, Geoffrey (1975) *Development of Underdevelopment: A Marxist Analysis*, New York: St Martin's.

Khor, Martin (2000) Speech made to the opening session of the Millennium Forum, UN General Assembly Hall, New York, 22 May, <www.twnside.org.sg/title/mk7.htm>.

Krueger, Anne O. (1974) 'The political economy of the rent-seeking society', *American Economic Review; Papers and Proceedings*, 64:291–303.

——(1981) 'Export-led industrial growth reconsidered', in W. Hong and L. B. Krause (eds) *Trade and Growth of the Advanced Developed Countries in the Pacific Basin*, Seoul: Korea Development Institute, pp. 3–27.

Lafer, Gordon (2004) 'Neo-liberalism by Other Means: The 'War on Terror' at Home and Abroad', *New Political Science*, 26(3): 323-46.

Lal, Deepak (1983) *The Poverty of 'Development Economics'*, London: Institute of Economic Affairs.

Larrain, Jorge (1989) *Theories of Development: Capitalism, Colonialism and Dependency*, Cambridge: Polity Press.

Liddle, William R. (1991) 'The Relative Autonomy of the Third World Politician: Suharto and Indonesia's Economic Development in Comparative Perspective', *International Studies Quarterly*, 35:403–25.

——(1992) 'The politics of development policy', *World Development*, 20(6):793–807.

Little, Ian (1981) 'The experience and causes of rapid labour-intensive development in Korea, Taiwan Province, Hong Kong and Singapore; and the possibilities of emulation', in Eddy Lee (ed.) *Export-Led Industrialisation and Development*, Geneva: International Labor Organization, pp. 23–46.

——,Tibor Scitovsky and Maurice Scott (1970) *Industry and Trade in Some Developing Countries: A Comparative Study*, London: Oxford University Press.

Lummis, C. D. (n.d.) 'The Myth of Catch-Up', *Third World Network*, <www.twnside.org.sg/title/myth.htm>.

Mahathir, Mohamad (1999) *A New Deal for Asia*, Kelana Jaya: Pelanduk Publications.

Matthews, Trevor and John Ravenhill, (1996) 'The neo-classical ascendancy: the Australian economic policy community and Northeast Asian economic growth', in Richard Robison (ed.) *Pathways to Asia: the Politics of Engagement*, Sydney: Allen & Unwin, pp. 131–70.

McNally, David (1999) 'Globalization on Trial: Crisis and Class Struggle in East Asia', *Monthly Review*, 50(4):1–14.

Micklethwait, John and Adrian Wooldridge (2004) *The Right Nation: Conservative Power in America*, New York: Penguin Press.

Miliband, Ralph (1989) 'Marx and the state', in Graeme Duncan (ed.) *Democracy and the Capitalist State*, Cambridge: Cambridge University Press.

Moon, Chung In and Sang-young Rhyu (2000) 'The state, structural rigidity, and the end of Asian capitalism: a comparative study of Japan and South Korea', in Richard Robison et al. (eds) *Politics and Markets in the Wake of the Asian Crisis*, London: Routledge, pp. 77–98.

Nesadurai, Helen E. S. (2000) 'In Defence of National Autonomy? Malaysia's Response to the Financial Crisis', *Pacific Review*, 13(1):73–113.

North, Douglass C. (1981) *Structure and Change in Economic History*, New York: W. W. Norton.

——(1994) 'Economic Performance Through Time', *American Economic Review*, 84(3):359–68.

——(1995) 'The New Institutional Economics and Third World Development', in John Harris, Jane Hunter and Colin M. Lewis (eds) *The New Institutional Economics and Third World Development*, London: Routledge, pp. 17–26.

Olson, Mancur (1982) *The Rise and Decline of Nations: Economic Growth, Stagflation and Social Rigidities*, New Haven: Yale University Press.

Panitch, Leo and Colin Leys (eds) (1999) *The Socialist Register 1999: Global Capitalism Versus Democracy*, Woodbridge: The Merlin Press.

Parsons, Talcott (1951) *The Social System*, New York: Free Press.

Peet, Richard (2003) *Unholy Trinity: the IMF, World Bank and WTO*, London: Zed Books.

Peters, B. Guy (1999) *Institutional Theory in Political Science. The 'New Institutionalism'*,

London: Pinter.

Putnam, R. (1993) *Making Democracy Work: Civic Traditions in Modern Italy*, Princeton: Princeton University Press.

Raghaven, Chakravarthi (n.d.) 'The Perils of Excessive Financial Liberalisation', *Third World Network*, <www.twnside.org.sg/peril-cn.htm>.

Robison, Richard (1986) *Indonesia: The Rise of Capital*, Sydney: Allen & Unwin.

——(1996) 'The Politics of 'Asian Values', *Pacific Review*, 9(3):309–27.

——(2004) 'Neo-liberalism and the Future World: Markets and the End of Politics', *Critical Asian Studies*, 37(3): 405–24.

——and Andrew Rosser (2000) 'Surviving the Meltdown: Liberal Reform and Political Oligarchy in Indonesia', in Richard Robison et al. (eds) *Politics and Markets in the Wake of the Asian Crisis*, London: Routledge, pp. 171–91.

——, Mark Beeson, Kanishka Jayasuriya and Hyuk-Rae Kim (eds) (2000) *Politics and Markets in the Wake of the Asian Crisis*, London: Routledge.

Rodan, Garry (1989) *The Political Economy of Singapore's Industrialization: National State and International Capital*, Basingstoke: Macmillan.

——(1996) 'The internationalization of ideological conflict: Asia's new significance', *Pacific Review*, 9(3):328–51.

——(2004a) 'Political Regimes and the "War on Terror" in Southeast Asia', First International Sources of Insecurity Conference, 17–19 November 2004, Melbourne: Globalism Institute, Royal Melbourne Institute of Technology.

——(2004b) 'International Capital, Singapore's State Companies, and Security', *Critical Asian Studies*, 36(3): 479–99.

——(2004c) *Transparency and Authoritarian Rule in Southeast Asia: Singapore and Malaysia*, London: RoutledgeCurzon.

——and Kevin Hewison (2004) 'Neo-Liberal Globalisation Conflict and Security: New Life for Authoritarian Regimes in Southeast Asia?', *Asia Research Centre Working Papers*, No. 106, August, Perth: Murdoch University.

Roubini, N., G. Corsetti and P. Pesenti (1998) 'What Caused the Asian Currency and Financial Crisis?', unpublished paper, <www.stern.nyu.edu/~nroubini/asia/AsiaHomepage.html>.

Roxborough, Ian (1979) *Theories of Underdevelopment*, London: Macmillan.

Schamis, Hector E. (1999) 'Distributional Coalitions and the Politics of Economic Reform in Latin America', *World Politics*, 51 (January):236–68.

Soesastro, Hadi M. (1989) 'The political economy of deregulation in Indonesia', *Asia Survey*, 29(9):853–69.

Stiglitz, Joseph (1998) 'Towards a New Paradigm for Development: Strategies, Policies, and Processes', Prebisch Lecture at UNCTAD, Geneva, 19 October, <www.worldbank.org/html/extdr/extme/jssp101998.htm>.

——(1999) 'Participation and Development: Perspectives from the Comprehensive Development Paradigm', Paper at International Conference on Democracy, Market Economy and Development', Seoul, 27 February, <www.worldbank.org/html/extdr/extme/js-022799/index.htm>.

Tabb, William K. (1998) 'The East Asian Financial Crisis', *Monthly Review*, 50(2):24–39.

——(1999) 'Labor and the Imperialism of Finance', *Monthly Review*, 51(5):1–13.

Thelen, Kathleen and Sven Steinmo (1992) 'Historical Institutionalism in Comparative Politics', in Sven Steinmo, Kathleen Thelen and Frank Longstreth (eds) *Structuring Politics. Historical Institutionalism in Comparative Analysis*, New York: Cambridge University Press, pp. 1–32.

Wade, Robert (1990) *Governing the Market: Economic Theory and the Role of Government in East Asian Industrialization*, Princeton: Princeton University Press.

——(1998a) 'The Asian Crisis and the Global Economy: Causes, Consequences, and Cure', *Current History*, November:361–73.

—— (1998b) 'The Asian Debt-and-Development Crisis of 1997–?: Causes and Consequences', *World Development*, 26(8):1535–53.

——and Frank Veneroso (1998) 'The Asian Crisis: The High Debt Model Versus the Wall Street–Treasury–IMF Complex', *New Left Review*, 228:3–23.

Weiss, Linda (1997) 'Globalization and the Myth of the Powerless State', *New Left Review*, 225, September–October:3–27.

——(1998) *The Myth of the Powerless State*, Cambridge: Polity Press.

——(1999) 'State Power and the Asian Crisis', *New Political Economy*, 4(3):317–42.

——and John M. Hobson (1995) *States and Economic Development: A Comparative Historical Analysis*, Cambridge: Polity Press.

——and John M. Hobson (2000) 'State power and economic strength revisited: what's so special about the Asian crisis?', in Richard Robison et al. (eds) *Politics and Markets in the Wake of the Asian Crisis*, London: Routledge, pp. 53–74.

Williamson, John (1994) 'In Search of a Manual for Technopols', in J. Williamson (ed.) *The Political Economy of Policy Reform*, Washington, DC: Institute for International Economics, pp. 11–28.

Wolfe, Charles Jnr. (1998) 'Blame Government for the Asian Meltdown', *Asian Wall Street Journal*, 5 February:14.

World Bank (1991) *Managing Development: The Governance Dimension. A Discussion Paper*, Washington, DC: World Bank.

——(1993) *The East Asian Miracle: Economic Growth and Public Policy*, New York: Oxford University Press.

——(1997) *World Development Report 1997*, New York: Oxford University Press.

——(1998) *East Asia: The Road to Recovery*, Washington, DC: World Bank.

Wright-Neville, David (2004) 'Dangerous dynamics: activists, militants and terrorists in Southeast Asia', *Pacific Review*, 17(1): 27-46.

Wu Yu-Shan (1996) 'Away from Socialism: the Asian Way', *Pacific Review*, 9(3):410–41.

Zysman, John (1994) 'How Institutions Create Historically Rooted Trajectories of Growth', *Industrial and Corporate Change*, 3(1):243–83.

Newspapers and Journals

Asian Wall Street Journal (AWSJ)
atimes.com
Australian Financial Review (AFR)
BBC News
Far Eastern Economic Review (FEER)
Malaysiakini
New Democrat
New York Times
Straits Times
washingtonpost.com

2 Poverty of Politics in the Philippines

Jane Hutchison

KEY TOPICS

Introduction
Political economy perspectives
Economic transformations
Social structure and development
A weak state
Securing stability?
Conclusion

INTRODUCTION

CAPITALIST development in the Philippines has not delivered sustained economic growth or substantially eased massive poverty and inequality. While these features are linked (Balisacan and Hill 2003:32), this chapter stresses the political foundations of each. Essentially, in both its democratic and authoritarian forms, the Philippine state has failed to attain the developmental attributes that, elsewhere in Asia, have produced industrial dynamism and comparative social equality.[1] Today, this situation exists despite concerted civil society activism against vested interests that have long stood in the way of vital reforms. These vested interests are embodied in the new and old elites that control political society and use that control to protect their personal and class privileges through patronage networks and violence against opponents.[2] An important instrument of that violence in the postwar period has been the Armed Forces of the Philippines (AFP), through its deployment in a number of domestic conflicts. Linked to this has been the 'special relationship' with the US, which, until 1992, centred on the Philippines hosting two major air and naval bases in return for substantial military and development assistance. Since September 11, that special relationship has been renewed in an altered form, but there are real concerns that bringing the AFP into the global war on terror at home will only exacerbate domestic conflicts while further advancing corruption and human rights abuses within the military (see Glassman, this volume). In short, this is not a scenario that is conducive to progress on the political and institutional reforms that are needed for the Philippines to match the economic performances of many of its neighbours over recent decades.

The chapter begins by comparing different political economy perspectives on the Philippines' development. Thereafter, the discussion falls into four sections. The first and second cover significant economic turning points and the social forces that these have produced. The third section deals with the weak nature of the Philippine state and the main factors behind political and policy reforms vis-à-vis democratisation, market liberalisation, and state capacity in the post-Marcos era. The fourth section covers the war on terrorism and its current and future consequences for the Philippines.

POLITICAL ECONOMY PERSPECTIVES

Neoclassical economists attribute the generally poor economic record of the Philippines to a policy and institutional mix that 'misallocates' resources to areas of inappropriate and inefficient economic activity (Kongsamut & Vamvakidis 1999; Ranis 1974; Shepherd & Alburo 1991). They argue that, for most of the postwar era, protectionist trade and macroeconomic policies promoted inefficient manufacturing for the domestic market, while also encouraging a form of business behaviour known as 'rent-seeking'. Rents are defined in the economic literature in a number of ways; however, in this context, they are understood as additional returns from government interventions in the market. Rent-seeking is, therefore, the effort applied to competition in the political arena over sources of rent—particularly quotas, tariffs, and public monopolies (Buchanan 1980; Krueger 1974). The neoclassical criticism is that 'by substituting political for economic criteria in many allocative decisions', rent-seeking is antithetical to the operation of market forces and, hence, to the development of an internationally competitive economy (Shepherd & Alburo 1991:155–6). However, in recent years neoclassical economists have paid more heed to the institutional foundations of market success. Accordingly, current economic commentary on the Philippines is more than ever concerned with the governance-related issues of corruption, poor regulatory performance, and policy incoherence (see *ADB* 2003:41; World Bank 2001). But these good governance approaches look to preferred technical institutional changes without properly addressing the power relations that these involve.

The role of rent-seeking in the political economy of the Philippines has also been highlighted by state-centred historical institutionalists. However, these writers are less concerned with its distorting effects on the market than they are with its consequences for state capacity. Drawing on the example of developmental states in East Asia, they maintain that the Philippines' poor economic record is the direct result of a 'weak' or 'patrimonial' state (Evans 1994; Hutchcroft 1994, 1999; Rivera 1994a). Particularly indebted to Weber (1968) on bureaucracy and rational action, they argue that the Philippine polity is unable to steer the course of national economic development because it is constantly subject to the particularistic demands of a wealthy elite or oligarchy. This high level of political patronage (or cronyism) compares with the strong 'institutional autonomy' of developmental states, 'which is derived from the differentiation of state institutions from the private interests of individuals within society' (Weiss & Hobson 2000: 54). Historical institutionalists pay more detailed attention to the social and political factors involved in the institutional arrangements that shape economic behaviour, but there are two key criticisms of their approach with respect to the Philippines. The first is that it is 'only the elite ... are attributed with political agency' (Pinches 1997:109; Quimpo 2004). The second is that the concern with patrimonialism has seen other forms of wealth accumulation neglected and, with this, many of the important, ongoing social transformations from capitalist development (Billig 2003; Pinches 1999). In relation to this last point, the political economy of state–business elite relations need to be examined more broadly in terms of the nature of corporate governance. Corporate governance 'focuses on who controls corporate assets and the decision-making process regarding where capital funds are allocated' (Unite & Sullivan 2000:192). As such, it raises issues around corporate structure and behaviour that are not confined simply to rent-seeking. These include matters pertaining to disclosure, the associated monitoring of corporate activity, and the enforcement of corporate regulations (Unite & Sullivan 2000).

A separate literature on civil society and democratisation deals with the political mobilisation of non-elite actors through non-governmental organisations (NGOs) (Clarke 1998; Coronel Ferrer 2004; Estrella & Iszatt 2004; Racelis 2000; Reid 2005; Silliman & Noble 1998).[3] Interest in this is sparked by questions around the possible transformative role that NGOs might play in deepening democracy—making it more broadly representative—as a condition of poverty alleviation and a more equitable distribution of wealth. Progressive NGOs in the Philippines have been long committed to achieving socioeconomic *and* political rights for the poor and marginalised. In society, as Racelis (2000:182) explains, 'one is necessarily a part of the other' under circumstances where there is 'a modicum of democracy and a highly skewed income distribution'. In other words, poverty in the Philippines is widely viewed as 'a *political* problem' requiring regime change to address (Clarke & Sison 2003:225). But frustrations over the ability to achieve regime change from a civil society base have led to efforts to create new political parties to challenge the elite domination within political society more directly (Eaton 2003; Quimpo 2004; Rocamora 2004). At the same time, political events around President Estrada's departure from office in 2001 have highlighted class divisions in civil society over democratisation priorities that stand in the way of the emergence of broad-based political parties.

Finaly, poverty and wealth disparities have been of particular concern to dependency theorists as well; however, more than most, their writing emphasises the injustices resulting from national dependency—which itself arises from 'neocolonial' ties with the US, international financial institutions, and the global economy (Bello et al. 1982, 2004; Stauffer 1974). Domestically, this perspective has made an important contribution to analyses on the Left, but in ways that tend to stress the inherent economic exploitation in external linkages. The political economy of the Philippine–US security relationship is raised again by the war on terrorism. While dependency theorists have stressed the role that this relationship has had in protecting US economic interests in the Philippines (Mackie 1988:25), it is more fruitful to view it, more broadly, in terms of US hegemony in the region and the political economy of globalisation (see Glassman, this volume). But as Glassman also makes clear, of equal significance in the war on terror are the domestic political agendas of the Phillipine elite.

ECONOMIC TRANSFORMATIONS

Export agriculture and import-substitution industrialisation

The modern economy of the Philippines began with the commercialisation of agriculture for export in the later part of the nineteenth century. As imports of manufactures from Europe and the US also expanded there soon developed a colonial pattern to the country's trade. This persisted into the early part of the twentieth century when, as a colony of the US, the Philippines was granted preferential access to that country's large and lucrative market for agricultural commodities. Notably, in the 1930s, the sugar industry expanded to contribute 30 per cent of national income, 43 per cent of government revenue (directly or indirectly), and 65 per cent of the value of total exports (Brown 1989:204). During the Pacific War, the Philippines was occupied by the Japanese and its economy virtually destroyed. Thereafter, notwithstanding a renewed free trade agreement with the US, export agriculture was slow to recover at a time when imports of manufactures were fuelled by inflows of war rehabilitation funds. In only three years, a resultant imbalance in trade threatened to bankrupt the country by draining its reserves of foreign currency. In response, the government introduced import and currency exchange controls in 1949.

The impact of these controls was dramatic. The country entered an era of rapid industrialisation as manufacturing expanded from 8 per cent of GDP in 1950 to 20 per cent in 1960; agriculture fell from 42 to 26 per cent over the same period (Jayasuriya 1987: 85) (see table 2.1 below). In the region at the time, this level of structural change and economic growth was unprecedented and the Philippines was touted as Asia's second newly industrialising nation after Japan. This form of protectionism altered the composition of imports rather than reducing their actual levels (Ranis 1974:4). As restrictions were mainly placed on non-essential consumer items, imports of raw materials and capital goods continued to grow. At the end of the 1950s, the Philippines thus continued to experience balance-of-payments problems. Meanwhile, manufacturing growth slowed once the limits of the domestic market were reached as income levels for the bulk of the population failed to rise.

TABLE 2.1 Structure of GDP of the Philippines (%)

	Agriculture	Industry (manufacturing)	Services
1950	42	14 (8)	44
1960	26	28 (20)	46
1970	28	30 (23)	42
1980	23	37 (25)	40
1990	22	35 (25)	43
2000	15	32 (23)	53
2004	15	32 (23)	53

Sources: Jayasuriya (1987:85); NSO (2004)

In the early 1960s, controls on foreign exchange were lifted and the peso was devalued by almost half against the US dollar. These changes had a 'serious but not devastating effect' on the manufacturing sector (Snow 1983:26). Profits fell, leading to the closure of some firms, but there seems to have been no major sectoral or intrafirm restructuring as a result. Import-substitution manufacturing thus 'stagnated rather than declined' into the late 1960s, largely because tariffs were introduced that reproduced a structure of protection in favour of consumer items over intermediate and capital goods (Shepherd & Alburo 1991:206). Although the lifting of controls and devaluation favoured exports of primary products, they coincided with a fall in the world price of these commodities. As a result, the value of imports continued to rise against the value of exports (Boyce 1993:253).

Export restructuring

During the 1970s, various transformations in the world economy converged to influence the later course of economic development in the Philippines. The first of these were ongoing falls in international prices for agricultural commodities. Then, in 1974, the United States government responded to its own domestic pressures by not extending the allowable quota on sugar imports from the Philippines. When the world price for sugar fell from 67 cents per pound in 1974 to a low of 7 cents in 1978, the industry was hit very hard. Billig (1994:666) reports that the people of the southern island of Negroes 'recall these years as the time when [unsold] sugar was stored in swimming pools, on basketball courts, and even in schools and churches'. World sugar prices rose again in the early 1980s but, by that time, President Marcos had installed one of his cronies as head of the government sugar-marketing authority. Price increases were not passed on to the growers, production was halved, and sugar workers were squeezed to the point of starvation (Billig 1994:666–7).

To a small extent, the decline in the value of traditional exports such as sugar has been compensated by the expansion of exports of plantation crops (particularly pineapples and bananas), fish, and livestock. However, of greater significance has been the growth in exports of non-traditional manufactures, especially garments and electronics. Between 1970 and 1985, the contribution of non-traditional manufactures to the value of total exports increased from 7 per cent to 60 per cent, at the same time as the value of traditional exports fell from 92 per cent to 28 per cent (Montes 1989:71). By the late 1990s, the contribution of non-traditional exports had lifted further to 88 per cent, where, in 2004, it virtually remained (see table 2.2 below). A feature of this restructuring in the 1990s was the growth in exports of electronics, which the World Bank (1999:47) describes as marking 'a clear long-term tendency' for the composition of exports from the Philippines to 'shift from technologically simple to complex products'. However, this is not universally accepted; Hill (2003:234) points out that the country is still mainly engaged in labour-intensive assembly processes alone. In contrast to electronics, the garments industry is losing international competitiveness at both the price-sensitive and quality ends of the market, as are other labour-intensive manufactures (ADB 2000:21).

TABLE 2.2 Structure of Philippines exports (by value) (%)

	1970	1990	1994	1998	2004
Fuels	23	18	13	6	1
Other primary commodities	70	11	7	3	7
Manufacturing	7	70	79	88	89
(Electronics)	–	(24)	(37)	(59)	(67)
Other	–	1	1	3	3

Sources: Montes (1989:69); World Bank (1999:85); BSP (2005a)

Despite this export restructuring, industrial development in the Philippines has stagnated, with the contribution of manufacturing to GDP and employment actually falling since 1970 (see table 2.3) (Hill 2003:221).

This means that the industrial sector remains small in regional terms—less than half the size of that in Indonesia and Thailand, and two-thirds that of Malaysia in 2000 (Hill 2003:225). Moreover, the structure of manufacturing output has little changed since 1970. It continues to reflect the history of protectionism and domestic market orientation, with there being only a small increase in the contribution of labour-intensive industries, with this coming mainly from one—electronics (Hill 2003:227–9). While there is now undoubtedly more competition in manufacturing than there was two decades earlier, high ownership concentration is still a feature (Hill 2003:238). In the case of services, exports are a fraction of the level for goods, but the sector has experienced growth since liberalisation efforts in the early 1990s (Abrenica & Llanto 2003:257). Much of this liberalisation involved the easing or removal of restrictions on the participation of non-national firms; however, changes of this kind remain uneven across the services sector. Nevertheless, Balisacan and Hill (2003:28) argue that the Philippines' main international comparative advantage indeed lies in labour-intensive services over manufacturing and that this is demonstrated by exports of contract labour and the hosting of outsourced services.

TABLE 2.3 Structure of employment in the Philippines (%)

	Agriculture	Industry (Manufacturing)	Services
1970	52	16 (11.9)	31
1980	51	15 (10.9)	34
1990	45	16 (9.7)	39
1995	44	16 (10.0)	40
2000	39	16 (10.0)	46
2005	34	16(10.0)	50

Sources: Balisacan and Hill (2003:14); NSO (2005)

Labour also became a major Philippine export in the 1970s. At that time, the oil boom generated demand for contract workers in construction and domestic service in the Middle East, especially in Saudi Arabia. Subsequently, workers have also been employed on fixed-term contracts in East and South-East Asia, especially in Japan, Hong Kong, and Taiwan (see table 2.4 below). While construction, domestic services, and entertainment remain the major land-based sources of overseas employment, there are also some growing areas of demand in business and professional services. By 2003, there were 3.85 million Filipinos working temporarily on fixed-term contracts overseas on both land and sea (POEA 2003). This number is equivalent to one-tenth of the employed domestic workforce. However, that equivalent increases to 25 per cent when workers employed overseas on permanent and irregular bases are included as well.[4] The bulk of those working overseas on a permanent basis are located in the US (70 per cent); the largest concentrations of irregular workers are in the US (34 per cent) and Malaysia (24 per cent) (POEA 2003). Remittances from all overseas workers have helped to boost consumer spending in the domestic economy through times of crisis and high unemployment and underemployment. In 2004, these remittances topped US$8.5 billion, an amount that correspond to approximately 10 per cent of GNP in the same year (BSP 2005b). But overseas workers are not only of great significance to the national economy, politically they have also become important players—as shown later in the government's varied responses to the war on terrorism.

TABLE 2.4 Geographic distribution of land-based overseas workers (% of the total for each category) (2003)

	Permanent	Temporary	Irregular
East & South-East Asia	3	23	32
Middle East	<1	43	7
Europe	6	14	10
US and Canada	82	4	34
Others	9	16	17

Source: POEA (2003)

Finally, in the last five years, the international outsourcing of business services to the Philippines has also grown. In 2004, investments in call centres, medical transcription, and digital animation amounted to about US$144 million (US State Department 2005). Although still well short of the earning figures for overseas workers, it is thought that this kind of IT-enabled outsourcing will be an important area of investment and employment expansion in the near future.

Foreign debt and investment crises

Despite the expansion of export manufacturing, growth in the Philippine economy in the 1970s was largely financed by international loans to government (Montes 1989:75–9). Public overseas borrowing began in the mid 1960s, but greatly expanded in the following decade as commercial bank lending increased and the Marcos regime sought to obtain credit for a range of development programs. Consistent with the cronyism of the regime, many of the loans were dispensed for entirely political ends, and inadequate controls meant that a large proportion simply went offshore as capital flight (Boyce 1993). By the end of the 1970s, sources of cheap commercial loans were disappearing and the government found it more difficult to cover existing debt with new borrowings. Consequently, it became increasingly dependent on the IMF and the World Bank, and therefore more vulnerable to pressures for structural reform. A crucial juncture in the debt crisis was reached in

1983 when the government was forced to place a ninety-day hold on its debt repayments. Over the next two years, the economy went into recession. GDP fell by 6 per cent in 1984 and by 4.3 per cent in 1985. Industry fared the worst with falls of 10.2 per cent in both years (World Bank 1989:3). President Marcos was finally driven from office in early 1986, but foreign debt contributed greatly to the fiscal difficulties of the next administration. President Aquino made debt repayment a high priority—often reducing public spending in areas such as infrastructure development—to retain access to multilateral and Japanese bilateral funds (Jayasuriya 1992:57).

Debt repayment was made more manageable by a restructuring agreement in the early 1990s. But the prolonged economic and political crisis saw the Philippines mostly miss out on the considerable wave of direct foreign investment that entered South-East Asia from the mid 1980s. Keen not to have this scenario repeated, in the early 1990s the Ramos administration sought to attract foreign investment by liberalising the financial sector and removing a range of equity restrictions more generally on foreign investors. In an improved political climate, net foreign direct investment (FDI) grew 1.6 times in three years—mostly targeting the electronics industry—while net portfolio investment increased almost 17 times over the same period—to levels 2.3 times above that for FDI (de Dios 1998:66). In addition, borrowing by the corporate sector rose more than 100 per cent as a share of GDP between 1990 and 1997 (Noland 2000:403). Therefore, in contrast to the Marcos era, it was the private corporate sector, not the state, that was doing most of the overseas borrowing (de Dios and Hutchcroft 2003:57). All these changes set the scene for the financial crisis of 1997–98. Yet, for several reasons, the Philippines initially came through that crisis rather better than a number of its neighbours. One, this was because the country's late exposure to speculative investment and private debt accumulation meant that it simply had 'less far to fall' (Noland 2000; World Bank 1999:16). Two, in regional terms, the Philippine financial system was comparatively robust after earlier reforms, particularly in relation to levels of capitalisation, the percentage of non-performing loans, and exposure to the property market (Noland 2000: 405–7). In short, the Philippines did better in the initial stages of the 1997 crisis because it had emerged only relatively recently from its own national economic and institutional crisis under Marcos.

However, since the financial crisis, public debt has again ballooned—to over 130 percent of GDP (including all liabilities of poor-performing government-owned or controlled corporations, which are a major source of the growth in government debt) (Rivera 2005:131). As a result, debt repayments climbed to just under 30 per cent of government expenditure in 2004 (ADB 2005). Fifteen percent of the external debt is owed to multilateral agencies, compared to double that for bilateral loans, most prominently from Japan (BSP 2005c). The fiscal burden of debt repayment is increased by the falling state revenues with, for example, tax collection dropping as a proportion of

GDP from 17 to 12.5 percent between 1997 and 2003, despite this being a period of some economic growth (de Dios et al. 2004:2). Congress passed new legislation to increase taxes on alcohol and tobacco at the end of 2004, but this is expected to deliver only one sixth of the additional revenue needed for the government to reduce its dependence on borrowing (ADB 2005). The effect of this has been cuts to public spending in the vital areas of infrastructure, health, and education (ADB 2005; US State Department 2005). Meanwhile, as shown in Table 2.5, in regional terms, the country continues to attract low levels of FDI as a proportion of total investment and especially of GDP. These figures betray the dependency theorists' long-held assertion that FDI assumes a dominant role in the Philippine economy and is a direct cause of developmental failures.

TABLE 2.5 FDI inflows as a percentage of gross fixed capital formation (GFCF) and gross domestic product (GDP) (2002, 2003)[5]

	Percentage of GFCF		***Percentage of GDP***	
	2002	**2003**	**2002**	**2003**
Philippines	13	3	15	16
Indonesia	<1	−2	33	28
Malaysia	14	11	60	57
Singapore	26	46	154	161
Thailand	4	5	28	26
Vietnam	11	15	50	51

Source: de Guia (2005)

Inequality and poverty

Something of the depth of the Philippines' development malaise over many decades is revealed by the observation that, between 1950 and 1996, national per capita income fell from one-seventh to one-tenth of that of the US, whereas for the same period 'all of its neighbours improved, some spectacularly' (Kongsamut & Vamvakidis 1999:10). In 2003, six years after the regional financial crisis, about 11 per cent of the Philippine population was living on less than US$1 per day, which is well above the 5.8 per cent average for South-East Asia as a whole (Schelzig 2005:27–8). In domestic terms, the proportion of individuals in the Philippines living in absolute poverty (as defined by the official income–poverty line) fell from 49 to 40 per cent between 1985 and 2000, but over the same period the actual number of people in absolute poverty increased by over 4 million due to population growth (Schelzig 2005:17–18). Since then, all signs indicate still more individuals living in poverty, coupled with a further fall in the income of the poorest 30 per cent (ibid).

Yet if poverty is defined more broadly, beyond low income, to include 'capacity deprivation' (Sen 1999:87–110) and 'asset vulnerability' (Moser 1998), then poverty is even more widespread in the Philippines. To give one example, while 20 per cent of the urban population is officially classed as income-poor, double that figure suffer great deprivation through living as squatters in generally substandard dwellings and environments (ADB 2004). The point of this is that access to residential land is not merely tied to income, but also is limited by a taxation system that encourages land-hording by owners, the reform of which is a contentious political issue. Further, while unemployment is chronically high in the Philippines, only some 17 per cent of the income-poor are, in fact, in this group (UNDP 2002). This indicates how much poverty in the Philippines is linked to low labour remuneration. Again, given the failure of the state to enforce even its own legislated minimum labour rights and protections, this is a political matter.

SOCIAL STRUCTURE AND DEVELOPMENT

Land and industrial elites

Commercial agriculture enabled the development of a small, land-owning elite. Industrialisation in the 1950s largely reproduced the resultant oligarchic structure of the economy. Given the importance under import substitution of having access to import licences and foreign exchange through the state, between one-third and one-half of the then new industrialists were members of the politically well-connected landed elite—the other major group being those that had an existing foot in commerce or manufacturing (Carroll 1965; Rivera 1994b: 159–64). As well as import-substitution manufacturing, the postwar period brought new investment and rent-seeking opportunities for the elite in finance, real estate, and construction. This facilitated the development of 'diversified family conglomerates' as 'the leading segment of Philippine capital' (de Dios & Hutchcroft 2003:48). As these writers observe, there consequently developed 'a substantial homogeneity of [elite] interests', particularly in opposition to redistributive reforms, with the result that major intra-elite conflicts were those confined to 'the factional and personal issues that arose in the quest for favourable access to the state machinery'. At a time of significant economic restructuring, these conflicts were similar to those in the pre-war period, with the result that they served to reproduce many of the same socioeconomic inequalities.

Under Marcos, the dominant force in key sectors of the economy were the presidential cronies. Mostly the cronies were not from the ranks of the traditional elite, as Marcos himself was not. Yet they also developed or expanded their business operations through privileged access to government-issued licences, monopolies, and loans—in short, through patronage (Koike

1989: 127–9). Significantly, the cronies were inconspicuous in export manufacturing, largely because it afforded them little opportunity to form local monopolies (Hawes 1992:157). The old elite was meanwhile 'harassed but not destroyed' by the Marcos regime (Doherty 1982:30). Their direct political power was largely broken; however, they remained sufficiently influential to protect their private economic base from trade and land reforms (Crouch 1984). Consequently, in tandem with a few surviving cronies, many of the traditional elite returned to economic prominence in the late 1980s. In the post-Marcos era, there have been two major changes in this regard.

First, while many of the same individuals and families remain prominent in business, their primary base has long shifted from rural areas and agriculture to urban-based industry and commerce (Billig 2003; Pinches 1999). Many of the names are familiar, but the economic elite in its current manifestation has different interests and ways of achieving influence. As Billig (2003:27) argues:

> Although patrimonial capitalism endures in the Philippines ... the shift from landlord dominance to the dominance of urban businessmen [*sic*] is critically important as a harbinger of future change in politics, economy, and culture. While it may appear at first glance that all Philippine elites are alike, that elites from different sectors pursue different strategies of domination and advocate different sorts of policies has consequential implications.

The second development is the parallel emergence of some new business players. In particular, investors of Chinese descent have benefited from the easing of discriminatory legislation under Marcos, to emerge with a significant presence in most sectors of the economy. With some exceptions, this group has not been as closely associated with political cronyism on a major scale and is well positioned to promote and gain from ethnic Chinese investment networks in the region (de Dios 1998:79; Pinches 1996:120). Notably, in the 1990s, the Chinese in business experienced a major status reversal with their perceived 'values of diligence and thrift' now being regarded as desirable traits for the nation as a whole to adopt (Billig 2003:241–2 ; Pinches 1999:287). As discussed below, these changes are part of broader transformations in Philippine society that have seen greater domestic support for economic liberalisation now than in the past. In short, while family-owned companies still 'control a large proportion of productive assets' in the domestic economy (Unite & Sullivan 2000:196), the families involved and the environment in which they operate have undergone important changes in recent decades.

Rise of wage labour

The commodification of labour through the rise of wage labour is an important feature of capitalist development. In agriculture, from the start, the forms of labour control exerted by the landowners varied according to region, crop type, farm size, and so on. In Central Luzon, for example, work in rice growing was originally organised largely on a *kasamá* or share-cropping (share-harvest) tenancy basis. As the lot of tenants worsened, relations with landlords also became more overtly conflictual and even violent (Kerkvliet 1979; Wolters 1984). In the 1930s, a peasant resistance movement emerged in Central Luzon, which, just after the Second World War, waged a seven-year armed rebellion against landowners, until eventually they were crushed by government forces in a counterinsurgency program that had US backing (Kerkvliet 1979; McCoy 1988). Subsequently, in an attempt to ameliorate such unrest, some land reforms were introduced, but these did little to alter the basic balance of power in the region. From the 1950s, a number of landlords introduced more machinery-intensive forms of rice growing, largely to circumvent their labour-control problems. These changes set in place an accelerating trend towards greater wage labour and landlessness in agriculture (Kerkvliet 1991:34–58).

In the 1970s, international funds were deployed for a green revolution in Philippine agriculture through the introduction of high-yield varieties of rice. As these new rice strains required more water, chemical fertilisers, herbicides, and pesticides for growth, they transformed the social relations of production—generating new sources of surplus extraction that have tended to decentre the landlord–tenant relationship (Wolters 1984: 207–10; Lim 1990: 123–6). In particular, although the main lines of credit and indebtedness for the direct producer still involve landowners, they now also include rural banks and commercial traders. This changed pattern of production relations in rice agriculture has generated new socioeconomic inequalities that land reform alone cannot address.

In the sugar industry, on the other hand, land (and mill) ownership has also been concentrated, although wage labour was originally more widespread than in rice growing (McCoy 1982). Given the relative abundance of cheap labour, the industry remained labour-intensive—by overseas standards—for a long period. In the 1960s, cheap loans from state and international sources were made available to lift industry productivity through mechanisation. The employment and income consequences for workers were severe and, with falling prices on the world market and the creation of a marketing monopoly under Marcos, they worsened (Boyce 1993:195–8). In the 1990s, labour conditions were generally less extreme as the industry recovered somewhat on the back of strong domestic demand (Billig 2003).

In the other important export industry, coconuts, the pattern of land ownership has been less concentrated and small-scale farming is more common. The use of wage labour is also growing, but the level of political organisation in this sector is less than in the sugar industry (Boyce 1993:189–92). Finally, many of the newest sectors in agriculture—bananas and other fruit, fish farming, and poultry and livestock production—have high levels of corporate involvement and contract farming, often through vertically integrated, transnational agribusinesses (Boyce 1993:199–203). In all, agriculture is a less important contributor to the rise of wage labour than industry or services, as today it accounts for only 16 per cent of the total (NSO 2005). By contrast, industry contributes 25 per cent; services—by its sheer size—contributes just under 60 per cent (NSO 2005).

Industry before the Second World War was a site of conflict as independent (and often radical) trade unions formed in the sectors where workers were congregated in their hundreds and even thousands—in large-scale agricultural processing (especially the sugar mills), cigar and cigarette factories, and in land transport and stevedoring (Kunihara 1945:72). During the 1920s, the number of unions and their reported memberships increased rapidly (Wurfel 1959:584). Cuts to wages and rising unemployment in the 1930s resulted in unprecedented levels of industrial action. Significantly, during this era there was an almost fourfold increase in the ratio of organised to spontaneous strikes (Kunihara 1945:65). By 1940, an estimated 5 per cent of the workforce was organised—although, less than 2 per cent was in registered unions (Kunihara 1945:72). Just after the war, the labour movement was briefly reconstituted under radical leadership until, in the early 1950s, at the height of state action against the peasant rebellion in Central Luzon, the peak organisation was declared illegal and its affiliated unions deregistered (Infante 1980:110).

With import-substitution industrialisation, the proportion of the labour force in manufacturing grew, peaking at almost 12 per cent (see table 2.3, page 45). This stimulated an increase in the number of unions, although many were company-controlled, ineffective, or simply inactive (Snyder & Nowak 1982:48–53). Three and a half decades later, still only 6 per cent of the workforce belong to a union, while less than 1 per cent is covered by a collective bargaining agreement (DOLE 2005). The 1950s saw some increases in real wages in industry in Manila, but declines over subsequent decades meant that, in the mid 1980s, wages were just below the 1950 levels (Ofreneo 1994:279). In the 1990s, wages rose nominally, but, due to inflation, not in real terms. Moreover, while there are region-based minimum wages, lax government enforcement means that some 60 per cent of the workforce does not receive its legal entitlement in this regard.

Services are characterised by great homogeneity. Within and between subindustry groupings there are large differences in the proportion of wage and salary workers, with some—such as domestic services—having only this class of employee, whereas others—such as retailing—have a greater share that are self-employed (see table 2.6 below). In 2005, just over half the total employed labourforce were on wages, with another third in the self-employed category (see table 2.6 below). In absolute terms, wage workers are concentrated in their millions in agriculture, manufacturing, construction, wholesale and retail trade, transport and communication, defence, and domestic services, although, as mentioned before, not all these areas are as wage-labour intensive as others. Yet the experience of wage labour is not confined to the domestic economy: at the very least, the number of Filipinos employed in this way expands by 20 per cent if one counts in those on temporary contracts overseas.[6]

TABLE 2.6 Class of worker by selected major industry group (%) (2005)

	Wage/Salary	Own Account Self-employed	Employer	Unpaid Family
TOTAL	51	33	5	11
Agriculture	23	45	9	23
Industry	79	15	2	4
(Manufacturing)	72	20	3	5
Services	60	31	3	6
(Wholesale/retail trade)	30	53	5	12
(Transport/communications)	55	42	2	1
(Public admin/defence)	100	–	–	–
(Domestic services)	99	–	1	–

Source: NSO (2005)

Middle class and new forces

In agriculture and industry in the postwar era, the number of medium-sized landholders, salaried workers in public and private sectors, professionals, and the like, has grown. This heterogeneous stratum is often termed 'middle class' according to level of income, occupation type and status, pattern of consumption, and so on. Pinches (1996:109) argues that sections of the middle class first came to national political prominence over their endorsement of government protectionism in the 1950s and 1960s. Since then, they have been a strong presence in the people power revolutions against two presidents. But, most significantly, since the fall of Marcos, middle-class disaffection with the traditional elite and its sources of power has increased, contributing to domestic pressures for economic and institutional reforms (Pinches 1996:123).

The middle stratum of Philippine society has proven to be a vital source of medium-scale investment in export manufacturing, particularly garments, footwear, and the like. Through international and local subcontracting arrangements, it has been possible for relatively small investors to set up in manufacturing, sometimes as a means to supplement or substitute professional incomes (Pinches 1996:121). In the last decade, this phenomenon has extended into consumer and business services and construction (Pinches 1999:277–8). Pinches' research shows that a significant proportion of these 'new capitalists' are 'women, former salaried professionals, middle-class Filipinos' who have returned 'from periods of residence in North America or Europe', especially when the economy picked up in the early to mid 1990s.

Alternatively, they are individuals 'with a background in small businesses' who, over time, have been able to expand those businesses (Pinches 1999:278). With the easing of restrictions on foreign investment in areas such as banking, insurance, telecommunications, and parts of retailing in the 1990s, new employment openings have developed in management and other professional areas. In all this, Pinches (1999:279) observes that it is worth noting 'the absence of a clear divide between the salaried new middle class and the new capitalist entrepreneurs' due to the extensive overlapping among families and individuals. However, throughout, the business interests of the middle classes are generally less dependent on political patronage than those of the traditional elite and are certainly not on any grand scale.

A WEAK STATE

The Philippine state is often characterised as weak. There are two facets to this (see Migdal 1988). The first centres on the relative distribution of power between state and society or, more particularly, between the state and dominant interests in the private sector of the economy—hence the question of state autonomy. As Caporaso and Levine (1992:191) put it, this view assumes that causality can be located either inside or outside the state: a weak state is one that is consistently acted upon by external social forces. The second facet is often expressed as state capacity and, as previously discussed, draws heavily on the Weberian distinction between patrimonial and rational-bureaucratic polities. On this basis, a weak state is one in which relatively little distinction is made between the personal interests and official duties of decision-makers in the executive legislature and/or bureaucracy, and, therefore, is one in which the policy-making process is constantly thwarted by particularistic demands. In this interpretation, the origins of the weak state are associated with the elite nature of democracy in the Philippines. The essential point here is not elite domination *per se*, but the fact that this kind of weak state is one 'which does not produce radical changes' to that pattern of domination (Crone 1993:59–60; Kraft 2003:138).

Elite democracy

Democratic political institutions were introduced in the early part of the twentieth century by the US's colonial administration, but they did not deliver representative government. Without concomitant socioeconomic reforms, the landed oligarchy was able to exercise its wealth and influence to dominate the national legislature. In power, members of this elite protected their own class and individual interests, not least by appropriating the resources of the state in particularistic ways. As Paul Hutchcroft (1994:230) explains, economic returns from public office in the Philippines thus largely fell to politicians of private means, rather than to an elite within the bureaucracy:

> In contrast to 'bureaucratic capitalism', where a powerful bureaucratic elite is the major beneficiary of patrimonial largesse and exercises power over a weak business class, the principal direction of rent extraction is [in this case] reversed: a powerful oligarchic business class extracts privilege from a largely incoherent bureaucracy.

For this reason, the Philippines state has not been an effective appropriator of domestic economic surpluses—through the taxation system, for example—and nor has it effectively regulated the relations of production in agriculture and industry that generate such surpluses. Instead, the political economy of rent-seeking in the Philippines has often been fuelled by the state's interface with the international arena, through policies in relation to trade and currency exchange, and in its role as a conduit for foreign development assistance and loans (Hutchcroft 1994:222). Given the enormous drain on public resources caused by political patronage, the state has been able to survive only by having further access to overseas funds. Thus, the tendency has been, 'While the state is plundered internally, it is repeatedly rescued externally' (Hutchcroft 1994:226). As we will see later, this has implications for the Philippine government's current response to the war on terrorism.

It is important to stress that 'Philippine legislatures have been hospitable to the entry of the newly affluent' (Coronel et al. 2004:5). In other words, reflecting broader economic diversification since the 1950s, the backgrounds of politicians and their families have become considerably more varied and urban-based. Yet, as Coronel et al. (ibid) explain, political participation is today 'still limited to a narrow range of Philippine society'. Accordingly, 'Congress remains a fortress of privilege, its gates open to the new and aspiring rich, but closed—except for some narrow openings—to the poor and the powerless.'

While privileged elites have held on to their power, the forces opposing them in society have lacked direct representation in political society and government. The political party system, for example, is notoriously characterised by affiliations centred on the shifting terrain of personality-based loyalties among the elite, rather than on 'policies aimed at meeting the interests of particular categories of citizens' (Crouch 1984:43; see also Montinola 1999). Pressures for significant reform, as a consequence, have taken mainly extra-parliamentary—even extralegal—forms. This is seen with both the militant campaigns of leftist groups and Muslim separatists, and the more civil strategies of NGOs. Nowadays, there are more concerted moves to counter this situation through the formation of new, programmatic parties with links to progressive movements in civil society.

Authoritarianism

The state's brokerage role in the distribution of international funds contributed to the rise and fall of authoritarian rule in the 1970s and 1980s as, earlier, it helped to create certain centralist tendencies in Philippine politics (Doronila 1992; Wolters 1984:194–5). As summed up by Gary Hawes (1992:150), the locus of power in the 1960s

> was shifting in favour of the government; and within the government the balance of power was shifting towards the executive branch. The president had always controlled the release of government funds, but with an increase in the role of economic planners, the new emphasis on technical expertise in the control of the economy, growing economic and military assistance from abroad, and an increased resort to foreign borrowing ... the power of the executive branch grew, and for the first time began to extend out into the countryside and into local politics.

This structural trend was greatly magnified by the political ambitions of Ferdinand Marcos. After his election to the presidency in 1965, he used public funds to win congressional support, at the same time reorganising the bureaucracy to facilitate more direct links with the rural masses, then 70 per cent of the population (Doronila 1992:127–31). When he faced constitutional barriers to a third term in office in 1972, Marcos entrenched himself in office by declaring martial law, in the process shutting down the legislature, limiting press and civil freedoms, expanding the police and the military, and bringing significant sections of the economy under state control.

Key actors in the Marcos era were his closest political supporters—who (as previously pointed out) were not, as a rule, members of the traditional elite—and the military. In addition to political repression, the interests of this group lay in the rent-seeking opportunities provided by favoured treatment from the state. Accordingly, authoritarian rule did not diminish political patronage, rather it became more centralised through the person of the president. As competition for political favours was more limited and the magnitude of rents increased by monopolistic controls and foreign borrowings, the scale at which public resources moved into certain private hands was thus unprecedented and the Marcos regime became synonymous with cronyism. But as the political economy of the regime was ultimately tied to the availability of overseas funds, this was a factor that also played a key role in its eventual overthrow

Another element in the toppling of the regime was the AFP, which, from 1972, played a key role in the enforcement of martial law against insurgents and civilians alike. This included their deployment against the then newly formed Moro National Liberation Front (MNLF) on the southern island of Mindanao. The separatist demands of the MNLF went back to 1946, when Muslim Mindanao was made a part of the newly independent Philippines; however, the demands intensified after extensive Christian migration to Mindanao and the associated loss of communal lands in the 1960s. An autonomy agreement was reached, but failed, leading to an MNLF split from which a second organisation, the Moro Islamic Liberation Front

(MILF), emerged. This saw the greater Islamisation—and radicalisation—of the separatist conflicts in the south. Given the military's role in defending the regime from internal threats, when Marcos was finally ousted from office by massive street demonstrations of people power, the loyalty switch of the military was crucial in ensuring that there was peaceful change, not further repression.

Contested democracy

Marcos's immediate successor, President Aquino, reintroduced democratic elections, restored the legislature, disbanded the agricultural monopolies, and privatised a significant proportion of public enterprises. However, the oligarchy survived the Marcos years, and Aquino established the institutional conditions for 'the restoration of elite democracy' (Bello & Gershman 1990). In the 1987 congressional elections, most of those elected were from families with a prior record of political incumbency, although, in keeping with the postwar trend, the main economic base of these dynasties was no longer in agriculture but in industry, banking, and real estate (Doronila 1992:83–9; Wurfel 1979). More broadly, the Aquino regime did little to enhance the class capacities of social movements seeking more fundamental change. In not pushing through land reform in agriculture, her administration succumbed to wealthy landowner resistance. In industry, disputation and wage bargaining was returned to the regional and enterprise levels, moves that contributed to the fragmentation of the labour movement. The regime also oversaw an escalation in the use of violence against political and community activists by failing to control the proliferation of paramilitary and vigilante organisations. With central control over the military now diminished, regional commanders often joined with local political and economic elites to harass and 'salvage' the members of legal, progressive organisations and movements (McCoy 1988: 60).[7]

On the other hand, Aquino did create new openings for sectoral consultation on policies via NGOs. As Clarke (1998:67) explains, martial law had seen the emergence of 'a new generation of NGOs'. In his words:

> Until 1972, NGOs worked in close collaboration with the Philippine state, and, elitist in nature, had weak ties to their beneficiaries. Under the authoritarian regime however, new NGOs worked closely with grassroots 'people's organisations' ... Implementation of development projects in local communities provided the means to mobilise opposition to the state and NGOs developed significant capabilities, both in delivering social services and in organising beneficiaries.

From that history of opposition to authoritarian rule, NGOs developed strategies 'to build an infrastructure of political power and a socioeconomic capacity that was autonomous from the government and has the potential to undermine it' (Clarke 1998:67). This vision of civil society as a 'counterweight' to an exclusionary regime is one that has remained influential since the restoration of democracy (Quimpo 2004:9).Thus, Quimpo (2004) argues that democracy in the Philippines is not merely elite-based; rather, it remains essentially contested due to the active engagement of these progressive forces. Towards the end of her term in office, Aquino also introduced the legislative conditions for what some commentators termed 'a new form of governance' (Magno 1993; see also Brillantes 1994). Under the Local Government Code of 1991, NGO representation in various facets of local government was institutionalised, at the same time that sizeable resources (including up to 40 per cent of internal revenue) and decision-making and regulatory powers were devolved from the national to the local level of the state. Assessments of the impacts of this decentralisation process on democratic deepening show that they are highly uneven across different sectors and local government areas, according to the level of available resources, political backing, and technical support (Estrella & Iszatt 2004).

At a national level, it is widely believed that Philippine democracy has been strengthened through the activism of NGOs, as the state is now 'less completely captive of elite interests than previously' (Silliman & Noble 1998:306; see also Clarke 1998). Yet citing the example of agrarian reform, José Magadia (1999:265–66) argues that, when NGOs are consulted over major policy matters, in many cases their inputs have little or no effect on the final outcomes. In his view, many of the traditional features of political decision-making based on patronage thus still remain (see also Eaton 2003:482; Hutchcroft 1999). Evaluating more recent trends in this regard, Reid (2005) also sees little change. He argues that the appointment of progressive individuals to key posts in Cabinet has only produced 'new relationships of patronage and exclusion … as the state contains and co-opts privileged layers of "civil society" while largely excluding critical voices' (2005:30).

The 1987 Constitution made provision for expanded political representation by requiring that 20 per cent of the 250 seats in the House of Representatives be filled by party-list candidates through proportional representation (Eaton 2003:475). However, it took another eight years for the enabling legislation to pass through Congress, and by then no one party was allowed to win more than three seats in order to prevent the formation of a single progressive bloc (Eaton 2003:477–8). In the first general elections held after this, only one-quarter of the available seats actually filled (Montinola 1999:137–8). Six years later, in 2004, still only twenty-four party-list politicians were elected, just under half the possible number (US State Department 2005).

Yet despite their failings, democratic institutions have a high degree of popular legitimacy in the Philippines. Public opinion surveys show regularly that there is 'little authoritarian nostalgia' and 'high levels of efficacy and idealism regarding voting' (Linantud 2005:87). Accordingly, twice in the post-Marcos period, proposed revisions to the Constitution that would have enabled the incumbent president to stand for a second six-year term were defeated by public protest. Significantly, even President Ramos was not able to use his performance as an economic manager to obtain more years in the office. In part, this was because a sizeable section of the population was yet to receive personally the trickle down from economic growth. More importantly, the authoritarian alternative did not deliver material improvement to the general population and so, in comparison to some other South-East Asian nations, there is little public faith in the economic credentials of a strongman. But as the history of democracy in the Philippines reveals, this is not to say that the broad support for elections means that civil and political rights are secure; nor does it imply that the political system functions free from violence (Linantud 2005). In other words, as stated before, the real political contestation today is over the depth of democracy rather than the presence or absence of elections.

Economic reform

As well as progressing democratic consolidation, the Aquino administration took steps to liberalise trade. As intimated previously, some of the pressure to do so came externally from the World Bank and the IMF. At the same time, there was domestic support in line with the administration's promise to dismantle all vestiges of the Marcos regime, particularly import controls and trading monopolies in agriculture (de Dios & Hutchcroft 2003:53). Yet, these authors add, another important factor was 'the overall weakness of the economy' and the desperate need to do something about this (2003:54). After his election in 1992, President Ramos instituted further measures to liberalise the economy. These included the privatisation of a number of major state-owned enterprises; the break-up of monopolies and cartels in sectors such as agricultural marketing, air transport, interisland shipping, telecommunications, and power generation; the lifting of restrictions on foreign investment and the repatriation of profits; and further tariff reductions in trade. Also, the Bangko Sentral ng Pilipinas was recapitalised and given more independence from government, foreign banks were let in, build–operate–transfer arrangements were introduced to facilitate private investment in various infrastructure developments, large tracts of government land were sold off, and reforms to the taxation system were achieved.

Contests over government protectionism are 'often depicted as the epitome of struggle between political and economic forces in the Philippines' (de Dios 1998:57–8). This is the case for both neoclassical and economic nationalist (dependency) perspectives. But given that a close relationship has existed between rent-seeking and dirigisme in trade and investment, market liberalisation in the Philippines might be assumed to put an end to political patronage on a grand scale. As we have seen, in the minds of state-centred historical institutionalists, this outcome is equivalent to the state acquiring greater institutional coherence and autonomy.

Was this the case under Ramos? Did market reforms proceed because the state increased its authority over oligarchic interests? Or were there other factors at work?

It is argued here that some strengthening of the state did occur vis-à-vis protectionist interests under Ramos (Balisacan & Hill 2003:40). However, more than there being a marked reversal of causality between state and society, the policies of the Ramos administration were mostly a reflection of the different climate for economic liberalisation that is a legacy of the Marcos years. Of particular note is the fact that elite interests have also proved to be quite adaptable and opportunistic in their responses to these changing circumstances (de Dios 1998:74).

President Ramos was personally quite skilful in negotiating the politics of policy reform through Congress, a task made easier by changes to the socioeconomic composition of the legislature after the 1992 election, as a result of incumbents having a more diverse set of backgrounds (Velasco 1999:187). These changes are consistent with previously discussed social and economic transformations that have created new allegiances and interests in the business community and the professional middle class. In general, the new interests are more oriented towards an open economy, most particularly with regard to recent expanded foreign investment in industry, services, and property (de Dios 1998:78). Although it is a mistake to assume that such interests are unambiguously aligned with a free market, it is also the case that they can no longer simply be encompassed by the general categories of 'crony' or 'patrimonial capitalism' (Pinches 1996:124–7). On the other hand, the popular forces more resistant to market liberalisation generally lack the political capacity to oppose such policy changes outright.

To repeat, aside from these changes to the composition of the political elite, the pull back of the state has been a direct reaction to the Marcos dictatorship. To quote Pinches (1996:126):

> Not only did the Marcos regime take cronyism to extremes, but it also succeeded in greatly discrediting it as a developmental model in the eyes of the broad population, including the non-crony business community, and also in the eyes of foreign bankers and investors.

At a time when other South-East Asian countries were embarking—or so it seemed—on their own development miracles, the Philippines looked to be missing the boat. Market reforms under Ramos were not especially the result of any major socioeconomic upheaval, rather, they gained wide support as a way to break with the perceived roots of past economic failures. What is more, oligarchic interests had the class capacities to adjust to the altered circumstances of a changed role for the state (de Dios 1998:74).

But market liberalisation was not the natural policy alternative to what had gone on before. That the economic planning bureaucracy was dominated by neoclassical economists is particularly significant (Bello 2000:243–44;

Velasco 1999:189–94). Known widely as the technocrats, these economists have been actively advocating market reforms for a number of decades. They are said to have been a force behind the 1972 declaration of martial law to quash social opposition to a more open, exporting economy (Crowther 1986; Hawes 1987; see also Hawes 1992). Yet it was not until the early 1980s that Marcos was, in fact, obliged to meet the conditions of a World Bank 'structural adjustment' package due to the looming debt crisis by introducing a number of market reforms (Bautista 1989; Broad 1988). Crucially, this was 'an unwanted and forced agenda' that was made necessary by the need to access international funds (Montes 1989:80; see also Jayasuriya 1992:60). In other words, under Marcos, the technocrats gained policy ground through the fiscal dependency of the state on foreign sources of income and, therefore, not surprisingly, had their greatest influence during times of severe fiscal crisis. In the early 1990s, similar pressures were at work on the Ramos regime due to debt repayments and the loss of US financial assistance after the 1992 closure of the military bases (Hutchcroft 1994:234). But, by this time, the technocrats were also less marginalised politically, the support for market liberalisation now being more widespread. In this context, Bello (2000:243) admits that it is difficult to persist in characterising neoliberalism as having been imposed on the Philippines by the IMF and the World Bank. This is by no means to say that there is no domestic opposition to neoliberalism (see Bello 2000), simply that it lacks a strong political base.

After all, economic liberalisation is not necessarily the antidote to rent-seeking that neoclassical economists assume it to be. Moves to free the market have not been matched by institutional reforms to strengthen state capacities (Hutchcroft 1999). In his dealings with Congress, Ramos himself 'consistently relied on old-style "pork-barrel" and patronage politics in order to promote new-style liberal economics' (Hutchcroft 1999:458; see also Agpalo 1995:268). Thus, up to the 1997 regional financial crisis, government processes in the Philippines were still subject to considerable particularism and patronage because little attention had been paid to the bureaucratic reforms that state-centred historical institutionalists see as necessary. This is exemplified in political developments since the crisis, most notably with President Estrada being forced from office in 2001 over charges that he was personally corrupt. Meanwhile, the focus of liberal reform agendas is shifting to areas requiring extensive re-regulation and not merely the removal of instruments of protectionism. Here, for example, the Philippines is currently under pressure with regards to its 'relatively ineffective' stance in relation to intellectual property rights being guaranteed (US State Department 2005). Despite being a party to the WTO and various international treaties on this matter, the Philippines is now considered to be 'a net exporter of pirated products, producing more illegal products than can be consumed on the domestic market' in areas such as brand-name clothing, medicines, consumer electronics, cosmetics, toys, and books (US State Department 2005). More broadly, regulatory agencies in the Philippines are seen to lack statutory independence as they remain linked to departments or the office of the president itself. In the area of competition policy, laws that do exist are 'rarely enforced' (US State Department 2005). All these features are consistent with the state possessing a weak regulatory capacity.

Populism and renewed instability

Unlike in Indonesia, the 1997 financial crisis did not become a political crisis in the Philippines. Indeed, as the country came through the initial stages of the crisis rather better than most of its neighbours, President Ramos was able to claim some credit for what had ensued. Still, he was not able to achieve the Constitutional changes necessary to run for a second six-year term. Accordingly, in May 1998, a new president was elected, this time on a populist, pro-poor platform. He was the former movie star, Joseph Estrada. Estrada's election to the presidency was indicative of some new trends in Philippine politics. Although wealthy, he was not from the traditional elite and, as mentioned, his style was unreservedly populist. 'Political populism' refers to 'a pattern of top-down mobilization by personalist leaders that bypasses or subordinates institutional forms of political mediation' (Roberts 1995:85). In ideological terms, it draws a sharp distinction 'between "the people" and a "power bloc"' (Roberts 1995:84). As Pinches (1997:115-16) argues, since the toppling of Marcos, political elites have been forced to take greater account of 'popular political agency' by finding 'ways to harness or capture the potency of "people power"'. Presidents Aquino and Ramos displayed obvious tendencies in this regard; however, Estrada is the one who has most obviously embodied this phenomenon in clearly populist terms in recent times. A key point here is the '*deinstitutionalization* of political authority and representation under populism' and, hence, its reliance on mass mobilisations and the like (Roberts 1995:87; emphasis added). This form of populism is labelled political (and ideological) rather than economic to highlight the lack of coherent wealth distribution policies and, hence, its affinity with neoliberalism (Roberts 1995).

Estrada indeed committed himself to further market liberalisation. His time in office saw the passing of laws to strengthen the regulation of banking and the securities market, to expand foreign investment opportunities in retailing, and promote e-commerce, although there was also some backpedalling in the area of trade and the protection of monopolies (US State Department 2005; de Dios 1999). Nevertheless, his administration soon came to embody the old-style politics of patronage and cronyism (Wurfel 1999:29). The implementation of some market reforms, for example, involved the disbursement of favours through government. As de Dios (1998:80) points out, this reminds us that 'some processes in a liberalizing agenda, especially deregulation and privatization, yield substantial rents'. During the two and a half years that Estrada held the presidency, the transfer of state assets into private hands followed a pattern more consistent with political patronage than the pursuit of market forces (Bolongaita 1999:248). Like Marcos before him, Estrada was eventually forced from office in January 2001 by People Power 2 and the withdrawal of military support.

The duly elected Estrada was succeeded by his then vice-president, Gloria Macapagal Arroyo.[8] Despite Supreme Court endorsement of the Constitutional correctness of the succession, the Arroyo presidency has been burdened by doubts over its legitimacy. Most visibly, this was demonstrated some months later in 2001 through a third display of people power on Manila's streets. This demonstration in support of Estrada was more agitated and more clearly representative of the city's urban poor. Significantly, many commentators from the middle class classes were dismayed by this 'uncivil' display of populist support for a corrupt politician, arguing that it demonstrated the poor's lack of proper political and moral judgment (Banzon Bautista 2001). But, as Estrada's supporters from the city's sprawling squatter settlements asserted, he was hardly the only corrupt figure in Philippine politics and his being singled out for prosecution was more about the protection of elite privilege than putting a stop to corruption *per se*.

Three years later, in 2004, Arroyo won the presidential election, but allegations of vote rigging have dogged her claims to legitimate authority. Unfortunately, many of the accusers are political rivals, bent more on discrediting her personal integrity than they are in achieving actual political reforms.

The main legacy of all these events is twofold. On the one hand, there is widespread, genuine disquiet that people power has become a threat to constitutional democracy when used to challenge the legitimacy of electoral outcomes for personal political advantage (Linantud 2005). Beneath these concerns, there are also class divisions over the use of people power. Essentially, middle class progressives tend to consider that its status as a moral act has been degraded by populism, whereas urban poor communities are often inclined to view it, in more instrumental terms, as one of the few political openings available to them (Karaos 2003; Murphy 2005).[9] While some middle class commentators claim the moral high ground, they continue to regard the urban poor as a threat to needed institutional reforms to strengthen the state against patrimonialism. In the face of heightened political uncertainty, the military is in a stronger position to exercise greater influence over the current government (Linantud 2005). While there is little risk of a full military takeover, Linantud (2005) notes that the environment makes it more difficult for military and police to be charged over human rights violations and corruption, evidenced by President Arroyo's failure to severely punish the some 300 soldiers who seized buildings in the main Makati business district for almost a day in July 2003.

SECURING STABILITY?

The manner of the Philippines' involvement in the US-led war on terrorism is best understood in terms of this political climate against the longer-term backdrop of the political economy of US–Philippine relations in the past (Glassman, this volume, p. 219). In both respects, the AFP's involvement in the domestic affairs of the nation is crucial. Indeed, in the postwar period, the Philippine military has been principally an internal actor as, up to 1992, the country's external security threats were covered by its security alliance with the US (de Castro 1999:119). Central to this alliance was the Philippines' hosting of two major US bases on the island of Luzon, for which, in return, it received substantial US military and development assistance. As stated before, this flow of funds helped to serve elite interests over many decades. In the 1980s, US military expenditure in relation to the bases was totalling some US$350 million per year—and this did not include the spending of service personnel on after-hours 'entertainment' (May 1988:37–8). However, the bases were also a target of considerable church and nationalist opposition, both in relation to their social impacts on local communities and violations of national sovereignty. In 1992, three key factors converged to see the bases closed—shifting US priorities at the end of the Cold War, damage from a nearby volcanic eruption, and, more crucially, the failure of the Philippine Senate to ratify a new bases agreement the year before.

For a period after the bases were shut down, the US–Philippine alliance was in an 'essentially moribund' state (de Castro 2003:978). Without perceived external threats to the nation, then President Ramos was more concerned to advance economic recovery while also opting for negotiations with the communist New People's Army (NPA) and Muslim separatists in the south. In 1994, this approach led to the offering of a general conditional amnesty 'covering all rebel groups, as well as Philippine military and police personnel accused of crimes committed while fighting the insurgents' (US State Department 2005). In this period, Ramos also looked to reshape the AFP to perform the less conventional military functions of a disaster relief and environmental protection (de Castro 1999). But then, fresh concerns over China's stepped-up presence in the contested Spratly Islands, off the coast of the Philippines, saw some resumption of closer security ties with the US in the form of a new Visiting Forces Agreement in 1998 (Capie 2004:234). Glassman argues that this is evidence of US intentions to rebuild its presence in the South-East Asian region prior to September 11 (this volume, pp. 223–6). After this there was a more complete resumption of the security relationship. Glassman's point is that, from a US perspective, the war on terrorism enabled the fulfilment of plans hatched before September 11.

For the Philippine government, the timing of the war on terrorism was also opportune. In the same year as she originally assumed the presidency under controversial circumstances, Gloria Arroyo was quick to commit the AFP to a familiar, 'low-intensity' war on Philippine soil. [10] To that end, in the following year, the country joined the US in placing the NPA and the Abu Sayyaf on the latter's growing list of international terrorists. In addition to receiving more than US$100 million in military training, financing, and equipment, the Philippines was granted 'a huge package of trade credits, tariff reductions and debt write-offs, potentially worth more than US$1 billion' (Capie 2004:233). Kraft (2003:144) argues that it is a demonstration of the weakness of the Philippine state that, 'in moments of political difficulty, it goes back to traditional relations of dependency with the United States'. Arroyo depended on the support of the military to stay in office and so the renewed security alliance's most obvious beneficiary was always going to be the AFP (Capie 2004:234). However, corruption in the military is known to be 'deeply institutionalized' (Rivera 2005:13). Renewed US military and financial assistance is bound to only further facilitate this problem. Indeed, as Glassman (this volume, page 219) notes, senior officers in the military have been accused of encouraging the escalation of armed conflict in the south: no wonder; they have an industry to protect.

But, struggling for greater popular legitimacy and support, the Arroyo government has also been forced to respond to domestic opposition to some facets of her engagement with the war on terrorism. In 2003, for example, a planned joint operation with US troops on Philippine soil was cancelled amid fears that those troops were to be involved in direct combat, which is in violation of the Philippine Constitution (de Castro 2005). Significantly, President Arroyo has shown greater willingness to have the AFP fight 'terrorists' at home than she has in supporting the war in Iraq. The Philippines did commit a small contingent of humanitarian forces to Iraq, but these were withdrawn early after the kidnapping of a civilian truck driver, Angelo de la Cruz, who was one of the nearly 4 million Filipinos working overseas on short-term contracts. Given the political pressures on successive governments in recent years to ensure the safety of these national heroes, his kidnapping, not surprisingly, drew a strong and anguished public response. Politically, Arroyo could not refuse to act to save Angelo de la Cruz, despite her actions invoking a sharp rebuke from the US and a number of its allies.

In short, Arroyo was motivated to allow a war against terrorism at home, largely to deal with her administration's own current political and economic difficulties. However, her response is also in keeping with the nature of the longer-term, special relationship between the Philippines and the US. As Kraft (2003) argues, instability in the Philippines is the result of a weak state, one with little or no capacity to produce radical change in the pattern of domination in society. Chances are, the war on terrorism will do nothing to change this.

CONCLUSION

After some optimism in the 1990s that the economic fortunes of the Philippines might be turned around, the new century has renewed doubts about the political system and its capacities for reform (de Dios & Hutchcroft 2003). More than ever, there is international scrutiny of the country's record on governance and poverty. As this chapter has shown, on both scores, the Philippines has not done well. Corruption is considered to be 'a pervasive and long-standing problem' (US State Department 2005), but measures to address this have not seriously confronted the unrepresentative nature of political society. Instead, on the whole, transnational policy agendas around democratisation and participatory development have stressed the transformative capacities of civil society organisations. Yet, one of the take-home lessons from the Philippines case is that progressive civil society organisations find it difficult to build needed fundamental reforms if the state is not particularly strong and responsive (Walzer 1992). Elite democracy in the country has accommodated a level of social activism that is unusual in South-East Asia; however, this itself has contributed to political instability because, currently, there is no mechanism to consolidate the reformist forces in electoral contests over government (Coronel Ferrer 2004:558–64). Alternative political parties remain too small and numerous to achieve this objective, the result being that political society in the Philippines continues to feature shifting, short-term, tactical coalitions and alliances (Abinales 2001; Coronel Ferrer 2004:562), with political populism being a key means of directly engaging the electorate. Thus, with apologies to Marx (1975), the title of this chapter aims to highlight major deficiencies in Philippine democracy that have undoubtedly contributed to persistent poverty and wealth inequalities.

NOTES

1 A partial exception to this was the period of the Ramos presidency between 1992 and 1998 (Balisacan and Hill 2003:40).

2 'Political society' here refers to the arena of contestation over 'the legitimate right to exercise control over public power and the state apparatus' (Linz and Stepan 1996:8, in Eaton 2003:471).

3 In the Philippines, a distinction is often made between NGOs and peoples' organisations (POs) on the grounds that the latter tend to be more membership-based and localised, whereas the former are generally more professionalised and claim to serve others, or at least represent their interests (see Clarke 1998:2–3).Here I use NGO more broadly to include POs; however, later in the chapter I point to current political divisions between urban POs and NGOs in Manila over the legitimacy of the Arroyo presidency.

4 Permanent workers are 'immigrants or legal permanent residents abroad whose stay does not depend on work contracts', whereas irregular workers are those 'not properly documented or without valid residence or work permits, or who are overstaying in a foreign country' (POEA 2003).

5 'The share of FDI to GFCF measures the relative weight of FDIs in the total aggregate investment (both public and private) in the country while the share of FDI inward stock to GDP provides an indication of the importance of inward stock in relation to the aggregate economic activity in the country' (de Guia 2005). McCoy (1988) argues that 'low-intensity conflict' against insurgence was a largely AFP invention in the war against the Huk peasant rebellion in the late 1940s and early 1950s, which the US later adopted and supported in Latin America and, again, the Philippines in the 1980s.

6 See Pinches (2001) for an insightful discussion of the overseas contract workers' experiences of wage labour. Pinches (2001: 187) argues here for an approach that takes more account of workers' class experiences 'beyond the workplace, the trade union or the political party' than the conventional literature generally does.

7 'Salvaging' is a term widely used in the Philippines for summary killings.

8 In addition to being a trained economist, Gloria Arroyo is the daughter of past President Diosdado Macapagal (1962–65), who lost the 1965 presidential election to Ferdinand Marcos.

9 McCoy (1988) argues that 'low-intensity conflict' against insurgence was a largely AFP invention in the war against the Huk peasant rebellion in the late 1940s and early 1950s, which the US later adopted and supported in Latin America and, again, the Philippines in the 1980s.

10 As Karaos (2003:2) explains, this is especially true of squatter communities living on government-owned land as the president has the power to proclaim such lands for disposition to the communities that live on them.

REFERENCES

Abinales, Patricio N. (2001) 'Coalition Politics in the Philippines', *Current History*, 100(645): 154–61.

Abrenica, Ma. Joy V. and Llanto, Gilberto M. (2003) 'Services' in Arsenio M. Balisacan and Hal Hill (eds) *The Philippine Economy: Development, Policies and Challenges*, New York: Oxford University Press, pp. 254–77.

Agpalo, Remigio E. (1995) 'The Philippines: Remarkable Economic Turnaround and Qualified Political Success', *Southeast Asian Affairs 1995*, Singapore: Institute of Southeast Asian Studies, pp. 259–72.

Asian Development Bank (ADB) (2000) *Asia Recovery Report 2000: May 2000 Update*, Manila: Regional Economic Monitoring Unit, Asia Development Bank.

——(2003) *Country Assistance Program Evaluation in the Philippines*, January, Manila, <www.adb.org/Documents/CAPEs/PHI/cap_phi_200304.pdf>.

——(2004) *Development of Poor Urban Communities Sector*, <www.adb.org/Documents/Profiles/LOAN/32499013.ASP>.

——(2005) 'Philippines' in *Asian Development Outlook 2005*, <www.adb.org/documents/books/ado/2005/phi.asp>.

Balisacan, Arsenio and Hal Hill (2003) 'An Introduction to the Key Issues', in Arsenio M. Balisacan and Hal Hill (eds) *The Philippine Economy: Development, Policies and Challenges*, New York: Oxford University Press, pp. 3–44.

Bangko Sentral ng Pilipinas (BSP) (2005a) 'Exports by Major Commodity Group', <www.bsp.gov.ph/statistics/spei/tab1.1a.htm>.

——(2005b) 'Overseas Workers' Remittances', <www.bsp.gov.ph/statistics/spei/tab11.htm>.

——(2005c) 'Total External Debt', <www.bsp.gov.ph/statistics/spei/tab6.htm>.

Banzon Bautista and Cynthia Rose (2001) 'People Power 2: The Revenge of the Elite on the Masses?', in Amando Doronila (ed.) *Between Fires: Fifteen Perspectives on the Estrada Crisis*, Manila: Anvil Publishing and Philippine Daily Inquirer, pp. 1–42.

Bautista, Romeo M. (1989) *Impediments to Trade Liberalization in the Philippines*, London: Trade Policy Research Centre; Aldershot: Gower.

Bello, Walden (2000) 'The Philippines: The making of a neo-classical tragedy', in Richard Robison, Mark Beeson, Kanishka Jayasuriya and Hyuk-Rae Kim (eds) *Politics and Markets in the Wake of the Asian Crisis*, London and New York: Routledge, pp. 238–57.

——and John Gershman (1990) 'Democratization and Stabilization in the Philippines', *Critical Sociology*, 17(1):35–56.

——, David Kinley and Elaine Elinson (1982) *Development Debacle: the World Bank in the Philippines*, San Francisco: Institute for Food and Development Policy.

——, Mary Lou Malig, Herbert Docena and Marissa de Guzman (2004) *The Anti-Development State: The Political Economy of Permanent Crisis in the Philippines*, Department of Sociology, Manila: University of the Philippines and Bangkok: Focus on Global South.

Billig, Michael S. (1994) 'The Death and Rebirth of Entrepreneurism on Negros Island, Philippines: A Critique of Cultural Theories of Enterprise', *Journal of Economic Issues*, 28(3): 659–78.

——(2003) *Barons, Brokers, and Buyers: The Institutions and Cultures of Philippine Sugar*, Manila: Ateneo de Manila University Press.

Bolongaita, Emil P. (1999) 'The Philippines: Consolidating Democracy in Difficult Times', *Southeast Asian Affairs 1999*, Singapore: Institute of Southeast Asian Studies, pp. 237–52.

Boyce, James (1993) *The Philippines: The Political Economy of Growth and Impoverishment in the Marcos Era*, London: Macmillan.

Broad, Robin (1988) *Unequal Alliance: the World Bank, the International Monetary Fund, and the Philippines*, Berkeley: University of California Press.

Brillantes, Alex B. (1994) 'Decentralization: Governance From Below', *Kasarinlan*, 10(1): 41–7.

Brown, Ian (1989) 'Some Comments on Industrialisation in the Philippines during the 1930s', in Ian Brown (ed.) *The Economies of Africa and Asia in the Inter-War Depression*, London and New York: Routledge, pp. 203–20.

Buchanan, James M. (1980) 'Rent Seeking and Profit Seeking', in James M. Buchanan, Robert D. Tollison and Gordon Tullock (eds) *Towards a Theory of the Rent-Seeking Society*, Texas: Texas A&M University Press, pp. 3–15.

Capie, David (2004) 'Between a hegemon and a hard place: the "war on terror" and Southeast Asian–US relations', *Pacific Review*, 17(2): 223–48.

Caporaso, James A. and David P. Levine (1992) *Theories of Political Economy*, New York: Cambridge University Press.

Carroll, John (1965) *The Filipino Manufacturing Entrepreneur: Agent and Product of Change*, Ithaca: Cornell University Press.

Clarke, Gerard (1998) *The Politics of NGOs in South-East Asia: Participation and Protest in the Philippines*, London and New York: Routledge.

——and Marites Sison (2003) 'Voices from the Top of the Pile: Elite Perceptions of Poverty and the Poor in the Philippines', *Development and Change*, 34(2):215–42.

Coronel, Sheila, Yvonne T. Chua, Luz Rimban and Booma B. Cruz (2004) *The Rulemakers: How the Wealthy and Well-Born Dominate Congress*, Manila: Philippine Center for Investigative Journalism.

Coronel Ferrer, Miriam (2004) 'The Philippine State and Civil Society Discourse and Praxis', *Korea Observer*, 35(3):535–71.

Crone, Donald K. (1993) 'States, Elites, and Social Welfare in Southeast Asia', *World Development*, 21(1):55–66.

Crouch, Harold (1984) *Domestic Political Structures and Regional Co-operation*, Singapore: ASEAN Economic Research Unit, Institute of Southeast Asian Studies.

Crowther, William (1986) 'Philippine Authoritarianism and the International Economy', *Comparative Politics*, 18(3):339–55.

de Castro, Renato Cruz (1999) 'Adjusting to the post-U.S. bases era: The ordeal of the Philippine military's modernization', *Armed Forces and Society*, 26(1):119–37.

——(2003) 'The Revitalized Philippine–U.S. Security Relations', *Asian Survey*, 43(6): 971–88.

——(2005) 'U.S. War on Terror in East Asia: The Perils of Preemptive Defense in Waging a War of the Third Kind', *Asian Affairs*, 31(4):212–231.

Department of Labor and Employment (DOLE) (2005) 'Existing Labor Organizations and Collective Bargaining Agreements (CBAs) as of March 2005', <www.blr.dole.gov.ph/>.

de Dios, Emmanuel (1998) 'Philippine Economic Growth: Can It Last?', in David G. Timberman (ed.) *The Philippines: New Directions in Domestic Policy and Foreign Relations*, New York: The Asia Society, pp. 49–84.

——(1999) 'Crisis without consequence: recovery without reform', *Philippine Daily Inquirer*, 25 August 1999, <www.inquirer.net/issues/aug99/aug25/business/bus_10.htm>.

——et al. (2004) 'The deepening crisis: The real score on deficits and the public debt', University of the Philippines, School of Economics Discussion Paper No. 04–09, accessed at <www.econ.upd.edu.ph>.

——and Paul Hutchcroft (2003) 'Political Economy', in Arsenio M. Balisacan and Hal Hill (eds) *The Philippine Economy: Development, Policies, and Challenges*, New York: Oxford University Press, pp. 45–73.

De Guia, John Frederick P. (2005) 'Foreign Direct Investments: Why do we need them?', National Statistics and Census Board (NSCB), <www.nscb.gov.ph/headlines/StatsSpeak/061305_rav_jpd_fdi.asp>.

Doherty, John F. (1982) 'Who Controls the Philippine Economy: Some Need Not Try as Hard as Others', in Belinda Aquino (ed.) *Cronies and Enemies: The Current Philippine Scene*, Philippine Studies Occasional Paper No. 5, University of Hawai'i, pp. 7–35.

Doronila, Amando (1992) *The State, Economic Transformation, and Political Change in the Philippines, 1946–72*, Singapore: Oxford University Press.

Eaton, Kent (2003) 'Restoration of Transformation? *Trapos* versus NGOs in the Democratization of the Philippines', *Journal of Asian Studies*, 62(2):469–96.

Estrella, Marisol and Nina Iszatt (eds) (2004) *Beyond Good Governance: Participatory Democracy in the Philippines*, Manila: Institute for Popular Democracy.

Evans, Peter (1994) *Embedded Autonomy: States and Industrial Transformation*, Princeton: Princeton University Press.

Hawes, Gary (1987) *The Philippine State and the Marcos Regime: The Politics of Export*, Ithaca: Cornell University Press.

——(1992) 'Marcos, His Cronies, and the Philippines' Failure to Develop', in Ruth McVey (ed.) *Southeast Asian Capitalists*, Ithaca: Cornell University Press, Southeast Asian Program, pp. 145–60.

Hill, Hal (2003) 'Industry', in Arsenio M. Balisacan and Hal Hill (eds) *The Philippine Economy: Development, Policies and Challenges*, New York: Oxford University Press, pp. 219–53.

Hutchcroft, Paul D. (1994) 'Booty Capitalism: Business–Government Relations in the Philippines', in Andrew J. MacIntyre (ed.) *Business and Government in Industrialising Asia*, Sydney: Allen & Unwin, pp. 216–43.

——(1999) 'After the Fall: Prospects for Political and Institutional Reform in Post-Crisis Thailand and the Philippines', *Government and Opposition*, 33(4):473–97.

Infante, Jaime (1980) *The Political, Economic, and Labor Climate in the Philippines*, Industrial Research Unit, Philadelphia: University of Pennsylvania, Wharton School.

Jayasuriya, Sisira (1987) 'The politics of economic policy in the Philippines during the Marcos era', in Richard Robison, Kevin Hewison and Richard Higgott (eds) *Southeast Asia in the 1980s: The Politics of Economic Crisis*, Sydney: Allen & Unwin, pp. 80–112.

——(1992) 'Structural Adjustment and Economic Performance in the Philippines', in Andrew J. MacIntyre and Kanishka Jayasuriya (eds) *The Dynamics of Economic Policy Reform in South-East Asia and the South-West Pacific*, Singapore: Oxford University Press, pp. 50–73.

Karaos, Anna Marie A. (2003) *Populist Mobilization and Manila's Urban Poor: The Case of SANAPA in the NGC East Side*, Occasional Paper No. 22, Manila: Institute for Popular Democracy.

Kerkvliet, Benedict J. Tria (1979) *The Huk Rebellion: A Study of Peasant Revolt in the Philippines*, Quezon City: New Day Publishers.

——(1991) *Everyday Politics in the Philippines: Class and Status Relations in a Central Luzon Village*, Quezon City: New Day Publishers.

Koike, Kenji (1989) 'The Reorganization of Zaibatsu Groups under the Marcos and Aquino Regimes', *East Asian Cultural Studies*, 28, March, pp. 127–43.

Kongsamut, Piyabha and Athanasios Vamvakidis (1999) 'Economic Growth', in Markus Rodlauer and Prakash Loungani (eds) *Philippines: Selected Issues, IMF Staff Country Report No. 99/92*, Washington, DC: International Monetary Fund, pp. 10–37.

Kraft, Herman Joseph S. (2003) 'The Philippines: The Weak State and the Global War on Terror', *Kasarinlan*, 18(1–2):133–52.

Krueger, Anne O. (1974) 'The Political Economy of the Rent-Seeking Society', *American Economic Review*, LXIV(3):291–303.

Kunihara, Kenneth K. (1945) *Labor in the Philippine Economy*, Stanford: Stanford University Press.

Lim, Joseph Y. (1990) 'The Agricultural Sector: Stagnation and Change', in Emmanuel S. de Dios and Lorna Villamil (eds) *Plans, Markets and Relations: Studies for a mixed economy*, Manila: Kalikasan Press, pp. 118–32.

Linantud, John L. (2005) 'The 2004 Philippine Elections: Political Change in an Illiberal Democracy', *Contemporary Southeast Asia*, 27(1):80–102.

Mackie, James (1988) 'An Overview: US Bases and Politics of the US–Philippines Relationship', in Desmond Ball (ed.) *US Bases in the Philippines: Issues and Implications*, Canberra: Australian National University, Canberra Papers on Strategy and Defence, No. 46, pp. 15–32.

Magadia, José (1999) 'Contemporary Civil Society in the Philippines', *Southeast Asian Affairs 1999*, Singapore: Institute of Southeast Asian Studies, pp. 253–68.

Magno, Alexander R. (1993) 'A Changed Terrain for Popular Struggles', *Kasarinlan*, 8(3): 7–21.

Marx, Karl (1975) *The Poverty of Philosophy: Answer to the 'Philosophy of Poverty' by M. Proudhon*, Moscow: Progress Publishers.

May, Ron (1988) 'The Bases Issue in Philippines Domestic Politics', in Desmond Ball (ed.) *US Bases in the Philippines: Issues and Implications*, Canberra Papers on Strategy and Defence, No. 46, Canberra: Australian National University, pp. 33–42.

McCoy, Alfred (1982) 'Introduction: The Social History of an Archipelago', in Alfred McCoy and Ed de Jesus (eds) *Philippine Social History: Global Trade and Local Transformations*, Quezon City: Ateneo de Manila University Press, pp. 1–18.

——(1988) 'Low Intensity Conflict in the Philippines', in Barry Carr and Elaine McKay (eds) *Low Intensity Conflict: Theory and Practice in Central America and South-East Asia*, Melbourne: Institute of Latin American Studies, La Trobe University and Centre of Southeast Asian Studies, Monash University, pp. 51–71.

Migdal, Joel S. (1988) *Strong Societies and Weak States: State–Society Relations and State Capabilities in the Third World*, Princeton: Princeton University Press.

Montes, Manuel F. (1989) 'Philippine Structural Adjustments, 1970–1987', in Manuel Montes and Hideyoshi Sakai (eds) *Philippine Macroeconomic Perspective: Developments and Policies*, Tokyo: Institute of Developing Economies, pp. 45–90.

Montinola, Gabriella R. (1999) 'Parties and Accountability in the Philippines', *Journal of Democracy*, 10(1):126–40.

Moser, Caroline O. N. (1998) 'The Asset Vulnerability Framework: Reassessing Urban Poverty Reduction Strategies', *World Development*, 26(1):1–19.

Murphy, Denis (2005) 'People go the other way', *Philippine Daily Inquirer*, July 13, p. A13.

National Statistics Office (NSO) (2004) 'National Accounts', <www.census.gov.ph/data/nationalaccounts/index.html>.

——(2005) 'Labor Force Statistics', <www.census.gov.ph/data/sectordata/datalfs.html>.

Noland, Marcus (2000) 'The Philippines in the Asian Financial Crisis', *Asian Survey*, 40(3):401–12.

Ofreneo, Rene (1994) 'The labour market, protective labour institutions and economic growth in the Philippines', in Gerry Rodgers (ed.) *Workers, Institutions and Economic Growth in Asia*, Geneva: International Institute for Labor Studies, pp. 255–301.

Philippine Overseas Employment Agency (POEA) (2003) 'Stock Estimates of Filipinos Overseas (Inter-Agency Report)', <www.poea.gov.ph/html/statistics.html>.

Pinches, Michael (1996) 'The Philippines: new rich: capitalist transformations amidst economic gloom', in Richard Robison and David S. G. Goodman (eds) *The New Rich in Asia: Mobile phones, McDonalds and middle-class revolution*, London and New York: Routledge, pp. 105–33.

——(1997) 'Elite Democracy, Development, and People Power', *Asian Studies Review*, 21 (2–3):104–20.

—— (1999) 'Entrepreneurship, consumption, ethnicity and national identity in the making of the Philippines' new rich', in Michael Pinches (ed.) *Culture and Privilege in Capitalist Asia*, London and New York: Routledge, pp. 275–301.

——(2001) 'Class and national identity: The case of Filipino migrant workers', in Jane Hutchison and Andrew Brown (eds) *Organising Labour in Globalising Asia*, New York and London: Routledge, pp. 187–213.

Quimpo, Nathan Gilbert (2004) *Contested Democracy and the Left in the Philippines after Marcos*, unpublished PhD thesis, Canberra: Australian National University.

Racelis, Mary (2000) 'New Visions and Strong Actions: Civil Society and the Philippines', in Marina Ottaway and Thomas Carothers (eds) *Funding Virtue: Civil Society, Aid and Democracy Promotion*, Washington, DC: Carnegie Endowment for International Peace, pp. 159–87.

Ranis, Gustav (1974) *Sharing in Development: A Programme of Employment, Equity and Growth for the Philippines*, Geneva: International Labor Organization.

Reid, Ben (2005) 'Poverty Alleviation and Participatory Development in the Philippines', *Journal of Contemporary Asia*, 35(1):29–52.

Rivera, Temario C. (1994a) *Landlords and Capitalists: Class, Family, and the State in Philippine Manufacturing*, Quezon City: University of the Philippines Press.

——(1994b) 'The State, Civil Society, and Foreign Actors: The Politics of Philippine Industrialization', *Contemporary Southeast Asia*, 16(2):157–77.

——(2005) 'The Philippines: New Mandate, Daunting Problems', *Asian Survey*, 45(1): 127–33

Roberts, Kenneth M. (1995) 'Neo-liberalism and the Transformation of Populism in Latin America: The Peruvian Case', *World Politics*, 48:82–116.

Rocamora, Joel (2004) 'Formal Democracy and Its Alternatives in the Philippines: Parties, Elections and Social Movements', in Jayant Lele and Fahimul Quadir (eds) *Democracy and Civil Society in Asia: Vol. 2*, Palgrave: Macmillan, pp. 196–221.

Schelzig, Karen (2005) *Poverty in the Philippines: Income, Assets and Access*, Manila: Asian Development Bank.

Sen, Amartya (1999) *Development as Freedom*, New York: Anchor Books.

Shepherd, Geoffrey and Florian Alburo (1991) 'The Philippines', in Demetris Papageorgiou, Michael Michaely and Armeane Choski (eds) *Liberalizing Foreign Trade Vol 2*, Oxford: Basil Blackwell, pp. 133–308.

Silliman, G. Sidney and Lela Ganer Noble (1998) 'Introduction', in G. Sidney Silliman and Lela Garner Noble (eds) *Organizing for Democracy: NGOs, Civil Society, and the Philippine State*, Honolulu: University of Hawai'i Press, pp. 1–25.

Snow, Robert T. (1983) 'Export-Oriented Industrialization, the International Division of Labor, and the Rise of the Subcontract Bourgeoisie in the Philippines', in Norman Owen (ed.) *The Philippine Economy and the United States: Studies in Past and Present Interactions*, Michigan Papers on South and Southeast Asia no. 22.

Snyder, Kay and Thomas C. Nowak (1982) 'Philippine Labor Before Martial Law: Threat or Nonthreat?', *Studies in Comparative International Development*, 17(3–4):44–72.

Stauffer, Robert B. (1974) 'Political economy of a coup: transnational linkages and Philippine political response', *Journal of Peace Research*, 3:161–77.

Unite, Angelo A. and Michael J. Sullivan (2000) 'Reform and the corporate environment in the Philippines', in Peter Drysdale (ed) *Reform and Recovery in East Asia: The Role of the State and Economic Enterprise*, London and New York: Routledge, pp. 191–213.

United Nations Development Programme (UNDP) (2002) *Human Development Report: Philippines*, New York: United Nations Development Programme.

US State Department (2005) *Philippines: 2005 Investment Climate Statement*, <www.state.gov/e/eb/ifd/2005/42102.htm>.

Velasco, Renato S. (1999) 'The Philippines', in Ian Marsh, Jean Blondel and Takashi Inoguchi (eds) *Democracy, Governance, and Economic Performance: East and Southeast Asia*, Tokyo, New York and Paris: United Nations University Press, pp. 167–202.

Walzer, Michael (1992) 'The Civil Society Argument', in Chantal Mouffe (ed.) *Dimensions of Radical Democracy*, London: Verso, pp. 89–107.

Weber, Max (1968) *Economy and Society: an outline of interpretive sociology*, Guenther Roth and Claus Wittich (eds), New York: Bedminister Press.

Weiss, Linda and John M. Hobson (2000) 'State power and economic strength revisited: what's so special about the Asian crisis?', in Richard Robison et al. (eds) *Politics and Markets in the Wake of the Asian Crisis*, London: Routledge, pp. 53–74.

Wolters, Willem (1984) *Politics, Patronage and Class Conflict in Central Luzon*, Quezon City: New Day Publishers.

World Bank (1989) *Philippines: Towards Sustaining the Economic Recovery*, Country Economic Memorandum, Washington, DC: World Bank.

——(1999) *Philippines: The Challenge of Economic Recovery*, Washington, DC: World Bank. Poverty Reduction and Economic Management Sector Unit of The World Bank, East Asia and Pacific Region.

——(2001) *Combating Corruption in the Philippines: An Update*, Washington, DC: World Bank.

Wurfel, David (1959) 'Trade Union Development and Labor Relations Policy in the Philippines', *Industrial and Labor Relations Review*, 12(4):582–608.
——(1979) 'Elites of Wealth and Elites of Power: The Changing Dynamic', *Southeast Asian Affairs 1979*, Singapore: Institute of Southeast Asian Studies, pp. 233–45.
——(1999) 'Convergence and Divergence Amidst Democratization and Economic Crisis: Thailand and the Philippines Compared', *Philippine Political Science Journal*, 20(43): 1–44. 3

3 Thailand: Boom, Bust, and Recovery

Kevin Hewison[1]

KEY TOPICS

INTRODUCTION

IN the first decade of the twenty-first century, Thailand is unequivocally a capitalist economy and society. This once agricultural society is now incorporated into a world system of production, exchange, and investment, subjecting its people to the many vagaries associated with international capitalism.

Most writers have tended to use 'capitalism' as a shorthand designation for the system of economic organisation that has taken place within a relatively free enterprise system. Industrialisation has been an important part of this, transforming a subsistence economy into one in which production involves the application of capital in enterprises that produce primarily for profit. Trade and commerce take on an increasingly significant role, while the industrial system sees producers separated from their products as they become waged workers, employed by the owners and managers of enterprises who control those products. Capitalist industry occurs within an environment where individuals or groups of investors own businesses and competition among businesses is the norm.

Conceptualising these fundamentals as integral to a system is important. Capitalism, as well as being a way of organising economic production, also structures society. Capitalist enterprise demands a social system in which the working class has at least some of its labour for sale and able to be purchased by a much smaller class of business owners and managers. As capitalists continually seek ways to reduce their costs, capitalist globalisation and production has increasingly been broken into its component parts, meaning that national borders are no longer obstacles to production and trade they once were. Finance, too, has had to become more mobile and huge sums of money are now invested internationally.[2]

It is sometimes argued that Thailand's capitalist transition has not matched the history of Anglo-American development (see, for example, Pasuk & Baker 1998:ch. 4). Indeed, Thailand's progress has not matched the trajectories of Britain, American and Japanese development. However, Thailand's capitalist path has much that is recognisable in other transition experiences. Thailand's capitalist development has been rapid and has deeply transformed society. Capitalist revolutions involve a rearrangement of the forces that rule a society. New elites are created, while old elites struggle to maintain their economic, social, cultural, and political power. At the same time, subordinated classes are reconfigured. Of course, such transformations involve considerable political activism and are inevitably highly contested.

Thailand's transformation was underpinned by a remarkable period of uninterrupted growth from 1957 to 1996 (Warr & Bhanupong 1996). While the Asian economic crisis ended this growth period, and dramatically demonstrated Thailand's integration into the global capitalist system, economic expansion again resumed from 1999. Contestation over the shape of this development and over the benefits that flow from it is both economic and political. It is these struggles that are the focus of this chapter. In examining contestation, the analysis will follow two main dimensions of struggle: the first is conflict between classes, focused on the contest between capitalists, workers, and other subordinated classes; the second is the conflict within the capitalist class itself. In outlining these contests, the accumulation regime of each of the epochs examined will be delineated. The analytical task is not so much to identify good and bad economic policy in each epoch, but to outline the ensemble of class forces and the conflicts that led to the emergence of particular policy outcomes. This means that emphasis will be on delineating the class relations involved in capitalist development, the changing international context of development, the role of the state, and the way in which policy reflects patterns of domination. The outline is necessarily schematic. It seeks to determine general patterns in periods of rapid change and to convey the essence of particular accumulation regimes.

This perspective is explicitly grounded in the social conflict approach outlined in chapter 1 of this volume. As was noted in that chapter, this is not the only interpretation of capitalist development in the region. It is, therefore, appropriate to begin this chapter with a brief outline and critique of the theoretical debates; however, as chapter 1 has detailed the general approaches that analysts have taken, this first section will elaborate upon these only for Thailand. Following this, the chapter turns to the story of contestation over the control and outcomes of Thailand's capitalist transformation over the last 150 years, paying particular attention to the last five decades.

A SKETCH OF THEORETICAL APPROACHES

Modernisation approaches

The dominant perspectives on Thailand's society and politics remain much influenced by modernisation theory. This theory characterises Thai society as 'loosely structured'; the mass of the population is apolitical, and politics revolves around the politicised elite. Hierarchy and status were important in binding the masses to the elite through a vast patronage network. Writing in the mid 1960s, Riggs famously analysed Thailand as a 'bureaucratic polity', a conception of the relations between business and government that remains exceptionally strong in the literature. Riggs (1966) saw business as having little political influence. The political elite of civil and military bureaucrats adopted a predatory attitude, making businesspeople their clients. Through its control of politics, the elite was able to dictate policy and establish corrupt patron–client relations that fed on economic development. Bureaucrats, especially those in the military, were able to maintain a degree of control over business that ensured that the benefits of development served the interests of the military and bureaucracy first and the masses second. Riggs used 'bureaucratic polity' as a theoretical conceptualisation of the transition from tradition to modernity, while most others who utilise the concept tend to use it as a descriptive category to identify a polity in which the civil and military bureaucracies retain considerable political power and privilege, and where society is relatively powerless.

By the 1980s, bureaucratic polity came to be seen as an inappropriate characterisation of a Thailand experiencing rapid economic growth and massive social change. The rise of a powerful and apparently independent business class, and the concomitant decline of the military, contradicted the Riggsian-derived description (see McVey 1992:20–2). As the bureaucratic polity was seen to be replaced by a system in which business had far more autonomy, historical institutionalist approaches surfaced (see below), where business–government relations were conceptualised as a partnership, albeit characterised by corruption that emerged from patronage (Anek 1992:13–15).

The 1997 economic crash saw a limited resurgence of modernisation perspectives. Unger (1998), for example, has taken a broadly modernisation perspective in his application of the notion of social capital to Thailand. He identifies the paradox of rapid growth being achieved where the bureaucracy is weak and policy implementation poor. Unger explains this as resulting from a lack of social capital among Thais. His analysis draws extensively on observations from modernisation theory, reviving bureaucratic polity in explaining cultural differences between ethnic Chinese and Thais. The former are seen as more sociable than the Thais, thus providing drive in the economy, albeit with limited inputs into the political system. Unger (1998:18) suggests that limited sociability among Thais has diminished the capacity of state officials to foster social change and the adoption of market strategies, and has led to factionalism and poor coordination among state agencies. In this approach, the 1997 crisis can be seen to have resulted from shortcomings that have deep cultural roots.

Like his modernisation predecessors, Unger operates with models of society, politics, and ethnicity that tend to downplay much of Thailand's diversity, political competition, repression, and struggle. Like his theoretical predecessors, Unger also pays too little attention to the international dimensions of capitalist development. The relative neglect of these factors means that revised modernisation approaches are unable to capture the full ramifications of Thailand's recent economic and political development.

Dependency approaches

As explained in chapter 1, dependency theorists argued that modernisation approaches were inadequate because they placed too much emphasis on elite behaviour and ignored predatory international capitalism. Dependency analysts regarded Thailand's business and state elites as tools of internationalised corporations, complicit in the exploitation of their own country (Suthy 1980).

A major problem emerged for this approach when a significant local capitalist class developed. Dependency approaches could only explain this as an artefact of foreign investment. Hart-Landsberg and Burkett (1998), for example, characterise such developments as tenuous and subject to the vagaries of business decisions made outside Thailand, meaning that it is 'false development'.[3] But this explained little about Thailand's capitalist development over several decades.[4]

The Asian economic crisis saw a resurgence of interest in dependency approaches. The attraction lay in its criticisms of the negative impacts of capitalist development and its nationalist economic rhetoric. Dependency analysts argued that high-speed growth, fuelled by foreign capital, had promoted the interests of international investors and technocratic and economic elites in the region, rather than the interests of the majority of the population. Thailand's development was considered as ultimately unsustainable and dependent on investment decisions made overseas. For these analysts, the 1997–98 crisis demonstrated the power of the major capitalist nations, especially the US, and Thailand's weakness. They condemned the IMF for taking advantage of the crisis to demand increased liberalisation that reproduced structures and approaches inspired by the US model of capitalist organisation (Bello 1998; Bullard, Bello & Malhotra 1998:124). Rejecting the IMF program, dependency analysts argued for a nationalist approach to development, including reorientating production to domestic markets and controls on international capital flows (Bello, Cunningham & Li 1998:249). This was seen as the only sure way to avoid domination by rich countries.

While the revised dependency approach directs attention to national responses to the negative impacts of liberalisation and capitalist globalisation, it does not indicate an approach that overcomes the theoretical problems noted by earlier critics and discussed in chapter 1. Importantly, the alternatives proffered appear unrealistic in the context of the embeddedness of capitalist development in South-East Asia (Hewison 2000a).

Neoclassical and neoliberal economic approaches

Despite fads and fashions in development theory, promoting and sustaining economic growth has been the central pillar of Thailand's public policy since the early 1960s. Indeed, international financial institutions have praised Thailand for its conservative economic policy and sustained growth (Warr & Bhanupong 1996). The official view has been that growth is best achieved through the operation of the free market, although this has not always meant adherence to all aspects of neoclassical and neoliberal economic doctrine. Indeed, while the discussion in chapter 1 shows that the neoclassical approach asserted the primacy of market over government, this had to be modified following the success of the East Asian development model. Government was seen as having a role in getting the fundamentals right and setting the legal and institutional frameworks that allow markets to operate.

The Asian economic crisis prompted neoclassical analysts to identify market distortions as contributing factors, reasserting their preferred theoretical and ideological position that market distortions resulted from state intervention. These analysts and their institutionalist allies identified poor policies, weak governance (state and corporate), inadequate institutions, cronyism (resulting in moral hazard), corruption, and resource misallocation as factors in the crisis. They argued that rent-seeking meant that state intervention prevented effective policy-making. It was argued that development would have been more rapid if industrial policy had promoted Thailand's comparative advantage through increased labour intensity and agriculture and processing (Christensen et al. 1993:1–8).

The crisis saw these analysts supporting IMF and World Bank market-enhancing reform. This meant considerable attention to issues of so-called good governance. Good governance is usually seen to involve the neoliberal policy orthodoxies of privatisation, liberalisation, and the development of institutions for a rules-based market system. The aim of many governance projects is public policy developed by technocrats, who are relatively insulated from political influences. It is assumed that there are universally applicable and technically correct policies available to capable technocrats.

These approaches suggest a narrow appreciation of the social or political nature of institutions and often fail to address the power relations inherent in programs that alter the existing arrangement of political and economic forces. The fact that the market and policies are socially and politically constructed is inadequately considered. Indeed, for Thailand, neoliberal reformers have sometimes suggested that parliamentary politics has been an impediment to good policy development because rent-seeking politicians have obstructed the work of able technocrats (see Christensen et al. 1993:19–20). This proclivity for technocratic solutions to economic problems, while bypassing or ignoring politics and power, is essentially anti-democratic and ignores the fact that democratic struggles have been—and remain—essential elements of Thailand's modern development. Since the 1980s, for all of these problems, orthodox theory has been transformed into an ideology that has driven the policy agendas of the international financial institutions and the governments of most developed countries, making it an exceptionally powerful doctrine and one that is difficult to challenge. As will be shown later in this chapter, following the Asian crisis, there was a Thai challenge to the orthodoxy, reflective of the economic and political contestation unleashed by the recession.

Historical institutionalist approaches

There was increased interest in historical institutionalist approaches as Thailand's economic performance during the boom was compared with that of East Asian economies. Analysts argued that the focus on only state and market drew too much attention away from an ensemble of non-state and non-market institutions that had determined Thailand's economic success. These included private-sector institutions such as commercial networks and business associations (Doner & Ramsey 1997). Specifically rejecting the bureaucratic polity approach, and differentiating Thailand and other South-East Asian economies from North-East Asian developmentalist states, Doner and Hawes (1995:168–9) argue that these countries have been successful due to their dynamic private sectors. They see a 'relative strength' in private institutions and comparatively weak states. Unlike the states of North-East Asia, these 'weaker' South-East Asian states have not been subject to the popular demands and challenges that led to the emergence of the developmental states (Doner et al. 2005). For Thailand, it is argued that some state elements, especially in fiscal and economic offices, were insulated from patronage, but that the private sector has also played a significant directing role (Doner & Ramsey 1997:273). Thus, in the face of market failures, a lack of popular challenge, and indifferent or predatory state policies, it has been business driving development.

The Asian crisis brought a re-evaluation. The more state-focused historical institutionalists argued that the extent of the impact of the crisis on Thailand demonstrated the state's incapacity to drive the changes required to improve the 'production regime' and to establish the resources required for this (Weiss 1999:319–22). As noted in chapter 1, these analysts also identified that external factors were responsible for deepening the crisis. Weiss (1999:329) adds that there was relatively limited insulation of state agencies from 'particularistic interest politics'. More society-focused institutionalists give attention to this latter aspect. Hutchcroft (1999:474), echoing Riggs, argues that Thailand has exhibited the characteristics of 'bureaucratic capitalism', where the state was relatively stronger than were business interests and 'relatively more patrimonial'. However, the economic boom of 1986–96 saw business establish its collective interest over that of the state. Market liberalisation occurred, with little attention paid to the building of appropriate institutions. This, together with an increasing tendency for rural politicians to enhance their patronage through access to state coffers and policy, set the framework for economic crisis. These politicians besieged the bureaucracy and expanded patrimonialism beyond the bureaucracy, making Thailand's system much more like the Philippines model of the patrimonial oligarchic state. This was reflective of a weakening of the state interests vis-à-vis those of business (Hutchcroft 1999:474, 495–7).

Such revised approaches were attractive for explaining differences between Thailand and developmental states, and for including historical arguments about the development of power and institutions. However, they have tended to emphasise trust, cooperation, and order among private-sector actors, while downplaying competition and conflict among them. Reform is often seen to be about establishing order, stability, and accountability. Where conflict is discussed, it is in the context of the state (and its officials) versus the private sector. Among other things, the crisis laid bare the contradictory relationships among the various fractions of capital and indicated that the state, although responsible for the interests of capital in general, was also cognisant of the shifting power relationships between domestic and international capital, and within domestic capital.

As noted above, neoclassicalists and historical institutionalists both favour technocratic solutions to economic and political problems. Hutchcroft (1999:488) argues that Thailand's reforms and appropriate policy require that conservative urban elites capture the state and parliament from unsophisticated 'country bumpkins' (elected rural constituency politicians) who engage in money politics and patrimonialism.

Social conflict approaches

If other approaches lack attention to conflict and attach too much significance to particular policies, this is not the case for the conflict perspective.

As explained in chapter 1, conflict theorists see markets, states, and institutions as products of interests and conflicts emanating from class relations and inequalities generated within societies and by the forces of global capitalism. The use of terms such as 'capitalism' and 'capitalist state' includes an identification of the nature of domination.

From this perspective, Thailand's growth and development during the past century is a part of a capitalist transformation that has irreversibly altered patterns of social, economic, and political relations. The period of growth from the late 1950s, which culminated in the 1986–96 economic boom, saw a rapid advance of capitalist relations throughout the country, and the rise and diversification of competing capitalist groups, together with increased attention from international capital.

Marxist political economists, then, saw the Asian crisis as a moment in this development process. In explaining the crisis, they pointed to issues sometimes ignored in other approaches—overexpansion, overproduction, declining profits, and the cyclical and crisis-prone nature of capitalism (see Hewison 2000b). Crises are thus unavoidable elements of the logic and contradictions of capitalist production. These analysts also recognise that a crisis will be associated with a recomposition of business. The tendency for competition among capitalists to become more intense and for capitalists to turn on each other in times of crisis means that crises invariably result in bankruptcies, mergers, and acquisitions. The crisis is thus seen as a part of global processes of capital accumulation and cycles of crisis. The boom emerged from the aftermath of an earlier crisis in the mid 1980s (see Robison et al. 1987), and the country was again consumed by crisis in the late 1990s. Although domestic capitalists did exceptionally well during the boom, the crisis saw a remarkable reconstruction of the local capitalist class, brought about by both the deepest recession since the 1950s and intense competitive pressure from international capital.

We may now turn to the examination of Thailand's capitalist development.

THE POLITICAL ECONOMY OF CAPITALIST DEVELOPMENT

Early development

While significant socioeconomic change was already underway in Thailand by the 1850s, the signing of the 1855 Bowring Treaty marked the emergence of modern Thailand and its enmeshment in trading patterns negotiated on Western terms and involving Western notions of free trade (Hong 1984; Nidhi 1982).

In 1855, Thailand's relatively small population was overwhelmingly a peasantry engaged in subsistence production that was within family and community units (Chatthip 1999). The links between these units and the royal state often weakened as distance from administrative centres increased, with state control manifested in obligations on the population to be met through slavery, corvée labour, military service, or in the delivery of valuable, often tradeable, commodities. External trade was controlled by royals and nobles who were also the state's officials (Reid 1995). Royals and nobles dominated the class and political structures, drawing their wealth and power not just from their control of trade, but also from their command over labour and land. The monarchy, often in competition with leading noble families, kept close control of government, developing a highly personalised state that was focused on the monarch.

Changes to this system emanated from a range of pressures. First, international trade patterns altered, driven by industrial production in the West and the need to sustain colonial empires. This saw Thailand's exports increase, initially of rice and later of timber, rubber, and tin. Second, colonial aggression in the region and the need to facilitate trade required that the Thai state modernise its administration and more carefully define its territory (Tej 1977; Thongchai 1994). A significant outcome of these changes and reforms was a greatly strengthened monarchy and state. By 1900, the monarchy, supported by a modernising military and bureaucracy, had become absolute. Any opposition to the regime was vigorously suppressed; political decision-making was controlled within the court.

Economic and political change was associated with a transformation of class relations. Slavery and the corvée were eventually discarded by the rulers, resulting in the emergence of a free peasantry. For the ruling class, the direct control of peasant labour became less significant as this class came to rely on land, taxation, and the control of business for their wealth and that of the state (Hong 1984). Hence, peasants were far more useful released from bondage and producing commodities for the export trade. The development of business saw the ruling class and state—with little distinction between state assets and those of the monarch—entering into alliances with foreign and local Chinese business. As trade grew, the ruling class expanded to include foreign and local Chinese businesspeople. Not only did they become partners with the Thai elite in business and trade development, but also became part of the administrative reforms, with some Chinese acquiring tax farms (and associated royal titles) and some Westerners participating in bureaucratic modernisation as senior officials.[5] Tax farming allowed the state to convert its revenue system to one based on money. In business, Chinese merchants, royals, aristocrats, and Western interests developed a supportive, yet still competitive, business structure that remained in place until 1932 (Suehiro 1989). Additionally, Chinese merchants and traders spread throughout the country, establishing businesses and shops, and enhancing commodity trade.

At the same time, a working class was being created and it was overwhelmingly Chinese. As trade and industry developed, labour was in short supply, especially in Bangkok and the southern tin mines. This was partly due to Thailand's small population, but also because Thais, freed from labour obligations, took advantage of opportunities in smallholder agriculture. The result was that, from the late 1880s to the 1930s, there was an addition of about 1 million Chinese to the population, and they dominated the working class until the 1960s.

Domestic and international events in the 1920s and 1930s brought dramatic economic and political change. Rising pressures for political reform were thwarted by King Vajiravudh, his successor Prajadhipok, and their advisers. Economic reform was also stifled, even as the government faced considerable fiscal problems through royal profligacy under Vajiravudh (Batson 1984; Copeland 1994). When combined with the world economic depression and international political instability, the stage was set for political change. In June 1932, a small group of commoners, organised as the People's Party, overthrew the absolute monarchy and established constitutional rule.[6]

The overthrow of the monarchy brought new economic and political ways. Although still not a fully fledged capitalist system, the commercialisation, monetisation, and commodification of the economy were well established by the 1930s. The overthrow of the monarchy's accumulation regime was an important step towards a modern economic system. Although unable to entrench the alternative constitutional form, 1932 was the year of a move against unrepresentative politics (Nakharin 1992). Initially brought together by economic nationalism and their opposition to the monarchical state, the People's Party split over economic policy and political representation. Even though no agreement could be reached, the regime held together through its resistance to a royalist restoration. For the population as a whole, the ousting of the monarchy promised an end to royal privilege and the possibility of a more rational economic system that might spread economic benefits more broadly in society.

The period from 1932 to 1957 saw considerable debate over economic policy, dominated by nationalist concerns and the role of the state in the economy and, especially, over industry policy and the lot of farmers. Indeed, this economic contest revolved around the struggle by the royalists to maintain their economic and political power. The competition that emerged was bitter. The royalists wished to preserve their privileges, as did those businesses that had done well from the royalist economic and political regime. The new political freedoms saw workers and peasants demanding a better deal. As more radical elements in the People's Party, supported by workers and students, proposed increased state intervention in the economy, the royalists countered with accusations of Bolshevism.

The political outcome of this dispute was an increased role for the military. Economic policies meant to promote ethnic Thai non-agricultural employment and investment were also developed. This sometimes meant investment by the state. When the military seized power following the Second World War, economic policy and practice became more closely associated with private benefits to senior political figures. Even so, there was no widespread opposition to private enterprise. It was this period that Riggs (1966) identified as the clearest expression of the bureaucratic polity, with military and bureaucratic leaders tapping into state enterprises and the resources of Chinese business for personal gain and to finance their political activity. Clearly, for those businesses that managed to link themselves to powerful political leaders, there were significant competitive advantages.

When the boom that had developed with the Korean War waned in the mid 1950s, business became concerned that this accumulation regime was no longer appropriate. For the capitalist class as a whole—as opposed to favoured individuals and firms linked to powerful leaders—the increasingly personalised arrangements required by the existing accumulation regime meant an uncertain investment climate. Demands that the state's investment role be limited received the support of foreign businesses. US companies, the largest foreign investors, also took the lead in pressuring the government to be more receptive to foreign capital and were supported by the use of official aid to encourage positive attitudes (Hewison 1985:276–7).

In two coups, one in 1957 and another in 1958, military leader General Sarit Thanarat seized political power. While a military-led administration was not new for Thailand, Sarit's coup established a government that set about altering the ways in which politics and economics had been organised. Sarit did this in the context of promises to improve the then struggling economy, proclaiming that his government would boost national income and improve standards of living. Sarit proclaimed that his government's authoritarianism—a system described by one analyst as 'despotic paternalism' (Thak 1979)—would deliver the political stability necessary for the expansion and strengthening of the middle class. The new government's economic approach represented a significant change from that of previous administrations, evidencing a determination to promote private rather than state investment and encouraging foreign participation; the state's economic role was to be limited to infrastructure. This enthusiasm for the private sector developed from the realisation that a number of state enterprises were in serious economic trouble and coincided with a range of reports by international organisations recommending increased support for the private sector and import-substituting industrialisation (ISI) (World Bank 1959).[7] These reports echoed a sentiment regarding development strategy that had emerged among a rising group of young technocrats who took important positions in Sarit's new economic agencies.

The system that the military promoted—Sarit called it a 'revolution'—required that a bargain or social contract be developed between the military leadership and domestic capital that demarcated their joint hegemony over the working and peasant classes. The military government would deliver political stability and support the further expansion of private capital while domestic capital was required to deliver the increased and sustained economic growth that would modernise the economy. The subordinated classes, who had no role in establishing this developmental deal, were involved through an assumption that enhanced capitalist development would permit a gradual trickle down of benefits to them.

The era of import-substitution industrialisation

When a World Bank (1959:94–106) country report urged an ISI strategy for Thailand, Sarit and his advisers seized upon its recommendations as a justification for their new economic model and moved quickly to expand manufacturing. The government established generous incentives for private investment and sought to attract foreign investors. The first national development plan (1961–66) saw a shift to policies that emphasised industrial development and the government welcomed US and World Bank assistance in implementing the plan, revising the Promotion of Investment Act (1960) and other policies that supported business, and directing state investments to infrastructure.

The US had provided substantial aid to Thailand prior to Sarit coming to power. This aid concentrated on military assistance (see Darling 1965) and increased and broadened with Thailand being centrepiece in the US's Cold War strategy in Asia. Thailand's authoritarian governments were firm US allies; they provided airbases supporting the US's Vietnam War efforts and strongly opposed communism.

The policy focus on industry did not mean that agriculture was neglected. Indeed, in addition to ISI, the first national plan emphasised agricultural development. The government was keen for agricultural exports to grow, as this permitted agricultural taxation and the extraction of household savings into the commercial banking sector to provide much of the domestic capital required for the development of industry (Jansen 1990; Silcock 1967b). Sarit's policies targeting industry and foreign investment saw substantial investment in manufacturing. For local business, the government's approach meant more room to invest free of state competition. For budding industrialists, the government granted the tariff protection required to develop domestic manufacturing. At this time, foreign manufacturers were also keen to establish themselves behind protective barriers (Hewison 1985:280–1).

The government created a number of agencies to support ISI, including the Board of Investment (BOI); a new national planning office, later named the National Economic and Social Development Board (NESDB); and a revamped Ministry of Industry. By the time of the second development plan (1967–71), ISI was embedded, with the bulk of capital invested with promotional privileges going to import-substituting industries.

Manufacturing's contribution to GDP rose significantly (see table 3.1, below). High rates of protection encouraged domestic investment and further strengthened local finance and banking. The banking and finance sector was also protected—foreign banks could not enter branch banking and were permitted to offer only limited services; policies to encourage saving also increased financial sector profitability. These were the big ISI winners. Large conglomerates resulted, many of them with commercial banks at their apex. Business control was consolidated within the fifteen to twenty families dominating commercial banks (Hewison 1989:ch. 8). These mainly Sino-Thai families also invested heavily in the expansion of manufacturing. It was their control of finance, when the stockmarket was in its infancy and raising capital overseas was tightly controlled, that permitted the building of oligopolies in a range of economic sectors. The families also maintained excellent relations with powerful political figures.

TABLE 3.1 GDP by industrial origin, 1960, 1971, 1980 (%)

Sector	1960	1971	1980
Agriculture	39.8	29.8	24.9
Mining and quarrying	1.1	1.5	1.6
Manufacturing	12.5	17.5	20.7
Construction	4.6	5.5	5.7
Electricity and water supply	0.4	1.8	1.9
Transport and communications	7.5	6.7	6.4
Wholesale and retail trade	15.2	17.1	16.5
Banking, insurance, and real estate	1.9	4.2	6.0
Ownership of dwellings	2.8	1.9	1.5
Public administration and defence	4.6	4.3	4.2
Services	9.6	9.7	10.6

Source: Bank of Thailand, *National Income of Thailand*, various issues

ISI resulted in a larger and more diverse working class, the expansion of which coincided with the class's ethnic and gender transformation. Following the cessation of large-scale Chinese immigration, it was Thais, mainly from rural areas, who moved into industrial employment, some temporarily, but increasingly on a permanent basis. Although agricultural activities remained the predominant occupation, the industrial labourforce expanded substantially. Between 1960 and 1979, the total workforce expanded by more than 20 per cent or almost 3 million people. The manufacturing workforce grew by 45 per cent over the same period (Hewison 1989:215). Increasingly, women moved into manufacturing employment.

ISI policies protected the big conglomerates. Funds deposited in the banks grew rapidly, enabling the banking families to expand their economic control. The protection of manufacturing and the banks ensured profitability. Support for ISI also came from some influential foreign investors, especially the Japanese, with investments in textiles and auto assembly and parts manufacture (Pasuk & Baker 1995:130–8).

Export-oriented industrialisation: the creation of an economic boom

Export-oriented industrialisation (EOI) is an approach to development that is meant to be based on a nation's advantage in producing commodities for a world market. For many Asian economies, this has meant utilising cheap labour. In Thailand, critics of ISI had long argued that ISI was limited by the relatively small domestic market and that the strategy created disincentives to export (see the summary of arguments in Hewison 1989:118–21). However, there was no strong pressure for change from business, especially as profits were maintained. In fact, under pressure from domestic capitalist groups, protection for import-substituting manufacturing actually expanded through the 1970s and into the early 1980s (Pasuk & Baker 1995:144–5). It was not until the mid 1980s and an economic downturn that the necessary policy momentum for a change to an EOI strategy was developed.

This downturn resulted from a confluence of events. First, from the late 1970s, the baht, being tied to the strengthening US dollar, began to climb. Second, agricultural commodity prices had been declining since the late 1970s. Third, the nature of international investment was changing, with a major relocation of East Asian firms to cheaper labour sites in South-East Asia. Fourth, the second oil crisis saw the government seeking loan funds, significantly raising public-sector debt. Fifth, military assistance had declined from the mid 1970s and, as counterinsurgency ended, the military embarked on a spending spree, buying new weapons, and further expanding public debt (Hewison 1987:61–76; Pasuk & Baker 1996:ch. 4).

The economic downturn had a substantial impact on business. Growth continued, but was at the lowest rate for years. Bankruptcies mushroomed, private investment collapsed, unemployment increased, and even the strongest companies reported flat profits or their first losses in years. The slump also highlighted problems with state policies. Budget deficits ballooned, public debt reached unprecedented levels, and trade and current account deficits increased. Agriculture was doing poorly. Reflecting the policy emphasis on industry, government and business were little interested in the agricultural sector, except to promote agro-industry and continue the exploitation of its output and labour. The downturn meant that farmers faced low prices, while workers' wages were eroded by inflation and increased government utilities charges.

As Pasuk and Baker (1996:65–6) point out, technocrats were split on the appropriate response to the economic slowdown, but even entreaties from the powerful banking and textile sectors and the World Bank brought few decisions. It was the belated recognition that there would be no rebound in agricultural prices to lift growth that resulted in a devaluation and a concerted move to embrace EOI. An important impact of the devaluation was to make Thailand's manufactured goods cheaper, emphasising the significance of cheap labour for export-oriented industries.

In terms of policy and production, EOI remained the dominant strategy until the 1997 economic crisis. The economic results of this emphasis were spectacular. There was a rapid expansion of exports, from average annual growth rates of 6 per cent in the 1960s and 11 per cent in the 1970s, rising to over 16 per cent a year in the 1980s, and remaining above 10 per cent through the first half of the 1990s. However, in a warning of things to come, there was no increase in 1996. The wider economic significance of the move to EOI can be seen in the data presented in table 3.2.

TABLE 3.2 GDP by industrial origin, selected years 1985–96 (%)

Sector	1985	1990	1991	1992	1993	1994	1995	1996
Agriculture	15.8	12.7	12.6	12.3	10.4	10.7	11.1	11.0
Mining and quarrying	2.5	1.6	1.6	1.5	1.4	1.3	1.2	1.4
Manufacturing	21.9	27.2	28.2	27.6	28.1	28.0	28.2	28.4
Construction	5.1	6.2	6.7	6.7	7.0	7.4	7.3	7.4
Electricity and water supply	2.4	2.2	2.1	2.3	2.4	2.3	2.4	2.3
Transport and communications	7.4	7.1	7.1	7.2	7.5	7.4	7.3	7.3
Wholesale and retail trade	18.3	17.6	17.0	16.7	16.7	16.5	16.2	15.5
Banking, insurance, real estate	3.3	5.5	5.3	6.4	7.3	7.8	7.5	7.6
Ownership of dwellings	4.2	3.0	2.8	2.8	2.6	2.4	2.4	2.4
Public administration and defence	4.6	3.5	3.5	3.7	3.7	3.5	3.7	3.7
Services	14.5	13.3	13.0	12.7	12.9	12.6	12.8	13.1

Sources: TDRI (1995; 1998); Bank of Thailand (2000, 2005)

The change in the relative shares of the manufacturing and agricultural sectors in the economy is remarkable (see figure 3.1, page 89). In 1960, agriculture was the most important economic sector. It accounted for 40 per cent of GDP, most exports, and employed the vast majority of the population. Manufacturing made a small contribution to production and employment. The transition took place in the early 1980s. By the mid 1990s, agriculture produced just 11 per cent of GDP, ranking lower than manufacturing, trade, and services. Rapid industrial growth saw manufactured exports expand from just 1 per cent of total exports in 1960 to a whopping 75 per cent by the early 1990s (TDRI 1992:6). This does not mean that agriculture had shrunk—it grew, but far less rapidly than manufacturing.

In 1960, 82 per cent of the economically active population was in agriculture. By 1996, this had declined to just 48 per cent (Economic Section 1998:9). These data understate the magnitude of change as most agricultural families now rely on income from off-farm sources. At the same time, employment in non-agricultural activities grew significantly. EOI saw the further development of the working class. Between 1979 and 1998, the workforce expanded by more than 50 per cent or almost 11 million people; the manufacturing workforce almost tripled over the same period (TDRI

FIGURE 3.1 GDP in agriculture and manufacturing, 1960–2003

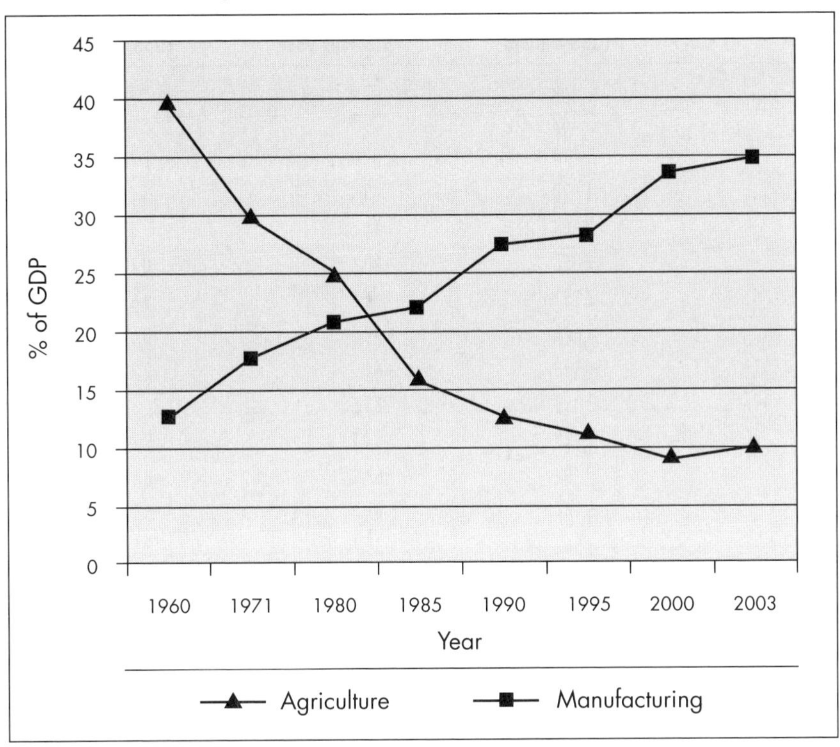

Source: Bank of Thailand, *National Income of Thailand*, various issues

1999:14) and, by 1992, women made up half the manufacturing workforce (Yada 1998:126).

Growth was driven by the private sector. Measured as a percentage of GDP, private investment in 1975 was about three times greater than public investment. The boom in private-sector investment following the policy changes of the mid 1980s saw private investment levels almost five times that of the state. Real gross fixed capital formation grew by an average 20 per cent annually during the boom of 1986–91, and by 10–15 per cent in 1992–96. The value of new business registrations and capital expansions also grew rapidly during these periods, averaging more than 50 per cent in the 1986–91 period. These levels were reduced after 1991, but remained high by international standards until 1996 (Board of Investment 1995, 2000).

These impressive results mirrored the expansion of a powerful domestic capitalist class and also saw this class become increasingly diverse. There was also considerable stimulus from foreign investors (Jansen 1997). Domestic investors remained positive towards foreign investment, often preferring joint ventures when entering new business sectors.[8] Foreign investment was seen as a barometer of business confidence, giving it considerable political significance. As seen in table 3.3, the inflows of foreign capital increased

TABLE 3.3 Flows of foreign capital, 1986–2004

Year	Net DFI (US$ million)	% Change on previous year	Total capital flows (US$ million)
1986	276	55.5	–376
1987	362	30.9	896
1988	1 118	209.2	2 926
1989	1 828	63.4	5 780
1990	2 588	41.5	9 910
1991	2 056	–20.6	10 726
1992	2 151	4.6	9 630
1993	1 675	–22.1	10 636
1994	598	–64.3	12 229
1995	1 995	233.6	21 803
1996	2 299	15.2	19 741
1997	3 752	63.2	–8 637
1998	5 547	47.8	–15 593
1999	3 562	–35.7	–13 541
2000	2 813	–21.0	–9 770
2001	3 873	35.5	–3 908
2002*	1 023	–73.6	–5 714
2003*	1 882	84.0	–8 766
2004*	835	–55.6	–211

Note: For the period 1986–96, US$1 was exchanged at about 25 baht. In 1997, after devaluation, US$1 was averaged at 31.37 baht, whereas for 1998, the figure was 37.84 baht and for the 1999–2004 period, US$ figures provided by the Bank of Thailand have been used.
* Preliminary figures.

Sources: TDRI (1992, 1995, 1998); Bank of Thailand (2000, 2005); Board of Investment (2000)

substantially in the late 1980s and remained high until 1996. It is of interest, however, that direct foreign investment (DFI) continued to increase during the early crisis period (discussed below).

The sources of DFI altered with the expansion of investment. In 1984, the US was the largest investor; by 1986, Japan held this position. Japan's net investments increased ninefold between 1987 and 1990, and accounted for about 44 per cent of all DFI. Japan, the US, and Hong Kong remained the largest investors throughout the period.

Although foreign investment was strategically important, local business investments were far greater. For most of the period between 1960 and 1994, although foreign investment increased steadily, its contribution to gross capital formation usually remained in a range of 1–8 per cent (Hewison 1989:112; Pasuk & Baker 1996:35). Even among BOI-promoted firms, approximately two-thirds of registered capital between 1960 and 1993 was domestic (Board of Investment 1995:11). These levels of DFI are relatively low when compared with other ASEAN states. As Pasuk and Baker (1996:35) observe, 'Foreign investment may have sparked the [post-1986] boom ... [but] Thai investments made it a big boom.'

The boom, driven by ballooning exports, pulled the domestic market along. Bangkok and other urban centres experienced investment booms that saw markets expand and diversify, especially in real estate, construction, and wholesale and retail trade. The outcome was the emergence of an expanded capitalist class (Pasuk & Baker 1996:chs 3 and 4). This resulted in a challenge to the financial dominance of the big banks. As noted above, the banks and their controlling families had long managed the supply of domestic investment funds. From the late 1970s, however, some technocrats sought to reduce the economic power of these families. It was decided that a limit on bank ownership in other business sectors and a widening of bank ownership would enhance growth (Hewison 1989:191). As some families were unable to keep pace with the capital expansion requirements of their banks, a dilution of family holdings began; however, it was only the expansion of the boom that was able to loosen banking-family control in other business sectors.

Although the Sino-Thai-owned banks did well from the boom and were aggressive in financing exports, a range of factors challenged their dominance.

First, the post-1985 increase in DFI saw foreign investors seeking local partners. The level of demand was such that it went well beyond the bank-dominated cliques.

Second, policy changes saw state controls on the finance sector and capital flows eased, meaning that domestic borrowers were no longer tied to domestic banks. Another important change was the ability to borrow overseas. At the same time, increased numbers of foreign banks were established in Thailand, and were particularly aggressive in their corporate and business lending. Merchant banking also expanded significantly, and several finance companies were in a position to expand their activities, especially as they were also freed from their previous reliance on the commercial banks.

Third, the banks were challenged by the expansion of the Stock Exchange of Thailand (SET). The SET had existed for years, but had been hampered by a lack of investor confidence, particularly after a finance sector crisis in 1979 (Hewison 1981). However, following the Wall Street crash of October 1987, the SET took off, and capitalisation and turnover expanded markedly (see table 3.4, below). Although still volatile, the SET became attractive to both local and international investors. It mobilised large amounts of capital, loosening the grip of the banks on finance and industry. An important factor in this was the establishment of international securities and brokerage companies in Bangkok (Pasuk & Baker 1996:39).

TABLE 3.4 Selected statistics on the Stock Exchange of Thailand, 1985–2004 (selected years)

Indicator	1985	1990	1996	1998	1999	2002	2004
Annual turnover (US$ billion)	0.6	25.1	52.1	20.7	42.5	51.2	125.6
Average daily turnover (US$ million)	2.5	101.6	213.6	84.7	173.6	208.9	512.7
SET Index (end of period)	134.9	649.4	910.3	331.3	395.5	356.5	668.1
Market dividend yield (%)	8.2	3.6	3.5	1.3	0.6	2.7	2.7
Number of quoted companies	97	214	454	418	392	389	439
Market value capitalisation (US$ billion)	2.0	24.5	102.4	30.7	58.0	49.5	113.1

Sources: Board of Investment (1990, 1992, 1995); SET (2000, 2005); Securities and Exchange Commission of Thailand (2000)

For many rising capitalists, the expansion of the SET and the liberalisation of the financial sector were perceived as freeing them from the control of the banking families. A range of companies and groups emerged to challenge those who were powerful during the ISI period. Many saw the SET as an unlimited source of funds and an expression of the free-wheeling spirit of capitalism. Manipulation was not unusual, especially as regulation was often deliberately loose (Handley 1997).

The result was a larger, more diverse, capitalist class. The dominance of banking and industry was challenged. These areas remained important, but remarkably wealthy capitalist groups were produced by the widened financial sector and by telecommunications, real estate, tourism, and a range of services (Handley 1997). Some of these new business groups even chose to challenge the big families on their own ground—in banking—and there were takeover battles among the smaller banks. Huge profits were made and, although much was reinvested, consumption and luxury spending increased markedly, further expanding the domestic market, but setting the scene for the 1997 economic collapse.

The accumulation regime of the ISI era had seen a small capitalist group dominate, buttressed by its relationships with powerful political figures. Technocrats tended to have control of economic policy-making, but this did not amount to independence. The EOI-driven boom disrupted these relationships. Although many of the links remained, the nature of Thailand's capitalism meant that technocrats were more concerned with managing an economy that enhanced expanded accumulation, being less particularistic and more concerned with the health of capital in general. This was a better strategy for dealing with a diversified business community; however, the expansion of electoral politics, where success depended on access to enormous quantities of money, saw business and elected politicians establishing relationships not unlike those between officials and business under ISI.

Thailand's consistent economic growth from the late 1950s to 1997 was not unreservedly positive. A range of negative issues was identified (see Medhi 1995), including a central problem of the boom period—wealth distribution.

Wealth distribution and the boom

The World Bank (1993) argued that one of the results of the East Asian miracle was increased equity. For Thailand, however, this was not the experience. As can be seen in figure 3.2 below, rapid increases in per capita incomes brought significant reductions in poverty. The downward trend has been consistent, with urban dwellers doing better than those in rural areas.[9]

FIGURE 3.2 Poverty incidence, 1975/76–2002

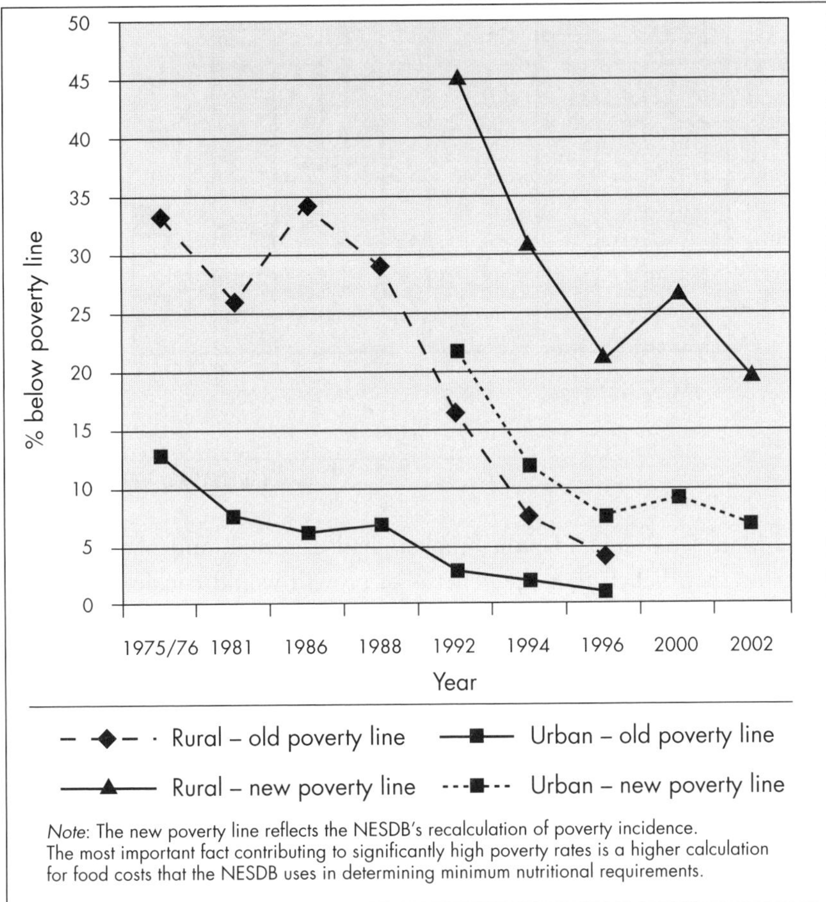

Note: The new poverty line reflects the NESDB's recalculation of poverty incidence.
The most important fact contributing to significantly high poverty rates is a higher calculation for food costs that the NESDB uses in determining minimum nutritional requirements.

Sources: TDRI (1992, 1995, 1998, 2003)

Significantly, however, income and wealth distribution became increasingly skewed (see figure 3.3 below). In urban areas, where workers have made significant contributions to economic growth, they have not gained adequate rewards for their labours. Indeed, workers' lives were characterised by low wages and poor working conditions. These conditions were necessary to maintain comparative advantage in both ISI and EOI strategies. In addition, there was widespread exploitation of women and children in sweatshops throughout the country (see Mathana 1995).

FIGURE 3.3 Income distribution, 1975/76–2002

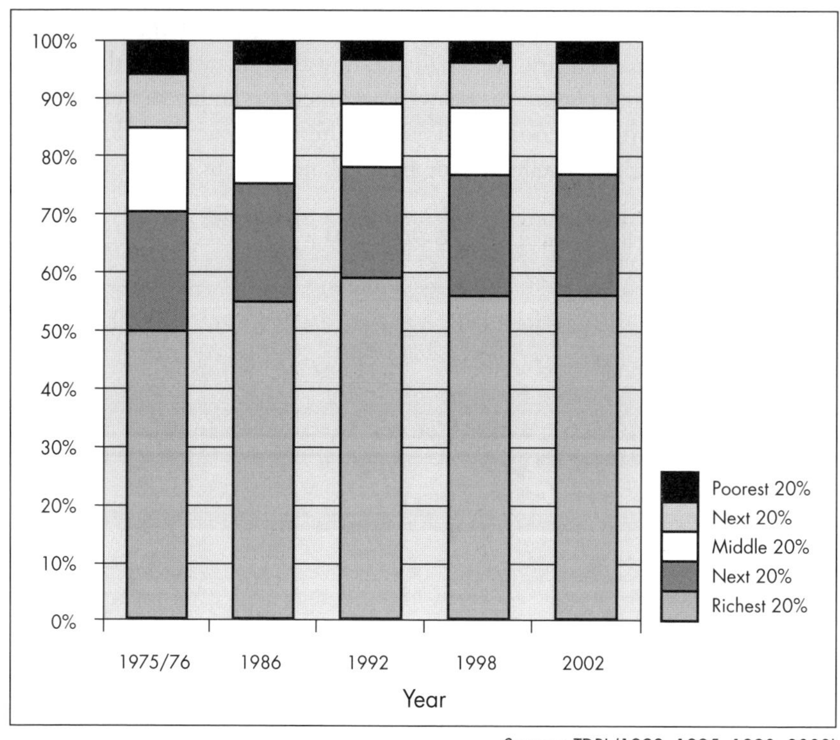

Sources: TDRI (1992, 1995, 1998, 2003)

Many analysts and policy-makers had expected, and had repeatedly restated their belief, that the benefits of growth would trickle down to all levels of society; few had predicted increased inequality. Distribution was most inequitable between rural and urban incomes. The principal reason for this is that smallholder agriculture had become a marginal way to make a living. This is illustrated by comparing the population and productivity of the various regions. Bangkok dominates. Most industry is clustered around the capital, meaning that the area is highly productive. Generally, as distance from the centre increases and agricultural activities become more significant, productivity decreases. This is most noticeable for the north-east, the most populous region and the region heavily reliant on agriculture. The result is that its productivity is low, poverty is high, migrant labour is common, and incomes are the lowest of all regions. Interestingly, despite governmental efforts to decentralise development, the gaps widened during the boom.

When some planners and politicians spoke of inequalities as a potential source of social conflict (*Nation* 14 December 1992), this was a shock for many as growth had been expected to solve social problems. Protracted debate led to a recognition that agriculture would continue to stagnate and income disparities were likely to worsen. The policy answer was to encourage industrial activity in rural areas and increase skills training in an effort to enhance the trickle-down effects of growth in provincial areas, while not compromising national growth (NESDB n.d.:99–104).

This approach failed. There was little consensus in business or government on the need for higher-level skills. The existing accumulation regime produced the boom and profits seemed to flow easily from both productive and speculative investment. In short, there was no imperative to look beyond existing patterns of investment and exploitation. Continued opposition to any expansion of the limited social welfare system reinforced this. These debates were temporarily abandoned when the 1997 crisis hit.

In addition to increasing inequality, there were other signs that the economy faced problems by 1996. From 1993, for example, the SET began a steady decline. Speculative attacks on the baht began in 1995, and there was a decline in property values, rising vacancy rates for office and condominium space, and deteriorating investor confidence. The 1996 failure of the Bangkok Bank of Commerce and the cessation of export growth confirmed that the economy was in trouble. But booms build confidence and many simply did not want to believe that the boom was ending.[10]

ECONOMIC CRISIS AND RECOVERY: ESTABLISHING A NEW ACCUMULATION REGIME

There have been a range of explanations for the Asian crisis (see chapter 1, this volume). Particularly significant for Thailand were downturns in investment and exports, partly attributable to the high value of the baht. There was also over-capacity in a range of sectors. Despite this, 'hot money' poured into unproductive areas and sectors with over-capacity (United States Embassy 1998:1). The result was a 'price collapse' and an erosion of 'the rates of return on new capital invested' (Bank for International Settlements 1998:35–6, 117). In addition, the 1996 troubles of the finance sector saw investor confidence weaken.

The 2 July 1997 devaluation marked the beginning of a downward economic spiral (see table 3.5 below). The IMF brokered a US$17 billion support package, demanding substantial reform and restructuring from Thailand's government in return.

Much has been written of the economic impact of the crisis (see Glassman 2004; Hewison 2000b; Pasuk & Baker 2000). The popular picture, especially outside Thailand, is that the crisis was a disaster for the country's corporate conglomerates and the middle class. Capitalists lost their business empires, while many in the middle class were thrown out of work. There is no doubt that the impact on business was considerable. Manufacturing firms struggled with overcapacity, which continued into 2003, and many firms were weighed down with debt, hamstrung by a liquidity squeeze and declining domestic demand. The finance sector was left in tatters, with only a handful of finance and securities companies remaining after 1997 and many banks closed, taken over by the state, or sold off to foreign investors. Thus, there is considerable truth in the popular picture. However, this is only a partial depiction of the broad impacts of the crisis. The principal impact was on the poor, who became poorer as a result of the crisis.

TABLE 3.5 GDP by industrial origin, 1997–2003 (%)

Sector	1997	1998	1999	2000	2001	2002	2003
Agriculture	9.4	10.8	9.4	9.0	9.1	9.4	10.0
Mining and quarrying	1.7	1.8	1.9	2.4	2.5	2.5	2.6
Manufacturing	30.2	30.9	32.6	33.6	33.4	33.6	34.7
Construction	5.7	3.9	3.6	3.1	3.0	3.0	3.0
Electricity and water supply	2.5	3.1	2.8	3.0	3.2	3.2	3.2
Transport and communications	7.8	7.8	8.1	8.0	8.3	8.3	7.8
Wholesale and retail trade	17.2	17.0	17.3	17.2	16.7	15.9	15.4
Banking, insurance, real estate	6.5	5.1	3.4	3.0	2.9	3.1	3.4
Ownership of dwellings	3.3	3.3	3.4	3.3	3.2	3.2	3.0
Public administration and defence	3.8	4.2	4.4	4.3	4.3	4.5	4.4
Services	11.9	12.1	13.1	13.1	13.4	13.3	12.5

Note: Categorisation for some sectors changed in the mid 1990s. This table modifies these so that they match earlier tables in this chapter. Data for 2003 are preliminary.

Sources: Bank of Thailand (2005)

It is worth recalling that, prior to the crisis, Thailand was seen by many orthodox economists as a success story (Warr & Bhanupong 1996:3), shepherded towards 'good' policies by capable technocrats. But in 1997, something went wrong with the orthodox success story and suddenly Thailand was at the centre of a regionwide economic crisis. The orthodox consensus was that the crisis was a result of poor policies, weak state and corporate governance, inadequate institutions, cronyism, corruption, moral hazard, resource misallocation, and failed liberalisation. While this conveniently ignored the existence of the same factors during the boom times of the early 1990s (Pasuk & Baker 1998:318), neoliberals were quick to reaffirm the critical differences between right and wrong policies, and the need for sound macroeconomic management that included further liberalisation. In Thailand, the post-crisis, neoliberal approach promoted by the IMF, the World Bank, the Asian Development Bank, and a range of bilateral partners, emphasised expanded liberalisation and more privatisation, fiscal austerity, deregulation, and decentralisation. A fundamental concern was to further reduce the economic role of the state.

Following the flotation of the baht, its subsequent and rapid devaluation, and the flight of capital (see table 3.3 above), the IMF had brokered a rescue package with the government led by Chavalit Yongchaiyudh. The devaluation saw many companies pushed into insolvency. Those that weren't insolvent, together with many small businesses, found they were unable to access a banking system that had all but collapsed (see Hewison 2000b; Regnier 2001). Thailand had little choice but to accept the IMF's US$17 billion standby facility and its demands for austerity and market-enhancing reform.

Initially, the IMF, drawing on Latin American experience, was concerned with stabilising the economy and negotiating policies that involved a tightening of monetary and fiscal policy. This was followed by attention to financial restructuring and reforms that demanded low wages, the privatisation of state enterprises (especially in communications, transport, and energy), civil service reform, improvements to corporate governance, regulatory reform, eased restrictions on foreign investment, and increased private sector participation in infrastructure projects (see Hewison 2005).

The outcome of this misguided reform strategy was a recession that was far deeper than might otherwise have been expected. Not only was the economic distress deep, but there were also negative political consequences. The crisis cut a swathe through the domestic business class, destroying or weakening all of the bank-based conglomerates that had long dominated the domestic capitalist class, and crushed many of the new business groups that had mushroomed during the boom. With the banking sector crippled by non-performing loans, even small enterprises found they had no access to capital. Foreign investment grew rapidly as joint-venture partners were bought out and cheap acquisitions completed. This was especially notable in the finance and industrial sectors. While business struggled, the greatest impacts of the economic downturn were on poverty, employment and wages, and inequality.

As mentioned, prior to the crisis, poverty had been reduced; however, the crisis saw more than 7 million people fall below the World Bank's poverty line of US$1.50 a day.[11] The impact was especially hard in already disadvantaged areas and the crisis meant that poverty re-emerged as a serious national problem.

In just a year following devaluation, unemployment and underemployment increased to about 10 per cent or almost 3.5 million people; a further half a million opted out of the workforce. Most affected were lower-skilled and semi-skilled urban workers in the construction, service, and manufacturing sectors. Contradicting popular views regarding traditional social safety nets provided by rural villages, not only were many of the unemployed found in rural areas, but people also continued to leave farms, just as they had during the economic boom. The already poor north-east region was hard-hit, accounting for almost 40 per cent of all unemployed.

Declining real wages had a substantial impact on Thai workers and farmers. Average monthly wages declined by 7.9 per cent between 1997 and 2000, and remained stagnant into 2004. Wages declined for all occupational categories, but most substantially in the agricultural sector, manufacturing, sales, transport, and clerical work. The most severely affected were workers with only primary school or lower education. Strikingly, as the World Bank (2000c:32) concluded, 'there was a shift in the distribution of aggregate wage earnings from groups with low pay to those with high pay'. This involved shifts in the distribution of aggregate wages from rural to urban areas, from poor to relatively wealthy regions, from shopfloor workers to technical and professional workers, and from those in small enterprises to those in large establishments.

The data on inequality are not so clear. The World Bank, using National Statistical Office data, indicates that inequality increased during the crisis, with the richest 20 per cent of the population seeing its share of wealth rise between 1996 and 1999, while that of all other quintiles declined. Part of the reason for this was that the poor had to transfer substantially higher proportions of their incomes to support their extended families than did the rich. The World Bank concluded that increased income inequality was associated with increased poverty and that inequality posed a threat to recovery. Surprisingly, given its ideological edge, World Bank analysis indicated that the source of inequality was profits. However, the TDRI (2003), using the same data set, reports that inequality was marginally reduced during the crisis. Even if the more conservative data are used, however, it remains the case that the poor have been unable to improve their situation (see figure 3.3 above).

All in all, it was the poor who were most severely affected by the economic downturn, with a movement of wealth and savings from the already poor to the already wealthy. This situation meant increased social conflict. While all workers suffered during the crisis, it was the lowest paid workers who suffered the most. Workers responded vigorously to their deteriorating situation and, while there were few strikes, officially reported grievances rose substantially (see Brown et al. 2002).

As the economic crisis worsened, a widespread and popular opposition to the IMF's strictures developed. This resulted in a loose alliance of workers, intellectuals, NGOs, politicians, domestic businesses, and even the country's monarch, drawn together in a broadly nationalist opposition to a perceived loss of sovereignty over economic policymaking, negative social impacts, and a fire sale of local assets to foreign interests. Domestic business was especially vocal and urged the government to implement measures to save the economy. Despite these pressures, the government continued to implement a neoliberal reform agenda. This steadfastness caused powerful elements of the local business class to conclude that the IMF-sponsored reforms would so weaken their control and reduce their wealth that the demise of their class was possible.

These political developments took place in a context in which domestic capital was restructuring under intense domestic competitive pressures and in the face of aggressive competition from international investors. The result has been a massive reorganisation of ownership and control, including the transfer of assets to foreign investors (see Hewison 2002b, 2004).

In terms of the discussion of economic regimes, a significant change was the relegation of the once powerful banking families and their conglomerates. Before the crisis, these families controlled the partially liberalised finance sector, including thirteen of the sixteen commercial banks. While the competitive reorganisation of banking capital had begun in the 1980s and continued through the 1990s, it was the crisis that ended the family control of a number of banks. By 1998, only five commercial banks remained outside state control and in majority Thai ownership, with each of these having foreign shareholdings of 40–49 per cent (Hewison 2004). This suggests the end of the control of the bank-based conglomerates that had been central for much of Thailand's capitalist development.

Domestic capital thus identified IMF-sponsored reforms as a threat to their power and control. The government was seen to be implementing a program that kept the IMF and its Western supporters on side. The government appeared determined to save capitalism, but this plan seemed to favour foreign investors rather than domestic capital, contrasting with previous policies in which domestic business had long been supported by international agencies and various Thai governments; now these agencies seemed intent on its destruction.

This threat to the power of local business forced the domestic capitalist class to take direct control of the state, parliament, and ministries. In this they were supported by a broad coalition that felt that Thai society was being torn apart by crisis and neoliberal reform. The political vehicle for local capital's fight was the Thai Rak Thai Party (TRT), established in 1998 by one of the few local tycoons to come through the crisis relatively unscathed, Thaksin Shinawatra.[12]

More than any previous party, TRT represented the interests of big domestic business. Previously, business leaders had remained aloof from corrupt electoral politics; they had not needed to be directly involved, for government had supported domestic business. It was the threat to their interests and power posed by neoliberal policy that caused the remaining tycoons to conclude that big domestic capital needed to take control of the state. Many long-standing rivalries were put aside as big business coalesced around Thaksin. TRT thus became the vehicle to give back a competitive edge to domestic business. This was symbolised in the TRT's runaway 2001 election victory.

TRT built an electoral platform that addressed the aspirations of many voters. It developed an inclusive message and nationalist policies, and pledged help for those suffering from the slump. This was appealing to poor, especially rural, voters. TRT also targeted small business, promising to make credit available to them. In economic policy, TRT caught the mood of an electorate that had suffered the welfare declines outlined above. The Party emphasised a dual track development strategy, in which the initial emphasis was on strengthening the domestic economy by boosting demand. Particular attention was paid to schemes that poured government funds into rural areas. Specific programs were developed to appeal to rural people: soft loans for every community in the country, a three-year debt moratorium for farmers, a 30 baht universal health care program, and a people's bank (Thai Rak Thai n.d.).

Not only did these promises deliver a handsome election victory in 2001, but they also rejected the IMF-brokered policies. To emphasise this, Thaksin extolled the virtues of managed development, drawing on the examples of Malaysia and Singapore (Thaksin 2001). Not only did Thaksin and TRT make promises, but, following the 2001 election, also moved quickly to implement them, emphasising its pledges to the poor. The political outcome was a landslide re-election in 2005.

These obligations to the poor should not conceal the fact that the TRT government was by and for the rich. Thaksin's cabinets included representatives of the most powerful post-crisis business groups and families, including his own Shin Corp, Jasmine, Charoen Pokphand, Bangkok Entertainment, the Thai Military Bank, Thai Summit, and others. The TRT government set about helping domestic business, including those associated with its own leaders, advisers, and supporters (see McCargo & Ukrist 2005:ch. 6).

To protect domestic business, the government slowed the pace of liberalisation in a number of areas, including in the telecommunications sector and the privatisation of state enterprises, and suggested limits on foreign ownership. In this the government ignored timetables and programs set by the previous government and the IMF. The government was also supportive of businesspeople who had come under investigation for deals done in the pre-crisis period and had state banks bail out a number of businessespeople (Pasuk & Baker 2004:18–19). That many of these were supporters of and advisers to TRT, and that there were serious conflicts of interest involved, was hidden in the language of economic nationalism.

Meanwhile, powerful nationalist rhetoric was not going to maintain political consensus for too long. As a result, TRT strengthened its political control. Thaksin and TRT attacked critics, neutered independent agencies, limited the media, managed news, managed mergers with smaller political parties, limited parliamentary scrutiny, and strengthened state security agencies (see McCargo & Ukrist 2005; Pasuk & Baker 2004). As Glassman (this volume) indicates, the government has also utilised the US-sponsored war on terror to shore up aspects of its political control. The intention has been to make the government of tycoons safe over the long term by minimising and managing opposition. Thaksin himself has argued that adversarial parliamentary politics is a betrayal of the people (Thaksin 2002:4).

Renegotiating social contracts

But this was not a simple case of domestic business seizing the state. Rather, Thaksin, TRT, and domestic capital, operating within a representative parliamentary system, established their political legitimacy through a new social contract that replaced Sarit's developmental social compact.

A political backlash against neoliberal economic policies had brought Thaksin his first election victory and, while TRT strategists clearly saw the need for alternative economic recovery strategies emphasising demand-driven growth, neither TRT nor Thaksin were natural enemies of liberal economic policies. Thaksin supports free trade and some of TRT's policies were congruent with those favoured by the international financial institutions (for example, on decentralisation, bureaucratic reform, and the promotion of small- and medium-scale enterprises). In essence, TRT's policies were designed to give domestic capital enough space to restructure and regather its strength before returning to policies that looked more like neoliberal orthodoxy. Without this breathing space, domestic capital would have been uncompetitive and foreign capital would have won substantial gains.

Once TRT had secured its 2001 electoral victory, Thaksin set about delivering on the promises that had him elected. The party came to power through policies that promised rapid economic recovery, targeted the poor, made social welfare a significant part of its platform, and allocated government a central role in reducing poverty. While the international financial institutions fretted over the increased role for the state and the impact of aggressive expansionary economic policies, this approach delivered growth and considerable political support for the TRT government. It also represented the establishment of a new social contract.

The deal implicit in TRT policies was that, if the electorate supported TRT, then TRT promised enhanced social protection and economic opportunities for the relatively poor majority of the population. This side of the bargain was targeted directly at those who would elect the government in the 2001 polls—small farmers, the working class, and those in the middle class who had been adversely affected by the economic crisis. The other side of bargain was support and protection for domestic capital as it faced restructuring and significant competition, especially from foreign investors (see Robison et al. 2005).

These policies raise an interesting question: How it is that a government that is representative of domestic capital developed a social contract that delivers state-supported social protection at a level never before considered possible for Thailand?

Interestingly, in the midst of competitive restructuring, the remaining elements of big local business were able to put aside their economic competition in order to cooperate politically. This was because they recognised that domestic capital needed a new social contract if it was to re-establish its economic power. In addition, domestic capital recognised that political and social unrest could result from crisis-induced rural stagnation, inequality, and poverty; it was keen to avoid the situation seen in Indonesia with the overthrow of the Soeharto regime.

At the 2001 elections, the domestic capitalist class allocated a high priority to achieving direct control of the state and to retaining control for a considerable time. This was indicated by the large expenditures it allowed the TRT government to allocate to the five major election policies—the 1 million baht village and community fund, the 30 baht universal health scheme, the people's bank, the one *tambon*–one product scheme, and farmers' debt suspension—more than US$3.6 billion. The most significant of these programs were the village and community fund and the 30 baht health scheme, accounting for about 90 per cent of the funding and claiming almost 52 million beneficiaries by 2002 (Worawan, 2003:3).

While much of the public support for Thaksin and TRT was generated from programs delivering benefits to the poor, the success of their broader economic policies was also important. While Thailand's growth rates have not returned to pre-crisis levels, the TRT government has presided over growth rates that increased to more than 6 per cent in 2002, which, despite a series of external shocks, were able to be maintained until 2005. Domestic capital benefited from a return to growth and other policies that supported recovery. The satisfaction of major business figures with the government was indicated during the campaign leading up to the 2005 election, when virtually all of them threw their weight behind TRT.

CONCLUSION

Thailand's economic development can be judged successful in growth terms. The crisis has not altered this judgment, even though it has prompted a reconsideration of the reasons for economic success and failure and the role of the state. Before the crisis, some concluded that Thailand offered little theoretical support for the efficacy of either interventionist or minimalist states. Others argued that Thailand's growth might have been higher had it not been for weak state institutions. The crisis focused attention on the institutions capable of facilitating markets through rules-based and predictable systems.

This chapter has attempted to demonstrate that this debate is not always enlightening. In general terms, it is not surprising that Thailand's development strategies and plans have supported the expansion of markets and capitalist accumulation. These policies were adopted not necessarily because politicians, bureaucrats, and technocrats were listening to capitalists or including them in policy-making—sometimes they did—but because structural imperatives demanded that the state support capitalist accumulation. In Thailand, from the late 1950s to the 1997–98 crisis, this has usually been translated as support for domestic capitalists. It has only been under Thaksin and TRT that a capitalist state controlled by capitalists has emerged.

The history of Thailand's development has seen the establishment of particular accumulation regimes. These regimes are an amalgam of economic, social, and political power, and structure the development of public policy. In other words, policy outcomes are not a measure of the abilities of institutions (state or private) or of the relative insulation of decision-makers from political interference. Rather, policy results from competition and conflict over production, profits, wealth, and power. These conflicts are intimately bound to the trajectory of various classes and class fractions, nationally and internationally. In Thailand, the conflicts unleashed by economic crisis and recovery have underlined the fact that markets are 'politically constructed by governments through a set of rules that enable rights and obligations to be allocated to different actors via markets' (Higgott & Nesadurai 2002:29). It is clear the government has been critical in shaping the accumulation regimes that have organised Thailand's markets and institutions from the time when monarchs were most powerful. It is the understanding of this fact that led Thailand's domestic capitalist class to seize control of the state in 2001. The importance of shaping the way markets will operate in Thailand has seen an attempt to reshape the accumulation regime through a social contract that delivers improved social welfare in a deal that also allows local capital to rebuild its competitiveness and avoid the bleak outcome that seemed likely under orthodox reforms proposed when the economic crisis began. Through intense struggle, particularly between domestic and international capital, the former appears to have achieved considerable success, re-establishing itself through the use of state power and authority.

NOTES

1 I am grateful to Andrew Brown, Richard Robison, and Garry Rodan for comments on an earlier version of this chapter.

2 These paragraphs are a characterisation; for more detail, see Bottomore (1985).

3 Writing from a different perspective, Yoshihara (1988), in arguing that South-East Asian capitalism is ersatz, develops an analysis that produces conclusions close to those of dependency theorists.

4 For a discussion of Thailand's capitalist development that points out these shortcomings, see Hewison (1989).

5 The history of the Chinese in Thailand is analysed by Skinner (1957, 1958) and Suehiro (1989).

6 The event is usually portrayed as the replacement of one elite by another in a coup. It was far more than this. The People's Party, although not cohesive or ideologically coherent, established the fundamentals of the new political and economic landscape and discourse. It defined a political opposition (royalists), brought the military to political prominence, and raised economic management, modernisation and progress, constitutionalism, representation, and opposition as important issues.

7 Sarit evidently had fewer links to state enterprises than did the leaders of the previous government; he had built his connections with the private sector (Silcock 1967a:20).

8 The BOI made no particular distinction between foreign and domestic investors. Promotional privileges to foreign firms have also been available to domestic investors, although a few areas of employment were reserved for Thais. The privileges have been generous. In addition to guarantees against nationalisation, state monopolies, or government competition, BOI promotion offers incentives such as tax holidays and other taxation relief, import bans on competing products, tax deductions, repatriation of profits, and substantial and additional benefits for exporters (Board of Investment 1995).

9 It needs to be noted that all of these data are based on unrealistically low poverty lines. The figure used to calculate these figures in 1996 was annual per capita income of the equivalent of 59 US cents per day for rural areas and 94 US cents a day for urban areas. In 2002, it was about 93 cents a day in rural areas and, in urban areas, about $1.29 a day (TDRI 2003).

10 The Bank of Thailand (1997a:5), for example, reporting the first nine months of 1997, referred to 'subdued' economic conditions, this when the crisis was underway. Shortly afterwards, the bank's annual report referred to 'severe difficulties' and a 'sharp economic slowdown' (Bank of Thailand 1997b:5–6).

11 This and the next two paragraphs are based on an analysis of World Bank crisis era research (World Bank 1999a–c, 2000a–c, 2001, 2005). For a detailed discussion, see Hewison (2002a).

12 It is unclear how Thaksin's businesses survived the crisis. His telecommunications businesses certainly continued to provide cashflow throughout the crisis. At the same time, it was said that, when deputy prime minister in the Chavalit government, Thaksin may have benefited from inside advice on the devaluation (Thitinan 2001:327). This allegation has been vigorously denied by Thaksin and his supporters. Thaksin's business success coincided with the economic boom. From a small computer business in the early 1980s, Thaksin was, by 1996, one of Thailand's wealthiest businesspeople and his companies were generally profitable (see Pasuk & Baker 2004). Even so, it is worth noting that much of Thaksin's business success was based on state concessions in telecommunications and related areas (see Ukrist 2002). He had excellent connections in the military, where relatives had powerful positions, and the police, where he had trained; also, he had married the daughter of a powerful police general (see McCargo & Ukrist 2005). Thaksin had dabbled in national politics from 1994 to 1997, although he had not been particularly popular or successful.

REFERENCES

Anek Laothamatas (1992) *Business Associations and the New Political Economy of Thailand: From Bureaucratic Polity to Liberal Corporatism*, Singapore: Institute of Southeast Asian Studies.

Bank for International Settlements (1998) *68th Annual Report*, Basle:8 June.

Bank of Thailand (1997a) 'Economic Developments in the First 9 Months of 1997', *Bank of Thailand Quarterly Bulletin*, 37(3):5–15.

——(1997b) 'Economic Performance in 1997 and Outlook for 1998', *Bank of Thailand Quarterly Bulletin*, 37(4):5–20.

——(2000) 'Bank of Thailand Statistics', <www.bot.or.th>.

——(2005) 'Economic Data', <www.bot.or.th/bothomepage/databank/EconData/EconData_e.htm>.

Batson, Benjamin A. (1984) *The End of the Absolute Monarchy in Siam*, Singapore: Oxford University Press.

Bello, Walden (1998) 'Testimony of Walden Bello before Banking Oversight Subcommittee, Banking and Financial Services Committee', US House of Representatives, 21 April, <www.igc.org/dgap/walden.html>.

——, Shea Cunningham and Li Kheng Poh (1998) *A Siamese Tragedy; Development and Disintegration in Modern Thailand*, London: Zed Books.

Board of Investment (1990), *Key Investment Indicators in Thailand*, various issues.

——(1995) *A Guide to the Board of Investment*, Bangkok: Office of the Board of Investment.

——(2000) *Thailand Information Database*, 19 July, <www.boi.go.th/english/tid/data/BOT Macro_e.htm>.

Bottomore, Tom (1985) *Theories of Modern Capitalism*, London: George Allen & Unwin.

Brown, Andrew, Bundit Thonachaisetavut and Kevin Hewison (2002) 'Labour Relations and Regulation in Thailand: Theory and Practice', *Southeast Asia Research Centre Working Papers Series*, No. 27, July, Hong Kong: City University of Hong Kong.

Bullard, Nicola, Walden Bello and Kamal Malhotra (1998) 'Taming the Tigers: The IMF and the Asian Crisis', in K. S. Jomo (ed.) *Tigers in Trouble: Financial Governance, Liberalisation and Crises in East Asia*, London: Zed Books, pp. 85–136.

Chatthip Nartsupha (1999) *The Thai Village Economy in the Past*, Chiangmai: Silkworm Books.

Christensen, Scott, David Dollar, Ammar Siamwalla and Pakorn Vichyanond (1993) *The Lessons of East Asia: Thailand: The Institutional and Political Underpinnings of Growth*, Washington, DC: World Bank.

Copeland, Mathew P. (1994) 'Contested Nationalism and the 1932 Overthrow of the Absolute Monarchy in Siam', unpublished PhD thesis, Australian National University, Canberra.

Darling, Frank C. (1965) *Thailand and the United States*, Washington, DC: Public Affairs Press.

Doner, Richard F. and Ansil Ramsey (1997) 'Competitive Clientelism and Economic Governance: The Case of Thailand', in Sylvia Maxfield and Ben R. Schneider (eds) *Business and the State in Developing Countries*, Ithaca: Cornell University Press, pp. 237–76.

Doner, Richard F. and Gary Hawes (1995) 'The Political Economy of Growth in Southeast and Northeast Asia', in Manochehr Dorraj (ed.) *The Changing Political Economy of the Third World*, Boulder: Lynne Rienner Publishers, pp. 145–85.

Doner, Richard F. Bryan K. Ritchie and Dan Slater (2005) 'Systemic Vulnerability and the Origins of Developmental States: Northeast and Southeast Asia in Comparative Perspective', *International Organization*, 59 (Spring): 327–61.

Economic Section (1998) '1998 Investment Climate Statement for Thailand', Bangkok, Department of State, United States Embassy, <http://usa.or.th/embassy/invcl98.htm>.

Glassman, Jim (2004) *Thailand at the Margins: Internationalization of the State and the Transformation of Labour*, Oxford: Oxford University Press.

Handley, Paul (1997) 'More of the Same?: Politics and Business, 1987–96', in Kevin Hewison (ed.) *Political Change in Thailand: Democracy and Participation*, London: Routledge, pp. 94–113.

Hart-Landsberg, Martin and Paul Burkett (1998) 'Contradictions of Capitalist Industrialization in East Asia: A Critique of the "Flying Geese" Theories of Development', *Economic Geography*, 74 (April):87–110.

Hewison, Kevin (1981) 'The Financial Bourgeoisie in Thailand', *Journal of Contemporary Asia*, 11(4):395–412.

——(1985) 'The State and Capitalist Development in Thailand', in Richard Higgott and Richard Robison (eds) *Southeast Asia: Essays in the Political Economy of Structural Change*, London: Routledge and Kegan Paul, pp. 266–94.

——(1987) 'National Interests and Economic Downturn: Thailand', in Richard Robison, Kevin Hewison and Richard Higgott (eds) *Southeast Asia in the 1980s: The Politics of Economic Crisis*, Sydney: Allen & Unwin, pp. 52–79.

——(1989) *Bankers and Bureaucrats: Capital and the Role of the State in Thailand*, Yale University Southeast Asian Monographs, No. 34, New Haven: Yale Center for International and Area Studies.

——(2000a) 'Resisting Globalization: A Study of Localism in Thailand', *Pacific Review*, 13(2):279–96.

——(2000b) 'Thailand's Capitalism Before and After the Economic Crisis', in Richard Robison, Mark Beeson, Kanishka Jayasuriya and Hyuk-Rae Kim (eds) *Politics and Markets in the Wake of the Asian Crisis*, London: Routledge, pp. 192–211.

——(2002a) 'The World Bank and Thailand: Crisis and Safety Nets', *Public Administration*

and Policy, 11(1):1–21.
——(2002b) 'Thailand: Boom, Bust, and Recovery', *Perspectives on Global Development and Technology*, 1(3/4):225–50.
——(2004) 'Pathways to Recovery: Bankers, Business, and Nationalism in Thailand', in Edmund T. Gomez and Hsin-Huang M. Hsiao (eds), *Chinese Enterprise, Transnationalism, and Identity*, London: RoutledgeCurzon, pp. 232–77.
——(2005) 'Neo-liberalism and Domestic Capital: the Political Outcomes of the Economic Crisis in Thailand', *Journal of Development Studies*, 41(2):310–30.
Higgott, Richard A. and Helen E. S. Nesadurai (2002) 'Rethinking the Southeast Asian Development Model: Bringing Ethical and Governance Questions In', *ASEAN Economic Bulletin*, 19(1):27–39.
Hong, Lysa (1984) *Thailand in the Nineteenth Century: Evolution of the Economy and Society*, Singapore: Institute of Southeast Asian Studies.
Hutchcroft, Paul (1999) 'After the Fall: Prospects for Political and Institutional Reform in Post-Crisis Thailand and the Philippines', *Government and Opposition*, 34(4):473–97.
Jansen, Karel (1990) *Finance, Growth and Stability: Financing Economic Development in Thailand, 1960–86*, Avebury: Gower.
——(1997) *External Finance in Thailand's Development: An Interpretation of Thailand's Growth Boom*, Houndsmill: Macmillan.
Mathana Phananiramai (1995) 'Thailand National Report: Employment Situation, Problems and Policy', *TDRI Quarterly Review*, 10(3):11–15.
McCargo, Duncan and Ukrist Pathmanand (2005) *The Thaksinization of Thailand*, Copenhagen: NIAS Press.
McVey, Ruth (1992) 'The Materialization of the Southeast Asian Entrepreneur', in Ruth McVey (ed.) *Southeast Asian Capitalists*, Ithaca: Cornell University Southeast Asia Program, pp. 7–33.
Medhi Krongkaew (ed.) (1995) *Thailand's Industrialization and Its Consequences*, Houndmills: Macmillan.
Nakharin Mektrairat (1992) *Kanpatiwat sayam ph.s. 2475*, Bangkok: Social Sciences and Humanities Project Foundation.
National Economic and Social Development Board (NESDB) (n.d.) *The Seventh Five-Year National Economic and Social Development Plan (1992–1996)*, Bangkok: Office of the Prime Minister.
Nidhi Aeusrivongse (1982) *Wathanatham kradumphi kab wannakam ton rattanakosin*, Bangkok: Thai Khadi Research Institute.
Pasuk Phongpaichit and Chris Baker (1995) *Thailand: Economy and Politics*, Kuala Lumpur: Oxford University Press.
——(1996) *Thailand's Boom!*, Chiangmai: Silkworm Books.
——(1998) *Thailand's Boom and Bust*, Chiangmai: Silkworm Books.
——(2000) *Thailand's Crisis*, Chiangmai: Silkworm Books.
——(2004) *Thaksin*, Chiangmai: Silkworm Books.
Regnier, Philippe (2001), 'Reform in Post-Crisis Thailand (1997-2001): Exploring the Contribution of Small Entrepreneurs to Socio-Economic Change, Democratization and Emerging Populist Governance', Paper presented to the EUROSEAS Conference, London, School of Oriental and African Studies, 6–8 September.
Reid, Anthony (1995) 'Documenting the Rise and Fall of Ayudhya as a Regional Trade Centre', in Kajit Jittasevi (ed.) *Ayudhya and Asia*, Bangkok: Core University Program between Thammasat University and Kyoto University, 18–20 December, pp. 5–14.
Riggs, Fred W. (1966) *Thailand: The Modernization of a Bureaucratic Polity*, Honolulu: East–West Center Press.
Robison, Richard, Kevin Hewison and Richard Higgott (eds) (1987) *Southeast Asia in the 1980s: The Politics of Economic Crisis*, Sydney: Allen & Unwin.
Robison, Richard, Garry Rodan and Kevin Hewison (2005) 'Transplanting the neo-liberal

state in Southeast Asia', in Richard Boyd & Tak-Wing Ngo (eds), *Asian States: Beyond the developmental perspective*, London: RoutledgeCurzon, pp. 172–98.

Securities and Exchange Commission of Thailand (2000) *Capital Market Performance, 1997–1999*, <www.sec.or.th/ann99/app4.html>.

Silcock, T. H. (1967a) 'Outline of Economic Development 1945–65', in T. H. Silcock (ed.) *Thailand: Social and Economic Studies in Development*, Canberra: Australian National University Press, pp. 1–26.

——(1967b) 'The Rice Premium and Agricultural Diversification', in T. H. Silcock (ed.) *Thailand: Social and Economic Studies in Development*, Canberra: Australian National University Press, pp. 231–57.

Skinner, G. William (1957) *Chinese Society in Thailand: An Analytical History*, Ithaca: Cornell University Press.

——(1958) *Leadership and Power in the Chinese Community of Thailand*, Ithaca: Cornell University Press.

Stock Exchange of Thailand (SET) (2000) *Fact Book 2000*, Bangkok: Stock Exchange of Thailand.

——(2005) *Annual Report 2004*, Bangkok: Stock Exchange of Thailand.

Suehiro, Akira (1989) *Capital Accumulation in Thailand 1855–1985*, Tokyo: The Centre for East Asian Cultural Studies.

Suthy Prasartset (1980) *Thai Business Leaders: Men and Careers in a Developing Economy*, Tokyo: Institute of Developing Economies.

Tej Bunnag (1977) *The Provincial Administration of Siam, 1892–1915*, Kuala Lumpur: Oxford University Press.

Thai Rak Thai (n.d.) 'Thai Rak Thai Party Policy', <www.thairakthai.or.th/policy_trt12.asp>.

Thailand Development Research Institute (TDRI) (1992, 1995, 1998, 1999, 2003) *Thailand Economic Information Kit*, Bangkok: TDRI.

Thak Chaloematiarana (1979) *Thailand: The Politics of Despotic Paternalism*, Bangkok: Thai Khadi Research Institute.

Thaksin Shinawatra (2001) 'Speech By His Excellency Pol. Lt. Col. Thaksin Shinawatra, Prime Minister of Thailand', 24 April, Putrajaya, <www.thaigov.go.th/news/speech/Thaksin/sp25apr01.htm>.

——(2002) 'Keynote Speech' to the 2nd International Conference of Asian Political Parties, Bangkok, 23 November, <www.thaigov.go.th/news/speech/thaksin/sp23nov02-2.htm>.

Thitinan Pongsudhirak (2001) 'Crisis From Within: The Politics of Macroeconomic Management in Thailand, 1947-97', unpublished PhD thesis, Department of International Relations, London: London School of Economics.

Thongchai Winichakul (1994) *Siam Mapped: A History of the Geo-Body of a Nation*, Honolulu: University of Hawai'i Press.

Ukrist Pathmanand (2002) 'From Shinawatra Group of Companies to the Thaksin Shinawatra Government: The Politics of Money and Power Merge', Paper presented to the International Conference on 'Crony Capitalism', Quezon City, University of the Philippines, 17–18 January.

Unger, Danny (1998) *Building Social Capital in Thailand: Fibers, Finance, and Infrastructure*, Cambridge: Cambridge University Press.

United States Embassy (1998) 'Thailand—Economic Trends and Forecast for 1998', Bangkok, <usa.or.th/embassy/eco.htm>.

Warr, Peter G. and Nidhiprabha Bhanupong (1996) *Thailand's Macroeconomic Miracle: Stable Adjustment and Sustained Growth*, Kuala Lumpur: Oxford University Press.

Weiss, Linda (1999) 'State Power and the Asian Crisis', *New Political Economy*, 4(3), pp. 317–42.

Worawan Chandoevwit (2003) 'Thailand's Grass Roots Policies', *TDRI Quarterly Bulletin*, 18(2):3–8.

World Bank (1959) *A Public Development Program for Thailand*, Baltimore: Johns Hopkins

Press, for the International Bank for Reconstruction and Development.
——(1993) *The East Asian Miracle: Economic Growth and Public Policy*, New York: Oxford University Press.
——(1999a) *Thailand Economic Monitor*, Bangkok: World Bank Thailand, October.
——(1999b) 'Thailand Macroeconomic Update', 13 July, unpublished paper.
——(1999c) *Thailand Social Monitor: Challenge for Social Reform*, Bangkok: World Bank Thailand.
——(2000a) *Thailand Economic Monitor*, Bangkok: World Bank Thailand, February.
——(2000b) *Thailand Economic Monitor*, Bangkok: World Bank Thailand, June.
——(2000c) *Thailand Social Monitor: Thai Workers and the Crisis*, Bangkok: World Bank Thailand.
——(2001) *Social Monitor VI: Poverty and Public Policy*, Bangkok: World Bank Thailand.
——(2005) *Thailand Economic Monitor*, Bangkok: World Bank Thailand Office.
Yada Praparpun (1998) 'Small and Medium Enterprises in Thailand: The Effects of Trade Liberalisation on SMEs and Women Workers', in Vivienne Wee (ed.) *Trade Liberalisation: Challenges and Opportunities for Women in Southeast Asia*, Singapore: Unifem and Engender, pp. 119–28.
Yoshihara Kunio (1988) *The Rise of Ersatz Capitalism in South-East Asia*, Singapore: Oxford University Press.

Newspapers

Nation

4 Indonesia: Crisis, Oligarchy, and Reform

Richard Robison and
Vedi R. Hadiz[1]

KEY TOPICS

INTRODUCTION

OF all the Asian economies, Indonesia's experience in the wake of the economic crisis of 1997 was to be the most intense and destructive. The downward spiral of the rupiah created a fiscal crisis for the government, while Indonesia's corporate moguls became mired in mountains of debt beyond their capacity to repay. Indonesia's banks were quickly paralysed by a deepening crisis of bad loans. This was to be much more than a financial or economic crisis. What has distinguished Indonesia from other countries in the region is the extent to which the crisis translated into social unrest, political violence, and the unravelling of state power. Soeharto, Indonesia's president of over three decades, found himself unable to stem the economic collapse and deal with its deepening social effects or to maintain the institutional underpinning of his political and economic power. The man who created Indonesia's New Order now became its greatest liability and the main obstacle to a resolution of the problem. With Soeharto's fall from power, the crisis claimed its most important political victim. The last of the Cold War capitalist dictatorships had come to an end.

There is no doubt that economic crisis in Indonesia was precipitated by speculation, panic, and capital flight in highly volatile and mobile global financial markets. But Indonesia was no innocent bystander in the disaster that was to take hold after the currency collapses of 1997. The extensive and destructive events that followed derived from contradictions deeply rooted within the economic and political regimes of the Soeharto era. The unconstrained exercise of political power in economic life, which generated rapid growth and provided the cement of a seemingly invulnerable architecture of political power, also created systemic faults. It was domestic capital, highly vulnerable because of overinvestment and overborrowing, that fled the rupiah when the crisis hit.

It is not a question of whether Indonesian capitalism contained fatal contradictions, but why it took so long for them to become manifest. As we shall see, crises in debt, banking, and corporate activities were already endemic in the decade preceding the 1997 crisis, propped up only by the political intervention of the government and continuing inflows of short-term loans. As Jeffrey Winters (1997, 2000) argued, because global capital was deeply implicated in this growing speculative bubble, its traders and fund managers were unwilling to put a halt to the process. The crisis ended the flow of these loans and undermined the capacity of the government to intervene on behalf of floundering companies and state agencies.

It is within this larger pathology of Indonesian capitalism that the turbulent events of the post-Soeharto era must be understood. But there is little agreement on the precise nature of this pathology. As we have seen in chapter 1 of this volume, neoclassical economists, particularly within the IMF, saw the crisis in functional terms: interventionist regimes simply collapsed under the weight of their inefficiency and dysfunction. It provided, in their view, a reminder that long-term growth in an era of globalisation required Asian economies and their governments to 'abandon their bad habits' and allow market signals to set prices (*Economist* 7 March 1998).

But the crisis in Indonesia did not usher in a smooth and frictionless transformation to markets and democracy in the liberal model. Indonesia's reformers have faced fierce resistance in their efforts to close insolvent banks and force powerful business groups to hand over assets to cover the costs of recapitalisation. Attempts to bring to court and successfully prosecute most of the major corrupt figures of the old regime have been almost entirely unsuccessful. Included among these are former New Order ministers Ginandjar Kartasasmita and Akbar Tandjung, businessmen Joko Chandra, Arifin Panigoro, and, most recently, Nurdin Halid, a former Golkar financier and businessman (*JP* 18 June 2005). Although many of the most notorious monopolies underpinning Indonesia's corporate moguls have been dismantled, monopolies, concessions, and off-budget funding persists. The shock of the crisis has been unable either to destroy the old relationships of corporate and political power or to bring to life a dominant neoliberal coalition.

This is not the first time that crisis and reform have produced outcomes unexpected by neoclassical economists. The dismantling of the command capitalism of the Soekarno era from 1965 and the opening of Indonesia to foreign investment and aid did not lead Indonesia down the path of a liberal market economy. Ironically, such reforms were to prove instrumental in the consolidation of political authoritarianism and state capitalism under Soeharto. Nor did the widespread programs of reform in financial and trade regimes and deeper integration within global financial markets, which followed the collapse of oil prices in the 1980s, result in the expected transformation to a liberal market economy. They precipitated, instead, a shift from public to private monopoly and the harnessing of state power to the interests of powerful coalitions of private and public oligarchies: an unconstrained form of robber baron capitalism.

How do we explain these divergent outcomes? If the costs of resisting the market are so high and the benefits of embracing it are so evident, why have successive Indonesian governments consistently resisted reform? More importantly, why have reformist initiatives in opening the economy and deregulating markets often strengthened the position of predatory officials and rent-seeking business interests? The answer to these questions, we suggest, can only be found in the constellation of social power and the nature of political conflict in post-Soeharto Indonesia. These have essentially determined the way in which the forging of new political and economic regimes has taken place following the demise of Soeharto's New Order.

A MATTER OF POLITICS

The demise of the New Order and the fall of Soeharto opened the door for a dramatic shift towards democratic politics in Indonesia. Neoliberals generally welcomed the changes that have, among other things, led to free and open elections in 1999 and 2004, as well as to the rise of parties and parliaments, nationally and locally. Though these changes were largely the product of domestic political dynamics—the heavily centralised New Order became impossible to keep intact without the man most responsible for its longevity—rather than any policy initiative by the IMF or the World Bank. Such agencies had, for some time, advocated breaking up centralised state power to make market reforms more possible. In the following years, these agencies came to advocate a number of policies in the area of good governance, mostly prominently that of administrative decentralisation. The latter has been linked to everything under the broad rubric of 'good governance', from public participation in politics and development, transparency and accountability, to facilitating the operations of free markets (USAID n.d). It is significant that the literature on decentralisation, as produced by international development agencies, typically implies that policy makers, if properly insulated from vested interests, can choose and craft the most appropriate form, pace, and sequencing of decentralisation (see, for example, World Bank Group n.d.). In this neoliberal worldview, just as markets need to be protected from politics, so the dysfunctional effects of politics and greater public participation in a democracy can be excluded from the real technocratic business of decentralisation (Hadiz 2004a).

It is undoubtedly significant that, after more than three decades in which politics was heavily regulated and controlled and civil society disorganised, the crisis of 1997–98 made possible a new political regime based on parliament and parties; however, it is now evident that the new Indonesian democracy has not been able to assert its authority over a state apparatus (and its corps of officials) that had evolved under Soeharto into a crude mechanism for allocating power and resources. Moreover, the power and influence of politicians, tycoons, and officials have not been subordinated to a rule of law and the authority of the courts, and thus money politics and the authority of political bosses have instead appropriated the institutions of democratic governance. At the same time, it is also clear that those interests nurtured at the middle and lower levels of the New Order's formerly vast system of patronage—local political operators and entrepreneurs, enforcers, and petty apparatchiks—have benefited immensely from the decentralisation of state power. They now predominate in Indonesia's local governments, parliaments, and the local branches of political parties, whose power and influence have grown as Jakarta's has waned.

Essentially, institutional change tied to the emergence of elections, party politics, and decentralisation of state power since Soeharto's fall has been determined by the way in which powerful entrenched interests were able to politically reorganise themselves. Thus, there was to be no swift or unambiguous transition to liberal democratic modes of governance. Some observers, such as Liddle, believed that, once the right institutions are in place, liberal democratic ideals and practices will slowly gain ascendance as a matter of institutional imperative (Liddle 2001). In this, he and others have been deeply influenced by the voluminous democratic-transitions literature pioneered by such theorists as O'Donnell and Schmitter (1986). In contrast, it is suggested here that the pervasiveness of a system of democracy run by money politics—and partly by political violence—in post-New Order Indonesia should not be understood as part of a journey that will ultimately lead to some form of liberal democracy, if only as a matter of time. Instead, money politics (and violence or thuggery) is understood to be fundamentally inherent to the logic of power relations in an illiberal form of democracy that fairly quickly came to be consolidated and entrenched as elements of the *ancien regime* scrambled to secure their interests and position in the immediate post-Soeharto era.

It should be noted, however, that this is far from an argument that maintains how nothing has changed in Indonesian politics. On the contrary, Indonesia recently held its first-ever direct presidential elections in 2004, and, in 2005, embarked on the first of a series of direct elections for provincial and district heads. Moreover, the Indonesian press is among the freest in the region, and political parties and parliaments have become genuine vehicles of political contestation, unlike during the New Order when they merely provided a convenient facade for an authoritarian and exceptionally stifling political regime. The military, though still a powerful force, does not enjoy the sort of influence it had during most of the New Order. Most, if not all, of these developments would have been quite unimaginable during the New Order.

Our argument, significantly, does lead to the question of why shifts in the institutional apparatus of power have not produced the liberal political and economic results many observers had expected in the immediate post-Soeharto period. In order to explain this, we must understand the sort of social conflicts and alliances that have forged the post-Soeharto political configuration. As mentioned, it was soon evident that many of the elements that had been nurtured under the authoritarian New Order could survive within the framework of a new, more democratic, regime, albeit necessarily through more diffuse alliances and vehicles than those that existed in the New Order. Crucially, it is the reorganisation of the old predatory power relations within a new system of parties, parliaments, and elections that has been the central dynamic of political change since 1998. Thus New Order-incubated interests remain highly influential in almost all of the major political parties in Indonesia today, from the now resurgent Golkar (the New Order's state party), the Indonesian Democratic Party for Struggle, and the National Awakening Party, respectively, of former Presidents Megawati Soekarnoputri and Abdurrahman Wahid, as well as a range of others. Moreover, a major feature of post-Soeharto political contests in Indonesia has been the rise of money politics—which has been highly prominent at the national level as well as in local elections, including the 2005 first direct polls for governor, mayor, and district head across Indonesia. As a general rule—although there have been important exceptions—it is the political actors who are most well endowed with the resources to play the game of money politics and best able to utilise an apparatus of violence or of selective mass mobilisations that have been the main beneficiaries of Indonesia's post-1998 democratisation. Reflecting the new emphasis on decentralised governance, contests over local office have becoming increasingly heated and, significantly, expensive. In turn, this provides a conducive environment for the proliferation of predatory rent-seeking activities as politicos typically seek to recoup the cost of investment in electoral campaigns while in office (Hadiz 2004b).

In this sense, it was significant to the post-Soeharto trajectory that the *reformasi* movement, due to its hesitancy, did not sweep aside the predatory and illiberal social and political forces nurtured by the New Order for three decades. Also significant is the fact that the legacy of authoritarian rule runs deep in Indonesia. Soeharto's New Order had systematically pursued a policy of disorganising civil society, effectively paralysing most independent capacity for self-organisation among groups such as the urban middle class and the working class, sections of which might have been expected to have an interest in more substantive reforms in the architecture of power. In reality, when authoritarianism finally gave way in Indonesia, it was the interests that had been nurtured by the New Order that were in the best position to take advantage of the opening up of political space and the mechanics of Indonesia's new democracy. The task for neoliberal reformers is thus a highly formidable one: to mobilise cohesive coalitions behind the neoliberal agenda within a political context that is clearly not conducive. Notwithstanding the support of the likes of the World Bank and the IMF, the building blocks for such a coalition appear quite limited to a smattering of intellectuals and officials in some government agencies and departments. At the moment, the task seems to be one that well beyond their capacities.

Thus our understanding of social, economic, and political change in Indonesia emphasises the elements of social conflict and power. It is in this respect that our analysis fundamentally challenges dominant interpretations of recent Indonesian developments, including that of neoliberal political economy.

INTERPRETING THE POLITICS OF ECONOMIC CHANGE IN INDONESIA

The emergence of neoliberal political economy in the 1980s and its complex fusion with structural functional variants of modernisation theory has given rise to a new orthodoxy for the analysis of change and reform. But neoliberal theory is not just another intellectual tradition. It became the ideology that drove policy agenda within Western governments and international financial institutions such as the World Bank and the IMF (Toye 1987:45–94). Its practitioners in Indonesia and elsewhere are well aware that imposing neoclassical economic prescriptions is a profoundly political process. But because markets are understood as abstract and universal self-regulating mechanisms driven by their own internal laws, it is the liberation of this natural market from the grip of rent-seeking and predatory coalitions that is the central dynamic in the neoliberal analysis of change. The major dispute is whether this is achieved by dismantling the very power of the state to intervene in economic life or by constructing a rational regulatory state insulated from politics.

From the very beginning of the New Order in 1966, close attachments were forged between Indonesia's economic technocrats and neoclassical economists in the World Bank and various Western universities. Western liberal economists heralded the rise of Soeharto's New Order as the victory of rationality over ideology and of economics over politics (Arndt 1967). The rational credentials of Soeharto's New Order were confirmed as it reopened the door to Western investment and appointed Western-trained economic technocrats to the key economic ministries. It was the capacity of these technocrats to adopt pragmatic policies based on rational technical calculation, transcending the demands of vested interests, that was seen as the critical factor in three decades of successful development (Hill 1996).

Despite the enthusiasm of neoclassical economists for the way in which Indonesia's technocrats managed fiscal and monetary policy, they nevertheless recognised that they did not have the political muscle to overcome rent-seeking interests. The process of liberal reform was understood as a war of attrition in which economic crises and shocks provided the opportunities for technocrats to convince the government of the need for change and progressively to erode interventionist policies. It was a case of 'good policies in bad times' for these economists (Bresnan 1993; Schwarz 1994; Soesastro 1989).

The idea of the New Order as an essentially modern and developmental regime was given its fullest expression in the political analysis of structural functional modernisation theory. Whereas the authoritarianism of the previous (Soekarno) regime had been portrayed as atavistic in nature and defined by traditional culture, the authoritarianism of Soeharto's New Order was to be understood as a modernising force; in the context of the Cold War, a regime that was, in its essence, anti-communist and opened its doors to Western investment could hardly be regarded as anything else. In Huntingtonian terms, the New Order provided the strong institutional cement for a disintegrating society and performed the historical role of the middle class—it was its 'advance guard', its 'spearhead into modern politics' (Huntington 1968: 222). Not surprisingly, it was a thesis seized upon with alacrity by the theoreticians of the New Order, providing the perfect legitimation for authoritarian rule (Moertopo 1973). For Donald Emmerson and William Liddle, two of the leading political scientists of Indonesia, the New Order was the only alternative to chaos and disorder, a return to a parliamentary system offering only anomic and untrusting behaviour, instability, and impotence (Emmerson 1976:250; 1978:104, 105; Liddle 1989:23).

It was Liddle who subsequently tied this profoundly anti-liberal political ideology with neoclassical economics. Soeharto, he argued, successfully drove economic growth because he was able to rise above the predatory and patrimonial attachments of others within the regime. In his own person, he established a relative autonomy from distributional coalitions and escaped the suffocating cultural lenses that forced many Indonesians to resist capitalism. This behaviour, Liddle suggested, is based on rational calculations about political survival, in particular, Soeharto's recognition that his long-term political self-interest lay in a neoclassical policy agenda able to deliver the economic growth and prosperity that would reinforce the legitimacy of the regime and provide a strong revenue base (Liddle 1991:403, 404; 1992:796–8).

Given the faith they had placed in the New Order and its technocrats, and their conviction that the economic fundamentals were good (Hill 1996), it is not surprising that the crisis came as a shock to many neoliberals. Their explanations emphasised shifts in capital flows, panic in global capital markets, and events after the crisis that made things worse—including inappropriate IMF policies and the collapse of political authority (Hill 2000). But there were also reflections on flaws internal to the regime. Garnaut (1998) argued that Indonesian policy-makers made the mistake of pursuing fixed exchange-rate policies at a time of growing capital mobility and business exuberance resulting from the economic boom. For McLeod (1998), the Indonesian economy unravelled as its economic managers tried simultaneously to control more than one of the nominal macroeconomic variables of prices, money supply, nominal exchange rate, and nominal interest rate.

For Liddle, the unexpected turn of events was explained by a sharp shift in the behaviour of Soeharto in the latter years of the regime. Liddle argued that Soeharto's actions had deviated recently from the pragmatic and rational concerns of earlier years, determined increasingly by an indulgence of the rapacious demands of his children as they rampaged through the business world (Liddle 1999). But attempts to protect their earlier assessments of the Soeharto regime by talking about policy errors, global market failure, or aberrations in behaviour, were soon to wear thin. Some neoclassical economists began to give more weight to the view that the dynamics of collapse were indeed embedded within the political arrangements and power relations of the regime itself (McLeod 2000).

If the evolution of Indonesia's economic regimes is more than just a matter of good policy choices prevailing over vested interest, what factors might explain why there has been no inexorable advance to a liberal market economy? MacIntyre (1999, 2001) brought an institutional perspective to bear, arguing that the lack of institutional constraints on the arbitrary authority of the Soeharto regime prevented effective policy responses and precipitated a downward spiral of investor confidence in the critical weeks following the crisis. The World Bank itself had recognised for some time that effective institutions were necessary for a liberal transformation, and institution-building has been an important part of its policy agenda in Indonesia and elsewhere (World Bank 1993:135–64). But how do institutions emerge and change, and why have liberal market institutions failed to take root in Indonesia? Again, neoclassical economists within the World Bank and elsewhere assumed that the supply of institutions is primarily a technical or policy matter—that capacity, transparency, and accountability flow from the introduction of efficient procedures and processes (World Bank 1997:2, 3, 28, 106). In a highly voluntarist approach, institutions can simply be supplied.

We argue instead that trajectories of change cannot be understood within the concept of a history that has no telos except efficiency (see Chaudhry 1997:11). What is required, we propose, is an explanation of how conflict over power and its distribution shapes change, and why the advent of markets and the rise of the private interest may lead to liberal markets in some cases and to the money politics of predatory capitalism in others.

Indonesia's economic regimes, we also propose, have been forged in a series of violent episodes of conflict among and within fluid and shifting coalitions of power and interest. Populism, social radicalism, state and predatory capitalism, as well as liberalism, have been central agendas in the struggles to define Indonesian capitalism. What was significant about the 1997 economic crisis is the damage it inflicted on the coherence of those politico–business coalitions that had become the central pillars of the state-centred predatory systems of the Soeharto era. But the collapse of the old system of highly centralised state authority did not mean a spontaneous transition to liberal markets and democracy. It merely opened the door to a new struggle to reforge coalitions and build regimes. The question in Indonesia is not whether markets and democracy will emerge but what kind of markets and what kind of democracy. How have the dominant interests of the Soeharto era reorganised their ascendancy within new alliances and in the context of different institutions? Can a new reformist coalition ultimately establish its authority and subordinate the entrenched oligarchy to legal and democratic constraints? What kinds of coalitions can yet be mobilised behind the neoliberal agenda?

HISTORICAL CONTEXT: STATE CAPITALISM AND THE INCUBATION OF OLIGARCHY

As the old colonial economy decayed around them in the 1950s, Indonesia's new political and economic power brokers were plunged into a struggle to shape the economic regimes of the new republic. In a world without large landowning elites or a powerful urban bourgeoisie, social radicalism and a reactionary form of petty bourgeois populism were to emerge as central threads in the ongoing conflicts that would drive economic change for the coming decades. But reactionary populism was focused around a declining rural propertied class and small-town businesses heavily influenced by anti-Chinese xenophobia and resentful of what they perceived to be growing domination by big business and foreign interests. Liberalism was only a minor political current in the early decades of Indonesia's postcolonial economic history. In the end, it was to be a complex amalgam of state-centred economic nationalism and predatory oligarchy revolving around the state and its corps of politico–bureaucrats that was to prevail.

As political power was assembled in the hands of Soekarno in the late 1950s, the path to fight liberalism was firmly rejected in favour of the principle that the state has a legitimate economic role in ensuring the national interest and that market forces should be tempered by social objectives. Although themes of populism and nationalism were to triumph, they did so under the umbrella of a highly centralised state and its corps of officials in the guise of state capitalism and an authoritarian form of organic corporatism. It was the state, in the three decades from 1960 to the mid 1980s, that embarked on an ambitious program to construct an autonomous industrial base. Nationalism and populism were ideologies sustained by deep-rooted and concrete, vested interests. They lay at the heart of the organic notions of power that legitimised de facto possession of the state by its officials and relieved them of problems of accountability and representation. At the same time, an extensive state sector and pervasive industry policy were the perfect mechanisms for entrenching the authority of the state and its officials in the economic sphere.

In 1965 and 1966, this uneasy alliance of national populism was confirmed by its final and violent victory over the Partai Komunis Indonesia (PKI) and the later petty bourgeois populism of Islamic politics. The new rulers of Indonesia under Soeharto set about entrenching a system of highly centralised military rule and state capitalism. Western powers provided an inflow of official foreign aid and foreign investment into a growing resource-based and import-substitution manufacturing economy. State capitalism was to reach its peak during the oil boom years of 1973–82, when state coffers were overflowing with petrodollars.[2] As part of a broad drive to expand Indonesia's industrial base (Kartasasmita 1985), the state invested heavily in steel, fertilisers, aluminium, petroleum refining, cement, and paper. Funding to the state-enterprise sector increased from Rp41 billion in 1973 to Rp592 billion in 1983 (Hill 1996:102–3). According to one estimate, the state controlled almost 60 per cent of the equity in all domestic investment and a further 9.2 per cent of the equity in foreign investment projects during these years (*Tempo* 14 March 1981:70–1).

The economic authority of the state was extended through a range of highly interventionist policies in foreign investment, trade, and banking. In the wake of the anti-Japanese riots of 1974, for example, the range of sectors closed to foreign investors was extended and all foreign investors were required to adopt local partners. In the trade sector, a wide array of restrictions, especially in the form of non-tariff barriers was introduced, including the establishment in 1982 of the approved traders program, a system of import monopolies that quickly fell into the hands of well-connected private and state companies (Robison & Hadiz 1993). In the banking sector, the government introduced credit ceilings and a variety of subsidised lending programs, significantly increasing its control over the allocation of credit (MacIntyre 1994:250–1; Hill 1996:99–116).

At the same time, powerful corporate conglomerates and politico–business families began to emerge under the umbrella of nationalist policies of protection and subsidy, and within monopolistic structures controlled by patrons with their hands on the levers of state power. Protected from international competition by restrictive trade, licensing, and investment policies, these conglomerates expanded from forestry, trade, and sole agencies into a variety of industries, including the manufacture of auto components, tyres, batteries, cement, electronics, steel, and the engineering industries that grew around the oil sector. Conglomerates with strong political connections, notably the Soeharto family companies, began to dominate the import and distribution of oil products and to secure the contracts for supply and transportation of oil for the state oil corporation, Pertamina (Jones & Pura 1986; Robison 1986; Shin 1989).

By the early 1980s, clear contradictions had begun to emerge within the very structures of authoritarian state capitalism. A new alliance of politico–bureaucrats and corporate moguls, with interests that extended beyond those of protecting and preserving state power, were now intent on using state power to construct and protect new corporate empires of private interest. Through the State Secretariat (Sekneg), Soeharto and powerful politico–bureaucrats, including Ginandjar Kartasasmita, secured institutional control over the allocation of supply and construction contracts for government-funded projects under Presidential Decisions 10 and 14 of 1979 and 1980. Under the flag of economic nationalism, it provided off-budget revenue for the regime and was an important channel for the distribution of state patronage. Under its patronage, an important group of indigenous (pribumi) capitalists was nurtured (Pangaribuan 1995:51–67; Winters 1996:123–41).

At this stage, however, the prevailing system of state capitalism was ruptured by the collapse of oil prices in 1981–82 and again in 1986. This led to a decline in the value of Indonesia's gas and oil exports from US$18.4 billion (or 82 per cent of total exports) in 1982 to US$8.3 billion (or 56 per cent of total exports) in 1986. In the same period, government revenues from oil and gas fell from Rp8.6 trillion to Rp6.3 trillion, or from 70 per cent to 39 per cent of total revenues (Robison 1987). The oil price collapse dramatically shifted the options for the players. It signalled the need to mobilise new sources of investment funds from the private sector, develop new export industries, and build new revenue bases. Influence over economic policy was to shift from economic nationalists within the government to the economic technocrats.

THE TRIUMPH OF OLIGARCHY

From 1986 onwards, Indonesia's technocrats introduced a raft of important policy reforms. Several trade monopolies were abolished, including politically sensitive import monopolies in steel and plastics. Extensive reductions in tariffs and import duties were introduced. In the banking sector, restrictions on domestic interest rates were eliminated in 1981 and, in 1988, the door was opened wide for the establishment of private banks. Public-sector monopolies in utilities, power generation, ports and roads, telecommunications, and television, sectors long regarded as strategically sensitive, were also opened selectively to private entry (World Bank 1995:40–2).

Such changes were reflected in the changing structure of investment and ownership. Between 1990 and 1995, foreign investment approvals surged from US$9 billion to US$39.9 billion, continuing to climb as the flood of money from North-East Asia into low-wage export manufacturing in South-East Asia followed the Plaza Accord in 1985 (World Bank 1996:12–14). Private domestic banks proliferated. By 1995, they numbered approximately 240, holding 53 per cent of the outstanding bank funds and 47.7 per cent of outstanding bank credit compared with 37 per cent and 41.9 per cent respectively for the state banks (World Bank 1995:17). Public fixed investment declined from 69 per cent of the total in 1979–80 to 27 per cent in 1993–94, although public-sector corporations continued to hold book assets of US$140 billion and produce 15 per cent of GDP in 1995 (World Bank 1995:29, 51). Deregulation created the opportunity for extensive growth in the private sector.

Yet this was not to be a flowering of business within liberal markets defined by common law and regulation. Instead, deregulation opened the door to a world of business controlled by layers of political gatekeepers within the state and its banking system. Large sectors of the economy remained controlled by politically sponsored cartels, and public monopolies simply became private monopolies still backed by the authority of an authoritarian state. Such unexpected outcomes were explained by neoclassical economists within the World Bank and elsewhere as the consequence of technical errors in sequencing reforms: deregulating trade and finance regimes before the real sector (Bhattacharya & Pangestu 1992).

But the sequencing of reforms was not a matter of technical choice. Indonesia's technocrats deregulated when the political opportunity presented itself. Structural pressures might have forced state planners and gatekeepers to give way in export-competitive sectors, but not in sectors related to domestic markets (Robison 1997:35–6). Financial deregulation, as Jonathan Pincus and Rizal Ramli have pointed out, was often a strategy to outflank state banks and other gatekeeping institutions, otherwise immune to regulation and control, rather than a technically calculated option (1998:728–32). It is also important to recognise that deregulation now also suited many of the corporate interests incubated within the structures of state capitalism. The heavy hand of the state had become a constraint where it prevented their access to lucrative opportunities in banking, public infrastructure, television, and air transportation. Ultimately, deregulation was a necessary step for these politico–business conglomerates.

Reform did not pervade all sectors of the economy. Domestic trading cartels continued to exist in cement, paper, plywood, and fertiliser. Apkindo, for example, a compulsory association of plywood producers presided over by Soeharto business partner Bob Hasan, set pricing and export quotas in the industry (Pura 1995a:1, 4; 1995b:1, 4). Liem Sioe Liong retained his lucrative monopoly in flour milling (Schwarz 1994: 110–12; World Bank 1995:43–4). In 1992, the Ministry of Trade awarded Tommy Soeharto monopoly rights to purchase and sell Indonesia's clove crop, a gift that came with a US$350 million low-interest loan from Bank Indonesia and a government requirement that cigarette manufacturers purchase exclusively from the new board (*Prospek* 7 March 1992:70-81; *Tempo* 25 September 1993:88–9).

Forestry concessions awarded without transparent tender continued to be a lucrative source of profit for powerful corporate groups and political families. Relatively free of attempts to constrain illegal or damaging logging practices and subject to minimal taxes, forestry companies also attracted large state and foreign loans to finance expansion into plantations and pulp and paper manufacture (Ramli 1992; *Tempo* 28 October 1991:26–32; World Bank 1993:44–9). Another refuge was found in the automobile industry where sole appointed agents for major auto producers operated behind tariffs of between 100 and 300 per cent applied to the import of completely built up (CBU) vehicles. Efforts to dismantle these tariffs or require greater levels of local production failed (*Jakarta Jakarta* 16–22 March:1; *Warta Ekonomi* 11 March 1996:19).

But it was in the former areas of state monopoly that the conglomerates and the families were provided with the most lucrative opportunities. Entering the deregulated banking sector, corporate conglomerates and the political families operated with little regard for legal lending limits. These banks were to channel the bulk of their loans to other companies within the group (*Infobank* 12 October 1995:14–34; Rosser 2002). The same inadequate regulatory frameworks made the Jakarta Stock Exchange a place where the conglomerates and family groups could raise capital without adequate disclosure (Kwik 1993; *Tempo* 10 April 1993:14–16).

While the state's grip on economic monopolies loosened, this did not mean the end of monopolies themselves. These remained, but increasingly were the possession of well-connected private groups. The Soeharto family stamped its position as a major corporate player as it secured key contracts and licences in the power-generation industry, road and port construction, and refinery construction in the petrochemical industry (Robison 1997:39–41).

These involved large capital outlays made available through the state banks as well as through international banking institutions. Commercial finance capital now replaced oil as the driving force of growth and investment. A private-sector borrowing spree began in the late 1980s as the conglomerates geared up for investment in the projects, prompting warnings from several sources (*Infobank* February 1997:38–43; December 1995:160–1; Nasution 1992). Serious economic problems began to emerge. Although the economy grew strongly, so did the foreign debt burden and the level of non-performing loans at domestic banks. In the petrochemical industry, for example, foreign investors and banks rushed into arrangements with well-connected licence holders who were guaranteed protection from foreign imports—provided with subsidised inputs from Pertamina—and markets with downstream producers (*AWSJ* 6-7 January 1995:1, 4; *JP* 16 February 1996:1, 4; Robison 1997:53–5). Investors and lenders in the power-generation industry were similarly guaranteed subsidised inputs and sales to Perusahaan Listrik Negara (PLN) at above-market prices and in a situation of oversupply (Robison 1997:40; World Bank 1995:71; 1996:56). These were both classic examples of the moral-hazard problem—the deregulation of the finance sector contributing to a growth in non-performing loans as banks made increasingly risky loans to well-connected individuals, not only in infrastructure projects, but also in sectors such as property, consumer finance, and the stockmarket.

Further cracks were to emerge as Indonesia's economic technocrats proved unable to enforce much needed regulatory reform in the face of opposition from the conglomerates and the politico–business families. A series of scandals in the early 1990s revealed a picture of collusion among officials, borrowers, and powerful political patrons in the allocation of credit by state banks (Kwik 1993; *Tempo* 9 March 1991:86–90; *Tempo* 21 February 1994:26–30; World Bank 1995:19). Within the private banking sector, several banks began to encounter difficulties through their exposure to overextended companies that collapsed when they defaulted on their loan repayments. In several cases, the government stepped in to rescue these banks (Rosser 2002).

Indonesia's technocrats were well aware of the potential debt problems. Although introducing tighter legal lending limits in 1993 and threatening offenders with legal action, the Central Bank governor found himself without the capacity to enforce these initiatives. Efforts to contain the growth of Indonesia's foreign debt through the establishment of a special team (Team 39, or COLT) to regulate foreign borrowing was ignored by well-connected conglomerates. Attempts to halt massive borrowing for the Chandra Asri petrochemical venture, for instance, were sidestepped when the government allowed it to proceed as a foreign investment. Protests by the technocrats over this decision were met with the announcement in 1994 that the existing COLT team was to be abolished and replaced by one under Industry Minister Hartarto (Robison 1997:54). Subsequently, its function was further reduced to one of regulating state-related foreign borrowing (World Bank 1997:14, 15). In the meantime, the technocrats found themselves with only one weapon to combat growing debt and inflation. In the so-called Sumarlin shocks of 1987 and 1991, monetary policy was used to slow growth, sending interest rates to more than 30 per cent and precipitating a capital flight. Several companies simply took their money offshore (*Tempo* 17 August 1991:86).

In the post-oil decade of deregulation, private interest not only established its ascendancy over the state and its officials, but also achieved a wider political dominance as part of a coalition of power built around the presidential family. This meant that the authority of the state was now increasingly harnessed to the commercial interests of the new politico–business coalitions, rather than to the institutional interests of state officials or liberal objectives such as the creation of a level playing field. This ascendancy was achieved only by coercive means and opened important political tensions within Indonesian society and politics.

As the new oligarchies seized former public monopolies, high-ranking officials were pushed aside as they attempted to resist demands by Soeharto family members and their associates for the allocation of trade monopolies and contracts for supply (Robison 1997:61). A struggle for control of state procurement saw various ministries and the military lose this authority to the State Secretariat and to the Board for Research and Technology under B. J. Habibie (Pangaribuan 1995). Tensions erupted into a public squabble among Habibie, Finance Minister Mar'ie Muhammad, and Armed Forces Chief Faisal Tanjung over an attempt by Habibie to purchase old German warships and allocate US$1.1 billion for their repair in his shipyards (*Tempo* 11 June 1994:21–7).

Political struggles also began to spill into society. As monopolies were put together with breathtaking speed by the Soeharto family and its associates, other business interests were squeezed. Plywood producers became increasingly agitated at the constraints of Apkindo as prices plummeted and Japan found new suppliers (*Tempo* 4 December 1993:83–4). A bizarre attempt to provide Soeharto's grandson Ari Sigit with rights to impose tax on beer in Bali propelled him into a collision with brewers and hoteliers that included his uncles. As Tommy Soeharto's state-enforced clove monopoly, Badan Penyangga dan Pemasaran Cengkeh (BPPC), began to encounter difficulties, he was plunged into a deepening spiral of dispute with the clove producers and the cigarette manufacturers who were the ultimate losers in this adventure (Robison 1997:44, 45; Schwarz 1994:153–7). The decision of the government in 1996 to grant to Tommy Soeharto exemptions from import duties and luxury goods taxes as part of a plan to produce a national car, led to a new wave of dispute. It brought condemnation from the US and Japanese governments and reignited the conflict between economic nationalists and liberal reformers within Indonesia. It set the scene also for bitter protest from Indonesia's other car producers, precluded from importing CBU vehicles by 300 per cent taxes (*JP* 18 March 1996:4; Robison 1997:55–7).

Corporate conglomerates now began to attract increasing criticism and resentment in Indonesian society. For liberal critics within Indonesian's growing urban middle class and the World Bank, conglomeration was the result of corruption, collusion, and nepotism, not only inefficient, but also concentrated in the protected non-tradeable goods sector, adding nothing to Indonesia's global competitiveness (*Tempo* 4 December 1993:93, 94; World Bank 1993:91, 92; 1995:49, 50). Anti-conglomerate feeling spread beyond the urban liberal critics into the wider countryside as land and labour disputes became entangled with the inexorable spread of big business. Apprehensive that this resentment would mobilise underlying currents of anti-Chinese xenophobia, Soeharto was forced to move. He was to distinguish his policies publicly from those of free-fight liberalism and to point to the strides made over the years in reducing poverty (ISEI 1990; Soeharto 1990:31, 32). In a highly symbolic gesture, he met with thirty-one of Indonesia's leading business figures at his private ranch in 1990, inviting them to transfer 25 per cent of their company shares to cooperatives, still the symbol of the New Order's commitment to egalitarian ideals. Predictably, this proposal was never implemented (*Editor* 31 March 1990:11–23).

While the increasing economic and political cohesion of this new polit-ico–business alliance now constituted the social base of the Soeharto era, it also laid the seeds of economic and social volatility. The economic crisis of 1997 and 1998 ignited the smouldering flames.

THE DESTRUCTION OF THE NEW ORDER

Indonesia's 1990s debt crisis was driven largely by a private sector whose foreign debt was revealed to be more than US$81 billion, of which more than US$34 billion was due in 1998. Much of this was unhedged. When the government abandoned attempts to defend the rupiah in August 1997 and floated the currency, it was no surprise that the currency attacks set in train a massive capital flight. Faced with a rapidly collapsing corporate and banking sector and looming fiscal crisis, the Indonesian government called in the IMF on 8 October (*AWSJ* 9 October 1997:1; *FK* 8 September 1997:24–5). Although Soeharto appeared to be under the impression that the entry of the IMF would be enough to soothe the waters and end the crisis, this was not to be the case. The rupiah kept tumbling, reaching more than 16 000 to the US dollar in January 1998. Nor did it appear that Soeharto considered seriously the sorts of conditions that the IMF might impose in return for its US$43 billion bailout. Yet, from October 1997, the Indonesian government had been forced to sign successive letters of intent to the IMF, outlining its agreement to various reform conditions (Government of Indonesia 1997, 1998, 1999, 2000).

Such agreements, which were to strike at the very heart of the Soeharto regime, included a range of fiscal reforms: the postponement or cancellation of several large industrial projects, the abolition of various state trading monopolies in flour, sugar, soy beans, and other commodities, and the liquidation of insolvent banks. Also on the IMF list was the abolition of the clove monopoly, the cancellation of the national car project, and Habibie's Industri Pesawat Terbang Nusantara (IPTN) jet aircraft project. Later provisions included a requirement for greater independence of the Central Bank; the elimination of cement, paper and plywood cartels; and phased elimination of subsidies for fuel and electricity. Perhaps the central feature of the IMF plan was the restructuring and recapitalisation of the banking system. These agreements meant, in effect, that the frameworks of state protection and privilege that sustained the major corporate conglomerates and politico–business families were to be eliminated. Officials of the US government and the IMF made it clear that funding would cease if the terms of agreement were not met (*JP* 10 January 1998:1; *JP* 14 January 1998:1).

A period of conflict and negotiation between the Indonesian government and the IMF commenced, punctuated by periodic halts to funding disbursement and concessions to the terms of agreements. Just days after the October 1997 package was announced, Soeharto reversed the cancellation of several the large infrastructure projects belonging to his own family members. The IMF realisation that Soeharto was not genuinely committed to reform was reinforced in dramatic fashion when Soeharto family members reacted angrily to the closure of sixteen insolvent banks by Finance Minister Mar'ie Muhammad, alleging a plot to bring down the Soeharto family. Despite legal action against the government and a disingenuous scheme to reopen a bank owned by Soeharto's son, Bambang Trihatmodjo, under another name, the banks were closed (see Robison & Rosser 1998).

A further concern for the government was the budget. Under pressure from the IMF to contain spending, a contradictory budget held real dangers for Soeharto, potentially forcing many Indonesian companies into bankruptcy, including those owned by his family and its close associates. Sharp reductions in food and fuel subsidies brought with it the risk of social unrest and rioting. Yet, immediately after the government's introduction of a mildly expansionary budget in January 1998, the rupiah collapsed to more than 16 000 to the US dollar. This sparked a rush on supermarkets and traditional markets to stock up on food in anticipation of an inevitable inflationary surge. With no apparent way out of the dilemma, and facing increasing pressure from overseas creditor nations, Soeharto was to turn to the idea of a currency board as the last hope. Lashing out at foreign currency speculators and accusing them of trying to destroy the Indonesian economy, Soeharto announced plans to fix the exchange rate and establish legislation necessary for the introduction of a currency board (*AWSJ* 9–10 January 1998:1; Robison & Rosser 1998:1601, 1602)

For Soeharto, protecting the architecture of power rather than introducing the IMF reforms was clearly the priority concern, even at the cost of a continuing decline in international confidence and the downward spiral of the rupiah. Yet, for the first time, Soeharto found himself unable to dictate the course of events, halt the economic collapse, or protect the political and economic interests surrounding him. As the ruling alliance began to unravel, demonstrations became bolder and criticism grew. In a last desperate gesture, Soeharto appointed a bizarre cabinet made up largely of close cronies, including his daughter Siti Hardijanti Rukmana (Tutut) and his long-time business associate Bob Hasan. In the end, events were overtaken by the resignation of a besieged Soeharto in May 1998 as his former supporters drifted away and following a period of violent rioting in Jakarta.

Unable any longer to call upon a powerful centralised state apparatus to secure their interests, the formerly dominant political and business oligarchies were now forced to reinvent their ascendancy within a new system. It was a system in which politics was mediated through parties and parliament, and in which political brokers and fixers—rather than generals and the apparatchiks of the state—were increasingly the conduits of power. The survival of politicians, too, depended upon the construction of new and wider political alliances. In this task they were not badly placed. The system of predatory relations among officials, business, and political entrepreneurs continued to pervade Indonesian politics from Jakarta down to the regions and local towns. Breaking up these old power structures was to be a difficult task. No inflow of foreign investment poured in to replace the old centres of corporate power. No new domestic bourgeoisie emerged to drive the neoliberal revolution or embrace a system of markets governed by transparency and accountability in its rules.

In their quest for survival, the old politico–business interests now had to contend with a raft of structural and policy reforms set in place by the IMF. Revitalised state audit agencies and a panoply of private organisations dedicated to the scrutiny of political and business activity now emerged, complemented by a vigorous and intrusive mass media. Several high-profile critics of the former regime and the conglomerates were to assume strategic ministerial positions in subsequent governments. But the reformist alliances formed initially under President Abdurrahman Wahid, who replaced Soeharto's immediate successor, B. J. Habibie, in 1999, proved to be neither politically cohesive nor ideologically coherent. Their authority over the state apparatus was to prove shaky. Although dedicated to the ending of arbitrary rule and the gross excesses of corruption, there was no broad commitment to liberal market reform within the diverse coalition that underpinned Wahid's government. Instead, the mix of populist, nationalist, and even social democratic ideals that initially prevailed became lost in the everyday tasks of brokering deals to stay in power.

It is within this political context that the reorganisation of Indonesian capitalism was to take place in the period following Soeharto's downfall. There was little prospect of a return to a centralised authoritarian rule. Things had gone too far for that. Instead, it was a contest to decide what sort of markets and what sort of democracy would prevail. In the economic field, two major struggles were to be decisive in the battle to break up the old politico–business alliances and reconstitute the configuration of power in Indonesia. One involved to the attempt to recapitalise Indonesia's moribund banking system and enforce debt restructuring on its corporate conglomerates. A second concerned attempts to dispossess the corporate and political oligarchies of the economic monopolies that sustained them and dismantle the very strategic gatekeeping institutions that had been the terminals of predatory capitalism.

THE STRUGGLE TO RECAPITALISE BANKS AND RESTRUCTURE DEBT

As Indonesia's private corporate sector began to founder under a mountain of debt, domestic banks were quickly paralysed by a surge in non-performing loans, estimated by Standard and Poor's to be 85 per cent of total loans at the end of 1999. A banking restructuring agency (the Indonesian Banking Restructuring Agency, IBRA) was established in January 1998 to implement a comprehensive recapitalisation plan that would eventually cost an estimated US$87 billion, or approximately 82 per cent of Indonesia's GDP (*AWSJ* 11–12 June 1999).[3] By mid 1999, a large number of the 240 private banks that had existed in July 1997 had been closed and twelve had been taken over by the state and recapitalised. The most difficult aspect of the exercise was not to be the closure and recapitalisation of banks. In the long term, the crucial question was who would pay the bill for recapitalisation and whether it would precipitate a broader restructuring of Indonesia's corporate sector.

Despite their efforts to avoid debt restructuring and retain control of their companies, Indonesia's leading tycoons lost control of some of the most important banks and corporations. In the Master Settlement and Acquisition Agreements (MSAA) signed between the IBRA and its largest creditors in September 1998, the latter were forced to hand over assets valued at Rp112 trillion to cover their debt to IBRA banks. Yet, by mid 2000, it was clear that many of the leading conglomerates were not only able to retain the core assets of their economic empires, but they had also been able to pass much of their debt to the government, which effectively now carried the main cost of a massive bailout through the banking recapitalisation program.

How did this happen? First, investigations by the Supreme Audit Agency (BPK) and the state comptroller of Finance and Development (BPKP) revealed that the Rp146 trillion (US$11 billion) in liquidity funds (BLBI) allocated by Bank Indonesia to the bank owners in 1997 to guarantee deposits and meet interbank loan commitments had been used for new overseas investment, currency speculation, and debt servicing on other companies. In other words, the BLBI was a lifeline for the struggling groups and a means of capital flight (*JP* 20 January 2000:1; *Kontan Online* 3 July 2000).

Second, when it came to negotiating the transfer of corporate assets to the IBRA, it proved difficult to penetrate the opaque financial statements of companies and soon became clear that the government faced a huge shortfall in its asset recovery program. To cover a debt of Rp47.7 trillion, for example, the Salim group surrendered purported assets of Rp53 trillion in September 1998 that were subsequently valued at Rp20 trillion, representing an effective loss of Rp30 trillion for the government (*Tempo* 11 June 2000:130). Yet, at the same time that they were stalling debt negotiations with the IBRA and foreign creditors, the conglomerates were able to insulate other highly profitable enterprises that provided strong cashflows for more strategic debt repayments and new investment (*AWSJ* 25–26 February 2000:1).

A third and decisive advantage enjoyed by the conglomerates has been the weakness and corruption of Indonesia's judicial institutions. In a series of startling acquittals in the Bankruptcy Court and the Supreme Court, high-profile business figures walked away from bankruptcy proceedings and criminal charges. It was an arena in which political influence and money were at a premium. Economics Coordinating Minister Kwik Kian Gie was to complain of ' "dark forces" who buy favours' (*Kompas Online* 6 May 2000; *Tempo* 26 March 2000:102, 103). So unsuccessful were both the IBRA and foreign creditors in the courts that it was soon recognised that debt had to be resolved through negotiation.

Fourth, as the government faced increasing pressure to cover the interest on bonds issued to finance recapitalisation of the banks, the urgency of speeding up the seizure and dispersal of assets increased (*JP* 1 July 2000; US Embassy 2000). On the one hand, this meant a tougher line against recalcitrant debtors among the big conglomerates; in several high-profile cases, property was seized and legal action taken or planned against forty-eight commercial banks for alleged misuse of Rp144.5 trillion of BLBI (US$17 billion). Among those targeted for prosecution were some of Indonesia's most politically prominent business figures. On the other hand, the government faced the reality that, if investment was to flow back into Indonesia and the banking and corporate sectors put back on track, the conglomerates were the key factors. From this perspective, the government was under pressure to drop its prosecutions, compromise on debt restructuring, and allow conglomerates to buy back their assets. The choice appeared to be one between justice and money. As Hong Goei Siauw of Nomura Securities observed that, in the present situation, no one wants to outlay US$2.5–3 billion to buy IBRA assets when they know the condition of these assets and Indonesia's circumstances. The re-entry of high-profile conglomerates would act as a magnate to foreign investors (*Tempo* 27 August 2000).

Forced to speed up the debt-restructuring and assets-sale processes, the government began to negotiate discounts to large debtors, including Chandra Asri, Texmaco, and other high-profile conglomerates. But the strategy was a dangerous one politically, raising claims of collusion and fears of a revival of the old predatory relations within the Wahid government. In particular, the government's provision of a US$96 million credit facility to Texmaco and the assumption of Rp19 trillion of its debts by the IBRA in March 2000 appeared to be a repeat of the indiscriminate allocation of state funds so disastrously undertaken by BI in 1997 and 1998. Like many of the recipients of BLBI only a year earlier, Texmaco was a company that appeared to be hopelessly bankrupted and without prospects. So puzzling was the rescue that the news magazine *Tempo* asked whether Tommy Soeharto might not now ask for credit to revive the Timor car project or Prajogo might not seek government assistance to re-enter Chandra Asri (*Tempo* 7 January 2000:98, 99). Perceptions of a return of collusion were reinforced as Liem and other tycoons were reported to be negotiating to buy back into their businesses (*AWSJ* 13 January 2000:1, 10). President Wahid announced that he had asked prosecutors to delay legal proceedings against key debtors, including Sinivasan, Prajogo Pangestu, and Syamsul Nursalim (*JP* 20 October 2000:1).

For the IMF and the World Bank, the situation was contradictory. Although supporting the need for speed in restructuring, they also expressed their concern at the opaque nature of the negotiations between the government and the debtors, and at the generous terms given to companies with poor-quality assets. They warned of future burdens on the public purse (*JP* 16 September 2000:1). Within parliament, resistance to the perceived bailouts grew. Legislators blocked the planned divestment of IBRA assets in Bank Central Asia and Bank Niaga. Such resistance was driven by the fear that assets were being sold off cheaply. More precisely, it was the prospect that assets would go to foreign investors cheaply or return to the conglomerates at a discount that propelled nationalist sentiment in the parliament (*JP* 6 October 2000:1).

In the end, the return of the conglomerates appeared to be inexorable. Their ultimate strength lay partly in their economic indispensability to the economy at large and to politicians. At question was the institutional and policy frameworks within which they would operate.

DISMANTLING THE GATEKEEPING ARRANGEMENTS AND RENT-SEEKING APPARATUS OF THE STATE

Post-Soeharto Indonesian governments inherited a system of politico–business alliances built upon discretionary allocations of credit and preferential access to licences, contracts, concessions, and monopolies. These arrangements were concentrated around an array of strategic gatekeeping institutions. Central to these were the state banks, the sources of discretionary allocations of finance to well-connected business groups. Perhaps the most powerful was Pertamina, which presided over the allocation of drilling and exploration leases, contracts for supply and construction, crude oil and fuel distributorships, and insurance arrangements. As we have seen, the Ministry of Forestry had also been the conduit for allocating Indonesia's 61 million hectares of forest concession to large military and Chinese-owned companies and to companies close to the Soeharto family, such as those of Bob Hasan and Prajogo Pangestu. In the field of primary commodities, monopolies on import and distribution, directed through Bulog, had provided well-connected interests with lucrative opportunities over three decades, with Liem and the Soeharto family deriving huge profits from flour milling and the import of sugar, rice, and soy meal (*FK* 23 September 1999:88–9). With the deregulation of the power-generation industry, PLN was also to emerge as a strategically important cash cow for well-connected politicians. In all, twenty-six projects were signed between PLN and various consortia of private energy providers, all of which included members of the Soeharto family and their associates.

Following the fall of Soeharto, investigations into these gatekeeping institutions and the arrangements with political and business figures revealed the extent of corruption and propelled attempts to end these arrangements. At the end of 1998, accumulated, non-performing loans in state banks were estimated at Rp150 trillion or 50–60 per cent of outstanding loans. A Price-WaterhouseCooper audit revealed losses of US$4.69 billion for Pertamina between April 1996 and March 1998, and losses of US$840 million for Bulog in the same period. In the forestry sector, USS$5.2 billion had been lost in the collection and utilisation of the Forestry Fund in the five years to March 1998 (*JP* 31 December 1999:1).

In 1998, Pertamina management admitted that 159 companies had received contracts through dubious means, most of which were associated with the Soeharto family. Huge mark-ups and overpricing imposed substantial costs on Pertamina (JP 12 October 1998:12; October 1999:1; Kompas 1 August 1998:11). The director-general of PLN, Djiteng Marsudi, was to claim in 1998 that contracts had been 'given without tender. I was in one way or another forced to sign the contracts' (quoted in JP 8 June 1998:1). At a time of overcapacity, PLN had been forced to buy electricity in US dollars at prices higher than it was permitted to charge public consumers (FK 29 December 1997:12–21). It was no surprise that it faced heavy losses after the collapse of the rupiah (JP 28 October 1998:8).

Pressure to dismantle these arrangements and the gatekeeping institutions was driven by the government's growing fiscal problems. The state budget faced growing interest payments on Rp624 trillion in government bonds issued to cover the BLBI and recapitalise banks. These were expected to reach Rp77 trillion in 2001 (31 per cent of total budget) and Rp130 trillion in 2002 (*Bisnis Indonesia* 3 October 2000). As the reform agreements with the IMF came into effect, these institutions were subjected to increasing audit from government and private sector auditors.

In the early years after the fall of Soeharto, reformers were to address these problems with an apparent enthusiasm. Energy Minister Kuntoro and

Pertamina Director Soegianto began to cancel and renegotiate contracts within Pertamina. Soeharto family business interests, organised around the so-called Cendana business group, lost a raft of exclusive monopolies in insurance, the import of fuel and crude oil, the shipping of liquid natural gas (LNG), and crude oil, and the development of gas pipelines and refineries. By the end of 1998, Pertamina had scrapped contracts with a total of thirty-two firms, claiming a saving of US$100 million (*JP* 23 September 1998:8; *Kompas Online* 9 May 2000). Within the forestry industry, Minister Muslimin Nasution began a process of reviewing and cancelling the licences of companies with poor forestry management records and those involved in the misuse of reforestation funds. Earlier, in 1997 and 1998, Bulog's exclusive right to import and distribute soy beans, sugar, cooking oil, and wheat had been abolished. Confined to importing and distributing rice, and maintaining price stability in competition with private traders, it was required to adopt a system of open tenders (*JP* 24 December 1999:8). In PLN, Director Djiteng Marsudi took a bold stance, announcing that it would continue to purchase electricity from power suppliers at pre-crisis rates and cancelling several contracts, including that of the president's stepbrother, Sudwikatmono. The director threatened to review the contracts of the giant Paitons I and II projects in which Soeharto family members Bambang Trihatmodjo and Hasyim Djojohadikusumo were the central figures (*JP* 8 June 1998).

But these attempts soon stalled. It was clear that the sort of extra-budgetary funds these institutions could provide remained attractive sources of discretionary money and were likely to become more important if money politics became entrenched in Indonesia's fledgling democracy. Ministries and agencies, for example, reported the existence of off-budget funds of approximately Rp7.7 trillion (US$860 million) in July 2000 (Government of Indonesia 31 July 2000:8). A bizarre scandal, the appropriation of Rp35 billion from Bulog involving President's Wahid's masseur, Suwondo, and Bulog Deputy Chairman Saupan, drew attention to the difficulties involved in eliminating this factor. A BPKP audit reported approximately Rp2 trillion in non-budgetary Bulog funds still in existence, with disbursements still going to businesses controlled by the Soeharto family and former Bulog chief, Bustanil Arifin (*JP* 13 June 2000:9; *JP* 20 July 2000:4).

In the forestry sector, attempts to control the industry through progressive resources-rent taxes and cancellation of concessions were to be undermined by the sheer inability of the government to control logging. The World Bank estimates that illegal logging is now a bigger business than legal logging, imposing a US$650 million loss each year on potential royalty and Reforestation Fund payments. These illegal forestry businesses are backed by big money and powerful individuals, including the military, the police, local officials, and parliamentarians (*JP* 14 August 2000:3, 4; *JP* 4 October 2000:10; World Bank 2000:40). With the collapse of a powerful central state and the devolution of power, the rise of local and regional predators outside the authority of a central state is likely to be an increasing problem.

It is instructive that various foreign financiers and investors also stood to lose from reform. In the case of PLN, for example, these had entered into projects riddled with bribery, overpricing, and collusive subcontracting, and signed contracts in which the function of PLN was clearly to transfer private costs to the public purse (*AWSJ* 9 June 1998:3; 21 December 1999:1). PLN attempted to cancel agreements, suspend purchases, and renegotiate contracts. Foreign governments entered the fray, not least because their import and export banks and insurers had provided more than US$4 billion in financing to the big US, Japanese, and German companies involved (*FEER* 21 October 1999:63, 4; *AWSJ* 9 March 2000:1). As lawsuits were traded, the Indonesian government was forced to retreat into an ongoing process of negotiation.

The ultimate solution to the problem of predatory capitalism appeared deceptively simple—simply abolish the authority of the state to intervene in the market in specific cases. As we have seen, most of Bulog's control of the import and distribution of basic commodities was abolished. A new central banking law was introduced in May 1999 that established BI's independence from government and abolished its authority to channel subsidised liquidity loans to individual borrowers. Its authority to supervise banks was transferred to a new independent institution to be established by the end of 2002 (McLeod 1999:148, 149). Pertamina, too, was to be stripped of its authority to allocate licences for exploration and production, and for downstream distribution and marketing. Under the terms of legislation proposed by the government, Pertamina would become just another oil company (*Kontan Online* 5 June 2000). Yet, even these seemingly decisive moves proved inconclusive, appearing to become mired in a sea of vested interests and political intransigence, despite the momentum of reform embedded in the ongoing process of audit, institutional reform, legal prosecution of uncooperative debtors, privatisation, and deregulation that were part of the Indonesian government's letters of intent with the IMF. In spite of vast institutional changes in the late and post-Soeharto periods, the basic logic of Indonesia's political economy remains remarkably resilient—the virtually untrammelled appropriation of public resources and institutions for the purposes of private accumulation among powerful groups.

CONCLUSION

We have seen profound changes occurring in Indonesia since the end of the New Order. The political reforms that have taken place—leading to a functioning democracy—were difficult to visualise even as the Soeharto presidency was in its death throes in 1998. In the economic sphere, powerful international agencies, such as the IMF and the World Bank, have applied more or less constant pressure on post-Soeharto Indonesian governments to undertake serious institutional and market reforms. The question now is why predatory relations of power have not been extinguished by the not insignificant institutional changes described above. Again, the critical factor is essentially political. Reformers have up to now failed to overcome the old interests still entrenched within the state apparatus. Thus, they have not been able to halt the mutation of new policies as they concern markets and governance into new opportunities for still pervasive but more decentralised rent-seeking activities. They have also been unable to contain the new pressures for money politics building outside the state bureaucracy in the new institutions of party and parliament. Indonesia's democratisation has, therefore, not made a difference in terms of the survival of an essentially predatory system of power that has underpinned Indonesia's particularly rapacious form of capitalism since the advent of the New Order.

NOTES

1 Many of the themes in this chapter are also developed in much greater detail in Robison and Hadiz (2004).

2 The oil boom consisted of two main phases. Between 1973 and 1974, the international price of oil rose from approximately US$3 per barrel to US$12 per barrel. Between 1979 and 1981 the price rose again, from approximately US$15 per barrel to more than US$40 per barrel. As a result, Indonesia's gas and oil exports leapt from US$1.6 billion (or 50.1% of total exports) in 1973, to US$18.4 billion (or 82.6% of total exports) in 1982. At the same time, government revenues from oil and gas taxes increased from Rp382 billion (or 39.5% of total revenues) in 1973, to Rp8.6 trillion (or more than 70% of total government revenues) in 1981–82 (*Republik Indonesia* 1994/95; Robison 1987:28–9, 44–6; Winters 1996:120–1).

3 In contrast, the costs of recapitalisation in Thailand, South Korea, and Malaysia are estimated at 35 per cent, 29 per cent, and 22 per cent respectively. Levels of non-performing loans are also lower in these countries, estimated to be 55 per cent in Thailand, 50 per cent in South Korea, and 35 per cent in Malaysia (*AWSJ* 22 October 1998:1).

REFERENCES

Arndt, Heinz (1967) 'Economic Disorder and the Task Ahead', in Tjiu-kie Tan (ed.) *Soekarno's Guided Indonesia*, Brisbane: Jacaranda, pp. 129–42.

Bhattacharya, Amarendro and Mari Pangestu (1992) 'Indonesia: Development and Transformation Since 1965 and the Role of Public Policy', paper prepared for the World Bank Workshop on the Role of Government and East Asian Success, East–West Center, November.

Bresnan, John (1993) *Managing Indonesia: the Modern Political Economy*, New York: Columbia University Press.

Chaudhry, Kiren A. (1997) *The Price of Wealth: Economies and Institutions in the Middle East*, Ithaca and London: Cornell University Press.

Emmerson, Donald K. (1976) *Indonesia's Elite: Political Culture and Cultural Politics*, Ithaca: Cornell University Press.

——(1978) 'The Bureaucracy in Political Context: Weakness in Strength', in Karl D. Jackson and Lucian W. Pye (eds) *Political Power and Communications in Indonesia*, Berkeley: University of California Press, pp. 82–136.

Garnaut, Ross (1998) 'The Financial Crisis: A Watershed in Economic Thought About East Asia', *Asian Pacific Economic Literature,* May: 1–11.

Hadiz, Vedi R. (2004) 'Decentralisation and Democracy in Indonesia: A Critique of Neo-Institutionalist Perspectives', *Development and Change*, 35(4) September: 697–718.

——(2004) 'Indonesian Local Party Politics: A Site of Resistance to Neo-Liberal Reform', *Critical Asian Studies*, 36(4) December: 615–36.

Hill, Hal (1996) *The Indonesian Economy Since 1966: Asia's Emerging Giant*, Cambridge: Cambridge University Press.

——(2000) 'Indonesia: the Strange and Sudden Death of a Tiger Economy', *Oxford Development Studies*, 28(2):117–39.

Government of Indonesia, 'Letters of Intent and Memorandum of Economic and Financial Policies,' 1997, 1998, 1999, 2000, <www.imf.org/external/NP/LOI>.

Huntington, Samuel (1968) *Political Order in Changing Societies*, New Haven: Yale University Press.

Ikatan Sarjana Ekonomi Indonesia (ISEI) (1990) 'Penjabaran Demokrasi Ekonomi', Jakarta, 15 August.

Jones, Steven and Raphael Pura (1986) 'Suharto-Linked Monopolies Hobble Economy', *AWSJ*, 24 November.

Kartasasmita, Ginandjar (1985) 'Daya Tahan Ekonomi dan Kekuatan Dalam Negeri', *Prisma*, 6:42–7.

Kwik Kian Gie (1993) 'A Tale of a Conglomerate', *Economic and Business Review Indonesia*, 5 June:26–7 and 12 June:26–7.

Liddle, R. William (1989) 'Development or Democracy', *Far Eastern Economic Review*, 9 November: 22, 23.

——(1991) 'The Relative Autonomy of the Third World Politician: Soeharto and Indonesian Economic Development in Comparative Perspective', *International Studies Quarterly*, 35:403–27.

——(1992) 'The Politics of Development Policy', *World Development*, 20(6):793–807.

——(1999) 'Indonesia's Unexpected Failure of Leadership', in Adam Schwarz and Jonathan Paris (eds), *The Politics of Post-Suharto Indonesia*, New York: Council on Foreign Relations Press, pp. 16–39.

——(2001) 'Indonesia' Democratic Transition: Playing by the Rules', in Andrew Reynolds (ed.) *The Architecture of Democracy: Constitutional, Design, Conflict Management, and Democracy*, Oxford: Oxford University Press.

MacIntyre, Andrew (1994) 'Business, Government and Development: Northeast and Southeast Asian Comparisons', in Andrew MacIntyre (ed.) *Business and Government in Industrialising Asia*, Sydney: Allen & Unwin.

——(1999) 'Political Institutions and Economic Crisis in Thailand and Indonesia', in T. J. Pempel (ed.) *Politics of the Asian Economic Crisis*, Ithaca: Cornell University Press, pp. 143–62.

——(2001) 'Institutions and Investors: The politics of the Asian Financial Crisis', *International Organization*, 55(1):81–122.

McLeod, Ross (1998) 'Indonesia', in Ross McLeod and Ross Garnaut (eds) *East Asia in Crisis: From Being a Miracle to Needing One?*, London: Routledge, pp. 333–51.

——(1999) 'Crisis-Driven Changes to the Banking Laws and Regulations', *Bulletin of Indonesian Economic Studies*, 35(2):147–54.

——(2000) 'Soeharto's Indonesia: A Better Class of Corruption' *Agenda*, 7(2):99–112.

Moertopo, Ali (1973) *The Acceleration and Modernisation of 25 Years Development*, Jakarta: Centre for Strategic and International Studies, pp.83–8.

Nasution, Anwar (1992) 'The Years of Living Dangerously: The Impacts of Financial Sector Policy Reforms and Increasing Private Sector Indebtedness in Indonesia, 1983–1992', *The Indonesian Quarterly*, XX/4:405–35.

O'Donnell, Guillermo and Philippe C. Schmitter (1986) *Transitions from Authoritarian Rule: Tentative Conclusions about Uncertain Democracies*, Baltimore: Johns Hopkins University Press.

Pangaribuan, Robinson (1995) *The Indonesian State Secretariat 1945–1993*, Perth: Asia Research Centre, Murdoch University.
Pincus, Jonathan and Rizal Ramli (1998) 'Indonesia: from showcase to basket case', *Cambridge Journal of Economics*, 22(731).
Pura, Raphael (1995a) 'Bob Hasan Builds an Empire in the Forest', *AWSJ*, 20–21 January: 1, 4.
——(1995b) 'Indonesian Plywood Cartel under Fire as Sales Shrink', *AWSJ*, 23 January: 1, 4.
Ramli, Rizal (1992) 'Kayu', *Tempo*, 13 June:77.
Republik Indonesia (1994/95) *Nota Keuangan dan Rancangan Anggaran Pendapatan dan Belanja Negara Tahun Anggaran 1994/95*.
Robison, Richard (1986) *Indonesia: The Rise of Capital*, Sydney: Allen & Unwin.
——(1987) 'After the Gold Rush: the politics of economic restructuring in Indonesia in the 1980s', in Richard Robison, Kevin Hewison and Richard Higgott (eds) *Southeast Asia in the 1980s: the Politics of Economic Crisis,* Sydney: Allen & Unwin, pp. 16–51.
——(1997) 'Politics and Markets in Indonesia's Post-Oil Era', in Garry Rodan, Kevin Hewison and Richard Robison (eds) *The Political Economy of South-East Asia: An Introduction*, Melbourne: Oxford University Press, pp. 29–63.
——and Vedi Hadiz (1993) 'Privatisation or the Reorganisation of Dirigism? Indonesian Economic Policy in the 1990s', *Canadian Journal of Development Studies*, Special Issue, December:13–31.
——and —— (2004) *Reorganising Power in Indonesia: The Politics of Oligarchy in an Age of Markets*, London: RoutledgeCurzon.
——and Andrew Rosser (1998) 'Contesting Reform: Indonesia's New Order and the IMF', *World Development,* 26(8):1593–609.
Rosser, Andrew (2002) *The Politics of Economic Liberalisation in Indonesia: State, Market and Power*, Richmond: Curzon.
Schwarz, Adam (1994) *A Nation in Waiting*, Sydney: Allen & Unwin.
Shin, Yoon Hwan (1989) 'Demystifying the Capitalist State: Political Patronage, Bureaucratic Interests and Capitalist in Formation in Soeharto's Indonesia', unpublished PhD dissertation: Yale University.
Soeharto (1990) State Address, 16 August.
Soesastro, Hadi (1989) 'The Political Economy of Deregulation', *Asian Survey*, 29(9):853–69.
Toye, John (1987) *Dilemmas of Development*, Oxford: Basil Blackwell.
United States Agency for International Development (USAID) (n.d.) 'Transition to a Prospering and Democratic Indonesia', <www.usaid.gov/id/docs-csp2k04.html>.
United States Embassy, Jakarta (2000) 'IMI: Bank Restructuring Update: High Costs; Banks Still in Deep Freeze', 1 May, <www.usembassyjakarta.org/econ/imibank050100.html>.
Winters, Jeffrey (1996) *Power in Motion: Capital Mobility and the Indonesian State*, Ithaca: Cornell University Press.
——(1997) 'The Dark Side of the Tigers', *AWSJ*, 12–13 December:10.
——(2000) 'The Financial Crisis in Southeast Asia', in Richard Robison, Mark Beeson, Kanishka Jayasuriya and Hyuk-Rae Kim (eds) *Politics and Markets in the Wake of the Asian Crisis*, London: Routledge, pp. 34–52.
World Bank (1993) *Indonesia: Sustaining Development*, Jakarta: Country Department III, East Asia and Pacific Regional Office, May 25.
——(1995) *Indonesia: Improving Efficiency and Equity—Changes in the Public Sector's Role,* Jakarta: Country Department III, East Asia and Pacific Region, 4 June.
——(1996) *Indonesia: Dimensions of Growth*, Jakarta: Country Department III, East Asia and Pacific Region, 7 May.
——(1997) *World Development Report, The State in a Changing World*, Washington: Oxford University Press.

——(2000) *Indonesia: Accelerating Recovery in Uncertain Times*, East Asia Poverty Reduction Management Unit, 13 October.

World Bank Group (n.d.) 'Decentralization Net', <www1.worldbank.org/publicsector/decentralization/>.

Newspapers and journals

Asian Wall Street Journal (*AWSJ*)

Bisnis Indonesia

Economist

Editor

Far Eastern Economic Review (*FEER*)

Forum Keadilan (*FK*)

Infobank

Jakarta Jakarta

Jakarta Post (*JP*) <www.thejakartapost.com>.

Kompas Online <www.kompas.com>.

Kontan Online <www.kontan-online.com>.

Prospek

Tempo <www.tempo.co.id>.

Warta Ekonomi <www.wartaekonomi.com/we10/34lpt2.htm>.

5 Singapore: Globalisation, the State, and Politics

Garry Rodan

KEY TOPICS

INTRODUCTION

FOLLOWING the 1997–98 Asian crisis, there was an enthusiastic official embrace of globalisation and the so-called New Economy in Singapore, which gave rise to increased economic liberalisation and governance reforms. Speculation arose as to whether the beginnings of a major and necessary shift in development strategy was occurring that requires a dismantling of Singapore Inc. and the ushering in of more neutral market conditions and regulations (*AWSJ* 12 July 2000:10; *FT* 13 May 2000; Lian 2000; *STWE* 6 May 2000:14–15; Tessensohn 2000). In contrast with this speculation, it is argued here that Singapore is entering a new phase of state capitalism rather than retreating from it. In the process, a range of tensions are being generated that require a political accommodation and associated institutional changes to economic and political regimes. Yet these changes amount to a reconstitution of state structures so that the capacities for strategic economic and political controls by the ruling party are not surrendered.

The idea that Singapore's modern economic development has so far been accompanied by a pervasive state is not generally a matter of contest in the literature on Singapore. Debate centres instead on the significance of the state's role. Among neoclassical and political economists, the tendency has been to downplay this in favour of the impact of market forces, or to interpret the state's role as one of fundamentally facilitating markets. Lim Chong Yah (1983:6) thus contended, for example, that 'Singapore has been able to grow so spectacularly in the economic field throughout the period because it has allowed a free enterprise system to flourish with government support and intervention where necessary.'[1] An equally influential neoclassical political economy idea percolating through the literature on Singapore is the notion that politics has been kept in abeyance through the exclusion of rent-seekers and distributional coalitions from the policy process, resulting in sound (and, by definition) pro-market public policy. References to 'correct development policy' (Lim 1983:101) and 'an effective government' (Chen 1983:24) are reflective of such a technical conception of the policy process. This often leads to voluntarism, as in Chen's (1983:24) claim that 'the experience of Singapore's growth strategies provided a useful model for rapid growth for both developing and developed countries', arrived at without any analysis of the social and political basis of economic regimes under the ruling People's Action Party (PAP).

Once we branch out of the orthodox neoclassical camp, the literature does not fall neatly into the historical institutionalist and social conflict theory camps. Much of it is descriptive rather than explicitly theoretical, or it reflects conscious or unconscious eclectic theoretical influences. To complicate matters, there are neoclassical political economists who have broken ranks from the above thinking to concede more importance to the role of the state in economic development. Linda Low (1998), for example, recognises the state's historic economic importance but maintains now that a fuller embrace of market forces is required to ensure continued development. Then there is the work of W. G. Huff (1994), which essentially comes out of a classical political economy and Keynesian tradition, but has occasional neoclassical resonance.[2] Thus, although arguing that the Singapore government constantly 'intervened to set the right prices to clear labour markets, which enabled the island's economy to take advantage of opportunities for trade and industrialization' (Huff 1994:368), Huff also places store in 'good public administration' and what he regards as 'the relative absence of ideology' on the part of the PAP (Huff 1994:369).[3]

Remarkably, despite the widely acknowledged parallels among Singapore and the East Asian developmental states of Taiwan and South Korea in the comparative literature, there is little by way of explicit attempts among scholars specialising in Singapore to fit the city-state into an historical institutionalist framework. In 1990, Stephan Haggard (1990) incorporated Singapore into his influential study *Pathways from the Periphery*. But his observation that policy decisions were shaped by the instruments and mechanisms availed by state institutions received little detailed follow-up.[4] More recently, Henry Wai-chung Yeung (2000) has deployed concepts of institutional capacity and embeddedness into his work, but they are married with a wide range of other theoretical influences.[5]

What is discernible in the Singapore literature is a broad range of challenges to the orthodox neoclassical account. These challenges have an emphasis on the state and how it has contributed to economic development in common. This might loosely be termed 'statist', although we should be careful not to overlook the fact that there are divergent ways of analysing the state and different purposes for doing so. Some of this work is descriptive of the functional economic role of the state; it does not attempt to explain why this role is assumed or the politics that sustains it. There is also work that delves into the conflict and power relations associated with the state's economic role, such as Frederic Deyo's (1981) study on labour control, Chua Beng-Huat's (1991) analysis of public housing and consumption, and Christopher Tremewan's (1994) general study on social control. The approach here shares with this literature a conception of the state as inseparable from the market and extending to the social, political, and ideological realms. More particularly, and from a social conflict theory perspective, the aim is to explain how power relations and the interests embodied in them have, at every turn, been crucial to the path of capitalist development in Singapore (Rodan 1989, 1993a), and will continue to be so.

Like the decades of industrialisation behind it, the current juncture in Singapore's political economy cannot simply be explained in neoclassical economic terms as the irresistible power of free-market processes combining with rational policy choices. Instead, the latest phase in the development strategy represents a refinement in the state's longstanding strategic economic role, not an abandonment of it. The interests of the PAP—not least those tied up with the extensive stable of government-linked companies (GLCs)—are integral to the particular strategies for the engagement with globalisation. The role of the state in subsidising social and physical infrastructure has not diminished either but has instead increasingly targeted technological innovation. Meanwhile, through changes to corporate, labour, and other regulatory and governance regimes, the state also continues to exert a crucial and dynamic role in the social construction of markets.[6]

The attempt to exploit more fully the forces of economic globalisation poses various challenges for the ruling PAP and its interests. For one thing, the advance of globalisation has led to greater scrutiny by the international business community of Singapore's state-owned companies and statutory boards, and the implications of their relationships to government for a level economic playing field in the city-state. However, these entities are part of the PAP power structure and state control over economic and social resources is the basis of a political paternalism that shores up the electoral position of the ruling party. Authorities will thus strive to ensure that the new economic direction does not exert stress on the fundamentals of this structure. Another challenge concerns rising material inequalities that are compounded by globalisation and sharper differentiations between the skilled and unskilled in labour market rewards. The ideological hostility of the PAP to welfare-oriented redistributional policies places it under pressure to devise alternative measures to manage the social and political consequences of economic restructuring effectively.

In what follows, the above arguments will be elaborated and demonstrated via a chronological account of the different phases of capital accumulation in Singapore's development.

FROM ENTREPÔT TO INDUSTRIAL ECONOMY

Singapore was incorporated under the British colonial umbrella in 1819 and subsequently developed as an entrepôt economy. This fundamentally shaped the patterns of capital accumulation by the domestic bourgeoisie. Chinese merchants, who were attracted to the island, established an intricate network of domestic commerce and small-scale collection, distribution, and retailing to complement the ascendancy of British and European capital (see Buchanan 1972:33). This involved a progression from trade and commerce into finance (Puthucheary 1960), but no challenge to its comprador role.

It was only after the Second World War, when Singapore's more rapidly expanding population was becoming more stable and economic nationalism was rising in South-East Asia, that the question of economic diversification began to receive serious consideration by authorities (Turnbull 1982:234). These trends threatened to undercut the rate of economic growth to Singapore's entrepôt economy at precisely the time when employment growth was increasingly required. The first official investigation into the problem resulted in the commissioning of a report by the International Bank for Reconstruction and Development (IBRD), which was presented in 1955. The report recommended an import-substitution industrialisation (ISI) strategy to alleviate unemployment. Economic union with Malaya, it was envisaged, would generate a sizeable protected domestic market for manufactured goods that would attract investors. However, given the preoccupation with the issue of Singapore's self-rule, serious action on industrialisation was shelved.

The domestic bourgeoisie's alignment of interests with colonial capital resulted in a detachment by it from the anti-colonial movement. As a result, when self-government came in 1959, the domestic bourgeoisie found itself politically marginalised. The triumphant PAP was predominantly led by a small group of English-educated, middle-class nationalists who had formed an alliance of convenience with the closely coordinated leaderships of the labour and student movements, which were dominated by the Chinese-educated. The alliance was to prove a tempestuous and, ultimately, unsustainable one, but this was a crucial historical phase shaping Singapore's economic and political direction. In particular, the alliance kept the government insulated from pressures by established business interests in the formation of a manufacturing strategy. There was no political necessity for a domestic, rather than an international, industrial bourgeoisie to prevail in any program to attract private investment. In any case, the legacy of colonial Singapore's class structure meant that the state would necessarily play a critical role in industrialisation. If this did not take the form of a heavy direct investment role to compensate for the absence of an industrial bourgeoisie, it was at least to involve the state in extensive measures to attract or nurture private sector investment in industry.

The PAP government's first initiative towards industrialisation involved a request to the World Bank for advice. As a consequence, there were visits to Singapore in late 1960 from a United Nations Industrial Survey Mission headed by Dutch economist Albert Winsemius. The resultant *State of Singapore Development Plan* 1961–1964, or what was known as the *Winsemius Report,* recommended a program of ISI led by private capital investment, but involving an extensive role for the state in attracting and supporting that investment. This included control over labour and the holding down of wages, the provision of various industrial estates, upgrading of technical training, tax incentives, and free remittance of profits. In early 1961, the government announced the *Development Plan, 1961–64* (MoF 1961), which closely reflected the recommendations of the *Winsemius Report.* Central to this was the proposed Economic Development Board (EDB), which was entrusted with a range of responsibilities, including the development of industrial estates, the provision of industrial loans, and technical assistance. Some functions were intended to compensate for the lack of industrial expertise of domestic-based capital, others to lower the establishment and operating costs to capital. However, the government's left-wing critics saw a greater role for the state in direct investment to ensure more favourable conditions for workers.

Yet it was the prospect of political merger with the Federation of Malaysia that was to finally precipitate a showdown between the PAP's competing factions. Although the Left had, in principle, supported the idea of political merger with Malaya, when the Federation of Malaysia was proposed in May 1961 by Malayan Prime Minister Tunku Abdul Rahman, this raised the prospect of the Left's persecution by a right-wing federal government. The consequent intensification of internal PAP friction culminated in a permanent split that led, in 1961, to the formation by Prime Minister Lee Kuan Yew's opponents of a new party, the Barisan Sosialis (BS). Support for the newly established BS came not only from the left-wing labour and student movements, but also from elements of the domestic bourgeoisie who shared concerns about the diminished status of Chinese language and culture (see Bloodworth 1986:58–61). This did nothing to endear the PAP leadership to the local business class; instead, it engendered further suspicion about it.

The PAP was now not only insulated from political control or significant influence by the domestic bourgeoisie—which, incidentally, did not entirely exclude some personal links with and selective cooption of individual business figures, notably from among the financial bourgeoisie (see Hamilton-Hart 2000)—but it was also largely spared internal pressures by organised labour. This high degree of relative political autonomy also brought the legitimacy of the government into question. The PAP responded by contending that a party that sat above the pressures of particular interest groups or classes was the only one that could represent the national interest. This rationale evolved into a comprehensive ideological case for elitist, technocratic government in the years ahead.[7] Meanwhile, the challenge for the PAP was to hold office after having lost the organisational backbone that mobilised mass electoral support for the party. Although repression of opponents and state-controlled propaganda were core components of the strategy to maintain office, the PAP understood that only through real and substantive social and economic improvements for the working class could it survive electorally in the medium to long term. This rendered the success of the ISI strategy ever more critical.

Singapore's membership of the Malaysian federation was short-lived. Political differences and mistrust between the governments in Singapore and Kuala Lumpur escalated between 1963 and 1965, culminating in the city-state's abrupt separation from the federation. With this, the vision of industrial expansion through access to a common market seemed an unlikely possibility. Apart from the troubling fact that unemployment was nearly 9 per cent in 1965, the collapse of the merger also presented a political opportunity for the PAP's domestic opponents who had opposed it. Then, in 1967, the UK government announced its intention to withdraw its military bases from the island. In that year, spending from the bases accounted for 12 per cent of Singapore's total GNP. The spectre of economic crisis loomed large in policy-makers' minds.

In the re-evaluation of strategy, the PAP's relative political autonomy from both capital and labour was to prove especially important. Having remained committed to private sector-led industrialisation, Singapore's policy-makers looked to the experiences of Hong Kong and Taiwan, both of which had, by the mid 1960s, successfully embarked on export-oriented industrialisation (EOI) programs. Such a direction would necessitate close attention to labour costs. It would also require the attraction of international capital since the domestic bourgeoisie lacked capital and expertise in sufficient quantities to give serious effect to such a program. Despite some expansion in the 1960s, local industrialists lacked the political or economic clout to frustrate this policy direction.

Similarly, the government set about not only further blunting independent labour, but also marshalling the PAP-affiliated National Trades Union Congress (NTUC) in support of its social and economic policies. Against this background, the *Employment Act 1968* and the *Industrial Relations Act 1969* were introduced, thereby reducing wages and eroding conditions, increasing working hours, and severely curtailing union bargaining powers and the capacity for industrial action. Government intervention in the labour market was further institutionalised with the adoption in 1972 of the National Wages Council (NWC).

Additional measures to promote EOI included a range of specialised institutional initiatives. In this, the EDB assumed a greatly enhanced role in centralising and coordinating the government's investment drive. Among other things, the EDB oversaw a host of generous tax concessions targeting investors in EOI. However, in 1968, the Jurong Town Corporation (JTC) was established to relieve the EDB of responsibility for the rapidly expanding industrial estates that provided centralised infrastructural facilities at low cost. During the same year, the Development Bank of Singapore (DBS) was created to provide below market rate finance and engage in equity participation to stimulate industrial ventures. In the following year, the government established Neptune Orient Lines (NOL) to expedite foreign trade and ensure lower freight charges for Singapore-manufactured goods. Through the compulsory government-controlled superannuation scheme, the Central Provident Fund (CPF), and the Post Office Savings Bank, the government also appropriated a considerable portion of domestic savings, much of which was channelled into physical and social infrastructure. Direct productive investment was also undertaken by the government as a means of boosting manufacturing (Lee 1978:138–9).

In a concerted fashion, then, the government set about trying to generate the social, political, and economic preconditions for industrial investment in export production. This involved it in conscious efforts to influence the costs of the different factors of production. In effect, the government was helping to shape Singapore's comparative advantage in the production of labour-intensive manufactures.

The EOI strategy proved a spectacular success. Foreign investment in manufacturing rose from S$157 million in 1965 to S$995 million in 1970, and to S$3054 million in 1974. In this time, direct manufactured exports from Singapore jumped from a value of S$349 million to S$1523 million, and to S$7812 million by 1974. The contribution of manufacturing to GDP increased from just over 15 per cent in 1965 to 22.6 per cent in 1974. In this economic transformation, assembly work in the electrical and electronics industries was especially important, with international capital adopting Singapore wholeheartedly as an export base for US and European consumer markets. Other low value-added, labour-intensive industries—such as shipbuilding and the textiles, clothing, footwear, and leather group of industries —underwent significant expansion.

Consequently, by 1974, Singapore's unemployment rate was brought down to below 4 per cent. Indeed, by the early 1970s, some areas of industry were experiencing labour shortages, which soon led to a reliance on imported workers. In this context, consideration was given to an accelerated policy push into middle-level technologies involving higher value-added processes. However, the effects of the global recession hit Singapore hard in 1974–75, resulting in sizeable investment cutbacks and job losses. This quickly returned the policy priority to employment generation and wage control through the NWC. Between 1975 and 1978, however, Singapore's economy staged a spirited recovery under the aegis of international capital. Cumulative foreign investment climbed to S$5242 million by 1978 and industrial exports jumped to a value of S$13 633 million in the same year (see table 5.1, page 147). In fact, labour shortages now posed a more serious problem. For social and political reasons, the government was at the time disinclined to resolve the problem of labour shortages by simply accelerating the importation of guest workers. Instead, it took the view that a rationalisation of the manufacturing sector was in order: scarce labour should not be hoarded by low value-added, labour-intensive industries in which Singapore would be unable to maintain international competitiveness over the longer term.

What transpired was a two-pronged strategy, dubbed the 'Second Industrial Revolution', both to increase technological sophistication and to raise further the contribution of manufacturing to Singapore's economic growth. On the one hand, the strategy involved measures to discourage unskilled, labour-intensive production, but, on the other hand, it cushioned the costs for employers attempting to move towards more skilled, higher value-added production. The chief element of the former was the so-called corrective wage policy of the NWC. By the end of 1981, three years of the policy had resulted in wage-cost increases to employers of more than 50 per cent. Quite intentionally, this hit the most labour-intensive, unskilled operations the hardest. If these operations were to remain in Singapore, it was expected that technological upgrading would lessen the dependence on labour. Meanwhile, tax incentives, below-market rate finance, and subsidised training schemes were made available to investors gearing towards higher value-added production. Considerable sums were invested by the government in developing the physical and social infrastructure to support a technological transformation.

The Second Industrial Revolution also witnessed refinements in the role of direct government investment. By 1983, the Singapore government had extensive investments involving fifty-eight companies and S$3 billion paid-up capital (Hon 1983); however, they were now used more strategically to promote higher value-added production. In 1983, Singapore Technologies Corporation (STC) was created with a capital base of S$200 million pooled to promote advanced technologies. The government was also a substantial investor in S$2 billion worth of joint ventures; it put together the first fully integrated petrochemical complex in South-East Asia. A further initiative was the establishment in 1981 of the Government of Singapore Investment

Corporation (GIC), which invested some of Singapore's extensive foreign reserves overseas in leading high-technology multinational corporations (Rodan 1989:153–4).

The state's efforts to foster higher valued-added production extended to the social and political realms. The country's two largest trade unions, the Singapore Industrial Labour Organisation (SILO) and the Pioneer Industries Employees' Union (PIEU), were broken up into nine industry-based unions. Not only was this new structure more functional for the technical aspects of the new industrial program, but also it reduced any potential for organised labour (however constrained by its close relationship with the ruling party) to frustrate the restructuring process.

TABLE 5.1 Selected economic indicators, 1960–84

Year	GDP growth (1985 market prices)	Direct manufacturing exports* (S$ million)	Manufacturing value-added per worker* (S$)	Cumulative foreign investment in manufacturing** (S$ million)	Cumulative local investment in manufacturing** (S$ million)	Unemployment rate%
1960						
1961	8.5	824	6 100			
1962	7.1	1 158	6 924			
1963	10.5	828	6 900			
1964	–4.3	794	6 845			
1965	6.6	858	7 207	157		8.7
1966	10.6	841	7 732	239		8.7
1967	13.0	912	8 192	303		8.1
1968	14.3	1 014	8 146	454		7.3
1969	13.4	1 971	8 600	600		6.7
1970	13.4	2 044	9 029	995		6.0
1971	12.5	2 362	9 705	1 575		4.8
1972	13.3	2 911	10 388	2 283		4.7
1973	11.3	4 779	12 856	2 659		4.5
1974	6.8	8 520	17 127	3 054		3.9
1975	4.0	7 610	17 763	3 380		4.6
1976	7.2	10 160	19 168	3 739		4.5
1977	7.8	11 412	20 417	4 145		3.9
1978	8.6	13 087	21 179	5 242		3.6
1979	9.3	16 904	23 992	6 349		3.4
1980	9.7	19 875	30 027	7 090	3 471	3.5
1981	9.6	22 894	34 681	8 382	4 060	3.9
1982	6.9	22 227	34 218	9 618	4 910	2.6
1983	8.2	22 922	36 645	10 777	5 646	3.2
1984	8.3	25 058	40 476	12 651	6 798	2.7

* Data for 1960–83 include rubber processing and granite quarrying.
** Figure excludes rubber processing.

Sources: DoS *YSS*, various years; EDB *Yearbook/Annual Report*, various years; DoS (1983); Huff (1994)

BEYOND EXPORT-ORIENTED INDUSTRIALISATION

By the mid 1980s, it became apparent that there were structural limits to the expansion of the manufacturing sector in Singapore. From the start of 1980 to the end of 1984, the rate of manufacturing growth was 6.1 per cent, compared with Singapore's overall economic growth rate of 8.5 per cent (MT&I 1986:26). Consequently, the relative contribution of manufacturing to GDP dropped from 23.7 per cent in 1979 to 20.6 per cent in 1984 (DoS *YSS 1984/85*:78). The opportunities for Singapore as an export-manufacturing base were not as extensive in middle-level technology as they had been in the earlier phase of low value-added production. The EOI strategy was confronting a paradox: the further up the technological hierarchy Singapore graduated on the basis of lower labour costs—albeit in more sophisticated technologies and in competition with higher-wage countries—the lower the proportion labour became to overall production costs. The global recession compounded this problem by generally restricting investment and by exposing the vulnerability of Singapore's heavy dependence on the US consumer market, particularly in the all-important electronics industry. In 1985, the economy actually contracted by 2 per cent, the first experience of negative growth since independence. Manufacturing declined by 6.9 per cent and 3.4 per cent during 1985 and 1986 respectively (DoS *YSS 1990*:3). Even with the repatriation of 60 000 guest workers (Pang 1994:81), unemployment still rose to 6.5 per cent by 1986 (DoS *YSS 1994*:16).

TABLE 5.2 Selected economic indicators, 1985–95

Year	GDP growth (1985 market prices)	Direct manufacturing exports* (S$ million)	Manufacturing value-added per worker (S$)	Cumulative foreign investment in manufacturing (S$ million)*	Cumulative local investment in manufacturing (S$ million)*	Unemployment rate%
1985	1.6	24 276	42 216	13 160	7 100	4.1
1986	1.9	24 387	48 240	14 120	6 804	6.5
1987	9.4	30 380	52 372	15 830	6 827	4.7
1988	11.3	37 806	55 182	18 131	7 449	3.3
1989	9.4	42 388	58 285	21 524	7 957	2.2
1990	8.8	47 000	61 440	24 133	8 682	2.0
1991	6.7	45 913	65 452	25 831	9 839	1.9
1992	6.0	46 907	69 508	28 565	10 604	2.7
1993	10.1	53 022	79 643			2.7
1994	10.1	62 261	87 743			2.6
1995						2.7

*Figure excludes rubber processing.

Sources: DoS *YSS*, various years; EDB *Annual Report/Yearbook*, various years; DoS (1983); Huff (1994)

In response to the mid 1980s economic recession, there was a major revision of economic strategy and objectives, enunciated in the report of the Economic Committee (MT&I 1986) headed by then Acting Trade and Industry Minister, Lee Hsien Loong. The immediate priorities were to resurrect Singapore's cost competitiveness in manufacturing vis-à-vis other newly industrialised countries (NICs), and to generate employment. Thus, some of the pressures on manufacturers introduced under the Second Industrial Revolution, particularly wage costs, were relaxed. However, with the longer term in mind, a shift of emphasis towards the services sector was prescribed.[8] The essence of the new vision was for Singapore to become a total business centre. Accordingly, new tax and other incentives were introduced for companies, extending their commercial and manufacturing roles to include financial, marketing, technical, and other corporate services in their networks of related companies in the region or worldwide—that is, companies making Singapore their operational headquarters (OHQ).

TABLE 5.3 Sectoral contributions to GDP (%)

Year	1960	1970	1980	1985	1990	1994
Total GDP (S$ million, 1985 market prices)	5058	12 172	28 832	38 924	57 471	78 765
Commerce	26.0	22.1	18.4	17.8	16.5	16.6
Construction	5.6	9.5	6.9	11.4	5.0	6.7
Financial and business services	14.8	17.0	19.9	20.9	26.1	25.0
Manufacturing	17.6	24.9	28.6	22.2	27.2	26.6
Transport and communications	9.3	7.3	11.6	13.7	13.3	13.7

Sources: DoS *YSS*, various years; EDB *Annual Report/Yearbook*, various years; Huff (1994)

Compared with previous policy redirections, the views of the domestic bourgeoisie appeared on this occasion to be given more weight. The Economic Committee not only comprised representatives of the Singapore Manufacturers' Association, the Singapore Federation of Chambers of Commerce and Industry, and leading local entrepreneurs, but also incorporated other local businesspeople through the many subcommittees that were part of the process. The rhetoric in the Economic Committee's report championed entrepreneurship, decried the government's past interventionist economic policies, and recommended a program of privatisation.[9]

Fundamentally, however, the new strategy was informed by a reading of emerging trends in international patterns by transnational corporations (TNCs) in the Asia-Pacific region. This trend included an increasing preparedness by the mid 1980s for TNCs to locate a more comprehensive range of higher value-added processes and services in discrete geographic regions—North America, Europe, and Asia—as opposed to adopting a single, hierarchical global division of labour (Ng & Sudo 1991). Importantly, higher levels of manufacturing investment for regional markets required high value-added services, such as accounting, law, training, and management services; this opened up a potential niche for Singapore. For the domestic bourgeoisie, this meant increased competition and increased opportunity.

Singapore's economic recovery was swift and strong, with GDP growing by an annual average of 9.5 per cent from 1987 to 1990. Although this included the impressive revival of the manufacturing sector, it did not tempt policy-makers to shelve plans for a structural transformation of the economy. The general directions outlined by the Economic Planning Committee (1991) were confirmed and refined in the *Strategic Economic Plan* of 1991, which underlined the importance of continued heavy investment in social and physical infrastructure to position the city-state as a provider of high value-added services for the region.

In response to a new level of organisation and activism on the part of small and medium enterprises (SMEs),[10] in 1989 the government committed itself to a SME Master Plan, with a complementary boost in the number of schemes assisting the development of local entrepreneurs. Private-sector participation in the policy process was still largely at the behest of the state, but, during the late 1980s and early 1990s, there was a general increase in the level and institutionalisation of interaction between capital and state in the policy process.[11] To some extent, this was also functionally related to the emergence of a more sophisticated and diversified economy. From the perspective of the private sector, consultation was also an acknowledgment of state economic power—not least through approximately seventy statutory boards and more than a thousand state-owned companies in manufacturing companies and commercial enterprises.[12] Dependence on the state for contracts and awareness of the political nexus between the civil service and the PAP has promoted cooption rather than forceful and open interest representation to the government.

One of the Singapore government's most imaginative and symbolic policy initiatives in support of greater integration with regional economies was the Growth Triangle, the idea of which was for the Malaysian state of Johor and the nearby Riau Islands of Indonesia to combine with Singapore as a coherent, trans-state economic zone of complementary specialisations.[13] In the development of this so-called external economy (Arun 1994), the government saw itself playing a pivotal role, freely describing this in terms of a Singapore Inc. (see EDB *Yearbook 1994*:3). The most ambitious of these projects was the S$28 billion Suzhou Township of 70 square kilometres, involving a twenty-two-member consortium led by the Singapore GLC's Keppel Group in partnership with the Suzhou municipal council. However, this project turned sour, resulting in huge losses (*STWE* 25 September 1999:17) when it fell victim to a combination of competitive market forces and, ironically, the inability of GLCs to operate within an alien set of bureaucratic structures (Yeung 2000).

Despite such problems, total direct investment abroad rose from S$16.9 billion in 1990 to S$75.8 billion by 1997 (DoS 1994:5; DoS YSS 2004:71), approximately half of which went to Asia. This suggested that, during the 1990s, there was an increase in Singapore's economic integration with the region and that a concomitant diversification of the city-state's economic base was underway.[14] The advent of the Asian crisis exposed the limitations of this progress and prompted a new sense of urgency in the Singapore government on the need for a fuller embrace of globalisation.

ASIAN CRISIS, GLOBALISATION, AND THE NEW ECONOMY

Although Singapore was not as adversely affected as neighbouring countries by the Asian crisis of 1997–98 (see Cotton 2000), it was not unscathed. Economic growth dropped from 8.4 per cent in 1997 to a mere 0.4 per cent in the following year. Non-performing loans amounted to S$35.8 billion in September 1998 (S$31.2 billion involving regional countries) or 14.5 per cent of the total assets of Singapore-incorporated banks. In this context, unemployment levels rose from 1.7 per cent in 1997 to 3.6 by 1999 (see table 5.4 below), peaking at 4.3 per cent at one point in 1998 during which there was a record 29 100 retrenchments (*STWE* 11 September 2000:24). Cost-cutting measures in response to the crisis also significantly reduced the effective incomes of the lowest-paid workers. This included NWC-supported wage cuts in 1998 and a 50 per cent reduction in employers' contributions to the CPF (down from 20 per cent to 10 per cent of the wages bill). Nevertheless, the government seized on the crisis as an opportunity to enhance regional economic supremacy and extend restructuring.[15]

TABLE 5.4 Selected economic and social indicators, 1996–2000

Indicator	1996	1997	1998	1999	2000
GDP growth (per cent)	7.5	8.6	0.9	6.9	9.7
Unemployment growth (per cent)	2.2	1.7	2.5	3.6	3.5
Net foreign investment manufacturing commitments S$ million	5792	5964	5214	6257	7235
Direct manufacturing exports S$ million	72 964	76 450	75 530	85 395	93 861
Growth in financial services (per cent)	7.6	18.6	-8.6	0.8	4.1
Total direct investment abroad S$ million	75 807	75 622	92 720	98 291	
Total assets/liabilities of commercial banks (change)	12.5%	14.6%	6.6%	4.0%	4.6%
Official reserves S$ billion	101.75	119.62	124.58	128.46	139.26

Sources: DoS *YSS 2000*; DoS *YSS 2004*; Monetary Authority of Singapore, *Quarterly Bulletin*, October 2001.

In particular, plans hatched on the eve of the crisis to elevate the financial sector were boosted thereafter. When then Deputy Prime Minister

Lee Hsien Loong was appointed chairman of the Monetary Authority of Singapore (MAS) in 1997, he declared his intention to transform Singapore into an international (not just a regional) financial centre. It was an ambitious objective, especially with the conspicuous absence in Singapore of the free flow of information that is widely regarded as an essential ingredient in the success of centres such as London and New York. Transparency levels, whether viewed in strict commercial terms or broader political terms, have been low in Singapore; however, in its attempt to promote the city-state as a financial centre, the government embraced the rhetoric of transparency, and even introduced specific measures raising the extent and quality of certain types of market-relevant information (Committee on Banking Disclosure 1998). Meanwhile, state information control remained extensive, resulting in recommendations from the IMF for increased fiscal, monetary, and policy-making transparency (IMF 1999, 2000a, 2000b, 2004), and media control was being consolidated rather than weakened (see Rodan 2000, 2004a).

The promotion of the finance sector again involved complementary state initiatives and market reforms. This included the opening up of some state-controlled superannuation funds to private fund managers, the issuing of bonds by cash-rich statutory boards to promote Singapore as a debt-capital hub, the liberalisation of guidelines on the internationalisation of the Singapore dollar to facilitate the foreign exchange market, and the exposure of domestic banking to greater, albeit controlled, international competition.[16]

But it was the manufacturing sector that saw the Singapore economy through the recession. Strong demand for electronics exports, particularly semiconductors, underpinned growth. However, targeted areas of the finance sector—such as bonds, fund management, and equity markets— did experience some progress in Singapore,[17] appearing to contradict the idea that the absence of transparency would be a serious impediment for investors. Investors seemed to place greater weight on other governance factors, including the predictability and reliability of institutions and political stability (Rodan 2000, 2004a).

Importantly, the Asian crisis precipitated a more general reappraisal of Singapore's economic trajectory by policy-makers that was given detailed expression in the 1999 National Day Rally speech of then Prime Minister, Goh. 'A powerful force is sweeping across the world: globalisation, because of technology and the Internet', Goh (1999) asserted, converting the world into a single 'global shopping mall'. More specifically, he contended that, 'We have to transform ourselves—from a regional economy to a first-world economy' (Goh 1999). The strategy to achieve this must entail the building of 'world-class Singapore companies', a point Goh (1999) made with approving references to the existing achievements by state-owned entities in the provision of airlines, seaports, and airports. According to Goh, the regional push over the past decade had also been valuable, even if it had been adversely affected by the Asian crisis. But, Goh (1999) declared, 'We should now go global by forming strategic alliances or mergers with other major players. Indeed, we have no choice—where the industries are consolidating worldwide, we either become major players, or we are nothing.'[18]

As with regionalisation, the globalisation push is impossible to disentangle from the interests and pressures associated with the capital accumulation of GLCs. For these companies, consolidating and extending their influence in a globalising world does, indeed, necessitate the strategic alliances referred to by Goh; however, their capacity for this was brought into question following unsuccessful merger attempts and failed offshore takeover and acquisition bids in key sectors during 1999 and 2000.[19]A recurring theme in most of these attempted mergers was apprehension about possibly handing over strategic assets to companies under the direct or indirect control of the Singapore government.[20] Private-sector analysts, fund managers, business executives, academics, and journalists seized on these events to argue for a dismantling of state enterprises. State ownership and control must give way to private entrepreneurship, it was argued, to ensure the creativity and flexibility essential to prosper in the New Economy (*AWSJ* 12 July 2000:10; *FT 13 May* 2000; Lian 2000; Tessensohn 2000; *STWE* 24 June 2000:3; *STWE* 6 May 2000:14–15).

Thereafter, the Singapore government has been repeatedly trying to project GLCs as purely commercial entities and there have been some significant offshore takeovers and mergers by GLCs. However, as we will see below, criticisms of GLCs remain significant within and beyond the international business community.

RECESSION, RECOVERY, AND THE DIRECTION OF STATE CAPITALISM

After a dramatic recovery from the Asian crisis and with 9.7 per cent growth by 2000, in no less dramatic fashion the economy shrank by 1.9 per cent the following year in the worst recession since independence in 1965. The same acute export dependence on the US economy by manufacturers of electronics components that had largely underwritten recovery from the Asian crisis now dealt the economy a severe blow.[21] The adverse economic effects of severe acute respiratory syndrome (SARS) on Singapore and the rest of the region in 2003 added to the city-state's woes. Meanwhile, by the end of 2002, unemployment levels reached 4.3 per cent.

By 2004, though, a pick-up in the global economy and in the electronics sector in particular resulted in a spectacular 8.1 per cent growth rate in Singapore. Much of this was due to demand emanating from the US and China. Yet, despite this high economic growth, the unemployment rate was remarkably steady throughout 2004, hovering at around 4.5 per cent. In the first half of 2000, when Singapore had last experienced growth approximating double digits, 43 300 new jobs resulted, yet in the first half of 2004, only

24 100 new jobs were created (*FEER* 26 August 2004:46), which underlined the problem of structural unemployment inherent in the attempt to transform the economy towards a higher skill base. The government's objective of greater diversification within the manufacturing sector to reduce vulnerability to external shock appeared to be making some progress, with sectors such as biomedical and chemicals growing strongly.[22] However, diversification within and beyond manufacturing had a long way to go before Singapore's vulnerability to external shocks could be substantially reduced and it could be expected to generate a range of social and political challenges for the ruling party. Public disquiet over the government's decision in 2005 to establish casinos in Singapore as a way of generating employment was but one manifestation of this attempt at diversification, with many of the PAP's own socially conservative ideas used against the government by casino critics (*STI* 17 April 2005; *STI* 26 November 2004).

TABLE 5.5 Selected economic and social indicators, 2001–04

Indicator	2001	2002	2003	2004
GDP growth (per cent)	–1.9	3.2	1.4	8.4
Unemployment growth (per cent)	2.7	4.2	4.4	4.3
Net foreign investment manufacturing commitments S$ million	6 609	7 039	6 271	6 002 p.
Growth in financial services (per cent)	3.7	–6.3	3.7	
Direct manufacturing exports S$ million	84 209	88 384	98 725	115 171
Total direct investment abroad S$ million	133 612	148 923	153 484	
Total assets/liabilities of commercial banks (change)	11.3	–5.5	2.7	9.8
Official reserves S$ billion	139.94	142.72	163.19	183.84

p. = preliminary figures

Sources: DoS *YSS 2005*; MAS *Quarterly Bulletin*, October 2001, October 2004.

Meanwhile, reform advocates from within the international business community seized on the 2001 recession to bolster the case for a retreat of the state from the market. This now extended to arguments for a relaxation of social controls over consumer demand affecting the domestic economy (Lian & Chung 2001). Against this background, the government established the Economic Review Committee (ERC) in 2001, headed by then Deputy Prime Minister Lee Hsien Loong, to find ways to 'upgrade, transform and revitalize' the economy (*AWSJ* 5 December 2001:11). However, the ERC subcommittee report, *Entrepreneurship and Internationalisation*, while recommending a rationalisation of GLCs, advocated one that would assist the development of globally competitive GLC enterprises. Temasek subsequently produced a new charter, which delivered the same message.[23] Not coincidentally, Temasek poured as much as US$1.5 billion into overseas ventures between 2003 and 2004 alone, including acquisitions in China, India, Thailand, South Korea,

Indonesia, and Malaysia (*FEER* 26 August 2004:46).

In the same month as the charter's release, Ho Ching became the new executive director of Temasek. As Ho was the wife of then Deputy Prime Minister Lee Hsien Loong, the appointment rekindled critical attention on the nexus between Singapore's economic, political, and bureaucratic elites (Reuters 1 July 2002). The email circulation to international journalists in early 2002 of a document authored under the apparent pseudonym of Tan Boon Seng and entitled 'Why It Might Be Difficult for the Government to Withdraw from Business', helped crystallise much of this concern. The document provided an indepth listing of the extensive interests in GLCs held by present and former cabinet ministers and their relatives, active and retired senior military personnel, and serving and former members of the PAP (*SCMP* 7 March 2002:8, 8 March 2002:6). The essential observation here could be distilled from existing academic literature (see Hamilton-Hart 2000; Worthington 2002). The compilation and circulation of the material on GLCs in this exercise was presumably a political act that sought to embarrass the government into reforming the developmental state.

GLC dominance had long been a sore point for Singapore's domestic bourgeoisie, but critical interest from international capital was conspicuous by its absence. Why the change? Partly, this has to do with the worldwide progress of the neoliberal revolution that has raised reform ambitions in recent years everywhere. The Asian crisis and the 2001 recession in Singapore could also be exploited by interests attached to such a reform agenda to try to exert pressure for neoliberal reforms. The structural transformation of Singapore's economy is also a factor—investors in the expanding financial, high technology, and service sectors want to prise open more of the domestic economy than their manufacturing counterparts do, because they want to compete with these internationalising GLCs on a more level playing field.

The ERC's final report in early 2003 provided further cause for disappointment among those advocating a winding back of the state from the economy and society, although the report made some concessions to neoliberal ideas. It recommended the deferral of the restoration of employer contributions to the CPF to pre-Asian crisis levels as well as the refinement of the CPF system to reduce the costs on employers from employing older workers—those most affected by structural unemployment. The changes would also open up selective opportunities for more private banks, insurance companies, and financial service providers to get access to national savings. However, the complete overhaul of the CPF that various interests among international capital had been calling for was not countenanced.

With a view to the longer term, the ERC report emphasised the 'need to embrace globalisation and continue linking ourselves to the developed economies' (ERC 2003). It reconfirmed strong support for the WTO, but added, 'We need to supplement this with bilateral Free Trade Agreements (FTAs) with key trading partners, to secure our economic ties and access to their markets' (ERC 2003). Increased labour market flexibility and linking wages more closely to individual company profitability were also championed, portending a more uncertain and insecure environment for labour ahead. This was reinforced through the prescription that, 'We need to refocus safety nets on the truly needy, and minimise the people's dependency on the State. An individual's success must depend on his [*sic*] own efforts and abilities, rather than on handouts from the State' (ERC 2003). The ERC argued that only in this way could entrepreneurship, innovation, and creativity—all so crucial to the knowledge economy transformation—be promoted in Singapore. Ironically, qualities of entrepreneurship and creativity were to be promoted through the establishment of the new position of a designated minister (or minister of state) for such.

The ERC also tried to allay some of the concerns within the international business community about the political nature of GLCs, declaring that, 'All GLCs should be run on strict commercial principles and be subject to the discipline of the market' (ERC 2003). Disagreement over this principle was largely responsible for the protracted nature of negotiations towards the US–Singapore Free Trade Agreement (USSFTA), which dragged on for two years; negotiations were concluded in late 2002 and the agreement formally approved early the next year.[24]

The US lobby group, the Coalition of Service Industries (CSI), turned the PAP government's rhetoric of transparency against it in its arguments for greater access to Singapore's domestic markets. The CSI called, for example, for a more transparent regulatory and licensing regime in Singapore. (*AFP* 3 July 2001). The final version of USSFTA incorporated concessions to the interests represented by the CSI by way of improved market access for select US banks, insurance companies, and other service industries.[25] It also incorporated a range of commitments to improve the transparency and independence of decisions by regulatory authorities, including the establishment of an independent dispute-settlement body for the telecommunications sector.[26] The concern with arresting anticompetitive practices benefiting GLCs was further embodied in the Singapore government's commitment to establish a competition commission. Major additional commitments by the Singapore government in the USSFTA included, first, to divest its interests in SingTel and Singapore Technologies Telemedia and, second, to provide annual information to the US on Singapore government enterprises with substantial revenues or assets. The exact form and timing of some of these commitments was imprecise, meaning that further contention on such issues may resurface. Under the *Singapore Competition Act*, for example, which came into effect in 2005, key sectors dominated by GLCs and statutory bodies—such as telecommunications, media, postal services, transport, power generation, water, and waste management—were to be exempted from its scope.

The Singapore government's willingness to sign off on the USSFTA not only reflected pragmatic resignation to US pressure, but also an appreciation that greater competition in the domestic market may be a necessary discipline in the commercial transformation of the GLCs. Conceding more space to competition in the telecommunications sector, for example, not only forced SingTel to confront the need for internal changes, but it also benefited SingTel's customers—including other GLCs—by lowering costs and thus making it more competitive. Importantly, tension over governance issues during the FTA negotiations was also kept in check by geopolitical factors. From 11 September 2001 onwards, the willingness in Washington to reward Singapore for support in the war on terror and conclude a deal intensified (see Rodan 2004b:490–2).

Systematic critical attention to transparency shortfalls and other attacks on the GLCs through the FTA negotiations contributed to renewed attempts thereafter by the Singapore government to improve the image of GLCs. Thus, in February 2004, Ho Ching publicly revealed for the first time details of the financial performance of Temasek investments, declaring it had achieved a compound annual rate of return of 18 per cent in market values over the past thirty years (*SCMP* 18 February 2004:B18). Then, later that year, Temasek published its first ever public document detailing and reviewing its total investment performance over the last thirty years. The document revealed that Temasek owned S$180 billion (nearly US$110 billion) in assets and had an investment portfolio estimated at about S$90 billion (Temasek Holdings 2004).[27] Temasek Chairman, S. Dhanabalan, projected an increasing global spread of Temasek's investments: 'Over the next 8–10 years, we expect to see a portfolio with approximately one-third of our operating asset exposure in Singapore, one-third in the rest of Asia and the remaining third in the OECD and other economies' (quoted in Temasek Holdings 2004:12). Temasek's review document failed to provide an auditor's report, information on directors' pay, or a balance sheet as detailed as those provided by publicly traded Singaporean companies (*Bloomberg Markets* March 2005:54). Calls from the international financial community for improved GLC transparency continued (*AWSJ* 1–3 October 2004:A3). Nevertheless, the report constituted improved information, further suggesting that the Singapore government was prepared to make limited governance concessions to advance Singapore Inc.'s expanded capital accumulation strategies.

Just as the Singapore government's embrace of globalisation did not mean the diminution of GLCs, nor did it mean an abandonment of state measures to attract international investment. On the contrary, state investments in specialised physical and human infrastructure, tax incentives, low-cost loans, and sympathetic regulations are integral to the economic diversification strategy. There was no better example of this than in the measures taken to promote biomedical sciences in Singapore. In 2002, the EDB earmarked S$2 billion to invest in biomedical companies and for incentive packages to attract targeted corporations to research centres in Singapore. It also committed a further S$1.5 billion in biomedical research to the National

Science and Technology Board (*FEER* 11 July 2002:48). In 2003, the Biopolis research hub was opened, bringing together more than 2000 researchers from five public-funded biomedical research institutes and research laboratories of leading biotechnology and pharmaceutical companies. Generous scholarships have also been provided for local PhD training and overseas postdoctoral posts, with as many as 234 taken up since 2001. Among the prominent international drug makers successfully targeted by the EDB was Pfizer; there were other signs, too, that the government's strategy was bearing fruit within the biomedical sciences industry. Between 2002 and 2003, manufacturing output in the industry grew by 15.9 per cent and value-added increased by 17.8 per cent (EDB 2004).

SOCIAL AND POLITICAL CHALLENGES OF GLOBALISATION

Since the early 1990s, the increasingly unequal distribution of material rewards associated with Singapore's economic development has grown in social and political importance. A more complete embrace of globalisation and economic restructuring has the potential to intensify this inequality through structural unemployment and workplace reforms. This raises a number of questions. Can conflicts associated with such processes be managed effectively through the prevailing PAP–NTUC relationship? If the PAP remains adamant that social welfare must be avoided, will a new social contract be required? Can existing forms of political cooption absorb and deflect the discontent and anxiety associated with globalisation, or will inadequacies here translate into pressures for political pluralism and an erosion of the authoritarian regime?

Decline in the government's support at the 1991 election from the PAP's traditional social base—the ethnic Chinese working class—was the first manifestation of a sense of marginalisation among working and lower middle class Singaporeans in the face of rising material inequalities (Rodan 1993b, 1993c; Singh 1992). Subsequently, the government established the parliamentary Cost Review Committee (MT&I 1993) to address public concerns about rising costs of living and inequalities;[28] however, the Asian crisis and the fuller embrace of globalisation have only served to bolster the trend towards increased inequality. As a result of cuts and restraint in 1998–99, wage costs were reduced by 5.8 per cent and the relative unit labour costs fell a dramatic 19 per cent, taking them back to 1990–91 levels (*STWE* 3 June 2000:7).[29] More worrying was the broader trend. Between 1990 and 1997—before the crisis—Singapore's bottom 10 per cent of households suffered an average income decline of 1.8 per cent, while all other households, to differing degrees, experienced increases (*STWE* 10 June 2000:15).[30]

It was no coincidence that increases in ministerial salaries, already among the highest in the world,[31] precipitated public outcries in Singapore over the last decade.[32] In 2005, structural unemployment and moves to link wages more directly to market forces and productivity proved contentious. GLCs retrenching workers has also generated consternation among employees and officials within the NTUC (*STW* 2 August 2003:10–1). The government's response to rising discontent has been two-pronged. First, NTUC Secretary-General, Lim Boon Heng, has called for a 'new compact' whereby employers accept greater responsibility for boosting employee skill levels to cope with a changing economy, in return for which workers must cooperate in the ushering in of wage flexibility and productivity-based measures (*ST* 24 July 2004: H2). Second, the government has reminded workers of the consequences facing union militants, demonstrated in its reaction to the Airline Pilots' Association of Singapore (Alpa-S) voting out its entire executive in the wake of a wage agreement perceived to have conceded too much to management. The *Trade Unions Act* was promptly amended to remove the right of union members to ratify any collective agreement signed by elected representatives. The pilot accused by Lee Kuan Yew of being the instigator of the campaign against the executive had his twenty-six year permanent residency status revoked (*AWSJ* 22 December 2003:M3; *AWSJ* 11 March 2004:A11).

Ironically, in response to depictions by opposition parties of the government as lacking in compassion for the people least benefiting from Singapore's economic development, the PAP has, in the last decade, begun projecting itself as generous in public welfare provisions.[33] Most recently, in early 2005, Prime Minister Lee Hsien Loong announced a billion dollar's worth of initiatives to assist the old, the poor, and the jobless, explicitly portraying measures as buttressing the effects of economic restructuring (*STI* 20 January 2005).[34] Nonetheless, Goh has insisted that 'the disadvantaged do not expect and cannot demand that they be looked after by the State as a matter of right' (*STWE* 18 September 1993:1). The PAP's concern remains to preserve a paternalistic political relationship more than to avoid public spending. In this relationship, Singaporeans are effectively rewarded by a benevolent government; they are not citizens with intrinsic rights that the government is obliged to honour.

They can effectively be punished, too—as was emphasised at the general election in the 1997. The PAP foreshadowed priority in social-development programs, notably major upgrading of public housing estates in electorates that supported the PAP (Ganesan 1998:232). Over 80 per cent of Singaporeans live in properties purchased from the government on the basis of a ninety-nine year lease. Then Prime Minister Goh warned voters who were contemplating supporting the opposition that 'In 20, 30 years' time, the whole of Singapore will be bustling away, and your estate, through your own choice, will be left behind. They [*sic*] become slums' (quoted in *Asiaweek* 17 January 1997:17). In the 2001 election campaign, Goh also told voters in the opposition electorate of Potong Pasir that individual precincts supporting the PAP could also get priority ahead of other precincts in the same electorate (*STWE* 3 November 2001:5). PAP victories in 1997—when it secured 65 per cent of the vote and all but two parliamentary seats—and at the 2001 poll, at which the PAP's share of the vote climbed to 75.3 per cent and it took all but two seats, were resounding. What part, if any, fear of retribution played in these outcomes is difficult to ascertain, but the government's threats did not appear to help the opposition cause (see *AWSJ* 5 November 2001:3; da Cunha 1997).

In any case, the capacity of political opposition to exploit any disquiet arising from economic restructuring—or any other dissatisfaction with government policy—continues to be constrained by a range of obstacles to political competition and political pluralism. These are neatly encapsulated in—but certainly not limited to—the *Societies Act*, which bars political engagement by organisations not specifically registered (with the Registrar of Societies) for that purpose. This militates against the formation of interest and pressure groups so essential to the social base of political parties and the creation of a political space independent of state sponsorship and control. Further impediments for opposition parties include electoral gerrymandering, which has increasingly entailed the absorption of electorates where there have been government defeats or close calls into multiconstituency electorates (Manikas & Jennings 2001); the use of administrative procedures pertaining to the issuing of licences to restrict public meetings, as through the *Public Entertainment and Licensing Act*, which has resulted in the imprisonment of opposition politicians in 1999 and 2002 (Rodan 2005:118); tight controls over the domestic media, which are dominated by GLCs and unapologetically pro-government editors (Seow 1998); and the political persecution of more formidable opponents and critics through litigation involving astronomical damages (Lydgate 2003).

Importantly, dependence on the state for economic and social resources and the continued suppression of civil society have been accompanied by major refinements in political cooption in response to the emergence of new social forces and interests associated with advanced capitalist development. The strategy acknowledges increased social plurality but seeks to ensure that this does not translate into political pluralism. Initiatives in this vein include the establishment of a Feedback Unit run out of the Ministry of Community Development, the expansion of parliamentary select committees for wider consultation in the policy process, the sponsorship of, and consultation with, select organisations dedicated to public policy issues, and the nominated members of parliament (NMP) scheme (Rodan 1996). The most significant of these has been the NMP scheme, introduced in 1990 through a constitutional amendment to allow for up to six non-elected MPs to be appointed, extended in 1997 to nine MPs. Despite the official rationale that emphasises individual expertise, the scheme has tended to incorporate functional representation, notably from local business, professional, ethnic, environmental, and women's groups. The high profiles of various NMPs through the local media have compounded the difficulties already faced by the opposition in projecting their own messages.

Significantly, such initiatives have been accompanied by new ideological concepts of consensus, participation, and consultation (Chua 1995, 2004). There have been attempts by some groups to exploit this and related official rhetoric to prise open greater independent political space. The government's 1999 vision statement, *Singapore 21* (Singapore 21 Committee 1999), for instance, recommended 'active citizenship', wherein civic groups combine in a 'positive and co-operative way' with the private and public sectors to assist in the improvement and implementation of public policy. It was against this background that, in 2001, the Association of Muslim Professionals (AMP) revived its challenge to the monopoly right of *Mendaki*—the PAP-dominated council for the development of the Muslim community—to represent Malays. It suggested there be a 'collective leadership' comprising 'independent non-political' Malays to break the supremacy of government MPs—aspirations presented as consistent with the spirit of 'active citizenship'. The proposal prompted a stern rebuke from then Prime Minister Goh, who warned the AMP against straying into the political arena. After a protracted dispute (*STWE* 30 December 2000:3), the AMP retreated.[35]

The new PAP consensus politics was also in evidence in the deliberations and report of the Remaking Singapore Committee—a broad 'review of social, political and cultural policies, programs and practices' premised on the notion that Singaporeans need to 'meet the challenges arising from our economic restructuring and the stresses on our various social faultlines' (Remaking Singapore Committee 2003). The committee consulted a wide range of Singaporean individuals and organisations inside and outside the city-state. The final report contained as many as seventy-four recommendations, of which sixty were accepted by the government, including measures to simplify registration by social groups, a change that did not extend to political discussion and activist groups. Indeed, the most profound statement of political direction to be found in this document is in the appendix, which identifies proposals without consensus and therefore not incorporated into the committee's recommendations. These included changes to defamation laws to enhance free speech, liberalisation of the media to improve the range and accessibility of information, and changes to the political playing field, including that electoral boundaries be announced in a reasonable time in advance of elections and that a transparent process of redrawing electoral boundaries be introduced.

What significance should we attach, though, to the fact that, in August 2004, Lee Hsien Loong succeeded Goh Chok Tong as prime minister? Lee can be expected to consolidate and extend the refinements to the authoritarian regime in Singapore largely initiated by Goh. Like Goh, Lee recognises that refinements to political structures and ideologies are required to reproduce the PAP state in a rapidly-changing economic and social environment. In his swearing in speech, Lee declared that

> Our people should feel free to express diverse views, pursue unconventional ideas, or simply be different. We should have the confidence to engage in robust debate, so as to understand our problems, conceive fresh solutions, and open up new spaces
>
> *STI* 13 August 2004

However, he has been clear on the conditional nature of the spaces he intends to open up. Reviving a concept PAP colleague, George Yeo, adopted in the 1990s, Lee projected that 'The Government will therefore continue to do its utmost to build a civic society' (*STI* 7 January 2004). Unlike civil society, this does not entertain independent organisations engaging in political acts, but the building up of social organisations functional for the fine tuning of, and in cooperation with, the government's policy agenda. Moreover, where there is 'criticism that scores political points and undermines the government's standing', Lee warned oppositionists that 'the Government has to rebut or even demolish them, or lose its moral authority' (*STI* 7 January 2004).

CONCLUSION

There has been a remarkable continuity in the fundamental strategies and power relations defining the developmental state in Singapore since the mid 1960s. The state remains a pervasive force in all aspects of economic, social, and political life in the city-state. Without refinements to the economic, social, and political institutions through which state power is exercised, this would not have been possible. These refinements reflect the structural pressures associated with Singapore's dynamic capitalist development as well as the changing nature of the tensions and conflicts accompanying it. Most recently, this has included unprecedented critical attention paid to GLCs from elements of international capital, statutory bodies, and governance regimes pertaining to them, raising new challenges for the institutional make-up of the developmental state and the ideology accompanying its rationalisation. The PAP government has responded with some minor reforms and concessions to such voices, but it remains to be seen how far this process will go. The PAP is not facing a coherent coalition of neoliberal ideologues so much as an assortment of pragmatic interests seeking to enhance opportunities for capital accumulation in Singapore. Improved market access for these interests, without any fundamental erosion of the strategic role of GLCs at home, may prove an effective accommodation to these pressures. Certainly, the experience of the USSFTA thus far suggests this path is a likely one. Furthermore, selectively opening up more of the domestic economy to international competition is not necessarily incompatible with the consolidation and extension of GLCs and other forms of state economic power, not only because their entrenched domestic market positions will take some shifting, but also because offshore investments are assuming increasing importance for GLC capital accumulation strategies.

As Singapore's incorporation into processes of globalisation accelerates and poses new pressures of adjustment in the areas of economic policy and governance, the PAP also faces the challenge of managing the political and social consequences of differential impacts of development. Disparities of income and wealth across the Singapore population are likely to be compounded by globalisation. Here, the government is grappling with competing political and ideological impulses. On the one hand, it remains committed to an extreme elitism that it sees as a functional necessity for continued economic success. On the other hand, it is not indifferent to the plight of those least rewarded under this system and wants to ensure that they are not left behind. Being resistant to redistributive welfare measures, for fear of institutionalising the concept of citizenship rights and all that this implies for politics in Singapore, nevertheless necessitates the forging of some form of social contract, the details of which are yet to emerge. In such a context, the capacity of the ruling party to modify and develop institutions and ideologies fostering political cooption ahead of political competition will remain important. It is this capacity that underscores the durability of the authoritarian regime thus far and is likely to ensure its reproduction for years to come.

NOTES

1 Similarly, Mohamed Ariff and Hal Hill (1985) argued that state intervention has been non-distortionary by providing incentives and inducements to assist rather than confront the market.

2 For a discussion of classical political economy and Keynesianism and their contributions to development theory, see Toye (1987).

3 Huff's most distinctive contribution to the literature, however, is the argument that the origins of Singapore's contemporary success in manufacturing and services lies in historic patterns of economic activity that cumulatively generated suitable preconditions. He traces this process to Singapore's adoption as a staple port, which preceded the city-state's international entrepôt status. In subsequent work, Huff (1999) has drawn more on state-centred historical institutional literature and the concept of the developmental state.

4 One possible exception is the examination of local business groups by Chalmers (1992), which drew, in part, on a society-centred historical institutionalist perspective.

5 In the case of embeddedness, Yeung does not so much discuss the social coalitions constituting the political basis of institutional practices. Rather, he uses it for more abstract theorisation about the relationship between states and international capital. He argues, for example, that transnational corporations are critically dependent upon the 'action of embedded states because it is in the interests of the latter that the former succeeds in capital accumulation on a global scale' (Yeung 2000:139).

6 As the then Deputy Prime Minister—and now Prime Minister—Lee Hsien Loong (quoted in *BT Online* 22 September 2000) acknowledged, neither the New Economy nor the market system associated with it are possible without an activist state: 'It doesn't happen by itself. You can have a free market only if there's a government to manage the rules and enforce them.' For an analysis of the relationship between governance and

the regulatory role of the state within the context of contemporary globalisation, see Jayasuriya (2000).

7 This ideology also, in time, lent itself to the rationalisation of a type of developmental state referred to by James Cotton as an 'enterprise association' or 'purpose-governed community'. According to Cotton (2000:155), 'Such a community is to be distinguished from a 'civil association', which is a body of individuals governed by rules (legal, moral, conventional) that regulate their conduct *but which is not committed to any particular identified purpose*' (emphasis in original).

8 Transport and communications had already increased their share of GDP from 12 per cent in 1980 to 17 per cent in 1984; financial and business services rose from 20.5 per cent to 24 per cent in the same period (DoS YSS *1990*:87). Singapore's rapid development as a financial centre since the late 1970s had been aided by a host of provisions and incentives by the Singapore government (see Rumbaugh 1995:39–40).

9 Asher points out that the arguments for privatisation in Singapore have been quite different from those elsewhere. The broadening and deepening of the stockmarket has been an objective, but this has not necessarily meant a diminution of the public sector. Rather, it has opened up opportunities for younger technocrats in the civil service, thereby retaining talent that might otherwise have been lost to the private sector. Also, instead of promoting private firms outright, the process has more often fostered private sector–public sector partnerships (see Asher 1994:800–2).

10 This included the 1986 establishment of the Association of Small to Medium Enterprises.

11 Thus, in 1994, the EDB appointed an International Advisory Council (IAC) comprised of chairmen and chief executive officers of the world's leading TNCs. The EDB expected this forum to strengthen its capacity to ascertain the thinking of international capital and its plans and aspirations for the region. Similarly, in 1994, the Regional Business Forum (RBF) was established, bringing together leading local private-sector and public-sector figures to coordinate the regionalisation drive.

12 By 1990, for example, through the three holding companies—Temasek, Singapore Technology, and Health Corporation Holdings—the Singapore state was the sole shareholder of fifty companies, with interests in a further 566 subsidiaries. The total assets of these enterprises amounted to S$10.6 billion (see Soon & Tan 1993:23; STWOE 29 August 1992:20; Vennewald 1994:27–8). An analysis of the top 500 Singapore-based companies in 1988 also depicted government-linked companies responsible for 60.5 per cent of total realised profits (see Vennewald 1994:25–8).

13 This involved Singapore government-owned companies in enormous direct investments to establish the necessary industrial infrastructure in Indonesia's Batam and Bintan Islands, as well as in the development of heavy industry and tourist resorts in other parts of the Riau Islands (Parsonage 1992, 1997; Rodan 1993b). The government subsequently introduced various incentives to support a bigger regional investment and trade push (see MoF 1993:44–8).

14 In spite of this progress, Paul Krugman (1994:70) contended that Singapore's exceptional economic growth owed most to 'an awesome investment in physical capital'. Increased efficiency in the application of capital and labour, referred to as 'total factor productivity' (TFP), still eluded Singapore according to Krugman (see also Cardarelli et al. 2000; Young 1995).

15 George Yeo, the then minister of Information and the Arts, who subsequently became minister for Trade and Industry, declared, 'We intend to be a net winner in the crisis' (quoted in *AWSJ* 12 November 1998:1).

16 Under these changes, the 40 per cent foreign ownership limit on local banks was eliminated, provision was made for up to six foreign banks to be granted newly created

qualifying full banking (QFB) licences, and Singapore dollar lending limits for qualifying offshore banks rose from 300 million to 1 billion. A QFB licence requires that a majority of the members of a bank's board of management be Singaporeans or permanent residents of Singapore.

17 Between late 1998 and early 1999, for example, Ford and General Electric Capital Corporation made respective bond issues of S$500 million and S$300 million. Similarly, the total assets under fund management by the end of June 1999 stood at S$204.1 billion—having grown by 36 per cent in the first half of that year (*BT Online 3 November* 1999).

18 The ideas contained in Goh's speech were subsequently reinforced and amplified by prominent ministers (Lee Hsien Loong 2000; Lee Kuan Yew 2000; *STWE* 11 March 2000: 24; Yeo 2000a, b). They were also pushed through the local media around the theme of the challenges associated with the New Economy (see, for example, *STI* 4 March).

19 These included the failure by Singapore Airlines in a bid to procure 50 per cent of the private Australian carrier Ansett Airlines (Air New Zealand being the successful bidder), an unsuccessful merger bid by SingTel with Cable and Wireless (C&W) HKT in Hong Kong, the failure of Singapore Airlines to secure a controlling interest in Air New Zealand, and the abandonment by Malaysia's Time Engineering of a proposed alliance with SingTel.

20 In the failed SingTel merger with C&W HKT, the Singapore government's 78 per cent ownership, through its holding company Temasek, and the fact that Lee Hsien Yang, the second son of Senior Minister Lee Kuan Yew, headed the company, reportedly prompted several non-executive directors of C&W HKT to demand that Temasek reduce its shareholding in SingTel for the deal to go through. Similarly, in the failed Singapore Airlines bid, New Zealand Prime Minister Helen Clark commented that it was not acceptable for people to perceive the national carrier as 'effectively controlled by the Singapore Government' (quoted in *Australian* 2 May 2000:25). More generally, the perception of political influence is also informed by the knowledge that many board members and executives of GLCs are civil servants, military officers, or government MPs who are, by definition, part of the PAP establishment.

21 Exports of machinery and transport equipment that incorporate such components, and which had risen in value from S$113.4 billion in 1999 to S$141.1 billion in 2000, fell to S$123.9 billion in 2001 and S$122.6 billion the following year (DoS YSS 2004: 150). The overall importance of the US market to Singapore's economic fortunes was reflected in the sharp decline in total exports, from S$41.2 billion in 2000 to S$33.5 billion in 2001 (DoS YSS 2004: 147).

22 Whereas electronics accounted for 49.7 per cent of manufacturing output in 1997, this had fallen to 39 per cent in 2003 (*FEER* 26 August 2004:46).

23 According to the this charter, Temasek would now concentrate on two categories of companies: (1) those domestic businesses deemed strategic enough to warrant government involvement, such as those involved with critical resources—water, power and gas grids, airport and seaport facilities, and public goods, such as broadcasting, subsidised health care, education, housing, and assorted amenities, and (2), those with the potential for regional or international growth. As journalist Hugo Restall (*AWSJ* 5 July 2002: A5) noted, 'Almost all of Temasek's existing companies fit into one or the other [category] meaning there's not going to be much divestment in the near future.' Indeed, he added, the charter indicated that 'far from stepping back from the marketplace, the government seems to be trying to improve its performance as an investor' (*AWSJ* 5 July 2002:A5).

24 During the same period, a FTA was also negotiated with Australia and this, too, involved some contention over governance regimes in Singapore; see Rodan 2004b for details.

25 Improved access in the banking sector included lifting the ban on new licenses for full-service banks within eighteen months and within three years for wholesale banks that service only large transactions. Licensed full-service banks would also be able to offer their range of services at up to thirty locations in the first year and at unlimited sites within two years. Locally incorporated subsidiaries of US banks could also apply for access to local ATMs within two and a half years, while branches could apply in four years (US State Department 2002)

26 A clause stating that 'Regulatory authorities must use open and transparent administrative procedures, consult with interested parties before issuing regulations, provide advance notice and comment periods for proposed rules, and publish all regulations' was also included in the agreement (US State Department 2002).

27 The report indicated that investments within Singapore included 57 per cent of Singapore Airlines, 28 per cent of DBS Bank, 100 per cent of Media Corporation of Singapore, 68 per cent of Neptune Orient Lines, 100 per cent of PSA International (shipping ports and terminals), 31 per cent of Sembcorp Logistics, 60 per cent of Chartered Semiconductor Manufacturing, and 100 per cent of Singapore Technologies.

28 The official claim that income inequality was declining in Singapore was not consistent with the work of academics. This work either contended that the statistical evidence was too weak to claim a narrowing of the gap between rich and poor (Rao 1990; 1996a, b), or actually argued that the disparities were widening (Islam & Kirkpatrick 1986; Krongkaew 1994). In any case, then Prime Minister Goh conceded that significantly rising absolute inequalities, if not relative inequalities, were engendering a sense of deprivation among lower-income earners (*ST* 2 May 1996:1).

29 The ratio of wage share to GDP also plummeted, to 41.4 per cent—the same level as 1988. Furthermore, in 1999, household income of the top 20 per cent compared with the bottom 20 per cent was eighteen times more. This compares with fifteen times in 1998. The gini coefficient, an economist's measure of inequality, also rose, from 0.446 in 1998 to 0.467 in 1999 (*STWE* 3 June 2000:1,7).

30 Even the Department of Statistics' chief statistician, Paul Chueng, conceded that 'We are observing the beginning of a trend of increasing income disparity in Singapore and the gap may remain' (quoted in *STWE* 3 June 2000:1).

31 The Singapore prime minister's annual salary of S$1.1 million (US$812 858), for example, was already more than threefold that of the president of the US in the mid 1990s (*STWE* 10 February 1996:24).

32 There was a considerable public relations effort to justify further ministerial increases in 2000 (*STWE* 1 July 2000: 4; *AWSJ* 2 July: 5; *STWE* 15 July 2000: 23)—under which the prime minister's salary rose to S$1.94 million, more than five-fold that of the US president. Still, negative public reaction was even more intense on this occasion (see Webb 2000).

33 For a discussion of social security and its political significance in Singapore, see Ramesh (2000).

34 In March 1996, a total of S$1.6 billion was also disbursed through various schemes. This included S$800 million for the Share Ownership Top-Up and Central Provident Fund Top-Up schemes, S$770 million for students, the aged, and Housing Development Board (HDB) flat owners, shopkeepers, and stallholders, and S$80 million for welfare, charitable, and community self-help groups to assist the poor.

35 The AMP publicly announced that it 'never had any desire to step into the political arena' and challenge *Mendaki* (*STWE* 23 December 2000:2). This retreat under pressure did not change the fact that the representation of ethnic Malay interests within the existing political structures is inadequate. So long as this is the case, the appetite for some independent political action is likely to remain.

REFERENCES

Ariff Mohamed and Hal Hill (1985) *Export-Oriented Industrialization: the ASEAN Experience*, Sydney: Allen & Unwin.

Arun Mahizhnan (1994) 'Developing Singapore's external economy', *Southeast Asian Affairs 1994*, Singapore: Institute of Southeast Asian Studies, pp. 285–301.

Asher, Mukul G. (1994) 'Some aspects of role of state in Singapore', *Economic and Political Weekly*, 2 April:pp 795–804.

Bloodworth, Dennis (1986) *The Tiger and the Trojan Horse*, Singapore: Times Books International.

Buchanan, Iain (1972) *Singapore in Southeast Asia*, London: G. Bell and Sons.

Cardarelli, R., J. Gobat and J. Lee (2000) *Singapore: Selected Issues*, IMF Staff Country Report No. 00/83, July, Washington, DC: International Monetary Fund.

Chalmers, Ian (1992) 'Loosening state control in Singapore: the emergence of local capital', *Southeast Asian Journal of Social Science*, 20(2):57–84.

Chen, Peter S. J. (1983) 'Singapore's Development Strategies: A Model for Rapid Growth', in Peter S. J. Chen (ed.) *Singapore Development Policies and Trends*, Singapore: Oxford University Press, pp. 3–26.

Chua Beng Huat (1991) 'Not Depoliticised but Ideologically Successful: the Public Housing Programme in Singapore', *International Journal of Urban and Regional Research*, 15(1): 24–41.

——(1995) *Communitarian Ideology and Democracy in Singapore*, London: Routledge.

——(2004) 'Communitarianism without competitive politics', in Chua Beng Huat (ed.), *Communitarian Politics in Asia*, London: RoutledgeCurzon, pp. 78–101.

Committee on Banking Disclosure (1998) *Report on Banking Disclosure, Singapore*, Singapore: Monetary Authority of Singapore, May.

Cotton, James (2000) 'The Asian Crisis and the Perils of Enterprise Association: Explaining the Different Outcomes in Singapore, Taiwan and Korea', in Richard Robison, Mark Beeson, Kanishka Jayasuriya and Hyuk-Rae Kim (eds) *Politics and Markets in the Wake of the Asian Crisis*, London: Routledge, pp. 151–68.

da Cunha, Derek (1997) *The Price of Victory: The 1997 Singapore General Election and Beyond*, Singapore: Institute of Southeast Asian Studies.

Department of Statistics (DoS) *Yearbook of Statistics Singapore*, Singapore: various years.

——(1983) *Economic and Social Statistics 1960–1982*, Singapore: Department of Statistics.

——(1994) *Singapore's Investment Abroad 1990–1993*, Singapore: Department of Statistics.

Deyo, Frederic (1981) *Dependent Development and Industrial Order: An Asian Case Study*, New York: Praeger.

Economic Development Board (EDB) *Yearbook*, various years, Singapore: Economic Development Board.

—— (2004) 'Singapore's biomedical sciences initiatives on track to meet targets', 19 February, <www.sedb.com>.

Economic Planning Committee (EPC) (1991) *The Strategic Economic Plan: Towards a Developed Nation*, Singapore: Ministry of Trade and Industry.

Economic Review Committee (ERC) (2003) *New Challenges, Fresh Goals: Report of the Economic Review Committee*, Singapore: Ministry of Trade and Industry.

Ganesan, N. (1998) 'Entrenching a City-State's Dominant Party System', in Derek da Cunha and John Funston (eds) *Southeast Asian Affairs*, Singapore: Institute of Southeast Asian Studies, pp. 229–43.

Goh Chok Tong (1999) 'First-World Economy, World-Class Home', National Day Rally speech, Singapore, 22 August, <web3.asia1.com.sg/archive/st/1/one1/one1a.html>.

Haggard, Stephan (1990) *Pathways from the Periphery: The Politics of Growth in the Newly Industrializing Countries*, Ithaca and London: Cornell University Press.

Hamilton-Hart, Natasha (2000) 'The Singapore State Revisited', *Pacific Review*, 13(2): 195–216.

Hon Sui Sen (1983) 'Statutory bodies and government-owned companies', a response from the Minister for Finance to a question in parliament from Toh Chin Chye, *Parliamentary Debates Singapore*, 43(1), 30 August, columns 12–15 and 89–96.

Huff, W. G. (1994) *The Economic Growth of Singapore: Trade and Development in the Twentieth Century*, Cambridge: Cambridge University Press.

——(1999) 'Turning the Corner in Singapore's Developmental State?', *Asian Survey*, 39(2): 214–42.

International Bank for Reconstruction and Development (1995) *The Report of the International Bank for Reconstruction and Development on the Economic Development of Malaya*, Baltimore: Johns Hopkins University Press.

International Monetary Fund (IMF) (1999) 'IMF Controls Article IV consultation with Singapore', *Public Information Notice (PIN) No. 99/26*, 26 March, <www.imf.org/external/np/sec/pn/1999/pn9926.htm>.

——(2000a) 'IMF Concludes Article IV consultation with Singapore', *Public Information Notice (PIN) No. 00/46*, 30 June, <www.imf.org/external/np/sec/pn/2000/pn0046.htm>.

——(2000b) Singapore: Selected Issues, IMF Staff Country Report No. 00/84, July, Washington, DC: International Monetary Fund.

——(2004) 'Singapore: 2003 Article IV Consultation', *IMF Country Report No. 10/105*, April, <www.imf.org/external/pubs/ft/scr/2004/cr04105.pdf>.

Islam, Islam and Colin Kirkpatrick (1986) 'Export-led development, labour-market conditions and the distribution of income: the case of Singapore', *Cambridge Journal of Economics*, (10):113–27.

Jayasuriya, Kanishka (2000) 'Authoritarian Liberalism, Governance and the Emergence of the Regulatory State in Post-Crisis East Asia', in Richard Robison, Mark Beeson, Kanishka Jayasuriya and Hyuk-Rae Kim (eds) *Politics and Markets in the Wake of the Asian Crisis*, London: Routledge, pp. 315–30.

Krongkaew, Medhi (1994) 'Income distribution in East Asian developing countries: an update', *Asian–Pacific Economic Literature*, 8(2):58–73.

Krugman, Paul (1994) 'The myth of Asia's miracle', *Foreign Affairs*, 73(6): 62–78.

Lee Hsien Loong (2000) 'US Role in Asia in the 21st Century: An Asia in Recovery', speech at the Williamsburg conference, 3 March, <sgdaily@list.sintercom.org>.

Lee Kuan Yew (2000) 'How will Singapore Compete in a Global Economy', speech at Nanyang Technological University, Singapore, 15 February, <sgdaily@list.sintercom.org>.

Lee Sheng-Yi (1978) *Public Finance and Public Investment in Singapore*, Singapore: Kong Brothers Press for the Institute of Banking and Finance.

Lian, Daniel (2000) 'Singapore Inc.—New Economy Patron or Old Economy Saint?', *Morgan Stanley Dean Witter comment on Singapore's economy*, <www.msdw.com/GEFdata/digests/20000605-mon.html#anchor5>.

——and Anita Chung (2001) 'Singapore: External Economy—Low Return is a Concern', *Global Economic Forum*, <www.morganstanley.com/GEFdata/digests/20000914-thu.html>.

Lim Chong Yah (1983) 'Singapore's Economic Development: Retrospect and Prospect', in Peter S. J. Chen (ed.) *Singapore Development Policies and Trends*, Singapore: Oxford University Press, pp. 89–104.

Low, Linda (1998) *Political Economy of a City-State: Government-Made Singapore*, Oxford: Oxford University Press.

Lydgate, Chris (2003) *Lee's Law: how Singapore crushes dissent*, Melbourne: Scribe.

Manikas, Peter M. and Keith Jennings (2001) *The Political Process and the 2001 Parliamentary*

Elections in Singapore, Washington, DC: National Democratic Institute for International Affairs.
Ministry of Finance (MoF), Republic of Singapore (1961) *State of Singapore Development Plan, 1961–1964,* Singapore: Government Printer.
——(1993) *Final Report of the Committee to Promote Enterprise Overseas*, Singapore: Singapore National Publishers.
Ministry of Trade and Industry (MT&I), Republic of Singapore (1986) *The Singapore Economy: New Directions, Report of the Economic Committee*, Singapore: Ministry of Trade and Industry.
——(1993) *Report of the Cost Review Committee*, Singapore: Singapore National Publishers.
Monetary Authority of Singapore (MAS), *Quarterly Bulletin*, various years.
Ng Chee Yuen and Sudo Sueo (1991) *Development Trends in the Asia–Pacific,* Singapore: Institute of Southeast Asian Studies.
Pang Eng Fong (1994) 'Foreign Workers in Singapore', in Wilbert Gooneratne, Philip L. Martin and Hidehiko Sazanami (eds) *Regional Development Impacts of Labour Migration in Asia*, UNCRD Report Series No. 2, Nagoya: United Nations Centre for Regional Development, pp. 79–94.
Parsonage, James (1992) 'Southeast Asia's 'Growth Triangle': a subregional response to global transformation', *International Journal of Urban and Regional Research*, 16(2):307–17.
——(1997) 'Trans-state Developments in South-East Asia: Subregional Growth Zones', in Garry Rodan, Kevin Hewison and Richard Robison (eds) *The Political Economy of South-East Asia: An Introduction*, Melbourne: Oxford University Press, pp. 248–83.
Puthucheary, James J. (1960) *Ownership and Control in the Malayan Economy*, Singapore: Eastern Universities Press.
Ramesh, M. (2000) 'The Politics of Social Security in Singapore', *Pacific Review*, 13(1): 243–56.
Rao, V. V. B. (1990) 'Income distribution in Singapore: trends and issues', *Singapore Economic Review*, XXXV(1):143–60.
——(1996a) 'Singapore household income distribution data from the 1990 census: analysis, results and implications', in B. Kapur et al. (eds) *Development, Trade and Asia–Pacific: Essays in Honour of Professor Lim Chong Yah*, Singapore: Prentice-Hall, pp. 92–104.
——(1996b) 'Income inequality in Singapore: facts and policies', in Lim Chong Yah (ed.) *Economic Policy Management in Singapore*, Singapore: Addison-Wesley, pp. 383–96.
Remaking Singapore Committee (2003) *Changing Mindsets, Deepening Relationships*, Singapore: Remaking Singapore Committee, Ministry of Community Development and Sports.
Rodan, Garry (1989) *The Political Economy of Singapore's Industrialization*, London: Macmillan.
——(1993a) 'Preserving the one-party state in contemporary Singapore', in Kevin Hewison, Richard Robison and Garry Rodan (eds) *Southeast Asia in the 1990s: Authoritarianism, Democracy and Capitalism*, Sydney: Allen & Unwin, pp. 75–108.
——(1993b) 'Reconstructing divisions of labour: Singapore's new regional emphasis', in Richard Higgott, Richard Leaver and John Ravenhill (eds) *Pacific Economic Relations in the 1990s: Cooperation or conflict?*, Sydney: Allen & Unwin, pp. 223–49.
——(1993c) 'The growth of Singapore's middle class and its political significance', in Garry Rodan (ed.) *Singapore Changes Guard: Social, Political and Economic Directions in the 1990s*, New York: St Martin's Press, pp. 52–71.
——(1996) 'State–society relations and political opposition in Singapore', in Garry Rodan (ed.) *Political Oppositions in Industrialising Asia*, London and New York: Routledge, pp. 95–127.
——(2000) 'Asian Crisis, Transparency and the International Media in Singapore', *Pacific Review*, 13(2):217–42.

——(2004a) *Transparency and Authoritarian Rule in Southeast Asia: Singapore and Malaysia*, London: RoutledgeCurzon.

——(2004b) 'International Capital, Singapore's State Companies, and Security', *Critical Asian Studies*, 36(3): 479–99.

——(2005) 'Westminster in Singapore: Now You See it, Now You Don't', in Haig Patapan, John Wanna and Patrick Weller (eds), *Westminster Legacies: Democracy and Responsible Government in Asia and the Pacific*, Sydney: University of New South Wales Press, 2005, pp. 107–25.

Rumbaugh, Thomas (1995) 'Singapore's experience as an open economy', in Kenneth Bercuson (ed.) *Singapore: A Case Study in Rapid Development*, Occasional Paper 119, Washington: International Monetary Fund, pp. 34–41.

Seow, Francis T. (1998) *The Media Enthralled: Singapore Revisited*, Boulder, Colorado: Lynne Riennier.

Singapore 21 Committee (1999) *Singapore 21: Together, We Make the Difference*, Chaired by Teo Chee Hean, Minister for Education, Singapore: Singapore National Printers.

Singh, Bilveer (1992) *Whither PAP's Dominance? An Analysis of Singapore's 1991 General Elections*, Petaling Jaya: Pelanduk Publications.

Soon Teck-Wong and Tan C. Suan (1993) *The Lessons of East Asia: Singapore, Public Policy and Economic Development*, Washington: World Bank.

Temasek Holdings (2004) *Investing in Value: Temasek Review 2004*, Singapore: Temasek Holdings, <www.temasekholdings.com.sg/2004review/AR_Secured.pdf>.

Tessensohn, John (2000) 'The Pink Elephant & Merger Interruptus', 15 March, <www.sfdonline.org/Op%20pages/OPMar00.html>.

Toye, John (1987) *Dilemmas of Development*, Oxford: Basil Blackwell.

Tremewan, Christopher (1994) *The Political Economy of Social Control in Singapore*, Houndmills: Macmillan.

Turnbull, C. Mary (1982) *A History of Singapore 1819–1975*, Kuala Lumpur: Oxford University Press.

US State Department (2002) *Facts Sheet: Free Trade Agreement with Singapore*, 19 December, online posting, available email: <sg_daily@yahoogroups.com>.

Vennewald, Werner (1994) 'Technocrats in the State Enterprise System in Singapore', *Asia Research Centre Working Papers*, No. 32, Perth: Murdoch University.

Webb, Sara (2000) 'Singaporeans Protest Officials' Pay: Public Gets Vocal About Raises in Rare Demonstration of Anger', *Asian Wall Street Journal*, 10 July, p. 4.

Worthington, Ross (2002) *Governance in Singapore*, London: Curzon.

Yeo, George (2000a) 'In the Mind of a Minister', Interview with Irene Ng, *Straits Times*, 5 March, <sgdaily@list.sintercom.org>.

——(2000b) 'Sink or Swim in Ocean of Global League', Interview with Irene Ng, *Straits Times*, 6 March, <sgdaily@list.sintercom.org>.

Yeung Wai Chung (2000) 'State Intervention and Neo-liberalism in the globalizing world economy: lessons from Singapore's regionalization programme', *Pacific Review*, 13(2): 133–62.

Young, Alwyn (1995) 'The Tyranny of Numbers: Confronting the Statistical Realities of the East Asian Growth Experience', *Quarterly Journal of Economics*, August, pp. 641–80.

Newspapers, magazines, and news services

Agence France Presse (AFP)
Asiaweek
Asian Wall Street Journal (AWSJ)
Australian

Bloomberg Markets
Business Times Online (*BT Online*)
Far Eastern Economic Review (*FEER*)
Reuters
South China Morning Post (*SCMP*)
Financial Times (*FT*)
New Democrat
Straits Times (*ST*)
Straits Times Interactive (*STI*)
Straits Times Weekly Overseas Edition (*STWOE*) (renamed *Straits Times Weekly Edition*)
Straits Times Weekly Edition (*STWE*)

6 Malaysia: Balancing Development and Power

Khoo Boo Teik

KEY TOPICS

The Alliance and the failure of *laissez-faire* capitalism
New economic policy and state intervention
Rupture between state and capital
The state and Malay capital: power shifts and emerging conflicts
Early Mahathirism: a new state–capital alliance
Conglomerates and the consolidation of Malaysia Inc.
Semi-autarky: the state against the market
A new compromise
Conclusion

FOR much of the forty-eight years since it gained *Merdeka* (independence) from British colonial rule in 1957, Malaysia was held to be a moderately successful, middle-income, commodity-producing, and net oil-exporting country. A state-supported program of industrialisation, largely based on foreign direct investment in the labour-intensive and export-oriented manufacture of textiles, garments, and electronic products had commenced in the 1970s, a program that was followed in the 1980s by a state-sponsored drive towards heavy industrialisation in the automobile, cement, and steel sectors. However, it was in the span of almost a decade, beginning with the late 1980s, that high rates of export-oriented and manufacturing-led growth, averaging over 8 per cent annually, turned Malaysia into a second-tier, newly industrialising country (NIC). As the indicators in table 6.1 suggest, such

TABLE 6.1 Economic and social transformation 1960–2003, selected indicators

Sectoral share of GDP (%)	**1960**	**1998**	**2003**
Agriculture	40.5	12.3	8.2%
Manufacturing	8.2	34.4	30.6%
Share of total export value (%)	**1960**	**1998**	**2003**
Top 5 primary commodities	71.9		
Manufacturing products		82.9	83.4
Share of total labourforce (%)	**1960**	**1998**	**2003**
Agriculture	55.2	12.8	13.8
Manufacturing	6.4	27.0	27.9
Poverty (%)	**1970**	**1997**	**2002**
Incidence of poverty (households)	49.3	6.8	5.1
Share of corporate equity (%)	**1969**	**1997**	**2002**
Malay/bumiputera share	1.5	19.4	18.7

Sources: Jomo (1990: 43, table 3.4; 79: table 4.1); Malaysia (1965: 23–4, tables 2–2, 35, tables 2–10); Malaysia (1971: 40, table 3–1), Malaysia (1981: 33, table 3–1), Malaysia (1999: 41, table 2–3; 67, table 3–1; 80–81, table 3–5; 89, table 3–9; 208, table 7.1), Malaysia (2003: 32, table 2–3; 61, table 3–2; 65, table 3–5; 95, table 4–2; 204, table 7–3).

a transformation included a major structural shift in the economy typically associated with a transition from an agrarian to an industrial society, and social changes particularly significant to Malaysian society.

Indeed, by early 1991, Malaysia's political leaders and business elites were already confidently envisioning, in strategic planning terms, that the country would attain developed country status by 2020 (Mahathir 1991).

According to certain neoclassical economic arguments, notably those advanced by the World Bank, Malaysia's economic transformation, not unlike that of other Asian NICs, was the outcome of an intricate mix of market-augmenting macroeconomic policies (World Bank 1993). To that extent, the state has been lauded for adopting pro-growth, pro-investment, and pro-market policies that kept the economy open to domestic private investment, attractive to foreign direct investment, and integrated with international trade. Such an interpretation of economic transformation accords a central role to neutral techniques of planning and management, and rational choices of policy menus. It credits efficiently functioning market processes as the ultimate determinant of economic performance. Leaving aside academic criticisms of this interpretation (see chapter 1, this volume), it is doubtful that the Malaysian political, business, and bureaucratic elites would agree with it. Successive regimes have prided themselves on being pragmatic and non-ideological in economic matters, meaning they have been responsive to market needs and demands in their maintenance of a capitalist economy. Since 1969, they have governed the market through extensive state economic intervention, the many forms and details of which were conditioned by social circumstances and political pressures.

As this chapter demonstrates, a political agenda of social engineering underlaid the state's economic intervention. The agenda, officially described as a plan to restructure Malaysian society, was germane to the state's management of social and political tensions. Yet the pursuit of that agenda under economic vicissitudes and against the opposition of specific social classes, ethnic communities, and institutional centres of power and influence, continually led to political conflicts. That the conflicts, for Malaysia, are often exclusively posed in ethnic terms is understandable; interethnic economic imbalances—essentially, the wealth and income disparities between the Malay and Chinese communities—have long been a source of political contention. But the conflicts that state policies have sought to manage, or have even created, extend beyond ethnic problems. They encompass class conflicts, the emergence of Malay capital, the rise and decline of bureaucratic interests, the politicisation of business, the aggrandisement of powerful conglomerates, and the promotion of economic nationalism.

This chapter approaches these politico–economic developments by tracking state–market relations as they changed over several periods, here distinguished according to the *laissez-faire* attitude of the Alliance (1957–69), state economic intervention of the first New Economic Policy decade (197–80), early Mahathirism (1981–90), the consolidation of Malaysia Incorporated (1991–97), and the semi-autarchy in evidence since July 1997. This chapter also links major changes in state–market relations—characterised by the degrees to which the market was shaped by state regulation, intervention, or liberalisation—to shifts in the balance of power between different alliances and coalitions of state, bureaucratic, party, and capitalist interests. Hence, this chapter argues two principal points of theoretical interest. First, it contends that the main themes of Malaysian political economy cannot be understood by seeing economic transformation as an apolitical expression of rational choices, technocratic options, and market processes. Instead, policy choices, technocratic interventions, and market processes must be analysed in political terms because they embody the 'conflictual nature of economic development and the importance of the state as an arena for this' (Robison et al. 1997:15). Second, it holds that politics and agency of powerful coalitions have been critical to the construction and reconstruction of the market during various phases in the post-colonial transformation of Malaysian capitalism.

THE ALLIANCE AND THE FAILURE OF *LAISSEZ-FAIRE* CAPITALISM

On the eve of merdeka, the political economy shaped by colonial capitalism had created certain patterns of uneven development, economic disparity, and social division. The locus of advanced economic activity lay in foreign-owned plantations, mines, and agency houses, which produced and exported primary commodities (rubber and tin being the most important) to the rest of the world. James Puthucheary's pioneering study of ownership and control in the Malayan economy in the 1950s found that European-owned companies controlled 84 per cent of large rubber estates (each of over 500 acres), 60 per cent of tin output (65–75 per cent of exports), and 60 per cent of imports (Puthucheary 1960:xv, 26–7, 85–6). On the whole, 'foreign, especially British, interests dominated nearly every facet of the colonial economy, including plantations, mining, banking, manufacturing, shipping and public utilities' (Searle 1999:28). Domiciled Chinese capital maintained a sufficiently strong presence in comprador activities, banking, small-scale manufacturing, retailing, and services so that the 'ubiquitous activity of the Chinese middleman' lent weight to the 'popular misconception that commerce is controlled by the Chinese' (Puthucheary 1960:xv). Political control and the administration of the state apparatus had been mostly turned over to Malay aristocrats who had been trained for civil service by the colonial state. Hence, the social origins of the ruling elite were those of the expatriate representatives of foreign capital, indigenous Malay aristocrats, and domiciled Chinese capitalists and traders.

Malaya's west coast had a developed urban sector that stretched north–south from Penang to Singapore. This sector contained the towns, ports, public works, and major infrastructure that integrated the domestic economy with the global economy. Here lived a broad spectrum of middle and working classes, including lower-level bureaucrats, professionals, teachers, clerks, shopkeepers, petty traders, hawkers, and industrial and service workers. Their numbers had grown with economic diversification and bureaucratic expansion under colonialism. Nearly 60 per cent of the economically active population, however, worked in the rural sector, mostly as peasants cultivating rice on their own land or rented land, smallholders growing rubber and other cash crops, wage labourers working on plantations, and squatters illegally raising cash crops on state land.

The economic disparities and social divisions were complicated by an ethnic division of labour not uncommon to the social organisation of labour in other former colonies, such as Burma, Fiji, and the countries of East Africa. Colonial design (Lim Teck Ghee 1984) as well as the peasantry's 'refusal to supply plantation labour' (Alatas 1977:80) left the Malay peasantry chiefly engaged in food production. Migrant Chinese and Indian labour mainly worked the tin mines, and rubber estates and public works projects, respectively. As a consequence of this ethnic division of labour, the Malay peasantry escaped the harsh conditions of early colonial capitalism, which took a heavy toll on migrant labour. But the rural Malay community was locked into an immiserating sector, close to subsistence, while sections of Chinese and Indian migrants took advantage of an expanding urban sector to gain upward mobility through commerce, education, and the professions.

The first ruling coalition, the Alliance—comprising the United Malays National Organisation (UMNO), the Malayan Chinese Association (MCA), and the Malayan Indian Congress (MIC)—did not change the fundamental features of the political economy. This was largely because of the character of Malaya's decolonisation. The colonial state had defeated a post-Second World War insurrection of communists, left-wing nationalists, former wartime partisans, radical sections of the working class, and squatter-farmers. After that, the colonial state and the Alliance forged a merdeka compromise that protected foreign economic interests (which were not nationalised, as happened, say, in Indonesia under Sukarno), preserved the position of domiciled Chinese capital, and largely ceded the control of the state apparatus to the Malay aristocrats who led UMNO. More broadly, a federal constitution reserved a special position for the Malay community in recognition of its indigenous status but guaranteed the non-Malays a new found citizenship and accompanying rights.

The Alliance's compromise expressed a balance of power by which the state played a 'restrained role' in what approximated a *laissez-faire* capitalism (Jesudason 1989:52–67). To be sure, the Alliance regime made some departures from the colonial policy regime of minimal taxation, strict avoidance of budget deficits, and the maintenance of an unprotected market (Jesudason 1989:48). The state expanded, for example, its revenue base by raising export duties on rubber and tin, imposing an excess profit tax on tin, and introducing a development tax on company profits (Jesudason 1989:49). Public development expenditure was increased, to the point of incurring small budget deficits (Jesudason 1989:49). The Alliance progressively protected the domestic market, as shown by its removal of a Commonwealth preferential tariff rate that had favoured imports of British origin. It also promoted import-substituting industrialisation (ISI) by offering fiscal, tax, and other incentives to firms engaged in pioneer industries.

Beyond these measures, the Alliance adopted a conservative stance in economic affairs that continued to favour foreign and domestic capitalist interests. The ISI program attracted some foreign investment to manufacturing for the domestic market. Taking advantage of some degree of the Malaysianisation of the economy, Chinese capital expanded into banking, manufacturing, trade, construction, and property development. The thrust of development was directed at improving urban infrastructure, implementing limited rural development schemes, and providing small-scale assistance to incipient Malay business. The state's own involvement in development was limited by an underlying concern to restrain the levels of domestic borrowing and foreign debt. Few things more clearly showed the regime's commitment to leaving the market free than the regime's reluctance to intervene on behalf of sections of UMNO's Malay base. In a notable instance, the Alliance rejected Minister of Agriculture Aziz Ishak's proposal to adopt a populist scheme of turning the control of privately-owned rice mills over to farmer cooperatives when the scheme was opposed by Chinese business interests (Jesudason 1989:55; von Vorys 1975). The regime used institutions such as Bank Bumiputra, the Majlis Amanah Rakyat (MARA, or the Council of Trust for the Indigenous People), and the Rural and Industrial Development

Authority (RIDA) to assist nascent Malay businesses. Yet, despite a growing Malay frustration with the lack of progress in redressing their 'relative economic backwardness', the regime's orientation in this area was supportive rather than aggressive (Jomo 1988:253–4).

Left to itself, the market could not resolve problems of increasing unemployment, declining incomes, and widening inequalities. By the late 1960s, the Alliance was hard pressed to meet social expectations unleashed by decolonisation and mass politics. A marginalised Malay peasantry sought release from poverty, indebtedness, and landlessness, most dramatically by opening state land, as when Hamid Tuah led land seizures in Sungei Sireh, Teluk Gong, and Binjal Patah (Husin Ali 1975:157–9). A combination of Malay bureaucrats, intelligentsia, and the middle class wanted concerted state assistance and economic parity vis-à-vis the Chinese community, and Chinese capital in particular. The non-Malay middle and working classes refused to accept that their opportunities for employment, education, and upward mobility could be prejudiced by constitutional safeguards of the special position of the Malays. During the 1960s, too, disaffection among organised labour in the plantation and manufacturing sectors resulted in exceptionally high numbers of work days lost to strikes in 1962, 1964, and 1968 (Todd and Jomo 1994:48-53, tables 2.16 to 2.19).

These mass economic expectations became ethnically divisive and politically volatile as they coincided with real and imagined fissures in the areas of language, culture, and citizenship during the formative period of Malaysian nationhood. Despite being ethnically divided, the opposition to the Alliance crystallised into an electoral revolt, as a result of which, in the May 1969 general election, an informal electoral pact helped diverse opposition parties—the Pan Malaysian Islamic Party (PMIP, now Parti Islam, or PAS), the Democratic Action Party (DAP), and the Gerakan Rakyat Malaysia (Gerakan, or Malaysian People's Movement)—erode the Alliance's hold onto power. On 13 May, Kuala Lumpur was engulfed in interethnic violence. The Alliance's political framework collapsed and, with it, a 'ridiculous' (Mahathir 1970:15) *laissez-faire* formula of 'politics for the Malays' and 'economics for the Chinese'.

NEW ECONOMIC POLICY AND STATE INTERVENTION

A National Operations Council (NOC), headed by Deputy Prime Minister Tun Abdul Razak, ruled under a state of emergency from 1969 to 1971. Parliament was suspended while Prime Minister Tunku Abdul Rahman, the personification of Alliance consociationalism, was sidelined (he retired in 1970). Razak's regime had no more use for the *laissez-faire* capitalism and devised the New Economic Policy (NEP). The NEP would remake the political economy to manage the class pressures and ethnic demands that an unregulated market had not satisfied. As Malaysian economic planning was carried out via five-year plans, the NEP was designed to be implemented over two decades, beginning with the *Second Malaysia Plan* of 1971–75.

The NEP's premises were that poverty, the ethnic division of labour, and Malay resentment of interethnic income inequalities lay at the heart of the May 1969 eruption. The NEP's two major objectives were, 'eradication of poverty, irrespective of race', and 'restructuring to abolish the identification of race with economic function'. The state's *Outline Perspective Plan 1971–90* targeted a decline in the incidence of poverty, from 49 per cent of all households in 1970 to 16 per cent in 1990. Restructuring was planned to raise the bumiputera (indigenous, but predominantly Malay) share of corporate equity from 2.5 per cent in 1970 to 30 per cent in 1990. To eliminate the identification of race with economic function, the NEP envisaged affirmative action that favoured the bumiputera community. To accomplish these objectives, the state used ethnic quotas and targets to regulate access to state assistance, business opportunities, tertiary education, and civil service recruitment.

The NEP's subsequent elaboration and implementation encompassed several major developments. Restructuring was promoted as an exercise to redress interethnic imbalances by redistributing corporate wealth ownership as well as employment. It became a massive social engineering project that altered the class structure of Malaysian society by sponsoring the rise of a combination of Malay capitalist, professional, and middle classes (later described as a Bumiputera Commercial and Industrial Community). The state no longer confined its activities to 'limited programs aimed at ameliorating rural discontent and the frustrations of a rising Malay intelligentsia' (Khoo Khay Jin 1992:50). Rather, by becoming a provider of opportunities for Malays, the state enlarged the existing corps of Malay entrepreneurs, graduates, and professionals. It gave aspiring Malay entrepreneurs financial assistance, credit facilities, contracts, preferential share allocations, subsidies, and training. It established new public universities and all-Malay residential schools and colleges at home, and sent tens of thousands of Malays—young students and mid-career officers—to universities abroad. The result of this social engineering was a full range of Malay entrepreneurs and capitalists (Searle 1999:81–95), a sizeable Malay middle class (Abdul Rahman 1995), and a considerable '*bumiputera* participation rate' in the professions (Jomo 1990: 82–3, table 4.2; Malaysia 1999:85, table 3–7).

Simultaneously, the state became a determined regulator of local and foreign business, although the regulation of the former was politically more contentious. The state strengthened its regulatory powers and enforced compliance with the NEP's restructuring requirements by using legislative means (*Industrial Coordination Act* [ICA] 1975) and bureaucratic procedures (set by the Foreign Investment Committee). The NEP's restructuring requirements set a quota of at least 30 per cent bumiputera equity participation and employment in companies covered by ICA.[1] In 'expanding government power over firms', ICA gave the minister of trade and industry wide discretionary power over licensing, ownership structure, ethnic employment targets, product distribution quotas, local content, and product pricing (Jesudason 1989: 135–8). Even at the level of state and local government, (non-Malay) businesses came under stringent bureaucratic regulation. In a non-manufacturing area such as real estate development, for example, many authorities—including land offices, town and country planning departments, municipal councils, and state economic development corporations—imposed NEP requirements on such seemingly technical matters as land-use conversion or planning guidelines.

Finally, the state became a major investor. It expanded public sector ownership of corporate equity by acquiring assets on behalf of Malays. Public enterprises proliferated from twenty-two in 1960 to 109 in 1970, 656 in 1980, and 1 014 in 1985. State agencies, banks, and funds sought, bought, and otherwise held equity in trust for bumiputeras. Some of the best known of these state agencies were Bank Bumiputera, the Urban Development Authority (UDA), Perbadanan Nasional (Pernas, or National Corporation), the Permodalan Nasional Berhad (PNB, or National Equity Corporation), the Amanah Saham Nasional (ASB, or National Unit Trust Scheme), and the state economic development corporations (SEDCs) (Gomez & Jomo 1997:29–39; Searle 1999:61–6).

RUPTURE BETWEEN STATE AND CAPITAL

The state's economic intervention led to critical shifts in the tripartite balance of power among the state, foreign capital, and domestic capital. The fundamental shift was revealed by the state's economic nationalist attitude towards foreign and Chinese capital. The NEP targeted a 30 per cent Malay share of corporate equity by 1990, but also allowed for a rise in non-Malay ownership from about 34.3 per cent in 1970 (with the politically more contentious Chinese share accounting for 22.8 per cent in 1969) (Malaysia 1971:40, table 3.1) to 40 per cent in 1990 (Malaysia 1976:86, tables 4–16). Thus, increases in Malay and non-Malay shares were to be attained at the expense of foreign ownership, which was to decline from 63.3 per cent in 1970 to 30 per cent in 1990 (Malaysia 1976: 86, tables 4–16).

During the NEP's first decade, the state acquired foreign companies or foreign equity. State enterprises, led by Pernas and PNB, bought foreign companies—such as London Tin, Chartered Consolidated, Sime Darby and Guthrie—that had long dominated the mines, plantations, and trading houses. Faced with state acquisitions or restructuring, certain foreign companies chose to relinquish ownership or control of their Malaysian subsidiaries (Searle 1999: 72–4). One exception to the success of the state's acquisitive trend was the foreign oil companies' refusal to share management control with Petronas (Petroliam Nasional, or National Oil Corporation), as stipulated by the *Petroleum Development Act 1974* (Searle 1999: 69–70). In response to the *Petroleum Development Act*, 'which smells of nationalisation, and ... cannot be acceptable to any foreign interests ... foreign investment in Malaysia has come to a standstill' (Grace 1976, cited in Jomo 1988:281, fn. 69). Thus there was an investment strike, which ended only after the state had renegotiated with the oil companies and dropped the management conditions.[2]

Chinese capital was not averse to reducing foreign ownership, but the danger to Chinese capital was that the state's economic nationalism took the hues of a Malay nationalism that the Chinese business community and political parties were too weak to resist. Under the Alliance, MCA leaders had held the ministries of finance and trade, and exerted considerable Chinese influence over economic planning and policy-making. By 1974, however, when Razak replaced the Alliance with an enlarged coalition, Barisan Nasional (BN, or National Front), UMNO leaders had monopolised policy-making and the balance of power between Malay state and Chinese capital had swung to the former. Chinese capital could not match the state's penetration of key economic sectors. In banking, for example, where Chinese capital had expanded in pre-NEP years, the state enlarged its assets and restructured both foreign-owned and Chinese-owned banks. By 1990, the three biggest banks were the state-owned Malayan Banking Berhad, Bank Bumiputera Berhad, and the United Malayan Banking Corporation (Searle 1999:75, table 3.2). Nor could Chinese capital escape stricter regulation, as was demonstrated by the failure of MCA and the Associated Chinese Chambers of Commerce and Industry of Malaysia, despite repeated attempts to have the ICA repealed (Jesudason 1989:134–42).

Foreign and Chinese capital distrusted state intervention, disliked NEP's nationalism, and balked at ICA's regulations. Still, the relations between the state and capital were not always antagonistic. Foreign capital was mollified in at least two ways. First, the old foreign capital of the plantation houses, mines, banks, and trading houses was never threatened with outright nationalisation. Malaysianising the ownership of established companies by restructuring was accomplished by market transactions. The NEP's backdoor nationalisation, as foreign critics characterised the state acquisitions, was tantamount only to 'relatively gentle ... encroachments on the terrain of foreign capital' (Jomo 1988:281, fn. 68). Second, the new foreign capital of manufacturing multinational corporations (MNCs) was highly favoured as the state initiated a program of export-oriented industrialisation (EOI). Here, the NEP interfaced with a new international division of labour. The state's urgent need to create mass employment matched the MNCs' search for cheap labour in politically stable offshore production sites. The state offered the MNCs the comparative advantages of lower wages, prohibition of unionisation among a new industrial labourforce, subsidised physical and social infrastructure, and fiscal, tax, and other incentives. The state established export processing zones (EPZs), the best known of which was the Bayan Lepas Free Trade Zone on the island of Penang, which became a leading centre for the production of semiconductors for the global electronics industry. The MNCs were not subjected to NEP's wealth restructuring requirements, but they met the NEP's employment restructuring goal by proletarianising large numbers of rural, young, and often female Malays within the modern sectors of the economy. In this context, state intervention reshaped markets in labour, land, infrastructure, and services on behalf of foreign capital.

Chinese capital never enjoyed the MNCs' privileged treatment. Portions of Chinese old wealth—typically, family businesses controlled by individual tycoons—were unable or unwilling to adjust to the intensifying institutionalisation of NEP practices. These 'pursued easy and safe areas of expansion, investing heavily in property development and finance, and avoiding sectors like manufacturing which entailed larger risks and longer periods to recuperate investment outlays' (Jesudason 1989:163). Other Chinese businesses discovered opportunities that were, arguably, attributable to the NEP. During the NEP's first decade, real GDP growth averaged 7.6 per cent per year (or 7.3 per cent over the Second Malaysia Plan period of 1971–75, and 8.6 per cent in the Third Malaysia Plan period of 1976–80). Under such conditions, business in general prospered, and the non-Malay (predominantly Chinese) share of corporate equity rose between 1970 and 1985. Some, typically big, Chinese businesses adapted to the NEP-altered balance of power at elite levels. Offering varying combinations of capital, networks, and expertise, they courted, were courted by, or otherwise built commercial relationships with aspiring Malay capitalists or influential Malays in the aristocracy, bureaucracy, military, and dominant Malay political party (Heng 1992:132–4; Sieh 1992:110–11). Soon, a distinctive NEP creation, the 'bumiputera-non-bumiputera joint venture', emerged as a corporate platform from which adaptable Chinese capital—old wealth and new money—partook in the state-led demand and public enterprise investment enormously boosted by high commodity and oil revenues.

THE STATE AND MALAY CAPITAL: POWER SHIFTS AND EMERGING CONFLICTS

Away from ethnic considerations, the state-sponsored creation of Malay capital was dependent upon three critical factors. UMNO, as the dominant political party in government, supplied the political power to push through the NEP's social engineering. The Malay-dominated bureaucracy provided the capacity for implementing NEP programs. The performance of an incipient class of Malay capitalists had to vindicate the state assistance and nurture they received. Influential coalitions emerged from among the ranks of party, bureaucracy, and class. But as resources were controlled by bureaucrats and technocrats and, as UMNO entered business on a large scale and individual Malay capitalists emerged, these coalitions contended for power, access to resources, and opportunities for accumulation. Their agendas could less and less be amicably subsumed under NEP; all based their claims on restructuring, but each pursued its disparate interests. Many flashpoints of competition were created that continually strained the integrity of this party–bureaucracy–class axis.

Within only a few years of the NEP's beginning, one such flashpoint emerged between the party and the bureaucracy. Razak's regime had rapidly moved to enlarge its corps of bureaucrats and technocrats as Razak insisted that development required more administration than politics. A whole generation of Malay administrators, technocrats, and professionals was trained at state expense and equipped with the resources to take charge of economic development under the NEP. But the transition to an NEP state involved a power shift, too, from UMNO's old guard to younger UMNO politicians who were being groomed by Razak. Just as the NEP repudiated the Alliance's *laissez-faire*, so the rise of Razak's coterie of 'young Turks' marginalised UMNO's old style politicians who supposedly lacked 'the vision and technocratic skills to carry through the restructuring of society' (Crouch 1980:17, 32–3). Not coincidentally, Razak's protégées included Mahathir Mohamad and Musa Hitam, who had attacked Tunku Abdul Rahman's leadership after May 1969, and their associate, Tengku Razaleigh Hamzah. After Razak died in January 1976, a crisis developed in UMNO when the old guard struck at Razak's allies by accusing several of them of being communists (Crouch 1980); however, this bizarre witchhunt turned out to be the last gasp of an old guard being swept aside by the NEP's technocratic shift.

Another source of conflict lay in the bureaucracy as it expanded in terms of funding, resources, and personnel (table 6.2 below). Bureaucratic involvement in economic activities grew such that, by 1983, the state had taken over the commanding heights of the economy. Then, public enterprises controlled an estimated 45 per cent of modern agriculture, 50 per cent of mining, and between 70 and 80 per cent of banking (Parti Gerakan 1984:187, table 2). But the performance of public enterprises was itself a major problem. For political and other reasons, many public enterprises could not meet market criteria of efficiency and profitability (Gomez & Jomo 1997:76–7; Rugayah 1995:75–8). Many officers regarded their public enterprises as social enterprises whose goal of redressing interethnic imbalances was not readily measured in pecuniary values. As the price of providing the Malays with experience, employment, and skills, the state tended to accept or overlook the public enterprises' deficits, debts, and losses. But the scale of deficits and losses was daunting. Total public sector deficit rose from RM400 million in 1970 to RM15.2 billion in 1982. State governments, statutory bodies, and public enterprises owed the federal government RM8.743 billion in 1982 (Mehmet 1986:133–4), while 'approximately 40–45 per cent of all SOEs [state-owned enterprises] have been unprofitable throughout the 1980s', of which 'almost half (or 25 per cent of all SOEs) had negative shareholder funds' (Adam & Cavendish 1995a:25).

TABLE 6.2 Expansion of public sector, selected indicators, 1970–85

Public expenditure	
First Malaysia Plan 1966–70	RM4.6 billion
Second Malaysia Plan 1971–75	RM10.3 billion
Third Malaysia Plan 1976–80	RM31.1 billion
Fourth Malaysia Plan 1981–85	RM48.9 billion
Development expenditure as % of GDP	
1971	8.5%
1980	14.4%
Public sector employment (excluding military and police)	
1970	139,476 employees
1983	521,818 employees

Sources: Jomo (1990: 106, table 5.1); Mehmet (1986:9, table 1.3, 133, table 6.1)

A politically more contentious issue was the transfer of public enterprise assets. In principle, public enterprises run by political appointees and state managers held those assets in trust for the Malays, but the more commercially oriented trust agencies, such as PNB, were empowered to acquire profitable companies. Even such a powerful public corporation as Pernas was required to transfer eleven of its most profitable companies to PNB in 1981. Commercial imperatives became more urgent after PNB established Amanah Saham Nasional (ASN, or the National Unit Trust Scheme). ASN bought PNB's assets at cost, while individual Malays bought units of ASN shares. The companies remained within the community, while individual shareholders received returns on their investment. ASN was a novel solution to the problem of asset transfer. Yet some managers of public enterprises were reportedly burdened by a 'disincentive to profit-making' for fear of PNB's taking over their enterprises (World Bank, cited in Gomez & Jomo 1997:77). Public enterprises also faced pressure from Malay entrepreneurs who wanted the assets to be directly transferred to them, or complained of unfair state competition. Not a few state managers chose to become entrepreneurs, sometimes by acquiring the very enterprises they managed. Contention over the transfer of public assets grew acute as UMNO entered business and its managers used the party's dominance to compete for state projects, contracts, and assets. Within a few years of starting Fleet Holdings (for the purpose of generating party funds), UMNO had built up an economic empire that penetrated most economic sectors (Gomez 1990; Searle 1999:103–26). Subsequently, notable UMNO 'nominees, trustees or proxies'—people to whom the party assets were entrusted—became big capitalists in their own right (Searle 1999: 135–53).

EARLY MAHATHIRISM: A NEW STATE–CAPITAL ALLIANCE

The brewing conflicts along the party–bureaucracy–class axis intensified after Mahathir became premier in July 1981. Mahathir's approach to development may be summarised as a composite of bureaucratic reformism, economic nationalism, and privatisation. It was modelled after the East Asian developmental state and inspired particularly by the economic success of Japan and South Korea.

Mahathir set out to tackle the 'structural problems' arising out of the 'size and extent of the government's involvement in the economy' (Khoo 1995:129). He was ambivalent towards state expansionism. He favoured having an interventionist state implement the NEP's social engineering, but he was contemptuous of public sector inefficiency and persuaded by the private sector's supposed dynamism. His first administration introduced reforms to improve the performance of the bureaucracy. When, in the early 1980s, commodity prices and state revenues fell, he reduced the public enterprises' involvement in business. The pace of this curtailment of the bureaucracy's involvement in business was accelerated under Minister of Finance Daim Zainuddin during the recession of 1985. But the curtailment adversely affected the interests of the managers of public enterprises as well as a range of Malay businesses dependent upon state assistance and political largesse (Khoo Khay Jin 1992); their ensuing disaffection contributed to UMNO's split from 1987 to 1990.

Mahathir also launched a heavy industrialisation drive based on the production of steel, automobiles, motorcycle engines, and cement. Domestic capital being reluctant to bear the heavy costs, high risks, and long gestation periods, he chose a combination of state investment via the state-owned Heavy Industries Corporation of Malaysia (HICOM), technology sourced from Japanese and South Korean firms through joint ventures, and indigenous (that is, Malay) management (Machado 1989–90, 1994). HICOM's program began with an import-substituting character: its industries enjoyed credit facilities, subsidies, and tariff protection. Its intermediate objectives included upgrading technology and the creation of extensive links in the economy. Its eventual goal was export competitiveness.

As with East Asian state-led late industrialisation elsewhere, HICOM's program had a strong nationalist impetus. Mahathir, too, personified capitalist impulses that went beyond the ethnic fixations of other NEP advocates. For those reasons, Mahathir wanted to heal the rupture between the state and domestic capital. The NEP had not quite created an independent class of Malay capitalists, but it had produced Malay entrepreneurs and technocrats with business experience. State regulation had also rendered the NEP more acceptable to non-Malay capital. Thus, Mahathir encouraged a new state–capital alliance, one that provided a major role for Malay capital, which was revealed by Mahathir's privatisation and Malaysia Incorporated policies (Khoo 1995:129–36). Privatisation was originally justified as the means to reduce expenditure on unprofitable public enterprises and improve economic performance, but what it did was to shift the burden of investment and growth to the private sector and serve as the mode of transfer of assets held in trust to Malay entrepreneurs. Malaysia Inc. promised cooperation between the state and a national capital that was no longer synonymous with domestic Chinese capital.

In 1985, the economy contracted by 1.0 per cent and only grew by 1.2 per cent in 1986. Three factors were principally responsible—a huge decline in commodity prices,[3] an escalation in public debt,[4] and the reduction in the government's development expenditure at the same time that total private investment declined.[5] The recession's impact was particularly severe on Malay businesses, while austerity measures, including a job and wage freeze, and cuts in development expenditure were forced upon the bureaucracy and public enterprises. In a bold if desperate move to attract private and, especially foreign, investment, Mahathir suspended the NEP's restructuring requirements. As the 1987 UMNO party election approached, the ranks of the party, the bureaucracy, and Malay capital were polarised. At one end stood a pro-growth camp that supported the NEP's suspension to boost investment and growth; at the other was a pro-distribution camp that wanted to continue NEP restructuring. The former, pro-Mahathir, camp was backed by bigger and more successful Malay businesses, while the latter, the Razaleigh Hamzah-led, camp found support among smaller and less independent Malay businesses and disgruntled sections of the bureaucracy (Khoo Khay Jin 1992:67–71).

The crisis deepened when, in April 1987, Mahathir narrowly survived the combined challenge of Razaleigh Hamzah and Musa Hitam; in late October, deteriorating interethnic relations became the pretext for the regime's general suppression of dissent (Khoo 1995). Still, Daim's austere response to recession and Mahathir's authoritarian reply to opposition gave the regime time to recover. From 1985 to 1987, the state liberalised the investment regime, initially for foreign capital, but later for domestic (Chinese) capital, too. Limits on foreign equity ownership were removed and fresh investment incentives offered. These measures coincided with moves by Japanese and other East Asian MNCs to relocate part of their production because of the post-Plaza Accord yen appreciation, an anticipated loss of the generalised system of preferences (GSP) privileges, and escalating domestic labour and production costs. Subsequently, a wave of East Asian investment that began to arrive in the late 1980s helped to effect a trend of rapid economic growth that lasted until July 1997.

CONGLOMERATES AND THE CONSOLIDATION OF MALAYSIA INC.

With economic recovery, privatisation was 'entrenched in the policy matrix', and by 1991, a *Privatisation Masterplan* had been completed, the scope of which portended a 'radical shift to the private sector' (Adam & Cavendish

1995b:135). The reliance on a partnership between the private sector and the state—Malaysia Inc., in short—was promoted as 'the way forward' in Mahathir's *Wawasan 2020* (Vision 2020) (Mahathir 1991). Yet accelerating privatisation and the consolidation of Malaysia Inc. had several consequences for the economic structure, power alignments, and governance, which laid some of the conditions for another crisis.

The practice of privatisation came to encompass the sale of profitable state monopolies (in energy and telecommunications, for example), awarding of large infrastructural works (the North–South Highway and the Bakun Dam being the largest), and opening of new areas (social services, such as health care and tertiary education) to domestic capital. To the extent that more and more sectors, companies, and projects passed into private hands, privatisation entailed rolling back the frontiers of the state. But privatisation did not operate under market conditions. Huge privatisation projects were awarded without open competition, and often without any tendering process at all.[6] In this tightly controlled 'market', rent-seeking and money politics were rife as coalitions formed around domestic conglomerates and powerful politicians who competed to become privatisation's chief beneficiaries.

A new category of politically connected Malay, non-Malay, or often interethnic conglomerates arose and evolved into privileged oligopolies.[7] These conglomerates did not manufacture for the world market, where success relied on technological innovation, research and development, and international competitiveness. Some operated in primary commodity production, which could trace its competitiveness to colonial times, or in resource-based industries in which local sourcing was an obvious strength. Most of the conglomerates congregated in banking, resource exploitation, construction, property and real estate, gaming, tourism, transport, utilities and services, and selected import-substituting industries. These were precisely sectors in which state policies and protection made the difference between success and failure. The conglomerates adopted an almost standard business strategy (though not necessarily in the following order of activity): deal in property and real estate, build up construction capacity, lobby for infrastructural and utility works, secure a banking or finance arm or a brokerage licence, buy up plantations, diversify into tourism, and enter newly privatised areas like telecommunications and social services.[8]

Conglomerate after conglomerate followed a predictable mode of expansion: having a flagship in one area, they used takeovers, acquisitions, mergers, or applications to the state to build up a fleet of companies. Their expansion drew financial support from two main sources: external borrowings, and capital raised on the Kuala Lumpur Stock Exchange (KLSE). Since the late 1980s, the financial system had been reformed to liberalise the capital market, support its growth, and introduce some competition (Ariff 1996:328–31; *Financial Times* 1995:195–201; Zainal et al. 1996:318). The liberalisation made it easier for the conglomerates to raise external loans or internal capital. Between 1988 and 1990, the private sector's medium- and long-term

TABLE 6.3 Outstanding private sector external debt 1987–2004

Year	Medium- and long-term debt (RM billion)	Short-term debt) (RM billion
1987	5.559	n. a.
1988	4.855	2.464
1989	4.613	3.343
1990	4.943	4.415
1991	6.723	7.171
1992	10.471	13.157
1993	15.498	17.320
1994	24.203	14.244
1995	28.080	16.204
1996	32.973	25.170
1997	62.081	43.257
1998	67.991	35.820
1999	64.315	22.427
2000	65.077	17.600
2001	57.604	24.072
2002	52.612	32.435
2003	56.232	33.571
2004	58.874	43.997

Source: Bank Negara (2005:126, table VIII.11).

external debt was less than RM5 billion, but thereafter grew at an average annual rate of 33.8 per cent, or from RM6.723 billion in 1991 to RM38.650 billion in June 1997 (table 6.3 below).

From 1992 to 1996, net inflows of portfolio investment funds ranged from RM5.345 billion (1995) to RM24.667 billion (1993) (table 6.4 below) and helped to boost KLSE's growth (table 6.5 below).

TABLE 6.4 Portfolio investment in shares and corporate securities 1991–2004

Year	Receipts (RM million)	Payments (RM million)	Net inflow (RM million)
1991	13 645	15 524	−1879
1992	33 324	26 481	6843
1993	116 743	92 076	24 667
1994	129 953	115 521	14 432
1995	90 987	85 642	5345
1996	127 590	120 899	6691
1997	113 212	138 675	−25 463
1998	40 846	42 309	−1463
1999	33 266	32 747	519
2000	44 645	51 616	−6971
2001	24 112	26 670	−2558
2002	38 169	39 319	−1150
2003	52 408	44 108	8300
2004	76 169	60 437	15 732

Source: Bank Negara (2005:140, table VIII.16)

TABLE 6.5 Kuala Lumpur Stock Exchange, selected indicators 1990–2004

Year	Composite Index	Turnover (RM billion)	Number of listed companies	New share issues (RM billion)	Market capitalisation (RM billion)
1990	505.92	29.522	285	9463.5	131.66
1991	556.22	30.097	324	3160.4	161.29
1992	643.96	51.469	369	9546.3	245.82
1993	1275.32	387.276	413	3440.7	619.64
1994	971.21	328.057	478	8228.7	508.85
1995	995.17	178.859	529	13 057.9	565.63
1996	1237.96	463.265	621	14 958.0	806.77
1997	594.44	408.558	708	17 523.2	375.80
1998	586.13	115.181	736	1661.6	374.52
1999	812.33	185.250	757	6466.5	552.69
2000	679.64	244.054	795	5909.5	444.35
2001	696.09	85.012	812	4416.6	464.98
2002	646.32	116.951	865	12 883.4	481.62
2003	793.94	183.886	906	7667.5	640.28
2004	907.43	215.623	963	*	722.04

* Incomplete data from source; excluded.

Source: Bank Negara (2005:80, table V.12)

SEMI-AUTARCHY: THE STATE AGAINST THE MARKET

By 1991, the balance of power had settled upon fairly cordial relations between the state, foreign capital, and the domestic conglomerates. The NEP had been replaced with a National Development Plan (NDP), which emphasised growth rather than restructuring, although the NEP's ethnic considerations were retained in practice. State policies continued to privilege the MNCs and welcomed speculative capital that arrived as part of the international money market's investment in emerging markets. The conglomerates constituted a more self-confident national capital and enjoyed the status of the vanguard of Malaysia Inc. It took the 1997 East Asian financial crisis to threaten the survival of the conglomerates and upset the state's relations with the market or, more precisely, the international money market.

An understanding of the complexities of the origin and spread of the July 1997 crisis lies beyond the scope of this chapter (see chapters 1 and 10 in this volume). In Malaysia, the crisis depreciated the currency, reduced KLSE's market capitalisation, and sent the economy into recession. The ringgit fell from a peak exchange rate of RM2.493 to US$1 in April 1997 to its lowest rate of RM4.88 on 7 January 1998. KLSE's market capitalisation declined from RM806.77 billion in 1996 to RM375.80 billion in 1997 and RM182 billion in September 1998. These currency and share price falls spared few, whether they were businesses dependent on imports, middle-class punters who had channelled savings into KLSE, or students abroad whose state- or family-borne expenses were denominated in foreign exchange.

But the conglomerates seemed destined to collapse first and spectacularly. Their dependence on external borrowings and stockmarket capitalisation had exposed them to bloated loan repayments, plunging asset values, and imminent insolvency. The financial system was imperilled as the banking sector's non-performing loans (NPLs) rose from 4 per cent in 1997 to 15.8 per cent in August 1998.[9] Worse, the money market and the IMF insisted that crisis management required the remedies of currency floats, higher interest rates, restrained liquidity, market liberalisation, financial sector reform, and good governance. Any of these remedies, properly applied, would have been bitter medicine for the conglomerates. Taken together they would have been fatal to Malaysia Inc.: a free market would govern a non-interventionist state,

Those who led the state were compelled to negotiate a new stance vis-à-vis the money market. Their initial attempts backfired when, in August 1997, the KLSE banned the short selling of 100 index-linked stocks, hoping to arrest the share price decline (Hiebert & Jayasankaran 1997). In September, the regime announced a RM60 billion fund that would selectively buy stocks from Malaysians but not from foreigners (Hiebert & Jayasankaran 1998). Those measures were swiftly reversed or modified after share prices plunged as stocks were dumped by fund managers who feared being locked into a falling market. Then followed attempts by Deputy Prime Minister and Minister of Finance Anwar Ibrahim, and Daim Zainuddin (appointed executive director of the newly established National Economic Action Council) to placate investor confidence. The 1998 Budget, presented by Anwar in October, showed fiscal restraint, made budget cuts, and adopted some IMF-type structural adjustment measures.[10] In December, Anwar announced stricter austerity measures.[11] A month later, the Foreign Investment Committee changed corporate takeover rules. It permitted United Engineers Malaysia to acquire 32.6 per cent of its parent company, Renong Berhad (UMNO's holding company) without making a general offer to shareholders (Fox 1998; Lim Kit Siang 1998:45–7, 130–5; RAM 1997). Market dismay sent the ringgit and the Kuala Lumpur Composite Index to their lowest levels (Shameen 1998; Tripathi 1998). In March, Petronas took control of Malaysian International Shipping Corporation, while the latter acquired the shipping assets of Konsortium Perkapalan Berhad, which was 51 per cent owned by Mahathir's son, Mirzan Mahathir (Subramaniam 1998:2–5). Further plans were announced to rescue debt-ridden banks and companies (Jayasankaran 1998; Shameen 1998). In response, capital flight became a capital strike: the market would not return if the state could not be disciplined.

On 1 September 1998, the state showed a desperate resolve. BNM instituted 'exchange control mechanisms' that ended the free convertibility of the ringgit (*New Straits Times* [*NST*] 2 September 1998). The ringgit, traded at

RM4.0960 to US$1 on that day, was pegged at RM3.800 to US$1 the next day. Holders of offshore ringgit accounts were given a month to repatriate their funds to Malaysia: beginning 1 October, the ringgit could not be traded overseas. For the money market, the most serious controls were those that prohibited non-resident correspondent banks and stockbroking firms from obtaining domestic credit facilities, and residents from obtaining ringgit credit facilities from non-resident individuals. Non-residents were required to deposit their ringgit securities with authorised depositories and to hold the proceeds from the sale of such securities in external accounts for at least one year before converting them to foreign currency (*NST* 2 September 1998). BNM insisted that the controls would curb currency speculation but not affect the 'general convertibility of current account transactions' and 'free flows of direct foreign investment and repatriation of interest, profits and dividends and capital' (*NST* 2 September 1998). But had the state not acted, in BNM Acting Governor's words, to 'bring the ringgit back into the country' (*NST* 2 September 1998), the currency would have collapsed. Instead, the capital controls halted the trend of capital flight, if only by trapping remaining foreign funds for a year, and even reversed it, if only by forcing the return of offshore ringgit funds. The currency peg gave domestic businesses and foreign direct investment a measure of stability by which to plan, contract, and manage.

Mahathir and Daim's political priority was to save strategic economic sectors and the conglomerates by domestic initiative. They had nothing better. Capital outflow for 1998 was RM21.7 billion (Mahani 2000:185). And capital was still on strike. Rating agencies—Moodys, and Standard and Poor's—downgraded Malaysia's credit worthiness when the regime planned to issue new bonds, and the plan was abandoned. Thus the capital controls presaged a semi-autarkic regime of reflating the economy, relaxing monetary policy, and resuscitating local business.[12] The state established three institutions to deal with the financial system. Danaharta, an asset management company, took charge of 'remov(ing) NPLs from the balance sheets of financial institutions', thus 'free(ing) the banks from the burden of debts that had prevented them from providing loans to their customers' (Mahani 2000:186). In 1999, Danaharta purchased RM45.5 billion in NPLs from banks and financial institutions. Danamodal, a special-purpose vehicle, recapitalised the financial sector by giving credit injections totalling RM7.59 billion to leading banks. The Corporate Debt Restructuring Committee (CDRC) managed sixty-seven debt-restructuring applications involving RM36.3 billion. CDRC's best known and most controversial applications came from the UMNO-owned Renong, the state-owned Bank Bumiputra, and Sime Bank. Recapitalisation largely depended on three sources: public funds (notably the Employees Provident Fund and Petronas's reserves), external loans (from Japan and the World Bank), and bonds that were eventually issued. BNM increased liquidity and facilitated bank lending to the corporate sector. BNM steadily lowered the banks' statutory reserve requirements from 13.5 per cent to 4 per cent between February and September 1998. From June to October, the base lending rate was reduced from 12.27 per cent to 6.79 per cent. The classification of NPLs was changed back from three months (March 1998) to six months (September 1998). BNM directed a higher target for bank lending. It made credit more easily available for private consumption (and on more favourable terms than those of pre-July 1997) to support key sectors, such as the automobile industry and the property market.

A NEW COMPROMISE

The state's recapitalisation, rescue, and reflation scarcely accorded with the reforms the money market had demanded of Asian crisis-stricken regimes.[13] Yet, by late 1999, trade surpluses had built up the country's reserves and the economy began to emerge from recession. Share prices had recovered substantially with the support of domestic institutional funds. The regime claimed to have reversed 'the wrong turns taken during the initial stage of the crisis'[14] (by Anwar, that is, in his last year as minister of finance). Critics attributed the end of recession to a regional recovery and a fortuitous growth in exports. They insisted that the controls could not work in the long run and harmed Malaysia's position as a destination of foreign investment.[15] But the capital controls had already been relaxed in February 1999 to permit the repatriation of foreign funds subject to a graduated exit tax. Some investment funds (notably, Templeton) were adamant about staying away from Malaysia, even after September 1999 when the trapped funds could exit without penalty. Still, the government and Petronas were able to raise bonds of US$1 billion and US$500 million respectively from the money market, albeit with Japanese backing and at punitive premiums. And Morgan Stanley Capital International reincorporated Malaysia in its index by early 2000, which paved the way for fund managers to re-enter KLSE. In short, the money market had reached a rapprochement with the state despite disagreements in principle. Or, as an *Asian Wall Street Journal* editorial (23 June 1999) cajoled Mahathir, 'Now that the pressure of the Asian crisis has abated, it's time to declare victory and rejoin the global economy.'

As with the 1985–86 recession, July 1997 brought with it a political crisis. Mahathir and Anwar had subtly differed over the waiver of UEM's takeover of Renong, rescue plans for several conglomerates, monetary policy, and the need for reform. Anwar seemed to heed the sentiments of several non-unified constituencies: technocrats, small businesses, and part of the Malay and non-Malay middle classes.[16] The Mahathir–Anwar differences represented a 'policy gridlock' (Saludo & Shameen 1998:44) that showed the narrowing of options available to the political leadership. Mahathir himself despaired that market demands had changed from the management of economic fundamentals to acceptance of IMF conditions, forced closures of financial institutions, opening corporations to foreign ownership, and, ultimately, to changes of government (*Time* 15 June 1998). It was over this last point that Anwar fell. At the June 1998 UMNO general assembly, his allies staged a half-hearted criticism of Mahathir, which signalled Anwar's readiness to replace Mahathir—which was, coincidentally, the ill-disguised hope of the money market, international institutions, and media then. On 2 September, Mahathir sacked Anwar from the government.[17] After that Anwar was expelled from UMNO, prosecuted and convicted in two trials, and imprisoned for fifteen years. Rarely have technocratic policy choices so skimpily covered their political substance. An account of the Anwar affair, the movement for reform (*reformasi*) that it sparked, and UMNO's unprecedented loss of Malay support in the November 1999 election belongs elsewhere (Khoo 2003). What is relevant here is that Barisan Nasional's electoral victory, however flawed, left policy direction in Mahathir and Daim's hands, and left unreformed the conglomerates allied to them.

Many far-reaching, post-1969 developments were linked to the fluctuating fortunes of the Bumiputera Commercial and Industrial Community (BCIC). Political conflict, rooted in a complex matrix of ethnic aspirations, class ambitions, and changing state–market relations, frequently enmeshed the state's project to social-engineer a BCIC via the NEP and raise it to pre-eminence via Malaysia Inc. Likewise, instability dogged the state's efforts to reorient the BCIC by holding the NEP in abeyance and rescue it from disaster via an economic shield of capital controls and reflation. With its relative success in confronting the money market, the state gained a reprieve for the Malay conglomerates. Where they could, Danaharta, Danamodal, and the CDRC repaired the financial system and saved ailing, mostly Malay-owned, companies. Where it was unavoidable, the state re-nationalised previously privatised corporations and large-scale projects, including the Malaysian Airlines System, the sewage treatment company Indah Water Konsortium, and the light-rail operators PUTRA and STAR.

Still, so many of the Malay conglomerates had virtually collapsed at their first serious encounter with globalisation that Mahathir had to reconsider the wisdom of picking winners to spearhead the BCIC's progress. Moreover, the scepticism of investors over the regime's commitment to transparency and good governance prevented a full return of foreign investment (Rodan 2004:131–2). Thus, the final years of the Mahathir regime oversaw an obdurate but inconsistent defence of a hard-won foothold for Malay capital. Mahathir maintained the policy of privileging Malay entrepreneurs by seeking out promising ones, although there was no assurance that the newly chosen would not go the same way as the tainted ones, who had been lionised before they failed. Mahathir would not abandon NEP restructuring, but re-emphasised Malay self-reliance, competitiveness, and meritocracy. He posed a 'second Malay dilemma ... whether [the Malays] should or should not do away with the crutches that they have got used to, which in fact they have become proud of' (Mahathir 2002). In that ideological mood, apologising for having failed the Malays but exasperated that the Malays had failed him, Mahathir announced his retirement at the UMNO General Assembly in June 2002. A transition plan, hastily drawn up by the UMNO leadership, kept Mahathir in office until Abdullah Ahmad Badawi succeeded him in November 2003.

Political economy is not about state power and elite behaviour alone. But, given the thematic concerns of this volume, one might observe that Malaysian political economy under Abdullah's regime rests on a tripartite division of power—among the state, foreign capital, and domestic capital—as it has done since 1957. There have been significant changes, of course. Once, the state governed the market in the mould of an East Asian developmental state. Now, its scope of freedom has been curtailed. Foreign capital is not just the foreign direct investment welcomed by the state, but includes a globalising speculative capital that the state treats with caution. And domestic capital is not pre-NEP Chinese capital, but a conglomerate-dominated national capital whose ranks have been filled, however imperfectly, by the BCIC.

Hence, Abdullah Badawi's regime was bound to maintain the stability of the tripartite division of power while trying to resolve some problems of late Mahathirism—the alienation of the Malay electorate over the Anwar Ibrahim affair, the persistence of pump priming measures, and the stagnation of NEP restructuring. Beginning in November 2003, Abdullah de-Mahathirised the system, so to speak, by improving governance to check the excesses of Malaysia Inc. Two important examples of this trend were the indefinite postponement of a multibillion ringgit double-track railway project (controversially awarded to MMC-Gamuda just before Mahathir retired) and the delay of the listing of the Federal Land Development Authority on the Kuala Lumpur Stock Exchange (that Mahathir's last budget recommended in September 2003). Among other things, Abdullah's decisions signalled the regime's concession to foreign capital's demands for best practices that could not be ignored by a state already disadvantaged by external competition and investor scepticism in attracting new investment flows. Abdullah also began to reduce the budget deficits[18]—associated with mega projects, bailouts, and pump priming—and to use a show of fiscal prudence to enforce adherence to other prudential standards.

At the popular level, Abdullah indirectly responded to *reformasi's* attacks on corruption, cronyism, and nepotism by launching an anti-corruption drive—an investigation of an alleged award of thousands of taxi permits to an individual applicant (*NST* 5, 8, and 9 December 2003), an investigation of suspected collusion of Customs officers in the import of luxury cars without payment of duties (*NST* 18 November 2003), the arrest of the head of a Malacca government corporation for suspected bribery (*NST* 28 November 2003), and the removal of a bankrupt from a Malacca district council (*NST* 20 November 2003). Subsequently, a former minister, Kasitah Gadam, and

Eric Cheah, the former head of Perwaja, the state's steel mill, were charged with corruption. The low- to medium-level anti-corruption drive was popular even if it was unclear whether Abdullah would impose stronger regulation and stricter performance standards to remove or diminish significantly the rentierism and money politics of the elite politico–corporate networks. Equally popular were Abdullah's other decisions—to dismiss an Employees Provident Fund proposal to disallow its contributors to withdraw part of their contributions prior to their retirement (*NST* 11 December 2003) and to introduce a RM200 million tuition scheme designed to help 500 000 poor pupils, of all races, in urban and rural areas, to cope with the change from teaching science and mathematics in Malay to English. These initiatives, crucially plebeian in contrast to Mahathir's penchant for mega projects, bespoke a sensitivity towards rural Malay communities, the civil service, and the UMNO grassroots. In the March 2004 general election, UMNO recovered virtually all its losses in the previous election.

CONCLUSION

One problem remains intractable: the Malay share of corporate equity failed to reach 30 per cent (see table 6.1 above), as targeted by the NEP for 1990. At its general assembly in July 2005, UMNO claimed that the failure was caused by the leakage of Malay state-awarded assets owing to the prevalence of rent-seeking practices and money politics over thirty-five years. UMNO's stance was predictable: it demanded that the state should explicitly renew the NEP's 30 per cent restructuring requirement. Naturally, this demand provoked disbelief—not confined to non-Malays—that pre-UMNO general assembly rhetoric about nurturing highly competitive and self-reliant 'towering [Malay] personalities' should culminate in a demand for more crutches. By posing the failure of the conglomerates as the flaws of an entire community, UMNO under Abdullah aims to travel once more the route of promoting class interests in the name of ethnic backwardness. This time, however, the discussion of the NEP's renewal may take on starker class dimensions: there were formulaic references to Malay poverty and relative backwardness, but the focus was on corporate ownership—the only basis upon which Malay capital, backed by state power, knows how to consolidate itself. On 20 July 2005, the final remnant of the 1998 capital controls was removed: the ringgit was unpegged from the US dollar. But it remains to be seen whether, under global circumstances very unlike those of the original NEP, ethnic concerns can be unpegged from class interests.

NOTES

1 Originally, ICA provisions applied to any manufacturing firm having at least RM100 000 in shareholder capital and employing a minimum of twenty-five workers.

2 Tengku Razaleigh Hamzah, who led the passage of the offending legislation, resigned as head of Petronas.

3 Commodity export earnings were RM37.6 billion in 1985, instead of the RM63.1 billion forecast by the economic planners after a threefold increase in earnings in 1975–80 (Jomo et al. 1996:80).

4 Public debt rose from RM34.16 billion in 1981 to RM87.06 billion in 1986 because of NEP-based deficit spending, the HICOM projects, and the post-1985 Plaza Accord yen appreciation (Jomo et al. 1996:80).

5 Development expenditures were RM6.756 billion in 1985 and RM7.521 billion in 1986 compared with RM11.189 billion for 1982. Total private investment fell from RM13.3 billion in 1984 to RM10.1 billion in 1986, while foreign corporate investment fell from RM3.26 billion in 1982 to RM1.73 billion in 1985, and RM1.26 billion in 1986 (Jomo, Khoo & Chang 1996:80–1).

6 See Jomo (1995:44–8) for a discussion of the cases of the North–South Highway, Sistem Televisyen (Malaysia) Berhad, Sports Toto, Pan Malaysian Sweeps, Totalisator Board of Malaysia, Jalan Kuching-Jalan Kepong Interchange, Indah Water Konsortium, Bakun Hydroelectric Project, Food Industries of Malaysia, and Peremba Berhad.

7 For excellent profiles and case studies of some of the conglomerates, see Gomez (1990, 1994) and Searle (1999).

8 Gomez and Jomo (1997:179–80) observed of the contemporary conglomerate style of growth that it has increasingly involved 'mergers, acquisitions and asset-stripping, with scant regard for relevant experience and expertise' and that it reflected 'the greater attention to financial accumulation rather than the difficult but ultimately necessary development of internationally competitive productive capacities'.

9 The official working definition of an NPL changed twice in 1998.

10 These included reducing federal government expenditure by 2 per cent, postponing mega projects, reducing the current account deficit, reducing corporate tax by 2 per cent, limiting credit growth to 15 per cent by the end of 1998, and consolidating the prudential standards and regulations covering non-performing loans, liquidity within the banking system (Malaysia 1998:chapter 1).

11 Significant measures included a reduction of the current account deficit to 3 per cent of GNP in 1998, an 18 per cent reduction in federal government expenditure in 1998, a lowering of the projected 1998 growth rate to between 4 per cent and 5 per cent, deferment of non-strategic projects, stricter criteria for approvals of reverse investment, enhanced corporate information disclosure, and closer regulation of corporate restructuring (Malaysia 1998:chapter 1).

12 The government's policies are set out in the White Paper, *Status of the Malaysian Economy*, <www.topspot.com/NEAC/>.

13 Jorgen Borhnoft, outgoing president of the Malaysian International Chamber of Commerce and Industry, expressed MICCI's 'concern that there does not seem to be enough strong action against those people who were responsible for that massive spate of irresponsible borrowing, and just as irresponsible lending', mentioned that MICCI supported the capital controls of September 1999 'on the basis that they are clearly seen to be short-term measures', and urged 'serious structural adjustments' to some troubled companies (Dow Jones 1999) .

14 *Status of the Malaysian Economy*, Box 1 (see references, this chapter).

15 See 'Capital controls erode', <www.freemalaysia.com/economic/loss_of_control.htm> for a neoliberal criticism of the capital controls.

16 The BNM and Treasury technocrats offered economistic solutions—imposing budget cuts, reducing credit growth, raising interest rates, controlling inflation, and stabilising the ringgit. Small businesses, including small Malay businesses, were not indifferent to arguments for disciplining the conglomerates.

17 A few days earlier, BNM Governor Ahmad Don and his deputy, Fong Weng Phak, resigned over disagreement with Mahathir's decision to implement exchange controls (Keenan et al 1998:11).

18 Jayasankaran (2003) gives a summary of rising budget deficits, from 3.2 per cent of GDP in 1999 to an estimated 5.6 per cent of GDP in 2002.

REFERENCES

Abdul Rahman, Embong (1995) 'Malaysian Middle Classes: Some Preliminary Observations', *Jurnal Antropologi dan Sosiologi*, 22:31–54.

Adam, Christopher and Cavendish, William (1995a) 'Background', in Jomo K. S. (ed.) *Privatizing Malaysia: Rents, Rhetoric, Realities*, Boulder: Westview Press, pp. 11–41

——(1995b) 'Early Privatizations', in Jomo K. S. (ed.) *Privatizing Malaysia: Rents, Rhetoric, Realities*, Boulder: Westview Press, pp. 98–137

Alatas, Syed Hussein (1977) *The Myth of the Lazy Native*, London: Frank Cass.

Ariff, Mohamed (1996) 'Effects of Financial Liberalization on Four Southeast Asian Financial Markets, 1973–94', *ASEAN Economic Bulletin*, 12(3)(March):325–38.

Bank Negara (2005) *Monthly Statistical Bulletin*, June.

Crouch, Harold (1980) 'The UMNO Crisis: 1975–1977', in Harold Crouch, Lee Kam Hing and Michael Ong (eds) *Malaysian Politics and the 1978 Election*, Kuala Lumpur: Oxford University Press, pp. 11–36

Dow Jones (1999) 'Foreign investors want more reform: MICCI', 15 June, <www.freemalaysia.com/reformasi_investors.htm>.

Financial Times (1995) *Banking in the Far East 1995*, London: FT Financial Publishing.

Fox, Justin (1998) 'The Great Emerging Markets Rip-Off', *Fortune*, 11 May 1998, <www.pathfinder.com/fortune/1998/980511/gre.html>.

Gomez, Edmund Terence (1990) *UMNO's Corporate Investments*, Kuala Lumpur: Forum.

——(1994) *Political Business: Corporate Involvement of Malaysian Political Parties*, Townsville: James Cook University of North Queensland, Centre for South-East Asian Studies.

——and Jomo K. S. (1997) *Malaysia's Political Economy: Politics, Patronage and Profits*, Cambridge: Cambridge University Press.

Grace, Brewster (1976), 'The Politics of Distribution in Malaysia', *American Universities Field Staff Report*, 24(9).

Heng Pek Koon (1992) 'The Chinese Business Elite of Malaysia', in Ruth McVey (ed.), *Southeast Asian Capitalists*, Ithaca: Cornell University Press Southeast Asia Program, pp. 127–44.

Hiebert, Murray and S. Jayasankaran (1997) 'What Next?', *Far Eastern Economic Review*, 18 September: 62–64.

Husin Ali, Syed (1975) *Malay Peasant Society and Leadership*, Kuala Lumpur: Oxford University Press.

Jayasankaran, S. (1998) 'Art of the Bail', *Far Eastern Economic Review*, 30 April:62–3.

——(2003) 'Bated Breath', *Far Eastern Economic Review*, May 15:44.

Jesudason, James V. (1989) *Ethnicity and the Economy: The State, Chinese Business, and Multinationals in Malaysia*, Singapore: Oxford University Press.

Jomo K. S. (1988) *A Question of Class: Capital, the State, and Uneven Development in Malaya*, Singapore: Oxford University Press.

——(1990) *Growth and Structural Change in the Malaysian Economy*, London: Macmillan.

——(1995) 'Overview', in Jomo K. S. (ed.) *Privatizing Malaysia: Rents, Rhetoric, Realities*, Boulder: Westview Press, pp. 42–60.

——(1998) 'Malaysia: From Miracle to Debacle', in Jomo K. S. (ed.), *Tigers in Trouble: Financial Governance, Liberalisation and Crises in East Asia*, London: Zed Books, 181–98.

——, Khoo Boo Teik and Chang Yii Tan (1996) 'Vision, Policy, and Governance in Malaysia', in Leila Frischtak and Izak Atiyas, *Governance, Leadership, and Communication: Building*

Constituencies for Economic Reform, Washington, DC: World Bank, pp. 65–89.
Keenan, Faith (1998) 'Desperate Measures', *Far Eastern Economic Review*, 10 September:11–12.
Khoo Boo Teik (1995) *Paradoxes of Mahathirism: An Intellectual Biography of Mahathir Mohamad*, Kuala Lumpur: Oxford University Press.
——(2003) *Beyond Mahathir: Malaysian Politics and its Discontents*, London and New York: Zed Books.
Khoo Khay Jin (1992) 'The Grand Vision: Mahathir and Modernisation', in Joel S. Kahn and Francis Loh Kok Wah (eds) *Fragmented Vision: Culture and Politics In Contemporary Malaysia*, Sydney: Allen & Unwin, pp. 44–76.
Lim Kit Siang (1998) *Economic and Financial Crisis*, Petaling Jaya: Democratic Action Party.
Lim Teck Ghee (1984) 'British Colonial Administration and the "Ethnic Division of Labour" in Malaya', *Kajian Malaysia*, 2(2) (December):28–66.
Machado, Kit (1989–90) 'Japanese Transnational Corporations in Malaysia's State Sponsored Heavy Industrialization Drive: The HICOM Automobile and Steel Projects', *Pacific Affairs*, 62:504–31.
Mahani Zainal Abidin (2000) 'Malaysia's Alternative Approach to Crisis Management', in *Southeast Asian Affairs 2000*, Singapore: Institute of Southeast Asian Studies, pp. 184–99.
Mahathir Mohamad (1970) *The Malay Dilemma*, Singapore: Donald Moore.
——(1991) 'Malaysia: The Way Forward', *New Straits Times*, 2 March.
——(2002) 'The New Malay Dilemma', *New Straits Times*, 30 July.
Malaysia (1965) *First Malaysia Plan 1966–1970*, Kuala Lumpur: Malaysian Government.
——(1971) *Second Malaysia Plan 1971–1975*, Kuala Lumpur: Malaysian Government.
——(1976) *Third Malaysia Plan 1976–1980*, Kuala Lumpur: Malaysian Government.
——(1981) *Fourth Malaysia Plan 1981–1985*, Kuala Lumpur: Malaysian Government.
——(1998), *National Economic Recovery Plan: Agenda For Action*, Kuala Lumpur: Malaysian Government.
——(1999) *Kajian Separuh Penggal Rancangan Malaysia Ketujuh 1996–2000* (Mid-term Review of the Seventh Malaysia Plan 1996–2000), Kuala Lumpur: Malaysian Government.
——(2003) *Mid-Term Review of the Eighth Malaysia Plan 2001–2005*, Kuala Lumpur: Malaysian Government.
Mehmet, Ozay (1986) *Development in Malaysia: Poverty, Wealth and Trusteeship*, London: Croom Helm.
Parti Gerakan Rakyat Malaysia (1984) *The National Economic Policy—1990 and Beyond*, Kuala Lumpur.
Puthucheary, James (1960) *Ownership and Control in the Malayan Economy*, Singapore: Eastern Universities Press.
RAM (1998) 'The NEAC: Accountability Subverted', *Aliran Monthly*, 18(2):2–5.
Robison, Richard, Garry Rodan and Kevin Hewison (1997), 'Introduction', in Garry Rodan, Kevin Hewison and Richard Robison (1997) *The Political Economy of South-East Asia: An Introduction*, Melbourne: Oxford University Press, pp. 1–28.
Rodan, Garry (2004) *Transparency and Authoritarian Rule in Southeast Asia: Singapore and Malaysia*, London: RoutledgeCurzon.
Rugayah, Mohamed (1995) 'Public Enterprises', in Jomo K. S. (ed.) *Privatizing Malaysia: Rents, Rhetoric, Realities*, Boulder: Westview Press, pp. 63–80.
Saludo, Richard and Shameen, Assif (1998). 'How Much Longer?', *Asiaweek*, 17 July:36–44.
Searle, Peter (1999) *The Riddle of Malaysian Capitalism: Rent-seekers or real capitalists?*, Sydney: Allen & Unwin.
Shameen, Assif (1998) 'The Bailout Business', *Asiaweek*, 27 March:30–31.
Sieh Lee Mei Ling (1992) 'The Transformation of Malaysian Business Groups', in Ruth McVey (ed.), *Southeast Asian Capitalists*, Ithaca: Cornell University Southeast Asia Program, pp. 103–26.

Subramaniam, Pillay (1998) 'Bailout Blues', *Aliran Monthly*, 18, 3:2–5.

Todd, Patricia and Jomo K. S. (1994) *Trade Unions and the State in Peninsular Malaysia*, Kuala Lumpur: Oxford University Press.

Toh, Eddie (1998) 'Cutting rates will put M'sian financial system at risk: Anwar', *Business Times* (Singapore), 2 June.

Tripathi, Salil (1998) 'Savings at Risk', *Far Eastern Economic Review*, 30 April:60–1.

von Vorys, Karl (1975) *Democracy Without Consensus: Communalism and Political Stability in Malaysia*, Princeton: Princeton University Press.

World Bank (1993) *The East Asian Miracle: Economic Growth and Public Policy*, New York: Oxford University Press.

Zainal Aznam Yusof, Awang Adek Hussin, Ismail Alowi, Lim Chee Sing and Sukhdare Sing (1996) 'Financial Reform in Malaysia', in Gerard Caprio, Izak Atiyas and James A. Hanson (eds), *Financial Reform: Theory and Experience*, Cambridge, Cambridge University Press, pp. 276–320.

Newspapers, magazines, and news services

Asian Wall Street Journal (*AWSJ*)
Far Eastern Economic Review (*FEER*)
Financial Times (*FT*)
New Straits Times (*NST*)
Time

7

Vietnam: the Transition from Central Planning

Melanie Beresford

KEY TOPICS

INTRODUCTION

VIETNAM is unique among the countries covered in this book in that it is in the process of transition from central planning to a market economy. To understand the special characteristics of this transition we need first to comprehend the nature of the socialist economy as it developed between 1954 and 1980—the social basis of the state and the way in which interests of different groupings in society were represented within the state apparatus, which are what gave Vietnamese socialism its particular institutions and economic structure. During the 1980s, these began to undergo dramatic changes, partly as a result of spontaneous developments at the grassroots level and partly as a result of state efforts to manage the process. The structure and institutions that Vietnam has today can be understood only as the outcome of a protracted struggle among various interests over the shape of the socialist state, a struggle that necessitated constant reform and that has, ultimately, led to the demise of the planned economy. As one Vietnamese intellectual put it to this author, 'The system was patched and repaired so many times that it was eventually repaired out of existence. It became something quite different.' The relations of power that developed throughout this process of struggle and reform are evident in the existing institutions and structure that give the Vietnamese market economy its peculiar characteristics today. Although the ultimate result of the current market-oriented transformation might be some form of capitalism, Vietnam is still ruled by a communist party, the distinction between public and private property remains blurred, and there is continuing pressure from parts of the state to defend the rights of workers and poor peasants. This means that the path is still unclear and likely to be characterised by considerable social and political tensions in future.

This chapter first gives a brief outline of the division of the country between north and south during 1954–75 and the attempts to construct rival socialist and capitalist economies in the two halves (more detail can be found in Beresford 1988). There follows a discussion of the socialist reality in North Vietnam, focusing on the role that economic interest played in creating the north's economic structure and institutions and the forces generating the transition process, particularly after reunification of the country in 1976. The third section looks at developments since the Sixth Communist Party Congress in 1986 at which the historic decision to institute *doi moi* (renovation) was taken. It focuses on the interaction between interests and policy in promoting—or obstructing—change, and discusses the ways in which contending social forces organise and find expression within the framework of a communist party state. The final section discusses the major issues in contention today.

HISTORICAL BACKGROUND

For two decades, from 1954 to 1975, two separate regimes claimed sovereignty over the whole of Vietnam. The Democratic Republic of Vietnam (DRV) was based in the northern half of the country, with its capital at Hanoi. Following the surrender of Japan, the north was established on 2 September 1945 by an indigenous nationalist movement, the Viet Minh, led by the Vietnamese Communist Party. It had fought and won a nine-year war against France's attempt to retake its former colony, a war that culminated in the humiliating French defeat at Dien Bien Phu in 1954. During this war, the Viet Minh had extended its control over nearly three-quarters of the country, although the French and some indigenous anti-communist groups had managed to retain the main cities and some of the rural areas, particularly in the far south. The inability of the communist-led movement to win decisively in the south provided the basis for the formation of an alternative regime, initially led by the Emperor Bao Dai, who was favoured by the French to promote their own interests. As the French war effort faltered, the US increasingly took over the role of preserving Western interests in Indochina and, by 1955, had installed a political leader in Saigon, Ngo Dinh Diem, less subservient to the French. From that year, the southern regime became known as the Republic of Vietnam (RVN).

During 1954, an international conference held at Geneva had temporarily divided the country at the seventeenth parallel, with an agreement to hold reunifying elections in 1956. Knowing that the Viet Minh would have won easily, the Diem regime and its US supporters refused to hold these elections. Between 1956 and 1959, the struggle between the regime and the southern Viet Minh gradually escalated until, in 1960, the DRV officially formed the National Front for the Liberation of Southern Vietnam (NLF) and began a war to reunify the country. US combat troops were introduced in 1964 and systematic bombing of the DRV by the US Air Force began in 1965; it lasted until 1968. By 1969, the US had more than half a million troops in the country and yet it had become clear by then that no end was in sight. For all the expense and effort that the US had put into defending the RVN, the communists' Tet (Vietnamese New Year) offensive in early 1968 had driven home the lesson that US war strategies were not working. In the US itself, the war became increasingly unacceptable politically and, by 1973, the last US troops were withdrawn. Within two years, the RVN collapsed completely and, on 30 April 1975, DRV armed forces entered Saigon.

The economic policies pursued in the two halves of Vietnam between 1954 and 1980 reflected the different social bases of the regimes. In the case of the DRV, its economic structure was, initially, developed in response to the needs of the peasantry, who constituted more than 80 per cent of the population, although their interests and those of the state were later to diverge in ways that, as we shall see, led to pressure for reform. The RVN, on the other hand, drew its support from a much narrower base—large landowners, the small indigenous capitalist class, and the bureaucrats.

Popular support for the DRV in the northern half of the country was consolidated during the 1950s by agrarian reform policies, beginning with rent-reduction campaigns from 1951 and culminating in land reform during 1954–56 that saw 810 000 hectares redistributed from landlords and rich peasants to poor and middle peasants (Moise 1976; White 1983).[1] However, a push from the poorest farmers and more radical sections of the party spilled over into the collectivisation of agriculture, commencing as a spontaneous movement during 1957–58, but acquiring an element of compulsion during 1959. Collectivisation had advantages for poor peasants because, even after land distribution, plot sizes in the crowded northern river deltas were often too small to provide an adequate subsistence, let alone surpluses. Moreover, poor peasants lacked draught animals, equipment, and access to irrigation water, and therefore faced potential economic insecurity. Collectivisation guaranteed access to these necessities, and provided minimum standards of nutrition, health, education, and welfare. From the point of view of the state, collectives were seen as a means of increasing agricultural productivity (through consolidation of fields, rehabilitation, and construction of large-scale irrigation works, more equal distribution of equipment and animals; and improvements in social security and living standards). This, in turn, would provide agricultural surpluses to finance industrialisation. Support for collectivisation also came from other socialist countries, notably, China.

Cooperatives were established in the rural economy in three stages, basically following the Chinese model of the mid 1950s and beginning with the formation of production solidarity groups, then graduating to lower-level cooperatives, in which land and equipment were collectivised and a small rent paid to their former owners, and, finally, to higher-level cooperatives in which all income was distributed according to a system of workpoints (Beresford 1988:130; Gordon 1981). By the mid 1960s, virtually the whole rural population had been incorporated into these higher-level cooperatives.

Industrial development in the north was to be carried out through a series of five-year plans (FYPs). Following nationalisation of the remaining French-owned plants, the first FYP was instituted for 1961–65 and resulted in the establishment of much new industrial capacity, which, in turn, was brought progressively under the control of Soviet-type planning institutions. Output targets and prices, input supplies, domestic wholesale and retail trade, and imports and exports were determined by central government, usually via the intermediary of provincial and district authorities. The planners intended to establish a vertically integrated economy in which individual production units had no commercial contact with each other, exchanging goods only with higher levels, which, in turn, distributed them according to plan. The State Bank of Vietnam was responsible for recording the value of transactions against the accounts of individual units and transferring revenue among these accounts and the state budget, thus eliminating the need for cash.

Renewed warfare against the US-backed southern regime created many difficulties for this newly created socialist economy; however, as we shall see below, the economic system itself was responsible for many of the problems besetting the DRV during the 1960s and 1970s. An overwhelming focus of the authorities on fighting war, their ability to rely on extensive aid from the Soviet Union and China, and strong popular support for the objective of national reunification meant that many of these economic problems were not tackled—or even regarded seriously—until much later. Indeed, most in authority genuinely believed that the wartime emergency called for stronger centralisation and planning rather than less. In the meantime, there occurred numerous (mostly illegal) experiments by individual households and production units aimed at overcoming the day-to-day difficulties imposed by the system. These experiments were, ultimately, to provide the foundations of the reformed economy.

Meanwhile, the southern half of the country continued to develop a capitalist economy. Although the narrow political base of the RVN regime ensured that the demands of the peasantry were largely ignored in areas under its control during the 1960s, land reforms were carried out by the NLF. Land ownership remained a contested issue until 1970–73, when the RVN decided to distribute land to the tiller, effectively legitimising occupancy under NLF reforms and, finally, resolving a problem that had led the majority of farmers to give their support to the communists. This reform came too late to save the RVN from military defeat, but it did have the effect of boosting agricultural production in the fertile Mekong River delta region as, with the ending of landlord domination, farmers gained control over their surplus output (Beresford 1989:66–7, 101–3; Ngo Vinh Long 1984).

During the war, US economic aid flowed into the RVN, enabling high levels of consumption of imported goods, which might, under normal circumstances, have boosted economic growth; however, speculative investments were encouraged by insecurity and inflation while productive investment suffered. Commerce, services, and bureaucracy expanded while the economy as a whole stagnated. Corruption became a serious problem in both civilian and military life. Refugees flooded into the main cities to escape the devastation of US bombing and chemical warfare, leading to the growth of slums and a large unemployed or semi-employed population. The complete withdrawal of US aid in 1975 thus provided the basis for a serious crisis of the southern economy, although the reformed agricultural sector also implied the possibility of a fairly rapid recovery. This recovery failed to materialise, largely because, after the official reunification in 1976, the DRV attempted to impose its own economic model on the south.

VIETNAMESE SOCIALIST ECONOMY AND PRESSURE FOR REFORM

Tensions over agrarian policy were already evident during the land reform of the 1950s, as many in the party leadership would have preferred a reform less damaging to the interests of rich and upper middle peasants whom they regarded as more productive and likely to foster rapid agricultural development. A rectification campaign carried out in 1956 went some way to redressing this problem, but tensions between poor and rich peasants, and among party factions remained. Although subsequent collectivisation appears to have had an impact in reducing tension (Elliott 1974; White 1983), it proceeded throughout the 1960s against some resistance from local forces. During 1960–63, the number of peasant households belonging to cooperatives actually fell, while there was an apparent lack of interest from upper middle and rich peasants, who provided a high proportion of membership and cooperative management boards (Gordon 1981:30–5). The move towards establishing higher-level cooperatives was renewed in 1964, but Adam Fforde's

(1989) detailed study of the cooperative management system during the 1970s shows that few actually functioned as the government intended. Instead, a wide variety of arrangements existed, including the extension of household plots beyond the 5 per cent of land officially permitted (often in favour of cadres and their families and friends) and the refusal by cooperative managers to issue plan targets. As with other socialist economies, Vietnam developed an outside (in the Vietnamese terminology) or second economy that, as we shall see, fed on the socialist structures and tended to undermine them in the long run.

The basic problem with cooperatives, not only in the north, but also in the south after 1976, lay in the lack of incentives for increased output and productivity. At the root of this problem was the official pricing system, which offered low procurement prices to cooperatives to maintain low wages in the urban sector and to boost industrial profits of state-owned enterprises. Market prices for agricultural produce and industrial goods, on the other hand, tended to be above the official prices from 1960 onwards, encouraging the diversion of state-supplied goods on to black markets and leading farmers to devote more time and effort to production on their household plots, the output from which could be legally sold on the free market. Estimates of peasant income earned from these plots rose from approximately 40 per cent in the 1960s to 60–70 per cent by the late 1970s. Because those with priority access to state-supplied goods were, generally, party members and officials, the system created opportunities for capital accumulation and new class divisions within the countryside. It is important to note here that it was their position within the cooperative structures that gave cadres such opportunities to profit from outside activities, one of the key factors that led to a widespread perception of the unfairness of the system.

Distribution of income within the cooperatives also created problems for increasing output and productivity. It was, in a formal sense, highly egalitarian, because minimum supplies of food and security of land tenure were guaranteed, and health, education, and other welfare facilities (such as childcare) were also provided to all members. The advantages to poor peasants and women were enormous: life expectancy, infant mortality, literacy levels, and other social indicators were all better than for other countries at similar per capita income levels (Beresford 1995). But these benefits came at a high cost, as cooperative production stagnated in the long term and egalitarianism became a case of shared poverty rather than rising overall living standards. Moreover, as demands from the government for procurement to feed urban cadres and industry rose, the residual output available for distribution to cooperative members declined, creating further incentives to reduce labour in cooperative fields and to increase that labour applied to household plots and to commercial activities outside the plan (Beresford 1989; Fforde 1989).

Conflict of interest was very apparent in the actual functioning of the cooperative system in Vietnamese agriculture. The needs of the poorest families for a more equal distribution differed from those of households most able to benefit from outside activities, as did those of cooperative farmers as a whole and those of the government. Pressure on lower-level and middle-level cadres tended to increase as, on one side, farmers' demands to reform the cooperative system increased and, on the other, the centre's procurement requirements also rose.[2] These contradictions only sharpened after reunification, particularly in the Mekong delta–Ho Chi Minh City region, where the market economy was firmly entrenched. The so-called middle peasants, the chief beneficiaries of land reforms in the 1960s and 1970s, stood to lose substantially through the collectivisation campaign of 1977–78. Their passive resistance meant that available surpluses dropped sharply (Beresford 1989: 113–15) and that black market activities intensified, despite the massive government clampdown on mainly ethnic Chinese businesses during 1978.

As Vietnam entered the 1980s, the scope of outside economic activity in the rural areas continued to increase and a powerful coalition of rural interests in favour of system reform began to emerge. Southern provincial politicians, in particular, fearing the loss of their peasant support base, became vocal spokespeople for change within the party and government apparatus. They found allies among the generation who had earlier argued that collectivisation in the north had gone too far.

A similar state of affairs existed within the state-owned industrial enterprise system, which had expanded rapidly following implementation of the First FYP (1961–65), but problems were already emerging (Fforde & Paine 1987) before US wartime operations destroyed much of the capacity created. High investment rates in industrial capacity, particularly in heavy industry projects with long lead times, created demand for resources that could not be met by the existing stream of output (Beresford 1989). Although the resulting shortages were, to some extent, alleviated by foreign aid, they were never eliminated altogether, and the Vietnamese economy, like other socialist economies, became characterised by chronic disequilibrium between supply and demand. Moreover, shortages within the planned sector were aggravated by the difference between official and market prices, which diverted resources to the outside economy (Fforde & Paine 1987).

In the debates over the reform of the economic system that began in the 1970s, two basic positions can be identified. The first essentially accepted the ability of planners to achieve an equilibrium growth path within the framework of central planning and, in general, opposed high rates of capital construction and insufficient attention to the real financial and resource capacity of the economy. The second located the real problem of the planned economy precisely in the attempt to achieve equilibrium by administrative means, and pointed to a built-in tendency to disequilibrium that could not be overcome due to the existence of real conflicts of interest. Once established, the shortage economy provides incentives to managers and planners that ensure that the tendency to disequilibrium is exacerbated rather than overcome (see Beresford 1989, and de Vylder & Fforde 1988, for a fuller discussion).

In reality, large capital construction projects involved vested interests among the ministries, managers, and employees engaged on them, so that simply scrapping them became politically difficult. Although the use of market forces and loose planning norms to allow more local initiative could alleviate the shortages, they threatened the positions of those in the central ministries whose control over resources was reduced and who exerted pressure to recentralise control. Market forces, on the other hand, allowed for the accumulation of capital independently of the centre. Such capital could be private, especially in the farm and retail sectors, but was more likely to take the form of corporatisation (that is, the separation of legal ownership and control) in the state-owned enterprise (SOE) sector (Beresford 1993). The ability of the planning authorities to reimpose centralisation after a period of decentralisation, then, depended crucially on its power vis-à-vis such relatively independent loci of capital accumulation.[3] The emergence of such capital accumulation in the periphery in Vietnam introduced not only a systemic tendency towards the breakdown of the planned economy, but also structural changes that laid the foundations for a relatively successful transition to a market economy.

In the political sphere, the ability and willingness of the state to reimpose centralisation determined whether the planned economy continued to exist in a recognisable form, or whether an irreversible transition was to take place. The planned economy in Vietnam was not a straightforward top–down system, but one in which the plan emerged as the outcome of a process of negotiation among groups with differing, often conflicting, interests. The most important interests that can be identified here are: first, those of central authorities whose power derived from the planning system and whose control was threatened by outside activity; second, those of local authorities and enterprise managers (including cooperative managers) who strove to minimise surplus extraction to higher levels and to accumulate capital within their own sphere; and, third, those who drew little benefit from the planning system due to lack of access to the kinship and/or party networks that held local power.

The process of negotiation among the contending factions and interests led to a balance of power that began to shift in the late 1970s and early 1980s. During 1979–81, a number of key reforms were pushed through that essentially legalised some outside activities conducted by individuals and production units. The earliest reforms, carried out in the second half of 1979, gave limited autonomy to farmers and enterprises. More important were the introduction of output contracts in agriculture in 1981 that permitted the allocation of cooperative land to production groups and the sale of surplus product on the free market, and the so-called Three Plan System in industry, which, for the first time, sanctioned production for the market by SOEs. In the same year, prices and wages were brought closer to market prices. By early 1982, a recovery was underway and party fears of the re-emergence of capitalism were renewed, causing the party to take measures against further private-sector development, including a renewed attempt to collectivise southern agriculture. However, the structural changes that had taken place after the second half of the 1970s meant that these attempts were only partially successful, if at all. The outside economy continued to expand, whereas the difficulties of the planned sector continued, not least because, in reality, the bulk of state investment still flowed into large-scale heavy industry projects. Shortages in the planned sector were exacerbated by the attempted recentralisation, leading to higher inflation in the increasingly monetised outside economy (176 per cent in 1984, according to the World Bank 1994:131). Moreover, the necessity to subsidise unprofitable SOEs contributed to high budget deficits, an inability to finance the external debt, and renewed stagnation in the agricultural sector.

In the face of the new crisis, in September 1985 the government introduced a further round of reforms aimed at price liberalisation, ending the ration system and monetisation of wages for state employees. By that time, almost all of the southern and central provinces, as well as a number in the north, were refusing to implement plan directives and/or pressuring the government for wider reform. However, the impact of this reform was blunted by several different political pressures on the government at this time. The southern provinces were already at a more advanced stage of commercialisation, had a correspondingly higher cost of living, and demanded big wage increases for government workers that resulted in large budget deficits. SOE directors, especially those in the older, less-efficient northern sector, demanded retention of the two-price system for industrial inputs.[4] Within three months of the reform's implementation, Vietnam had galloping inflation,[5] and the reform was partially reversed. Nevertheless, a further substantial shift towards the commercialisation of the economy had been achieved.

DOI MOI (RENOVATION)

By 1986, the Vietnamese socialist economy had already undergone major structural and institutional changes towards the formation of a market economy. Official statistics on this period do not reflect these changes because they continued to measure only the planned economic sector. However, other evidence indicates strongly that transactions taking place outside the scope of the plan were of increasing importance (de Vylder & Fforde 1988). Not only was a large proportion of agricultural output being marketed, but there were also signs of a rudimentary capital market as SOEs sought ways to util ise capital accumulated through non-plan activities. Under the impact of these developments, and due to the fact that the rationing system had largely disappeared after the 1985 reform, political pressure for further changes to the system increased.

Not enough research is available for a full understanding of how the Vietnamese political system works and how pressures from interests associated with increased commercialisation of the economy are translated into policy changes at the top.[6] The major reason for this is the essentially closed character of this system, and the concern of party leaders from earliest times to present a unified front to the rest of the world. As a result, we have little understanding of how political positions were achieved or, in other words, how the leadership gained its political constituency. What we do know is that several of the top leaders in Vietnam have held different political positions in relation to key issues, and that alliances within the leadership have often been quite fluid (Beresford 1988:88–90). This suggests that, far from being communist ideologues, the Vietnamese leaders have behaved much like politicians elsewhere, and that their power is contingent upon building coalitions of interest that provide support for particular sets of policies. It follows from this that, if the structure of interests changes substantially, the position of political leaders on questions such as reform must change accordingly. Members of key party organisations who continue to reflect the dominant interests of the old system are likely to be replaced by representatives of the new dominant interest groups.

This appears to be what happened at the Sixth Party Congress in December 1986. Membership changed in favour of a younger generation who had less experience of revolutionary activity and were more versed in the problems of managing the socialist economy, particularly at the local level. There was also increased representation in the highest positions of those with long experience in the south (Beresford 1988:113), a change that seems to reflect recognition of the relative success of the more commercialised southern region in overcoming the constraints of the planning system. Moreover, the emergence of reformers at the top opened the way for many more junior cadres to freely express their views.

DOI MOI IN THE ECONOMIC SPHERE

The 1986 congress was a turning point for the reform process in the sense that it took a conscious decision to build a market economy in Vietnam, although this was—and still is—portrayed by the party leadership as a socialist market or a market economy under state guidance.

By the late 1980s, the planned economy had disintegrated to the extent that there was no longer sufficient strength of interest in attempting to make it work. Even within the SOE sector, which had strongly resisted the proposal to implement market prices in 1985, there were differences of interest between those enterprises that continued to depend heavily on price subsidies and those in which the majority of their activities were, by now, market oriented. The upsurge of inflation during 1986 forced state sector workers, who were unable to survive on their official wages, to devote more and more time and effort to outside activities. Productivity in the SOEs declined, requiring higher levels of subsidy and generating yet more inflation through rising budget deficits. Although Soviet aid continued to be available in the late 1980s, the rise of Gorbachev to power and the introduction of perestroika (restructuring) in the Soviet Union in 1986 meant that aid would no longer be provided on the same generous terms as before (being finally cut in 1991). The Vietnamese state was now faced with a looming fiscal crisis that convinced even the highest levels that further reform was their only option. Whereas reform before 1986 was largely spontaneous in character, with the state attempting to manage (sometimes even reverse) the process of change, it is only after 1986 that we can speak of the state playing a role in pushing the pace of change.

The reforms of the late 1980s are widely regarded in the Western literature as the only ones of importance. Indeed, several authors have described the reform package of 1989, in particular, as constituting a big bang or shock therapy type of reform that introduced a market economy in Vietnam for the first time. What we have seen in this chapter, however, is that a market economy had been developing in Vietnam since the late 1970s. To understand the relative success of these reforms in Vietnam (as compared, for example, with the results of shock therapy in some East European countries or in the Soviet Union), it is important to understand that, to all intents and purposes, the Vietnamese economy by the late 1980s was already a market economy. Policies designed for a market economy are more likely to work in a market economy than in a planned economy.

The first major reform of *doi moi* was the Foreign Investment Law, passed in December 1987 and implemented in the following year. By South-East Asian standards, this was a very liberal law, allowing for 100 per cent foreign ownership and profit repatriation, significant tax holidays, and concessions for enterprises investing in a number of priority areas, including exports, consumer goods, technology transfer, and processing of local raw materials. The resulting inflow was small at first but, by 1996, it amounted to US$8.5 billion in new project commitments per annum, and constituted approximately one-third of Vietnam's total investment effort. The majority was in joint ventures with Vietnamese partners, mostly SOEs. Moreover, in the 1990s, Western aid to Vietnam began to increase rapidly and brought with it a stream of foreign contractors. Foreign companies and aid donors now constitute an important interest group applying pressure for further market-oriented reforms and for changes to the legal system to bring it into line with international norms.

In March 1988, Resolution 10 of the politburo effectively led to decollectivisation in the Vietnamese countryside. Although many cooperatives continued to exist, their functions were severely curtailed and, most importantly, they were no longer given a role in production. Instead, land was distributed for a period of fifteen years (or fifty years in cases of perennial crops) to households who were put in charge of all decisions relating to production and investment. Government procurement contracts were abolished and all output could be sold at market prices, either to the government or to the open market. This reform had very positive effects on agricultural output, to the extent that, in 1989, Vietnam shifted from being a net importer of rice to being the world's third-largest exporter (although, as we shall see below, the immediate increase in supply was also related to the success of anti-inflation measures in that year). Even so, a number of the more useful functions pro-vided by the cooperatives were adversely affected. In particular, householders were reluctant to make contributions to cooperative health and welfare facilities, and the cooperative maintenance of irrigation schemes also tended to suffer. Responsibility for the provision of these, as well as for other local infrastructure, has shifted to the commune (village) and district levels of government, which also suffered severe cuts in revenue after 1989. The impact of these changes has inevitably fallen hardest on the poor; however, as overall living standards have risen, the potential for rural class conflict has been blunted.

During 1989, the government abolished official prices, except for a handful of government monopolies, floated the exchange rate, and introduced positive real interest rates in the banking system. The first two of these mean that all prices, including the exchange rate against foreign currencies, are now basically market prices, although the state bank does control the exchange rate through its market operations. Direct subsidies from the state budget to SOEs were effectively ended. Positive real interest rates,[7] temporarily reversed in 1990–91, were used to encourage savings, halt the dollarisation of the economy,[8] reduce SOE subsidies via cheap credit provision, halt the growth of the budget deficit, and bring inflation under control.

The impact of this package on the economy was dramatic. Inflation was reduced from 308 per cent per annum in 1988 to only 36 per cent in 1990 (World Bank 1994:131); the domestic savings ratio also improved. With the reduction in inflation, much of the incentive to hoard goods for speculative purposes disappeared and there was an increase in supply, particularly of rice, so that shortages were eliminated. Industrial output has also risen rapidly since the reform. At the same time, many of the least-profitable SOEs closed their doors—the number of enterprises still operating had been halved by 1993—and there was a significant reduction in industrial employment as formerly subsidised SOEs sought to become profitable. Within the state-owned sector, the total number of employees was reduced from 3.86 million in 1985 (approximately 15 per cent of the total labourforce) to 2.92 million in 1993 (9 per cent). Employment in the cooperative industrial sector declined even more precipitously—from 1.2 million in 1988 to 287 600 in 1992 (GSO 1994)—which affected mainly women workers. Unemployment initially rose to 13 per cent of the workforce, but many of those laid off were able to find work in the burgeoning household sector or in the informal sector, particularly in farming, trade, and services, which led to a substantial shift in the employment structure.

Control over inflation has seen a significant return of confidence in the

Vietnamese currency, increased savings ratios, and rapid growth of GDP (at over 8 per cent per annum in 1992–97 and around 6 per cent in the years after the Asian crisis). These sustained high growth rates in a labour-intensive economy mean that unemployment has diminished, although, given the irregular character of much informal-sector employment, underemployment remains a serious problem, especially affecting farmers. Nevertheless, the high growth rates have seen a very rapid reduction in poverty: whereas in 1993, half the population lived below the national poverty line, by 2002 the proportion had fallen to 29 per cent (World Bank 2005).

One of the implications of the above analysis is that the high growth rates of the early 1990s were brought about chiefly through improvements in efficiency. The elimination of hyperinflation reduced speculation and the waste of resources, and the abolition of subsidies to SOEs provided incentives for improved productivity and a shift of resources into more profitable areas of production. A major issue in the economic debates has, therefore, been how to improve rates of investment to sustain growth over the long run. This has a parallel in government concerns to improve revenue-collection—to finance much-needed infrastructure projects and to restore funding to education and health—without having to resort to inflationary deficit-financing. Reform of the financial sector and taxation system have thus been key priorities (see below).

SOCIAL AND POLITICAL IMPACT OF *DOI MOI*

The impact of this series of reforms on the politics and culture of Vietnam has been just as dramatic as that on the economy. As Vietnam has opened to the world market, there have been significant gains in the ability of individuals to become involved in decisions concerning their livelihood and in freedom of speech, although not without setbacks. Debates in the national assembly have become much more lively and in 1992, for the first time, candidates not approved by the party were permitted to run for election. The demise of the cooperative system in the rural areas has also enabled the revival of traditional Vietnamese cultural and religious practices. Kinship networks have become more important in village life. New types of cooperative organisation, such as the numerous credit groups, have also spontaneously arisen to fulfil some of the social functions previously carried out by the cooperatives. Independent trade unions are permitted and some have already emerged in private enterprises, although so far mainly of the house union type. There have been a number of strikes in foreign-invested enterprises where unfamiliar—and, to Vietnamese workers, harsh—labour-management systems have been introduced. The government has so far shown no inclination to interfere in the independent settlement of these disputes.

Vietnam is now a much more open society than at any stage in the so-called socialist period (Thayer 1991:26–33). The party's concern for political stability has ensured that such freedoms have not extended beyond the limits of what it considers acceptable at any given time, but these limits are still expanding. As in the 1980s, when policy tended to attempt to manage change but was unable to control it, the desire of party leaders to preserve legitimacy means that they have been forced to react to shifts in public opinion.

This was evident, for example, in the movement of the first half of the 1990s to create a society ruled by law. Rule by law (often mistranslated in English language sources as 'rule of law') represented the attempt to codify Vietnamese laws and regulations into a coherent and internally consistent system to increase the transparency of bureaucratic processes and to eliminate opportunities for corruption, nepotism, favouritism, and arbitrariness from their implementation. As such, it implied reform of the bureaucracy as well as the rewriting of many laws to make them applicable to a market economy. Unlike the Western concept of rule of law, law did not represent a higher authority than the party–state. It did attempt to create a level playing field in which the popular perceptions of unfairness in the application of law, which characterised the socialist and earlier transitional society, would be eliminated. In reality, rule by law has not been applied very rigorously, as it sits awkwardly with patterns of settling disputes by negotiation and personal relations inherited from the pre-market economy.

In the latter half of the 1990s, the pace of change tended to slow down, due, at least in part, to a perception by party leaders that increased freedom had brought a startling rise in corruption, smuggling, and other crime, as well as higher divorce rates, juvenile delinquency, and other signs of a breakdown in social cohesion. Recognising that those in positions of authority are often the source of these social evils, many commentators have interpreted the resulting clampdown simply as a measure to maintain party privileges and control. Such an interpretation was certainly borne out by measures taken in 1999 to restrict media criticism of the party and government. However, the leadership has also responded by taking steps to increase accountability by promoting grassroots democracy—in other words, by attempting to defuse conflict by channelling it into lawful avenues and restricting the capacity of individuals openly to flout the law. One reason for such apparently contradictory measures being able to operate side by side is that grassroots challenges to authority rarely take on the character of challenges to the regime, and tend to be soluble within the existing political framework. Intellectuals, on the other hand, are more likely to issue challenges to the political system itself.

CURRENT ISSUES

Sustainable growth

For the party and government, the main question is how to sustain economic growth at a sufficient rate to catch up to its South-East Asian neighbours in ASEAN.[9] This is seen as the surest way to avoid the potential for social conflict inherent in the reform process and to maintain Communist Party rule in the medium term.

There have been four main areas of concern in this search for sustainable growth. The first is efficient use of resources.

As mentioned above, high growth rates of GDP in the early 1990s came largely from improvements in the efficiency with which resources were used. Gross investment in the state sector in 1992 was approximately 8 per cent of GDP, which is far too low to sustain rapid economic growth and did not include investment in the private sector and in own-capital of SOEs. Raising the rate of savings and investment has, therefore, had a high priority. By 1997, the estimate for all investment had risen to approximately 27 per cent of GNP.

Although domestic savings rose in importance as a source of investment finance during the 1990s, foreign direct investment (FDI) also played a key role. During the Asian crisis, however, FDI fell dramatically and, by 1999, was back to its 1992 level. With hindsight, it is apparent that the foreign investment boom formed part of the bubble economy affecting the South-East Asian region as a whole and did not reflect the true attractiveness of Vietnam. In the early 1990s, there was something of a last frontier mentality among investors, yet, by the second half of 1996, the realities of red tape, poorly developed infrastructure, and conflicting regulations had led to a slowdown in the rate of new investments. Thus the onset of the Asian crisis in mid 1997 served only to accelerate the downturn; recovery in the rest of Asia has not returned it to its previous levels. Domestic investment was able, partially, to offset this decline and Vietnam was otherwise relatively insulated from the impact of the crisis by virtue of its lack of global financial integration, so that growth rates were maintained at approximately 4–5 per cent during 1998–99. However, the loss of foreign investment represented a blow to the government's growth strategy, which had largely depended on FDI to provide technology transfer and boost the efficiency of the SOE sector through joint ventures. Since there were also considerable domestic linkages deriving from FDI—in the form of subcontracting, components supply, and so on—the longer-term effects of the decline might be stronger than initially indicated.

The second main area of concern in the search for sustainable growth in the 1990s was reform of the financial sector. In 1990, the government separated commercial banking from the central bank functions of the State Bank of Vietnam and established four commercial banks, which, in principle, were to lend only according to commercial criteria. However, the process of commercialisation of the banking system has been slow. During the period of negative real interest rates, the demand for funds by SOEs remained high, and savings deposits were low with many banks being technically insolvent. When, in 1992, interest rates were raised again to positive levels, many SOEs were unable to repay their loans and the state bank was forced to provide funds to cover these non-performing debts—which meant that the system of subsidising SOEs continued through an indirect method. More recently, the Agricultural Bank, in particular, has been under pressure to shift its lending portfolio away from SOEs towards private farmers; it has made some progress. But given the lack of adequate accounting practices in all Vietnamese enterprises, banks have little genuine ability to assess commercial risk and therefore continue to prefer SOEs because of the greater certainty that they will be bailed out by the government. Private ventures have had to rely on informal borrowing, which is more risky and limits the capital available. This is one of the factors restricting the growth of large-scale private capitalists in Vietnam—a situation with which many in the party might be content if they see an emerging bourgeoisie as a threat to party rule.

A third area of concern in relation to sustained economic growth has been the fiscal system. As explained above, the main sources of finance for state-led industrialisation under central planning were the profits of industrial enterprises and foreign aid. However, by the 1980s the majority of SOEs were clearly unprofitable and, of more than 12 000 then existing, the government was forced to rely on only a few hundred to provide the bulk of revenue. The flow of aid from the West remained slow; Soviet aid was withdrawn in 1991. Expenditure needs, on the other hand, continued to grow, and the resulting large budget deficits could be financed only in an inflationary way. The need to stabilise the economy by reducing the budget deficit provided a strong impetus for reform of the fiscal system, both to increase revenue collection and to widen the tax base to include the private sector.

Revenues increased substantially, from a low of 11 per cent of GDP in 1988 to 26 per cent in 1994, and the deficit was greatly reduced. After 1986, some of the revenue burden shifted from SOEs to taxes on foreign trade and oil production; however, attempts to increase the private sector's tax share were less successful. Personal income tax provided only 1 per cent of revenue (IMF 1994:58; World Bank 1994:127). For this reason, the government introduced a value-added tax in 1999. While reliance on foreign trade taxes was reduced, VAT revenues failed to expand fast enough to offset the loss, forcing the budget to become overreliant on oil revenues.

One of the main factors leading to popular resistance to tax payments is that the severe compression of local budgets during the fiscal crisis led local authorities to extract 'contributions' from the population. This practice has, rightly or wrongly, often been tarred with the brush of corruption. These days, education and health care fees constitute the bulk of such local levies, since funds coming from the centre are insufficient (Beresford 2005). Such contributions tend to be highly regressive, impinging on the poor more heavily than on the rich.

A fourth issue of concern to the sustainability of growth is the environment. The socialist system was certainly not free of environmental problems (Beresford & Fraser 1992) but, given the priorities of the regime and the lack of countervailing power, these did not become an important issue. The emergence in the government's agenda of environmental issues in the 1990s is testimony both to its greater openness and to the increasing ability of the people to organise themselves. As the growth rate has accelerated, the socialist economy's legacy of poorly developed infrastructure and dirty industrial plants has proven highly inadequate. In rapidly expanding urban centres, such as Hanoi and Ho Chi Minh City, the drainage system of the colonial period can no longer cope with the volume of effluent. Old factories, new construction sites, and millions of motorbikes pour dust and chemical pollution into the atmosphere. Public transport systems are run down and traffic clogs the multitude of narrow streets. Despite rapid improvements in access to a better quality water supply since the mid 1990s, 27 per cent of the population, the group most vulnerable to pollution, continues to rely on hand-dug wells, rivers, lakes, natural springs, ponds, or rainwater (World Bank 2005).

Institutional frameworks for dealing with environmental problems remain weakly developed and, when conflicts of interest arise, solutions can be the result of an ad hoc public protest—as in the case of the successful campaign against construction of a coal-washing plant in a residential area (Bach 2004). The government has also acted firmly in cases where public safety is threatened; however, it seems more likely to act in favour of those with market power—that is, when pollution and congestion become evident as bottlenecks to growth. For the time being, environmental guidelines are often flouted.

Social equity

The distributional impacts of growth are very much on the agenda. Since *doi moi,* despite the rapid reduction in absolute poverty, there has been a significant widening of income differentials, most notably in the growing gap between urban and rural areas. In popular perception, increased inequality is also linked to corruption and a lack of transparency at all levels of the state apparatus. These issues are seen as central to the maintenance of the regime's legitimacy and its credentials as a leader of the transition to socialism. During the crisis period of the late 1970s and 1980s, the party suffered a loss of legitimacy and its attempt to rebuild is based largely on the simultaneous effort to sustain economic freedoms and promote growth while providing a social safety net for the poor. However, the party and government contain a diversity of views on the relationship of growth and equity, which has led to a continuing struggle over relative priorities.

Some of these concerns are reflected, for example, in the labour and land laws passed in 1993 and 1994. The Labour Law contained many provisions aimed at protecting the rights of workers, but is often not implemented, especially in the domestic private sector. The Land Law also prominently addressed the security needs of farmers and, consequently, contained a number of provisions inimical to the development of markets in land and to the development of capitalism in agriculture. This has also turned out to be difficult to implement in many areas.

The future of the health and education sectors is also a key equity issue. The legacy of the socialist system in this area was relatively high levels of literacy and public health indicators (Beresford 1995) as well as high popular expectations, particularly in relation to education. In the fiscal crisis of the late 1980s and early 1990s, however, public spending in both these areas dropped significantly. Teachers and health workers found it impossible to live on their state salaries and most took up second occupations or left the system completely. Schools began to demand contributions from parents to maintain classes, but, with staff frequently demoralised by their poor wages and conditions, standards fell and well-off parents found it necessary to pay for private tuition outside school hours. The rise of the household economy also led to higher school drop-out rates, particularly in the rural areas, and the gap between boys' and girls' education levels has increased, with girls tending to leave school earlier than boys. In health care, there has been a shift away from the use of clinics and private practitioners towards self-prescribed drugs, which are freely available in the new market environment. As state revenues have begun to recover, there are signs of some improvement in health-sector funding, especially at the local level; foreign non-governmental organisations are also now active. Education remains more problematic because it not only requires more funds (private sector education can take a small portion of the burden for this), but also requires extensive restructuring of the curriculum to adapt to the needs of a market economy.

Centre–local relations

Centre–local relations have been one of the most difficult areas of reform within the state apparatus. From the point of view of the centre, its capacity to manage the economy is affected by the distribution of power existing at the outset of the reform process, uneven regional development, and the degree of integration of local levels into the national administrative apparatus. Historically, national integration has been influenced by

- regional autarchy arising from the operation of the socialist system, with incomplete market reform giving rise to a situation in which regions were able to defy central policy directions (this also refers to the rise of local networks using family, party, and business connections to build quasi-independent control over a protected local economy)
- the emergence of wide regional disparities between provinces and regions together with essentially contrived attempts to equalise income differentials has led to resentment—by wealthier regions at having to subsidise the poorer ones and the poor regions at perceived privileges meted out to the more prosperous.

Under the impact of market-oriented reforms, competition between centre and localities over budget resources became a major issue. Under the traditional socialist system, local budgets of the poorer regions or those with a large number of political production units were heavily subsidised by the centre. After reform, these subventions were reduced as chronic fiscal deficits could no longer be tolerated because they fuelled inflationary tendencies. The problem was exacerbated by the low revenue-raising ability of the centre. However, the increased buoyancy of revenues since 1993, and corresponding deficit reduction, reduced the pressure on the localities. Nevertheless, a majority of provinces continues to require subsidies—which leads to tensions between these and the wealthier provinces.

The purpose of reforms that decentralised economic decision-making (as initiated in 1979) was to unleash the productive energies of individual units, and the new policies did not at first contain any well articulated regional dimension. However, a regional policy, known as the 'growth pole strategy' emerged as earlier autarchic policies were replaced by a more market-oriented system promoting trade and investment links with the international economy. In the 1990s, regional differences in growth rates began to emerge more strongly, with the southern region around Ho Chi Minh City significantly outstripping other areas in growth rate and per capita income. The northern industrial centres around Hanoi and Haiphong have, more recently, experienced similar rapid rates of growth, whereas some rural provinces, especially in the highlands and the central coast, have lagged behind. The two industrial regions have been able to retain much larger shares of revenues collected and have correspondingly higher levels of per capita expenditure than poorer regions. Subsidies provided by the centre to poor provinces are only weakly redistributive (Beresford 2003).

The normal expectation is that, with the spread of market influence, there will be a gradual erosion of the strength of regional political autonomy and the ability of local authorities to allocate resources independently of (or in contradiction to) the direction of central policy. Higher levels of regional integration will ensure that it is in the interests of localities to contribute to central budgets for the maintenance of interlocality infrastructure and macroeconomic stabilisation and growth policies. However, this will not occur if localities are, at the same time, denied resources needed to sustain local growth and social welfare systems. The answers will have implications for the distribution of accumulation and growth, the efficiency of resource allocation, and the longer-term ability of the centre to manage the economy. These questions are also closely related to the equity issues discussed above. At the present time, capital construction expenditures (including those financed by aid) by the central authorities are tending to be spent on large infrastructure projects that will have benefits primarily for the high-growth regions and for the centrally managed SOEs and foreign investments concentrated in those regions.

State enterprise reform

Financial autonomy of SOEs was progressively increased after 1981, thereby enabling the process of capital accumulation and cross shareholdings. In 1989, direct budget subsidies were ended and cheap credit was reduced, with the result that enterprises either had to restructure or close down. Although many assets of these enterprises are still owned by the state and a capital fee is charged, the growth of relatively autonomous capital accumulation has implied an increase in the proportion of own-capital, which is regarded by the enterprises themselves—although not by the bureaucracy—as their collective property. Workers may share in the enterprise profits in the form of bonus and welfare funds that grow in size as productivity rises and serve to reinforce the ethos of collective ownership. In at least a few SOEs, bonus funds have been distributed in the form of shares. Labour recruitment practices also reflect this ethos, especially in the north, where many enterprises try to provide employment security and recruit new workers from among family members of the existing workforce. The question of ownership of the SOEs is, therefore, very unclear. Increased autonomy from government control suggests a process of corporatisation of public enterprises (Beresford 1993); a corporatist, rather than a confrontational, model of labour relations has developed in many cases. The situation varies, however, and, in some sectors exposed to a more competitive environment (the garment industry, for example), there have been numerous confrontations.

Corporatisation of the state-owned sector does not necessarily represent the formation of a private sector. Administrative interference in the operation of enterprises still exists, directly via the line ministries and indirectly via the banking system. Soft budget constraints on enterprises, although considerably reduced since the beginning of the reform, are also still in existence. The political difficulties associated with imposing genuine bankruptcy on unprofitable SOEs mean that, in common with other reforming planned economies, Vietnam has been subjected to a stop–go cycle in relation to financial discipline. There still exists a lot of confusion between the macroeconomic management role of the government in a market economy (as the reformers see it) and the productive function of the state ministries and enterprises. Fforde (1993:310) speaks of a state 'business interest', which is distinct from the private sector because control over enterprises remains dependent on directors' positions within the state apparatus. In fact, attempts to use state positions to accumulate private capital have been clearly identified as corrupt and, where possible, been severely punished. The state business interest forms a powerful sectional interest within the state that prevents the establishment of a capitalist economy based on private property, most clearly, by creating barriers to entry for new capital. Moreover, given the power of the state business interest, the continuing low rate of investment by this sector must throw some doubt on the sustainability of growth. One indication of this problem is that output per worker in the state industrial sector at the end of the 1990s was only about half that of foreign-invested firms.

State enterprise reform remains one of the most sensitive areas. As market discipline on enterprises becomes greater, pressure on workers seems likely to increase, both for increased productivity and to end the sharing of profits between worker funds and investment funds. Also, foreign investors and international competition are likely to generate pressure to halt the real wage increases that state-sector workers have experienced in recent years. Development of a stronger labour market and the movement of new, inexperienced workers into the waged labourforce is also likely to see a dilution of the culture of social or collective enterprise ownership. Equitisation of enterprises is presently considered a more appropriate model of ownership reform than is privatisation, and implies that the state, along with managers, workers, other SOEs, and private capitalists, will retain a considerable share in enterprise ownership. Some small, non-core enterprises have been equitised to date, but large-scale equitisation has yet to happen. In most cases, the process has involved the state retaining a controlling interest, with the remainder of shares going to insiders—that is, directors and workers. Steps have also been taken to increase corporatisation through measures to remove the control of line ministries over production-related decisions; some of these ministries had been amalgamated or abolished. In several industries, enterprises were incorporated into large, vertically integrated corporations in an effort to rationalise production capacity, finance, and lines of management authority. To date, the reorganisation has shown few results.

CONCLUSION

The planned economy in Vietnam by no means corresponded to the command economy model favoured by Western commentators on actually existing socialism. Rather, it was a system in which the demands of conflicting interest groups within society were negotiated through the mediation of the state apparatus. These interests included sections of the state apparatus itself that derived power from their control over the planned allocation of resources; local authorities, enterprise and cooperative managers, and their dependants, who strove to minimise surplus extraction to higher levels and accumulate capital within their own sphere; and, last, those who lacked access to the networks holding local power. The fundamental legitimacy of the regime, due to its nationalist credentials and reliance on popular mobilisation during wartime, not only blunted any social conflict inherent in the system, but also created a tradition in which negotiated solutions were possible. After unification of the country in 1976, the shift in the balance of interests in favour of relatively independent capital accumulation led to an increasing erosion of the power of interests associated with the planning system as inflation tended to aggravate shortages generated within the plan. Serious economic crises between 1978 and 1980, and again in the mid 1980s, progressively destroyed the remaining legitimacy of the planning system within the central apparatus itself and led to the political consensus around *doi moi*. Moreover, by the end of the decade, structural and institutional change had proceeded far enough to ensure that abolition of the remaining vestiges of planning produced little serious dislocation of the economy.

State-led marketisation of the economy under *doi moi* has very much reflected the interests of those groups that rose to dominance during the early part of the transition: SOE managers (often in alliance with the new group of foreign investors), as well as local and provincial kinship networks, and political networks linked to relatively autonomous capital-accumulation processes. However, within the increasingly pluralist Vietnamese society, new groups are emerging that are not necessarily linked to these networks; they include private domestic capitalists and can also include wealthy farmers. Until now, their potential for expansion has been limited by discrimination in policy implementation and lack of capital, and they are unlikely to become a dominant class in the foreseeable future. Those SOE workers who remained in employment after the shakeout of the early 1990s have also benefited through their ability to share in the profits of enterprises that most still regard as collectively owned. However, as market discipline on enterprises increases, and as a labour market becomes more established, these benefits are likely to diminish.

At the bottom end of the scale are those who have not participated in capital accumulation and who are largely excluded from state power: poor peasants, the unemployed, and underemployed. Women are in the majority in all of these categories. For many, their livelihood has become increasingly precarious, although there is so far no evidence that this is true for the great majority. Nevertheless, the crisis in health and education, increasing regional differentiation, and increasing income differentials mean that there is potential for social conflict. Therefore, not only the sustainability of growth, but also equitable distribution of the benefits, are likely to remain important issues for some time to come. Within the party–state apparatus, the perceived need to maintain the legitimacy of Communist Party rule is also likely to ensure that the interests of the poor are not completely ignored. Although what might be called the state–business bloc remains powerful, there are many in the party and bureaucracy who see a continuing need for compromise with the interests of the poor in order to block the rise of opposition parties based on interests associated with private capital.

NOTES

1 The category of 'middle' peasants, defined as those producing 'on average' sufficient for household subsistence and not requiring hired labour, is problematical as it includes many above-average farms that produced a marketable surplus. In the southern region in the 1970s, it was the 'middle' peasants, accounting for 72 per cent of the rural population, who produced the bulk of the south's large marketed grain surplus (Beresford 1988:149).

2 In the late 1970s, for example, there were reports that procurement officials were sometimes arrested by cooperative members and their bicycles appropriated because the centre was unable to supply the contracted amounts of industrial goods in exchange for procurement quotas.

3 The term 'relatively independent' is used here because capital accumulation in the periphery remained, in many cases, contingent upon access to resources, supplied at low official prices within the plan, that could then be diverted on to parallel markets.

4 The system of subsidised input prices continued at approximately 60–70 per cent of the market price, while the government's wages bill rose by 220 per cent. The budget deficit rose from 24 per cent of expenditure in 1984 to 31 per cent in 1986 and 39 per cent in 1988 (Spoor 1988:125; World Bank 1994:126).

5 Inflation during 1986 was 487 per cent per annum (World Bank 1994:131).

6 Some insights are provided by Dang Phong and Beresford (1998).

7 Meaning that the rate was pegged a few points above the inflation rate.

8 One of the characteristics of high inflation in all the former socialist countries has been increasing use by the population of the US dollar as the preferred currency for domestic transactions because it holds its value better than the local currency.

9 Party Secretary Do Muoi, in delivering the political report to the Mid Term National Conference of the party held in January 1994, enumerated four basic challenges facing the country today: 'The challenges lie in the danger of our economy falling further behind those of other countries in the region and the world due to our low starting point, our still low and unstable growth rate and the fact that we have to develop in an environment of tough competition; the possibility of our going astray from the socialist orientation if we fail to correct deviations from the path laid down for its implementation; corruption and other social evils; "peaceful evolution" schemes and activities undertaken by hostile forces' (CPV 1994:24).

REFERENCES

Bach Tan Sinh (2004) 'Institutional challenges for sustainable development in Vietnam: the case of the coal mining sector', in Melanie Beresford and Tran Ngoc Angie (eds.) *Reaching for the Dream: Challenges of Sustainable Development in Vietnam*, Copenhagen: NIAS Press, pp. 245–87.

Beresford, Melanie (1988) *Vietnam: Politics, Economics and Society*, London: Pinter.

——(1989) *National Unification and Economic Development in Vietnam*, London: Macmillan.

——(1993) 'The political economy of dismantling the "bureaucratic centralism and subsidy system" in Vietnam', in Kevin Hewison, Richard Robison and Garry Rodan (eds.) *Southeast Asia in the 1990s*, Sydney: Allen & Unwin, pp. 213–36.

——(1995) 'Political economy of primary health care in Vietnam', in Paul Cohen and John Purcal (eds) *Health and Development in Southeast Asia*, Australian Development Studies Network, pp. 104–19.

——(2003) 'Economic transition, uneven development and the impact of reform on regional inequality', in Hy Van Luong (ed.) *Vietnamese Society under Economic Reform: Development and Conflict*, New York: Rowman & Littlefield.

——(2005) *Towards Gender Budgeting in Vietnam*, Hanoi: Women Publishing House.

——and Lyn Fraser (1992) 'Political economy of the environment in Vietnam', *Journal of Contemporary Asia*, 22(1): 3–19.

Communist Party of Vietnam (CPV) (1994): *Political Report of the Central Committee* (7th Tenure) Mid Term National Conference, Hanoi: Gioi Publishers.

Dang Phong and Melanie Beresford (1998) *Authority Relations and Economic Decision-Making in Vietnam*, Copenhagen: Nordic Institute for Asian Studies.

de Vylder, Stefan and Adam Fforde (1988) *Vietnam: An Economy in Transition*, Stockholm: SIDA.

Elliott, David (1974) 'Revolutionary Reintegration', unpublished PhD thesis, Ann Arbor: University of Michigan.

Fforde, Adam (1989) *The Agrarian Question in North Vietnam 1974–78*, New York: M. E. Sharpe.

——(1993) 'The political economy of reform in Vietnam—some reflections', in Borje Ljunggren (ed.) *The Challenge of Reform in Indochina*, Cambridge MA: Harvard University Press, pp. 293–326.

——and Suzanne H. Paine (1987) *The Limits to National Liberation*, London: Croom Helm.

General Statistical Office (GSO) (1994) Nien Giam Thong Ke 1993, Hanoi: Statistical Publishing House.

Gordon, Alec (1981) 'North Vietnam's collectivisation campaigns: class struggle, production and the "middle peasant" problem', *Journal of Contemporary Asia*, 11(1), pp. 19–43.

International Monetary Fund (IMF) (1994) *Vietnam: Recent Economic Developments*, Washington DC: International Monetary Fund, June.

Moise, Edwin E. (1976) 'Land reform and land reform errors in North Vietnam', *Pacific Affairs*, 49(1): 70–92.

Ngo Vinh Long (1984) 'Agrarian differentiation in the southern region of Vietnam', *Journal of Contemporary Asia*, 14(3): 283–305.

Spoor, Max (1988). 'State finance in the Socialist Republic of Vietnam', in David G. Marr and Christine P. White (eds.) *Postwar Vietnam: Dilemmas in Socialist Development*, Ithaca: Cornell University, Southeast Asia Program, pp. 111–32.

Thayer, Carlyle (1991). 'Renovation and Vietnamese society: the changing role of government and administration', in Dean K. Forbes, Terence H. Hull, David G. Marr and Brian Brogan (eds.) *Doi Moi: Vietnam's Renovation Policy and Performance*, Political and Social Change Monograph no. 14, Canberra: Australian National University, pp. 21–33.

White, Christine P. (1983). 'Mass mobilisation and ideological transformation in the Vietnamese land reform campaign', *Journal of Contemporary Asia*, 13(1): 74–90.

World Bank (1994) 'Vietnam: Public Sector Management and Private Sector Incentives Economic Report', 20 September.

——(2005) *World Development Indicators 2005*, <www.worldbank.org/data/wdi2005/index.html>.

8 US Foreign Policy and the War on Terror in South-East Asia

Jim Glassman

KEY TOPICS

INTRODUCTION

THE US war in Vietnam and, later, Cambodia and Laos, was the most sustained, deadly, and consequential US military intervention in South-East Asia, so it provides a useful reference point for discussion of recent US activities in the region. The Bush administration's declaration during October 2001 that South-East Asia was to constitute a front in the US-led war on terror thus invites comparison and contrast with US declarations after the Second World War that South-East Asia was to become a front in the US-led war on communism, which ultimately led to US intervention in Vietnam. Explaining similarities and differences between these two wars requires attention to the interconnected geopolitics and political economy—or, better, geopolitical economics—of US foreign policy. The US was a major geopolitical economic force in South-East Asia during the Cold War. It continues to be a major force in post-Cold War South-East Asia, but from a position of, arguably, more tentative overall geopolitical economic strength.

In explaining the continuities and discontinuities in US impacts within South-East Asia, this chapter utilises and distinguishes between the concepts of imperialism and hegemony. The first section of the chapter briefly explains these ideas. Next, there is a brief review of the basic motivations that drove US intervention in South-East Asia during the Cold War, and what circumstances have changed in the post-Cold War era. After this, it is demonstrated that US foreign policy planners, keenly aware of the changing terrain of power in Asia in the post-Cold War era, wanted to increase the US military presence in the region long prior to the terrorist attacks of 11 September 2001—an event that provided a convenient pretext for promoting a more aggressive US military role. Finally, it is shown that the US declaration of a war on terror within the region has created a context in which various South-East Asian elites have been able to pursue projects of their own, projects that often have comparatively little to do with either the US government's stated objectives in declaring the war or with its pre-September 11 plans. In consequence, it can be argued that US South-East Asian foreign policy in the post-September 11 era is marked by resurgent imperialism, but is confronted by real limits, which reflect slowly declining US hegemony. At the same time, the war on terror has provided opportunities for South-East Asian elites to re-package—and gain leverage in—a variety of domestic social struggles.

IMPERIALISM AND HEGEMONY

Imperialism is the term that has sometimes been used to refer to a situation in which one country dominates another. This conception is problematic because it implies a level of social unity within societies that rarely corresponds to reality. Even under colonialism, imperial powers have, typically, relied on active collaboration by various local groups within the dominated country to be able to rule effectively.

This does not mean that imperialism is a useless concept, but rather that it has to be interpreted in ways that allow for the recognition of social conflicts within states and transnational collaboration between different national elites across state boundaries. A productive way to view imperialism is to see it as involving varying forms of collaboration and conflict between social groups within and across international boundaries, conditioned by the globally uneven development of capitalism (Glassman 2004a:11–32). During the Cold War era, a typical form of imperialism in South-East Asia was military and economic alliance between US and South-East Asian elites—sometimes with support from groups such as peak US labour organisations (Glassman 2004b)—with these alliances being used by South-East Asian elites to strengthen their position in struggles against domestic opposition groups, such as leftist parties and militant labour organisations.

Forms of imperialism can change, depending upon the specific patterns of uneven capitalist development that underpin them; arguably, the forms of imperialism that the US was able to exercise in South-East Asia during the Cold War era have been undermined somewhat by the growth of competing centres of capitalist power within Asia, making Asian elites somewhat less likely to accommodate US projects that are not clearly perceived as being in their own interests today than they were during the Cold War. Cold War era forms of US imperialism have also been undermined somewhat by the more contentious relationship between US elites and US labour organisations that have developed because of declining wages and greater job insecurity for most US workers since the 1970s. This has made US labour support for overseas projects of the US state more tenuous, particularly where it seems that US policies encourage the 'hollowing out' of US industries and the relocation of US firms to overseas, 'cheap labour' production sites, such as those in Asia (Glassman 2004b).

These changes bear directly on the notion of hegemony. For Antonio Gramsci, hegemony did not mean just dominance—which is roughly what the term implies in many geopolitical analyses—but rather, the ability of a particular group to lead (Gramsci 1971). This implied that such a group—specifically, in Gramsci's analyses, a class or class fraction—was powerful enough to rule not only because it could repress opposition, but also because it could offer benefits to potential opposition groups in exchange for their consent to the dominant group's leadership. For Gramsci, this included the ability to offer a compelling ideological rationale for the existing social order.

Arguably, while US imperialism has remained a potent force in the world since the end of the Cold War (see Beeson, this volume), US hegemony, though still significant, has actually been in decline, particularly in regions such as East and South-East Asia. The rise of new centres of capitalist power in East and South-East Asia has made US leadership a more contentious issue and has turned erstwhile collaborators into sometimes competitors. Under these conditions, the US government seems increasingly focused on the projection of military force to counteract the growth of more geographically decentred capitalist power (Arrighi & Silver 1999; Wallerstein 2003).

US FOREIGN POLICY DURING AND AFTER THE VIETNAM WAR

While US projection of military power naturally attracts considerable attention, it is important to see the relationships between US military power and political economic factors shaping US foreign policy. By the end of the Second World War, US foreign policy makers were laying out detailed plans for post-war reconstruction, highlighting what came to be called by the influential Council on Foreign Relations (CFR) the 'Grand Area'. The Grand Area was the minimum amount of global economic space (or, as one planner called it, 'elbow room') the US economy was deemed to need in order to avoid major readjustments (CFR 1946). The problem that beset the US economy before the Second World War was understood by many planners to have been a crisis of either overproduction or underconsumption, which made the search for overseas markets for US goods central to postwar reconstruction efforts. US capitalism, in short, required what has come to be called 'globalisation' (Smith 2005).

The markets about which the US was most concerned were in Europe, but Asia was important because of Japan's role as a global industrial power and consumer of US exports, the contribution that Europe's South-East Asian colonies might make to Europe's postwar reconstruction, and longstanding hopes for the China market (Kolko 1988; Rotter 1987). This meant that, although South-East Asia was not directly crucial to most US exporters and investors, it was, nonetheless, indirectly crucial to the development of the Grand Area (Glassman 2004a:38–46).

The geopolitical significance of South-East Asia, which led the US to oppose communist-led and/or anti-colonial movements such as those in Malaysia, the Philippines, and Vietnam, was never unconnected to these concerns about postwar reconstruction. The US government was not focused on South-East Asia as a primary overseas market for US exports and investments, but neither was it narrowly concerned about South-East Asia as the source of a direct communist security threat to the United States. The threat that communist parties posed was more indirect and based on the momentum they might impart to broader efforts at reconstructing the postwar world in ways inconsistent with US objectives. As one US official put it, 'Today many peoples are striving to better themselves economically and politically and have thus accepted or are in danger of accepting the Communist movement' (Borden 1984:45). Non-aligned and/or communist groups in East and South-East Asia might thus inspire each other and collectively contribute to the development of a world in which the US economy no longer had adequate elbow room. As a report for the Woodrow Wilson Foundation put the matter in 1955, communism presented a problem for the US because it threatened 'a serious reduction of the potential resource base and market opportunities of the West owing to the subtraction of the communist areas from the international economy and their economic transformation in ways which reduce their willingness and ability to complement the industrial economies of the West' (Woodrow Wilson Foundation 1955:42). In this respect, the geopolitical danger presented by communism and neutralism in South-East Asia stemmed from US political economic demands for the postwar global economy.

A review of the specific policies that the US supported in South-East Asia during the Cold War is beyond the scope of this chapter, but what the foregoing points out are the basic underpinnings and aspirations of US–South-East Asia policies in that era. These basic underpinnings and aspirations have not changed fundamentally in the post-Cold War period. The US remains concerned about South-East Asia, not as an end in itself or as a destination for crucially large amounts of US exports or investment, but rather, as a link in a broader geopolitical economic chain that determines US elbow room and affects US elites' global prospects. Moreover, as during the Cold War, US concerns vis-à-vis East Asian countries, such as China and Japan, loom especially large.

Nonetheless, certain things have changed in the post-Cold War period. Paradoxically, some of what has changed is a reflection of problems that arise from the success of US Cold War policies. East and South-East Asian communism has been successfully thwarted, to the extent that virtually all of East and South-East Asia today is involved in capitalist development, even where this is nominally overseen by communist parties. Far from being a pure success story for the US state and Asian capitalists, the victory has proven in some respects pyrrhic.

For the US state, the victory is pyrrhic because it has led to the growth of forms of capitalist power in Asia that the US state cannot easily control, even where this growth is driven in part by investment from US-based corporations (Arrighi & Silver 1999; Harvey 2003; Wallerstein 2003). Even more so than during the Cold War, the new forces of competition unleashed by recent capitalist success in Asia have generated diverging projects among elites within the Cold War alliance, which have frequently led to strained relations between capitalists and state officials in the US and Japan, South Korea, and China, as well as between US elites and those in Singapore, Malaysia, and Thailand. Arguably, the US state has retained imperial dominance within East and South-East Asia, even as this growth of autonomous capital has occurred (Beeson 2004, and this volume). Nonetheless, leading US planners clearly feel threatened by the growth of competition in Asia, especially in China.

US imperial power in Asia, in a context of increasing competition, seems to be accompanied by gradually declining US hegemony. The US retains strong alliances with crucial East and South-East Asian elites, but there have been substantial challenges to US conceptions of appropriate forms of economic and social governance. Through much of the 1990s, these challenges became associated with Singaporean Premier Lee Kwan Yew's defence of Asian values—against Western calls for social liberalisation—and Malaysian Prime Minister Mahathir Mohammed's assertion of the need for more Japanese political and economic leadership in the region, including endorsement of Japanese-style industrial policies that are not in line with the Washington Consensus (Beeson 2000). Challenges also began to come from other quarters and were, in some respects, intensified by the Asian economic crisis. In Thailand, typically a strong bastion of support for Washington Consensus policies, popular antagonism towards neoliberal structural adjustment drove the US's closest allies, the Democrats from power, resulting in the rise of a quasi-nationalist, quasi-populist regime that formally rejects many aspects of neoliberalism and openly hews to models more like those of Singapore and Malaysia (Glassman 2004c; Hewison 2003; Pasuk & Baker 2004).

For South-East Asian capitalists, success in the Cold War has also been pyrrhic in certain respects. Although official state rhetoric has usually praised the growth of democratic forces in South-East Asia, this process of democratisation also poses challenges to class elites, thus eliciting new rounds of social struggle. While much of the literature on democratisation in South-East Asia has emphasised the role of the middle classes, the growth of democracy has, in fact, involved a broader range of social groups, many of whom are engaged in struggles to expand democracy in ways that pose threats to existing forms of class privilege and state practice. Notably, specific labour groups and non-governmental organisations (NGOs), which have rarely been encouraged by elites or the middle classes, have played important roles in opening up political space within post-Cold War South-East Asia, especially in countries such as the Philippines and Thailand, and, more tentatively, Indonesia (Brown 2004; Hewison 1997; Ji 1997; LaBotz 2001; West 1997).

As a result of these challenges to authoritarian rule and the changing social structures that enable these challenges, democratisation has not been a final outcome but rather a contested terrain on which elites struggle to retain privilege by restricting the forms of empowerment available to popular organisations. This kind of struggle over democratisation has shaped elite responses to the war on terror in South-East Asia.

POST-SEPTEMBER 11 US FOREIGN POLICY IN SOUTH-EAST ASIA

Policies encouraged by the US government as part of the War on Terror have to be understood against the background of these changing social relations in East and South-East Asia, instead of simply in relation to the terrorist forces emphasised publicly by the Bush Administration. After September 11, the Bush Administration announced al Qa'eda-inspired threats as the basis for extending the War on Terror to places like the Philippines. Yet prior to September 11, the US had already targeted South-East Asia for increased attention, based on issues that are independent of terrorism, especially US relations with East Asian powers like China.

China's growth has generated special concern for US planners and was given vastly greater emphasis than Islamic terrorist groups prior to September 11. Given that China's rapid economic growth over the past two decades has been part of its integration into the global capitalist economy, there has been no shortage of laudatory commentary. Yet for many US planners, a successful capitalist China is nearly as much of a threat as was a successful Communist China. In particular, while China's growth does offer new opportunities for profitable re-investment of capital by Western firms (Harvey 2003), it also generates new competition for US-based firms (CIA-NIC 2004). Moreover, a rapidly growing China generates increasingly large demands for shares of global energy resources (Andrews-Speed et al. 2002). Finally, though China is far from becoming a serious global military power, its increasing military capacities make it a significant regional force and a potential counterweight to unilateral US military dominance in Asia (Huxley & Willett 1999; Shambaugh 2002). Prior to September 11, it was primarily these concerns about China that led US planners to re-emphasise the importance of US policies in South-East Asia.

Indeed, the basic contours of post-September 11 US policies were articulated prior to September 11, as can be discerned by examining some of the policy literature, including the much-cited report by the Project for a New American Century (PNAC), *Rebuilding America's Defenses* (Kagan et al. 2000). PNAC is well known for its role in shaping the Bush administration's domestic and foreign policies, and has been supported since its inception in the 1990s by well-placed figures in the George W. Bush administration, such as Dick Cheney (vice-president), Donald Rumsfeld (secretary of defense), and Paul Wolfowitz (deputy secretary of defense and later, since 2005, president of the World Bank).

The PNAC report outlines a vision for building the post-Cold War US military to enable capitalisation on the historic opportunity presented by the collapse of communism. The goal is to preserve the Pax Americana, deterring the rise of a new great power competitor, while defending key regions and exploiting the transformation of war made possible by new technologies. Crucially for the PNAC authors, the geographic locus of strategic competition has shifted to East Asia (Kagan et al. 2000:2–3).

Expanding on this last point, the authors suggest that 'despite increasing worries about the rise of China and instability in South-East Asia, US forces are found almost exclusively in Northeast Asian bases' (Kagan et al. 2000:4). They assert the need to maintain US military bases in South Korea and Japan (Okinawa), and also the need for the expansion of the US military presence in South-East Asia, where, they note, 'American forces are too sparse to adequately address rising security requirements, particularly since the withdrawal of its troops from the Philippines in 1992' (Kagan et al. 2000:18). Moreover, the authors argue, 'the East Timor crisis and the larger question of political reform in Indonesia and Malaysia highlight the volatility of the region', which 'has long been an area of great interest to China' (Kagan et al. 2000:18–19). The authors conclude their overview of the challenges in East and South-East Asia by stating that,

> In sum, it is time to increase the presence of American forces in Southeast Asia. Control of key sea lines of communication, ensuring access to rapidly growing economies, maintaining regional stability while fostering closer ties to fledgling democracies and, perhaps, most important, supporting the nascent trends towards political liberty are all enduring security interests for America. No US strategy can constrain a Chinese challenge to American regional leadership if our security guarantees to Southeast Asia are intermittent and US military presence a periodic affair. For this reason, an increased naval presence in Southeast

> Asia, while necessary, will not be sufficient; as in the Balkans, relying solely on allied forces or the rotation of US forces in stability operations not only increases the stress on those forces but undercuts the political goals of such missions. For operational as well as political reasons, stationing rapidly mobile US ground and air forces in the region will be required (Kagan et al. 2000:19).

These PNAC visions of the US's role in South-East Asia can be seen as representing the views of a bloc of conservatives and neoconservatives, but they were shared across the political spectrum in Washington, DC, prior to September 11, as can be seen from other, contemporaneous reports, such as those of the conservative RAND Project Airforce division (for example, Sokolsky et al. 2000) and those of the more liberal Council on Foreign Relations (CFR) (for example, CFR 2001).[1] What had become the consensus project of such varied US elites before September 11 was thus to strengthen US leverage against China by restoring military relations with key South-East Asian countries. This involved utilising the 1999 Voluntary Forces Agreement to increase the US military presence in the Philippines, restoring aid and training to the Indonesian military (TNI), and expanding regional defence alliances with other countries, such as Singapore, Malaysia, and Thailand. These projects are precisely what the US has promoted in South-East Asia as a putative response to terrorism.

US imperialism in the Philippines

US activities in the Philippines after September 11 provide a clear example of the use of terrorism concerns to legitimise the kinds of activities called for in the PNAC, RAND, and CFR reports. Yet they have also enabled a somewhat autonomous project of local actors, namely, the use of the war on terror by Philippine military elites for their own benefit.

Shortly after September 11, US government officials announced that the Abu Sayyaf Group (ASG), which had been operating a terrorist racket on the southern Philippine island of Basilan, just southwest of Mindanao, had links to al Qa'eda and would become a focus of US anti-terrorism operations. Prior to this, ASG had primarily gained media exposure through small-scale violent acts such as the kidnapping for ransom—and occasional execution—of Catholic priests and foreign tourists (Eder & McKenna 2004:77). Long the most Islamicised region of the Philippines and the region with some of the highest levels of poverty, the south has also been the region most distant from Manila's rulers (be they Spanish, American, or Filipino) and the region that has been most susceptible to separatist struggles (Eder & McKenna 2004; Islam 1998).

The most recent phase of struggle in the south developed at the same time leftist activity against the Marcos dictatorship was rising, with the formation of the Moro National Liberation Front (MNLF) in 1971 (Eder & McKenna 2004:71). A nationalist front, the MNLF has been based in

Mindanao and has fought for greater regional autonomy within a broader framework of struggle against military dictatorship. Internal conflicts within the MNLF led, by the late 1970s, to the emergence of a group more committed to struggle for an Islamic state, the Moro Islamic Liberation Front (MILF), (Eder & McKenna 2004:73; Islam 1998:449–50). Some MILF members have reportedly received training in al Qa'eda camps in Afghanistan, as well as with Indonesian Islamist groups that received similar training (ICG 2002a, 2003a:6, 16–17). Yet, like the MNLF, the MILF has an indigenous base of social support in Mindanao and operates independently of these international networks (Rahim 2003:214). The MNLF and MILF have formed the most important regional opposition to leaders in Manila and, with the fall of the Marcos dictatorship, the 1990s regime of President Fidel Ramos had been able to move—if haltingly—towards some resolution of regional conflicts by carrying out negotiations with those involved (Eder & McKenna 2004:74–8; Islam 1998).

Against the backdrop of these major political manoeuvres, the appearance on the scene of ASG in the early 1990s was a barely-noticed event. In a semi-chaotic context, in which many different criminal and small-scale terrorist organisations operate alongside (and perhaps sometimes in connection with) insurgents, ASG was seen as little more than a group of bandits—in fact, prior to September 11, Philippine President Gloria Macagapal-Arroyo characterised ASG as 'a money-crazed gang of criminals' (International Peace Mission 2002:10). On the Philippine Left, ASG was widely suspected to have been a creation of the Central Intelligence Agency (CIA) and/or Philippine intelligence, formed to further splinter and undermine the southern insurgency.

In addition to this, many local activists and community members in Basilan testify to events that imply Philippine military collaboration with ASG leaders and tolerance of ASG operations (International Peace Mission 2002:15–17). Such accusations were largely the province of the Philippine and international Left until July 2003, when a mutiny by Philippine military officers brought to the fore parallel charges from the Right. The mutineers accused senior Philippine military officers of selling weapons to Islamic separatist groups in the south and staging bombings in Davao City so that they could receive more US military assistance in the name of fighting the war on terror (Klein 2003; Roberts 2003).

Such charges are difficult to prove or disprove completely, but what they help to reveal is something more important to the present argument, specifically, that the extension of the war on terror to the southern Philippines has been out of proportion to the actual threat of the insurgent forces and has created new opportunities for Philippine military elites. The military response to the claimed ASG threat has included joint operations that conform to the imperatives of the pre-September 11 US agenda for the Philippines (Arkin 2005:184–6). Beginning in 2002, the US military conducted expanded war games and joint training *balikatan* (shoulder-to-shoulder) exercises with the Philippine military. After being temporarily halted in 2003 because of the political controversy they aroused, further *balikatan* exercises were undertaken during 2004 on the island of Palawan and in central Luzon, involving the use of Clark Air Base (Arkin 2005:185). Moreover, intensification of the military struggle in the south has created a gravy train of military expenditures that encouraged corruption at the highest levels of the Philippine government. US military aid to the Philippines increased from $2 million in 2001 to $80 million per year in 2002–03; after September 11, the US government pledged a total of $100 million in security assistance to the Philippines (Arkin 2005:185; Klein 2003). The availability of these new, large military grants, according to the junior military officers involved in the July 2003 actions, has encouraged high-ranking officers to promote rather than reduce conflict in the south.

The fact that the US military has been able to state its desire forthrightly for renewed access to the Philippines and to gain such access on the basis of the September 11 pretext is, in part, a function of the US government's continued dominating influence in Manila (Tyner 2005). Such influence has to do with colonial and neocolonial legacies, as well as the ongoing economic dependence of Philippine elites—and the minimally successful economy they sit astride—on the US. But, as the corruption charges levelled by the junior officers attest, the autonomous interests of specific elites in endorsing the expansion of joint US–Philippine military exercises cannot be overlooked: September 11 not only provided US elites with a pretext for a re-assertion of a neocolonial presence, but it also provided Philippine elites who have battled against widespread nationalist and democratic sentiment with the opportunity to sell their own military collaboration with the US government as a project in the national interest.

US imperialism in Indonesia

In Indonesia, though the US has broadly similar designs to those it has for the Philippines, the situation is substantially different and has necessitated a different form of engagement with national elites. In particular, there is little possibility for the US military to gain rights to build bases anywhere in the archipelago, given fierce nationalist opposition to this in Indonesia, so the goal is rather to ensure tight and supportive relations between the US military and the TNI. The fact that most TNI members are Muslim, and that the overwhelming majority of Indonesians are as well, makes post-September 11 rationalisations of US actions a much more delicate matter in Indonesia than in the Philippines. Indeed, immediately after September 11, Indonesian President Megawati Soekarnoputri was unwilling to openly participate in a war on terror to the same extent as was Arroyo.

This provides the background for considering the US project of rekindling ties with the TNI. Particularly after the 12 October 2002 bombing of a Bali nightclub, in which 188 people (mostly Australians) were killed, the US government justified this rekindling of ties by playing up the threat to Indonesia posed by the political Islamist organisation Jema'ah Islamiyah (JI). As with ASG, uncertainty and speculation surrounds JI and the nature of its operations. Fortunately, there have been detailed reports on JI by the International Crisis Group (ICG).[2] The reports provide a useful picture of aspects of JI's operations, a picture that substantiates its credentials as a terrorist threat within Indonesia. At the same time, the reports make it impossible to cast the JI threat in the Manichean and selective terms that are central to the war on terror.

The ICG's reports on JI make several crucial points. First, JI is not an organisation that is unique or has come into existence *de novo*. Rather, JI is part of a broader political Islamist tendency that dates back to the Darul Islam rebellions of the 1950s; indeed, many JI members draw ideological inspiration from those struggles, while contemporary Darul Islam members have cooperated in JI activities (ICG 2002a:2–3, 7, 21, 25, 2003a:2, 12–14, 22–3). Second, JI is not merely a terrorist organisation created out of al Qa'eda's global aspirations. Indeed, the ICG states unequivocally that 'JI is not operating simply as an al Qa'eda subordinate' and that '[v]irtually all of its decision-making and much of its fund-raising has been conducted locally', while its focus 'continues to be on establishing an Islamic state in Indonesia' (ICG 2003a:1, cf. 2003a:15). Moreover, as an embedded part of the Indonesian social and political landscape, JI has built itself around Islamic schools that are an integral part of Indonesian culture (ICG 2002a:3, 25, 2003a:26–7). Third, precisely because it is embedded in a social and political landscape that is pervasively Islamic, JI is not a simple, unified, or regionalised phenomenon. Since Islam mediates and articulates most political positions taken in Indonesia, the sharing of a broadly Islamist agenda has not resulted in a uniformity of opinion among self-identified JI members (ICG 2002a:2, 3–4). Beyond this, even if JI is considered to be a coherent organisation with a clear identity, it is scarcely singular or unique; the ICG reports indicate the existence of a large number of other Indonesian organisations with overlapping, if sometimes conflicting, agendas.

Fourth, just as the ICG reports show that JI is not a distinctive, isolated, or homogeneous organisation standing apart from the rest of Indonesian society, it shows, too, that JI is by no means a straightforward antagonist of the TNI or Indonesian elites. ICG investigations found, in fact, that JI members have worked on the side of the TNI in its struggle against Acehnese rebels, attempting to woo and utilise defectors from the Acehnese independence movement, Gerakan Aceh Merdeka (GAM) (ICG 2002a:7–9). Indeed, because of these kinds of connections, the ICG concludes that military associations have likely been important to some JI operations (ICG 2002a:11).

In this context, it is not especially surprising that the war on terror in

Indonesia seems to have shown little in the way of success on the internal security front. Particularly after the Bali bombing, the US military pushed for increased military and intelligence cooperation and, in 2003, training under the US International Military Education and Training Program for Indonesian personnel was restored (Arkin 2005:134), as PNAC, RAND, and CFR analysts desired. Yet, even with increased cooperation from US and Australian intelligence as part of the war on terror, the TNI has seemingly had difficulty eliminating high-profile terrorist activities, such as the 5 August 2003 Jakarta Marriott Hotel bombing (ICG 2003a:11).

While Indonesia's participation in the war on terror has not eliminated terrorist activities in that country, the TNI has used national security rhetoric to legitimise very different projects, such as stepping up its operations in West Papua (ICG 2001, 2002b, 2003c). Meanwhile, the TNI has also used national security rhetoric to legitimise waging an intensified war on the GAM. Beginning in May 2003, the TNI launched a 'shock and awe' campaign against the GAM and its supporters, sending in 30 000 troops and 13 000 police and paramilitaries to take on the GAM's 5000 fighters (Symonds 2003). The campaign continued throughout 2003 and into 2004, with hundreds of civilian casualties, the forced evacuation of at least 100 000 people during the first three months of martial law alone, and the burning by Indonesian forces of as many as 500 schools (ICG 2003b). While the TNI has been able to legitimise such actions through reference to national unity and security, its interests include very lucrative returns from local resources and industries (see, for example, Kingsbury 1998:167; Robinson 2001:220–1).

In summary, whatever the precise realities of JI's threat to Indonesian security, the US-led war on terror has failed to undermine the possibility of terrorist actions in Indonesia, while at the same time US re-engagement of the TNI has facilitated the TNI to embark on newly intensified rounds of state repression in outlying regions, motivated by TNI leaders' autonomous projects of accumulation and political–military control. Like the US re-engagement of the Philippine military, this is understandable as part of a broader design for strengthened US–Indonesian military ties and for the suppression of regional separatist struggles. In this sense, US re-engagement of the TNI has enabled the TNI's subimperial project in Aceh and West Papua, an outcome that is driven by the agendas of TNI leaders but which the US government has been willing to facilitate for its own purposes.

US imperialism in Thailand

Thailand's position as a US ally in the war on terror was solidified after the arrest in Thailand of reputed JI operations leader Hambali in August 2003 (Nakashima & Sipress 2003). Since then, much of security rhetoric has focused on the issue of Thailand's three predominantly Islamic provinces on the border with Malaysia.

Indeed, immediately after September 11, various senior Thai military officials hinted at the need for an escalation of military activities in southern Thailand against criminal gangs—in the name of anti-terrorism. At the time, Prime Minister Thaksin Shinawatra proved somewhat resistant, instead re-directing public discussion from terrorism issues to issues of the south's development and Thailand's tourist attractions (Ukrist 2005:5). Thus, until 2003, Thailand participated in the war on terror in a somewhat different fashion than did the Philippine or Indonesian governments; Thaksin utilised the environment created by the war on terror for quite different ends.

To understand Thaksin's manoeuvres, it is necessary to note the orientation of his ruling Thai Rak Thai (TRT, Thai Love Thai) Party. TRT came to power in early 2001 on a populist and putatively nationalist platform that had wide support because of the impacts of the economic crisis and the International Monetary Fund (IMF) structural adjustment program imposed by the previous government (Hewison 2003, and this volume; Pasuk & Baker 2004). During TRT's first year in power, Thaksin's faction consolidated its position and implemented a series of spending measures that modestly boosted the fortunes of some groups hurt by the crisis and the IMF program. Then, during 2002, Thaksin reshuffled the governing coalition and moved the party more firmly in the direction of not only his own interests, but also those of dominant political and economic elites that provide crucial backing for TRT (Glassman 2004c:55).

Of particular significance in this regard was the change in relations between TRT and popular organisations that supported it during the election campaign. TRT had made various promises to such organisations, yet by 2002, TRT leaders had decided that these organisations had made demands that TRT was unable or unwilling to accommodate. Thus, during 2002, Thaksin asked foreign donors to suspend their support for some Thai NGOs, while simultaneously bringing fifty-three former military officers into his cabinet as special advisers on security issues, a warning to popular organisations that state relations with 'civil society' groups were returning to a more antagonistic orientation (Glassman 2004c:54–8; Hewison 2003; Pasuk & Baker 2004).

This antagonism was evident throughout 2002 and 2003. In a number of cases, TRT sent in police forces to repress actions by popular organisations. Moreover, by 2003, Thaksin made his intention to govern in a relatively militarised fashion clear, signified especially by the campaign to eradicate low-level drug dealers—the so-called war on drugs—in which more than 2000 people were killed within several months (Pasuk & Baker 2004:162). This led to condemnation from Thai and international human rights organisations, as well as expressions of concern from the US (Hewison & Rodan 2004:16). Thaksin shrugged off such criticism and the Bush administration took no action.

Through its turn against popular organisations during 2002 and 2003 and its re-engagement of a Cold War-era style of authoritarian politics, TRT thus placed itself in a better position to contain the popular forces it had attempted to coopt through its electoral agenda. Moreover, Thaksin and his strongest allies within TRT were also positioning themselves in ways that would make them the dominant class elites within Thailand. Here, however, the domestic politics of the war on terror became yet more complicated. Encouraged by the US government to play a more overt role in the war on terror, and lured by promises of inclusion in a free trade agreement with the US in return for doing so (Hewison & Rodan 2004:14–16), Thaksin's regime not only facilitated the arrest of Hambali, but it also began to pay more attention to the situation in the south, declaring martial law in early 2004. These actions did not take place against the background of established and agreed-upon security threats. Although various separatist and terrorist groups exist in southern Thailand and have maintained low-level activities over many decades (McCargo 2004; Surat 2003), nothing that had occurred up to 2003–04 signalled a noticeable upsurge in their activities. By 2003–04, however, there was a significant increase in violence, with more than 1000 deaths and injuries in 2004 alone (Ukrist 2005:3). Yet major political Islamist or terrorist organisations rarely stepped forward to take credit for the violence, and many of the killings—involving police, politicians, and criminal gangs—were of the sort that had gone on for decades, often centred in conflicts over corrupt activities (Pasuk & Baker 2004:237).

During 2004, there were three major exceptions to this generalisation, but they deepen rather than clarify the mysteries surrounding violence in the south. First, on 4 January, a military post was attacked; several people were killed and a weapons cache stolen, an action blamed on separatist groups, but with no organisation taking credit (Pasuk & Baker 2004:237). Second, on 28 April, in Pattani and Narathiwat, Thai military units attacked groups of machete-wielding youths who were putatively involved with separatist organisations; over 100 youths were killed, more than 30 of these at the Krue Se mosque in Pattani (Pasuk & Baker 2004:238). Third, on 25 October, Thai military units killed more than eighty southern protestors in Tak Bai district of Narathiwat, most of whom were killed when they suffocated after being forced into crowded police vans (Ukrist 2005:2).

Although all of these events spoke to an intensification of violence grounded in long-standing patterns of local activity and conflict between the Thai state and southerners, none of them clearly manifest the emergence of new and more powerful separatist groups; nor did any clearly manifest the hand of international terrorist organisations such as al Qa'eda (Fullbrook 2004). This being the case, what led to the intensification of violence in 2004?

Given the uncertainties surrounding the events, there is a variety of claims that have been put forward. One central factor that begins to emerge from various of the accounts, however, is that Thaksin's more open engagement with the war on terror became part of his own project for gaining leverage within the military and helped generate a conflict—centred, especially, in the south—with long-entrenched interests in the opposition Democrat Party, sections of the military, and Royalists connected to former Prime Minister Prem Tinsulanond (McCargo & Ukrist 2005:213–16). This conflict broke into the open with special force when Prem, speaking for the Privy Council in early 2005, criticised Thaksin's reliance on force to address the southern problem (Ukrist 2005:29).

Precisely how this conflict between Thai elites has spurred violence in the south is itself a matter of contention, but there is good reason to believe that the violence is very much a domestic affair and that neither international Islamic terrorist networks nor US policies under the war on terror have directly caused the problems, even though both may have indirectly affected it. Rather, acting in an environment created by the US's declaration of a war on terror, political elites in Thailand have carried forward struggles against popular organisations and struggles with each other—struggles that, in this case, happen to take place within the south. Thus, even more than the cases of the Philippines and Indonesia, the Thai case shows how local and national politics are being affected by resurgent US imperialism in South-East Asia and how, in a context of declining US, neoliberal hegemony, South-East Asian elites are acting autonomously to further their own objectives using the leverage provided by US actions.

CONCLUSION

During the Cold War, South-East Asian military leaders often played up the threat posed by communism in order to please US policy makers and thereby gain leverage in specific domestic struggles. In this regard, the political jockeying enabled by the US-led war on terror in South-East Asia is not deeply different from what occurred during the Cold War. But, during the Cold War South-East Asian elites also had legitimate reason for concern about local communist parties and about the regional dynamism that might be imparted to their efforts by China and the Soviet Union. Ferdinand Marcos (the Philippines), Soeharto (Indonesia), Thanom Kittakachorn (Thailand), and other such Cold War leaders certainly used state power to enhance their own economic fortunes and to counter moves by competitors, but they also used the state and US Cold War support to repress popular forces that might ally with—or that, in fact, were allied with—local communist parties and their Chinese or Soviet backers. In this sense, however opportunistic was the participation of South-East Asian capitalist elites in the Cold War, it was also grounded in very real concerns these elites had about leftist and popular threats to their power and privilege. The US-led war on communism—even where it became, in many respects, a war on anti-colonial nationalism, as in Vietnam—could attract the support of these elites and various other members of South-East Asian societies because the US interests it reflected also coincided with many of their own interests. The USA was not only an imperial power, but also a hegemon, in Gramsci's sense, and many South-East Asian elites accepted its rationale for the war on communism and its basic economic doctrines.

In this respect, the US-led war on terror is different, since South-East Asian elites are not deeply threatened by the official target of the US-led war, the Islamic terrorist networks; nor do they uniformly share fears of the bigger regional challenger to US dominance, China. In the Philippines and Indonesia, the kinds of internationally connected terrorist forces the US targets undoubtedly exist, but this existence does not explain long-standing domestic conflicts. In the Philippines, military elites may appreciate the access to increased funds and weaponry for battles in the south that the war on terror makes possible, but Moro struggles in the Philippines do not depend upon international connections, nor have they posed a serious threat to basic structures of power in the Philippines in recent years. Indonesian military elites may also relish the renewal of US military support made possible by the war on terror, but their will and ability to use this support to eradicate groups such as JI seems questionable, while the likelihood of their using it to suppress separatist groups in Aceh and West Papua is clear. In Thailand, it is questionable how important internationally linked terrorist organisations are to the violence that has erupted, while there is no doubt that significant domestic political conflicts are being played out in the environment created by the war on terror.

The locally conditioned autonomy and diversity of South-East Asian elites' responses to the terrorist threats announced by the Bush administration illustrates that, while the US still has the power to significantly affect geopolitical economic processes in South-East Asia, it does not necessarily do so as a force that South-East Asian leaders follow in the same way they did during the Cold War. This is even more clear if one looks behind the Bush administration's official reasons for declaring a war on terror in the region to US policy makers' broader and longer-standing concerns about Asia. The US desires to strengthen its military presence in South-East Asia as a counterbalance to growing Chinese influence are unambiguously central to the US response to September 11, but the South-East Asian leaders who have signed on to the war on terror do not, for the most part, share US concerns about China (Sokolsky et al. 2000:29–62). Most regard China as a new regional competitor, posing enormous difficulties for South-East Asian exporters, but most also see some economic opportunities in the growth of the China market; few would want to create potential military confrontations in the name of security.

How the tensions surrounding resurgent US imperialism in a context of declining US hegemony will play out is highly uncertain. What is certain is that they will be driven by the continuing—even if crisis-prone—growth of capitalism in Asia and the complex, internationalised social struggles that are central to capitalist development.

NOTES

1 For an analysis of the similarities and differences between conservative, neoconservative, liberal, and neoliberal tendencies in the US, see Glassman (2005a); for a more detailed account of the reports mentioned, see Glassman (2005b).

2 The International Crisis Group is a fundamentally conservative, US-backed organisation that includes on its board former Australian Foreign Minister Gareth Evans, former US National Security Advisors Richard Allen and Zbignew Brzezinski, Costa Rican Nobel Laureate Oscar Arias Sanchez, former NATO Supreme Allied Commander Wesley Clark, former US Trade Representative Carla Hills, Indonesian Human Rights lawyer Todung Mulya Lubis, former Thai Foreign Minister Surin Pitsuwan, former Philippine President Fidel Ramos, British journalist William Shawcross, and financier George Soros.

REFERENCES

Andrews-Speed, Phillip, Liao Xuanli and Roland Dannreuther (2002) *The Strategic Implications of China's Energy Needs*, Adelphi Paper 346, International Institute for Strategic Studies, New York: Oxford University Press.

Arkin, William (2005) *Code Names: Deciphering U.S. Military Plans, Programs, and Operations in the September 11 World*, Hanover: Steerforth Press.

Arrighi, Giovanni and Beverly Silver (1999) *Chaos and Governance in the Modern World System*, Minneapolis: University of Minnesota Press.

Beeson, Mark (2000) 'Mahathir and the Markets: Globalization and the Pursuit of Economic Autonomy in Malaysia', *Pacific Affairs*, 73(3):335–51.

——(2004) 'Southeast Asia and the Major Powers: The United States, Japan, and China', in Mark Beeson (ed.), *Contemporary Southeast Asia: Regional Dynamics, National Differences*, New York: Palgrave Macmillan, pp. 198–215.

Borden, William S. (1984) *The Pacific Alliance: United States foreign economic policy and Japanese trade recovery, 1947–1955*, Madison: University of Wisconsin Press.

Brown, Andrew (2004) *Labour, Politics and the State in Industrializing Thailand*, London and New York: RoutledgeCurzon.

Central Intelligence Agency (USA), National Intelligence Council (CIA–NIC) (2004) *Mapping the Global Future: Report of the National Intelligence Council's 2020 Project, Based on Consultations with Nongovernmental Experts Around the World*, Washington, DC: Central Intelligence Agency–National Intelligence Council, <www.foia.cia.gov/2020/2020.pdf>.

Council on Foreign Relations (CFR) (1946) Memorandum T-A14, June 17, 1941, in *The War and Peace Studies of the Council on Foreign Relations, 1939–1945*, New York: Harold Pratt House.

——Independent Task Force (2001) *The United States and Southeast Asia: A Policy agenda for the New Administration*, New York: Council on Foreign Relations, <www.cfr.org/publication.php?id-3979>.

Eder, James F. and Thomas M. McKenna (2004) 'Minorities in the Philippines: Ancestral Lands and Autonomy in Theory and Practice', in Christopher Duncan (ed.), *Civilizing the Margins: Southeast Asian Government Policies for the Development of Minorities*, Ithaca: Cornell University Press, pp. 56–85.

Fullbrook, David (2004) 'Thailand: Behind the Muslim "Insurgency" ', *International Herald Tribune*, 17 December.

Glassman, Jim (2004a) *Thailand at the Margins: Internationalization of the State and the Transformation of Labour*, Oxford: Oxford University Press.

——(2004b) 'Transnational Hegemony and US Labour Foreign Policy: Towards a Gramscian International Labour Geography', *Environment and Planning D: Society and Space* 22(4): 573–93.

——(2004c) 'Economic "Nationalism" in a Post-Nationalist Era: The Political Economy of Economic Policy in Post-Crisis Thailand', *Critical Asian Studies* 36(1):37–64.

——(2005a) 'The *New* Imperialism? On Continuity and Change in US Foreign Policy', *Environment and Planning A* 37(9): 1527—44.

——(2005b) 'The "war on terror" comes to Southeast Asia', *Journal of Contemporary Asia* 35(1):3–28.

Gramsci, Antonio (1971) *Selections from the Prison Notebooks of Antonio Gramsci* (ed.) Quinton Hoare and Geoffrey N. Smith (eds), New York: International Publishers.

Harvey, David (2003) *The New Imperialism*, Oxford: Oxford University Press.

Hewison, Kevin (1997) 'Introduction: power, oppositions, and democratisation', in Kevin Hewison (ed.) *Political Change in Thailand: Democracy and Participation*, New York: Routledge, pp. 1–20.

——(2003) 'The Politics of Neo-Liberalism: Class and Capitalism in Contemporary Thailand', *Southeast Asia Research Centre Working Paper No. 45*, May, Hong Kong: City University of Hong Kong, <www.cityu.edu.hk/searc>.

——and Garry Rodan (2004) 'Closing the Circle?: Globalization, Conflict and Political Regimes', *Southeast Asia Research Centre Working Paper No. 63*, May, Hong Kong: City University of Hong Kong, <www.cityu.edu.hk/searc>.

Huxley, Tim and Susan Willett (1999) *Arming East Asia*, Adelphi Paper 329, International Institute for Strategic Studies, Oxford: Oxford University Press.

International Crisis Group (ICG) (2001) 'Indonesia: Ending Repression in Irian Jaya', Jakarta/Brussels: ICG, 20 September, <www.icg.org>.

——(2002a) 'Indonesia Backgrounder: How the *Jemaah Islamiyah* Terrorist Network Operates', Jakarta/Brussels: ICG, 11 December; <www.icg.org>.

——(2002b) 'Indonesia: Resources and Conflict in Papua', Jakarta/Brussels: ICG, 13 September, <www.icg.org>.

——(2003a) Jemaah Islamiyah in South East Asia: Damaged But Still Dangerous', Jakarta/Brussels: ICG, 26 August, <www.icg.org>.

——(2003b) 'Aceh: How Not to Win Hearts and Minds', Jakarta/Brussels: ICG, 23 July, <www.icg.org>.

——(2003c) 'Dividing Papua: How Not to Do It', Jakarta/Brussels: ICG, 9 April, <www.icg.org>.

International Peace Mission (2002) *Basilan: The Next Afghanistan?* Report of the International Peace Mission to Basilan, Philippines, 23–27 March, <www.focusweb.org>.

Islam, Syed S. (1998) 'The Islamic Independence Movements in Patani of Thailand and Mindanao of the Philippines', *Asian Survey* 38(5):441–56.

Ji Giles Ungpakorn (1997) *The Struggle for Democracy and Social Justice in Thailand*, Bangkok: Arom Pongpangan Foundation.

Kagan, David, Gary Schmitt and Thomas Donnelly (2000) *Rebuilding America's Defenses: Strategy, Forces, and Resources for a New Century*, report of the Project for a New American Century, <www.newamericancentury.org/publicationsreports.htm>.

Kingsbury, Damien (1998) *The Politics of Indonesia*, Melbourne: Oxford University Press.

Klein, Naomi (2003) 'Stark Message of the Mutiny: Is the Philippine government bombing its own people for dollars?' *The Guardian* (UK), 16 August.

Kolko, Gabriel (1988) *Confronting the Third World: United States Foreign Policy, 1945–1980*, New York: Pantheon.

LaBotz, Dan (2001) *Made in Indonesia: Indonesian Workers Since Suharto*, Boston: South End Press.

McCargo, Duncan (2004) 'Southern Thai Politics: A Preliminary Overview', POLIS Working Paper No. 3 (February), Leeds: School of Politics and International Studies, <www.leeds.ac.uk/polis/research/pdf/wp3mccargo.pdf

——and Ukrist Pathmanand (2005) *The Thaksinization of Thailand*, Copenhagen: NIAS Press.

Nakashima, Ellen and Alan Sipress (2003) 'Tips, Traced Call Led to Capture of Al Qaeda Suspect: Hambali Tracked Through 4 Countries', *Washington Post* Foreign Service, 16 August, A14.

Pasuk Phongpaichit and Chris Baker (2004) *Thaksin: The Business of Politics in Thailand*, Chiang Mai: Silkworm Books.

Rahim, Lily Z. (2003) 'The Road Less Traveled: Islamic Militancy in Southeast Asia', *Critical Asian Studies* 35(2):209–32.

Roberts, John (2003) 'Military mutiny in the Philippines: a sign of deeper political tensions', World Socialist website, <www.wsws.org>.

Robinson, Geoffrey (2001) '*Rawan* is as *Rawan* Does: The Origins of Disorder in New Order Aceh', in Benedict Anderson (ed.) *Violence and the State in Suharto's Indonesia*, Ithaca: Cornell University Southeast Asia Program Publications, pp. 213–41.

Rotter, Andrew (1987) *The Path to Vietnam: Origins of the American Commitment to Southeast Asia*, Ithaca: Cornell University Press.

Shambaugh, David (2002) *Modernizing China's Military: Progress, Problems, and Prospects*, Berkeley: University of California Press.

Smith, Neil (2005) *The End Game of Globalization*, New York: Routledge.

Sokolsky, Richard, Angel Rabasa and C. Richard Neu (2000) *The Role of Southeast Asia in US Strategy Toward China*, Santa Monica: RAND, Project AIR FORCE division, <www.rand.org/publications/MR/MR1170>.

Surat Horachaikul (2003) 'The far South of Thailand in the era of American empire, September 11 version, and Thaksin's "cash and gung ho" premiership', *Asian Review 2003*: 131–51.

Symonds, Peter (2003) 'Indonesia launches "shock and awe" military offensive in Aceh', World Socialist website, <www.wsws.org>.

Tyner, James A. (2005) *Iraq, Terror, and the Philippines' Will to War*, Lanham: Rowman & Littlefield.

Ukrist Pathmanand (2005) 'Thaksin's Achilles Heel: Why did the South go wrong?', paper presented at the 9th International Thai Studies Conference, DeKalb: Northern Illinois University, April 3.

Wallerstein, Immanuel (2003) *The Decline of American Power*, New York: The New Press.

West, Lois (1997) *Militant Labor in the Philippines*, Philadelphia: Temple University Press.

Woodrow Wilson Foundation (1955) *The Political Economy of American Foreign Policy*, New York: Holt.

9 South-East Asia and the International Financial Institutions[1]

Mark Beeson

KEY TOPICS

INTRODUCTION

POLITICAL and economic development in South-East Asia has occurred in a unique set of historical circumstances. The period in which most of the countries of South-East Asia became independent nation-states following the Second World War was one that had very distinctive features. Undoubtedly, the most important factor in this period was the rise and rise of the US, first as part of a bipolar Cold War contest with the Soviet Union, and latterly, as the world's first hyperpower or global hegemon. But no matter how we describe US power in the postwar period, one thing is particularly noteworthy: the US's ascendancy has been closely associated with a simultaneous growth of a range of international financial institutions (IFIs), institutions that have had a major impact on the South-East Asian region. IFIs have assumed an increased importance and visibility as part of the emerging institutional architecture of what we have come to call 'global governance'. Imperfect as this term is, it does capture something of the novel ways in which political and economic activities have evolved over the past few decades. It is important to recognise at the outset that the foundations of the seemingly global processes we now take for granted were laid down in the aftermath of the Second World War; they have been consolidated by US hegemony and the powerful intergovernmental agencies that were created under its auspices. The IFIs that were established in the late 1940s—the World Bank, the International Monetary Fund (IMF), and the General Agreement on Tariffs and Trade (GATT)—became well known the world over, no small achievement given the nature of their responsibilities, and testimony to their importance, even if their precise roles have sometimes not been well understood.

Before considering the role and impact of the IFIs in any detail, it should be emphasised that, unlike most of the other contributions to this book, the focus of this chapter is primarily on the external realm—that is, on the actors and institutions that have sought to influence the course of economic and political development in South-East Asia from a distance. This does not mean that the orientation of the chapter is at odds with the social conflict approach adopted elsewhere in this volume, but it does mean that its principal interest is in the impact of exogenous forces on the political contests and social struggles that are generally considered within exclusively national frameworks. The potential importance and relevance of taking external influences seriously is clear when we remember the circumstances that underpinned the downfall Indonesia's Soeharto: not only did external controllers of financial capital arguably create the preconditions for the crisis that delegitimated Soeharto's rule, but the lack of support from the IFIs and the US also further undermined his regime, ultimately making his position untenable (Beeson 1998). True, Indonesia's particular social conflicts may have had domestic roots and revolved around nationally based struggles over resources and power, but external forces provided a catalyst for the upheaval and the IFIs played a crucial role in attempting to manage the aftermath of the crisis and the particular institutional milieu that emerged as a consequence.

Given the importance of external influences in the international system, the central argument of this chapter is as follows: political and economic development in South-East Asia has occurred within, and has been shaped by, a range of external actors and forces, the precise influence of which has itself been a function of particular geopolitical circumstances. Of pivotal importance in this context has been the evolving strategic position of the US. US foreign policy priorities have themselves been shaped by a shifting calculation of its own national interest, the best way of pursuing it, and—as elsewhere in the world—the relative balance of economic and political interests within the US itself (Trubowitz 1998). The influence of finance capital—for example, the liberalisation of which has been such a major goal of the IMF—has varied, dependent on a wider set of economic and/or geopolitical circumstances.[2] Significantly, political contests that were once primarily confined within national borders or expressed through the foreign policies of individual nations, have now assumed a transnational dimension. It is not necessary to agree with Robert Cox's (1992) assertion that the state everywhere has been reduced to a 'transmission belt' for the policy preferences of a transnational managerial elite, to recognise that all nations find their autonomy constrained and their policy preferences shaped by a range of external forces. The key point is, of course, that some countries have a far greater capacity than others to shape the external regulatory environment that influences national policy outcomes. In this regard, the US continues to exert an unparalleled influence (Foot et al. 2003).

This has major implications for friend and foe alike. On the one hand, it has meant that the US's willingness to support countries such as Indonesia has been partly dependent on a wider set of geopolitical factors (see Glassman, this volume). On the other hand, the precise way that the US has chosen to exert its influence over other countries has also varied. One of the most important long-term consequences of the US's evolving policy approach has been its influence over the IFIs. Although the US was the principal architect of the postwar international order of which the IFIs were such an influential and novel part, it has frequently allowed these bodies a good deal of autonomy at times and preferred to act at a distance through institutional auspices. For the countries of South-East Asia, the IFIs have come to exert a major influence over the course of development and frequently acted as an extension of US foreign policy, with the overall goal of encouraging not only successful capitalist development, but also, preferably, economic development along neoliberal lines. By including international political economy in our understanding of national development, we can further illuminate and explain sources of social conflict over the content of domestic public policy and the specific distribution of resources such policies help determine. As national economies[3] are reconfigured and the power of various political and economic actors fluctuates as a consequence of their ability to take advantage of changing circumstances, external forces like the IFIs can provide policy ideas, a crucial source of legitimacy, and tangible economic assistance. Conversely, of course, they can help to undermine opponents of their reform agendas.

There is plainly a debate to be had about the relative influence of internal and external forces, the relationship between sovereignty and globalisation, and the capacity of states and the political elites that control them to act autonomously—especially in South-East Asia. Historical institutionalists clearly have a point when they highlight the relatively limited state capacities of most South-East Asian states when compared to their North-East Asian counterparts. Equally important from the perspective of social conflict, however, is the fact politically-determined contests about 'appropriate' economic policy and institutional development are occurring in the context of a wider reconfiguration of the international political-economy. Not only have individual national economies been increasingly integrated into overarching, internationally-oriented finance and production structures, but the IFIs are emblematic of the way regulatory power and authority have become trans-nationalised, too. Because the IFIs are associated with a particular set of economic policies, and because such policies inevitably favour some political and economic interests over others (both domestically and internationally), they can directly influence the course of hitherto domestic social conflicts. Consequently, we need to take account of this transnational dimension of contemporary economic and political relations if we hope to obtain a complete picture of nationally-based social conflicts.

This chapter explains the development and roles of the IFIs, their relationship to US hegemony,[4] and their impact on South-East Asia. The first two sections of the chapter describe the establishment and evolution of the postwar international order and the very distinctive roles the IFIs have played within it. Both the roles of the IFIs and the geopolitical context in which they operate have changed significantly over the course of the last fifty or sixty years, and this has been reflected in the emergence of new policy initiatives on the part of the IFIs and—especially of late—important changes in US foreign policy. It will be argued that the IFIs have played a crucial role in promoting a broadly neoliberal policy agenda associated primarily with the US, and that this has been a key expression of US hegemony. The overall impact of these changes is considered in the final section of the chapter, where some of the impacts that the IFIs have had on the region, the ideas that have informed their evolving policy initiatives, and the responses these have engendered across the region are detailed.

THE POSTWAR INTERNATIONAL ORDER

Given some of the criticisms that have recently been levelled at the US, its current foreign policy style, and its impact on South-East Asia (Beeson 2004), it is easy to forget that US hegemony has had important beneficial effects as well. At one level, this possibility is evident in the way US influence over the former colonial powers actually assisted independence movements in countries like Indonesia (McMahon 1999). At a more indirect level, the particular international order that the US was instrumental in creating in the aftermath of the Second World War provided the conditions in which at least some parts of the wider East Asian region were able to rapidly industrialise. Although there is still some debate about the long-term impact of this process on different parts of South-East Asia,[5] it is striking that the first few decades after the war are now considered to be something of a golden age of contemporary capitalist development (Marglin & Schor 1990). Given the criticisms that are sometimes directed at the contemporary international order, it is worth spelling out how this system came into being and what role the IFIs played within it.

The postwar international order was largely created at an especially convened conference at Bretton Woods in 1944. The Bretton Woods institutions—the World Bank, the IMF and the GATT—were specifically designed to avoid the mistakes of the interwar years, when the world plunged into an economic depression made worse by beggar-thy-neighbour tariff barriers and a chaotic monetary system in which competitive devaluations further discouraged trade. The social, political, and, above all, economic trauma of the interwar period fundamentally undermined the credibility and legitimacy of capitalism as an economic system in many parts of the world. It was against this ideologically charged backdrop that the US actively promoted the construction of a liberal, open economic order that encouraged trade integration and expansion (Latham 1997). It was the job of the GATT to encourage trade liberalism and reduce tariff barriers. Significantly, and unlike the World Trade Organisation (WTO) that replaced it, the GATT had no capacity to enforce its policy preferences; rather, it had to rely on moral suasion and voluntary compliance.

While the IMF and the World Bank may not have undergone quite the sort of radical makeover that the GATT did, they have both changed in important ways that need spelling out. The World Bank—formerly known as the International Bank for Reconstruction and Development—was, as the name implies, established to provide the funds for postwar reconstruction. Although initially focused on European reconstruction, the World Bank rapidly became primarily associated with attempts to encourage economic development in the Third World.[6] While this may seem a relatively uncontroversial and worthy goal, the precise way the World Bank has gone about this—especially given its close association with the foreign policy objectives of the US during the Cold War—has made its actions the subject of heated debate and no small controversy (see Caufield 1996). Not only was the bank criticised for funding grandiose, socially, and environmentally inappropriate megaprojects, but it was also often seen as attempting to exercise an invasive ideological influence on the policies of supposedly autonomous governments. Structural adjustment policies, as they became known, worked on the basis of borrowers adhering to a set of demanding and carefully calibrated public policy reforms that were broadly in keeping with neoliberalism and the so-called Washington Consensus.

The term 'Washington Consensus' was coined by John Williamson in 1990 to describe what he considered to be the prevailing orthodoxy among policy elites in the IFIs. Central to the conventional wisdom of the time, as Williamson saw it, was agreement on the need for limited budget deficits, growth-oriented public spending, tax reform, financial liberalisation, competitive exchange rates, tariff reductions, unimpeded foreign investment, privatisation of state assets, removal of impediments to competition, and secure property rights (Williamson 1990). Williamson now contends that his original list was very much a 'product of its time', and not intended as a 'cookbook' (Williamson 2005). He also claims that the consensus has subsequently 'evaporated', with the World Bank and the IMF becoming more sensitive to questions of income distribution, while the highly influential US Treasury Department remained more doctrinaire. While the degree of this divergence may be overstated, it is clear that, during the course of the 1990s, when the declining importance of strategic issues decreased the need for ideological solidarity among the IFIs, and when the World Bank and the IMF came in for extensive criticism from a more assertive international civil society, we saw the emergence of a post or augmented Washington Consensus. The augmented consensus paid much greater attention to the need for social safety nets, sustainable development, poverty reduction, democratic participation, as well as to more conventional economic issues, such as public and private sector governance, regulatory harmonisation, labour market reform, central bank independence, and, perhaps most significantly, the strengthening of domestic financial sectors prior to liberalisation (Beeson & Islam 2005:202; Higgott 2000).

Policy towards the financial sector is emblematic of wider debates about economic reform and the context within which they have unfolded. In this regard, the IMF's role has, like the World Bank's, changed in ways that are simultaneously controversial and indicative of the way in which the international economic order has evolved. The IMF was originally an organisation charged with maintaining stability in a system of managed exchange rates. It maintained order by offering short-term loans to countries experiencing balance of payments difficulties and thereby discouraged the sort of competitive devaluations that wreaked such havoc in the interwar period. It was a system that worked remarkably successfully until the early 1970s when the US decided it was no longer in its perceived national interests to underpin the old system, which linked the value of the US dollar to gold. Put simply, foreign competition and the costs of the Vietnam War made devaluation an increasingly attractive option for US policymakers, but one that was foreclosed by the dollar–gold link. Consequently, President Richard Nixon unilaterally 'closed the gold window' (Gowa 1983).

A couple of points merit emphasis here. First, this period not only led to the emergence of a significantly different international order characterised by the massive growth of increasingly self-regulating money markets, but it also led to a significant change in the IMF's *rasion d'être*. From being the centrepiece of a regulated system of monetary relations, the IMF transformed itself into a champion of financial sector deregulation and capital account opening (Pauly 1997). The merits of such policies— especially for the emerging market economies—are hotly debated (see Kahler 1998), particularly following a series of financial crises that swept Latin America, Russia, and, most importantly for the purposes of this discussion, South-East Asia. But whatever one thinks about the merits of such policies, the fact that many observers see a clear link between the sorts of policies organisations such as the IMF advocated and particular financial sector interests based in the US, which stood to benefit from their implementation, made them highly controversial (Wade 2001).

The second point to make is that there has always been a tension in the international system between its unilateral and multilateral dynamics. This is important, as some observers claim that US dominance of the international system is accepted—or at least acquiesced to—because the very IFIs the US helped create are multilateral by nature, thereby enabling access for other countries to decision-making processes and institutionally constraining US power (Ikenberry 1998). Yet America's role in the collapse of the old system of managed exchange rates reminds us that there is nothing new about the most powerful country in the world attempting to exploit its position and act unilaterally if it perceives such action to be in its own national interests to do so.

Consequently, there is an even more fundamental general point to emphasise about the postwar international order and the US's place in it: the US has always been able to exercise more direct and indirect (through agencies like the IFIs) influence than any other country. The key difference between the old Bretton Woods regime was that it was embedded in, and a key element of, a specific Cold War regime that was designed to make capitalism work and undermine its socialist rival. The end of the Cold War and the abrupt demise of the Soviet Union means that this potential constraint on US policy no longer applies: not only can Third World states no longer try to play off one Superpower against another, but the only remaining global power is not obliged to tolerate economic and/or political practices of which it may not have approved, but which it felt obliged to overlook in the context of the Cold War. Consequently, the sorts of developmental states that have been so characteristic of East Asia generally, and which are closely associated with forms of non-democratic, authoritarian rule, are now being subjected to much closer negative scrutiny and reformist pressure.

GLOBALISATION AND THE POST-COLD WAR ORDER

To get a sense of how the Cold War order differs to the contemporary period, it is worth looking at the extent of, and motivations for, IFI and US interventions in South-East Asia during the 1960s and 1970s. Indonesia following the downfall of Soekarno and the accession of Soeharto in 1966 offers one of the most telling examples of the influence of the IFIs in South-East Asia during the Cold War period. Keen to shore up its pro-Western credentials, the newly installed Soeharto regime invited the IMF and the World Bank to work with Indonesian economists to establish an appropriate policy framework in return for aid and loans (Winters 1996:53–4). Far from being an obstacle to the development of a robust market economy, Soeharto's authoritarian regime was actually seen as an important source of stability. This symbiotic relationship, in which key IFIs provided crucial assistance and legitimation for the Soeharto regime's policies, was a pattern that persisted in one form or another until the East Asian crisis. True, there were occasional interventions from the US and the IMF in which they tried to discourage the sort of corrupt patrimonial practices that became synonymous with the Soeharto clan (Winters 1996:86), but on the whole it is remarkable how supportive and uncritical the IFIs remained long after the Cold War ended and the earlier ideological imperatives fell away (see Brauchli & Solomon 1998).

A similar story can be told of the Philippines. Significantly, as Paul Hutchcroft (1998:113) points out, it was his close connections with the US that allowed the dictator Ferdinand Marcos to cultivate good connections with the World Bank and the IMF, relationships that ensured continuing access to multilateral aid. Despite the fact that the IMF and the World Bank were intent on propping up the position of pro-market technocrats within the administration, as in Indonesia, they 'ended up providing enormous support to the crony system' (Hutchcroft 1998:114). While there has been a somewhat belated recognition of the perverse impact IFI policies had during the Cold War, as they effectively propped up and helped legitimate regional autocrats, this has not stopped the IFIs from more aggressively pushing their reform initiatives and ideas in the reconfigured political space opened up by the end of the Cold War. Indeed, the diminution of geopolitical and ideological imperatives has allowed the IFIs to promote a reformist agenda more forcefully as if it were set of apolitical technical issues, rather than an expression of a particular set of normative values and power relations.

At one level, these developments can be seen as part of a wider process of emergent global governance, in which a range of non-state actors and intergovernmental agencies have come to play a bigger part in the way increasingly transnational economic and political processes actually operate (Rosenau 1997). In part, this is simply a functional requirement of globalisation: the growth and sheer complexity of transborder interactions necessitates concomitant web of regulatory relationships to grease the wheels of global commerce (Cerny 1995). While such processes may have allowed a potentially larger group of actors access to decision-making processes, in reality, effective power in the international system remains predominantly with the developed industrialised economies in general and with the US in particular (Woods 2003). Indeed, it is striking how underrepresented East Asia generally is in the most important intergovernmental institutions (Rapkin & Strand 2003). More fundamentally in the long term, perhaps, the sort of pro-business agenda associated with neoliberalism and the Washington Consensus has been entrenched within many of the private sector agencies that have assumed regulatory responsibility in key areas of the global economy (Braithwaite & Drahos 2000).

As far as the IFIs are concerned, the new environment offers an opportunity for greater policy activism and the refinement of the policy discourses that accompany them. The World Bank has been at the forefront of developing a policy agenda that is still broadly in keeping with market-oriented reform, but which has been significantly re-packaged, partly as a response to widespread criticism from an increasingly active transnational social movement (see O'Brien et al. 2000). In place of structural adjustment policies, the bank and like-minded organisations employ the language of the augmented n Consensus. In the new paradigm, the key to economic develop- od governance', which means the rule of law, transparent political relationships, and capacity building (World Bank 1994). While seem worthy and uncontroversial goals, they fail to adequately ...e political context in which economic development occurs (Leftwich 2000). As other contributors to this book demonstrate in more detail, this is an especially important consideration given the historical experience of South-East Asia.

Even though the sort of developmental state that guided economic development in Japan, Taiwan, and South Korea may never have been as successfully or completely realised in South-East Asia, important elements of the underpinning economic and political relationships were (see Jomo 2001a). Economic development throughout South-East Asia has invariably been characterised by close relationships between political and economic elites; even if they were not as successful in achieving developmental goals as were their North-East Asian counterparts, a nexus of political and economic power has been a distinctive feature of many South-East Asian nations. In some cases—most notoriously, in Indonesia—close ties between political and economic elites were the glue that bound together a regime based on patronage (Robison & Hadiz 2004). Even in Malaysia, which has historically been less overtly corrupt, political elites and even party organisations have played central roles in the ownership and control of key economic assets (Gomez & Jomo 1997). The pattern is repeated across the region, albeit with subtle, contingent variations (see Gomez 2002). The point to emphasise here is that, in its ideal-typical form—epitomised by Japan in the first two decades after the war—state-guided development was facilitated rather than obstructed by close government–business ties, as the state was able to direct capital to strategically important industries and influence the course of industrialisation as a consequence. It is a development strategy that is fundamentally at odds with the dominant IFI view and helps to explain why it has been so controversial and the target of reformist pressures.[7]

Whatever we may think about the relationships that underpinned the developmental state from either a normative (are they ethical?) or pragmatic (do they work?) point of view, there is little doubt that close ties between economic and political elites have been a central part of the historical development experience in South-East Asia. They have become deeply institutionalised and entrenched as a result. The prospects for a reformist agenda based on good governance are, therefore, fraught with potential difficulty. The proposed reforms—especially the desire for a more accountable, transparent political class or state that is independent of economic interests—are a direct threat to the existing order. Equally important, the historical dominance of the state and the relative paucity of independent organisations and institutions in civil society means that it is difficult to replace the state as a central actor, even if there was a genuine desire to do so (Beeson 2001).

This is all rather surprising. Superficially, much of South-East Asia would seem to be broadly moving with the times. There has, for example, been a notable expansion in the number of democratic—or, at least, semi-democratic—regimes across the region (see Case 2002) and a concomitant decline in the sorts of strongman leaders personified by Soeharto, Marcos, Mohamed Mahathir, and Lee Kwan Yew. At one level, then, the potential for friction with ardent supporters of democratic expansion, such as the US, ought to have been reduced. And, indeed, this does seem to be the case, but not simply because there is an inevitable congruence of interests between like-minded democracies. On the contrary, the war on terror and the re-prioritising of security issues has seen the US reverting to Cold War practices, adopting an indulgent attitude toward more authoritarian-minded regional elites, and re-establishing closer ties with the region's militaries (Beeson 2004).

But even this apparent reversion to old ways in the security arena has not halted a continuing process of structural transformation across the region that is steadily changing political and economic relationships within countries, across the region, and between the region and the rest of the world. The IFIs have played an important part in this process.

THE IMPACT OF THE IFIs ON SOUTH-EAST ASIA

Important changes have occurred in the role of the major IFIs, the content of the policy regimes they have promoted as a consequence, and the way they have attempted to promote those ideas at particular historical moments. Although the changing geopolitical context has presented the IFIs with an opportunity to press change more forcefully upon their clients, they have become more sensitive about criticism of their roles and the efficacy of the policies they champion. The emergence of the augmented Washington Consensus was indicative of the contradictory impulses at work. Yet as long as East Asia generally and South-East Asia in particular were seen to be miraculous economic success stories, it was not easy for the IFIs to impose either version of the economic orthodoxy. When the economic crisis hit in 1997, it not only changed this underlying dynamic, but also exposed some apparent divisions among the IFIs over economic policy.

The significance of the crisis here lies in the impact it had on relations between South-East Asia, the IFIs, and, by extension, the US. A number of commentators have drawn attention to the inter-relationship between US policymakers in the State and Treasury Departments, their close connections with and influence over the IFIs, and financial sector interests based in the US (Beeson 2003a; Bhagwati 1998; Wade 2001). Controllers of mobile capital and financial market actors more generally are able to influence policymakers through lobbying, political donations, and overlapping career trajectories. The Treasury Secretary at the time of the Asian crisis, Robert Rubin, for example, was a former chairman of Goldman Sachs, and since leaving government has become a director of Citigroup, one of the largest financial institutions in the world. As Jagdish Bhagwati (1998: 11) points out

> Wall Street's financial firms have obvious self-interest in a world of free capital mobility since it only enlarges the arena in which to make money. It is not surprising, therefore, that Wall Street has put its powerful oar into the turbulent waters of Washington political lobbying to steer in this direction.

This is important for two reasons. First, following the crisis, the reformist agenda promoted by the IMF in particular was inevitably tainted by perceptions of self-interested and opportunistic behaviour. In this regard, there is no doubt that the US saw the crisis as a possibly unique opportunity to force compliance with a neoliberal agenda that it had long promoted with little success in East Asia. Equally damaging was the perception that US lenders were treated more favourably and with less opprobrium than were Asian borrowers (Jomo 2001b), which has sparked an important and continuing debate about how to manage crises, and raised the question of whether foreign lenders are equally culpable and should be bailed in rather than bailed out in the aftermath of a crisis.

The second major consequence that flowed from perceptions about the Wall St–Treasury complex was that the specific remedies or crisis-management strategies the IMF proposed were less credible as a consequence, in particular when they were widely perceived to have exacerbated economic conditions in Malaysia, Thailand, and, especially, in Indonesia. There were two further noteworthy impacts of the IMF's (mis)handling of the crisis and the perception of US influence on its policies. One consequence was that it gave opponents of IFI policies an opportunity to criticise them, the US, and the West more generally. Most prominent in this regard was Malaysia's Mahathir (1999), who characterised the crisis as a conspiracy to undermine the hitherto successful East Asian economies; he dismissed the IMF's advice as inappropriate and took the opportunity to promote an alternative regional monetary fund with which to ward off future crises. While such initiatives have not progressed far as yet (Lincoln 2004), what is most striking about Mahathir's position was that he saw the possibility of developing new, regionally based IFIs to act as a defensive buffer and potential vehicle with which to champion East Asian ideas, rather than as a Western-dominated mechanism with which to promote further neoliberal reform.

The other consequence of the IMF's role in the crisis was that it highlighted apparent divisions between the IMF and the World Bank. The principal spokesperson of the new thinking was Joseph Stiglitz, the (then) chief economist of the World Bank. Stiglitz wrote a series of stinging critiques of the IMF, which not only pilloried its approach, but which also actively championed the sort of state activism and intervention that had characterised development across much of the region. Stiglitz (2002:99) argued that premature capital account liberalisation was 'the single most important factor leading to the crisis', an argument that was a direct indictment of IMF strategies and priorities. He also pointed out that the IMF 'provided some $23 billion to be used to support the exchange rate and bail out creditors [but that] the far, far smaller sums required to help the poor were not forthcoming' (Stiglitz 2002:119). While Stiglitz was a source of intellectual inspiration, at least some elements of the bank seemed willing to fundamentally rethink aspects of the Washington Consensus that the IMF, by contrast, continued to promote in a doctrinaire and inflexible manner. Yet important, revealing, and unexpected as these differences over policy were, we should be careful not to overstate their long-term importance: not only has Stiglitz subsequently left the bank with the active encouragement of prominent US officials, but the US continues to exert a powerful influence over the bank and its policy direction (Wade 2002).

Nevertheless, opinions about and attitudes towards the IFIs within South-East Asia have been affected by the crisis. Changes in thinking about economic policy and the role of IFIs have occurred at a number of levels. While a number of countries appeared to want to detach themselves from the IMF's influence, this has proved difficult and is indicative of the continuing influence of the IMF in the region. Mahathir's Malaysia took the pursuit of independence furthest: from early on in the crisis, Malaysia adopted a series of initiatives—especially capital controls—that were at odds with IMF advice and designed to insulate the country from external influences (Beeson 2000). It has been noticeably more circumspect under Prime Minister Abdullah Badawi, however. Countries that either embraced (in Thailand's case) or were compelled to adopt (in Indonesia's case) the IMF's crisis management strategies, also expressed a desire to free themselves from the IMF's influence. Indeed, the IMF became a lightning rod for popular disaffection in Indonesia, leading President Megawati to accelerate the repayment of IMF loans in an effort to distance her government from an institution associated with a Western-inspired process she described as 'the marginalisation of the developing countries' (Powell 2003). While such rhetoric may have struck a chord with elements of her domestic audience, the reality is that Indonesia still has obligations of some US$10 billion to the IMF and little room to manoeuvre as a consequence. Even in Thailand, once the poster child of IMF-led reform, subsequent disillusion about the impact and effectiveness of the IMF reform agenda led the government of Thaksin Shinawatra to pledge and achieve the early repayment of unpopular IMF loans (Kazmin 2002).

For a region in which national autonomy or sovereignty has always been somewhat compromised and jealously defended as a consequence (Beeson 2003b), such high-level, state-led responses are unsurprising—despite the potential risks.[8] Yet while attitudes toward the IFIs may have hardened among some political elites, the agenda the IFIs promote, loosely captured by the rubric of market-driven globalisation, continues to gain ground. A number of studies have described the way in which national economic elites are being affected by processes associated with globalisation, and embracing an agenda of market-oriented, competition-enhancing reform as a consequence (Ravenhill forthcoming; Stubbs 2000). Unsurprisingly, perhaps, those companies and actors that are most externally oriented and plugged into the international economy are most supportive of reform. For countries with political economies based on a form of 'embedded mercantilism', in which states oversee delicate trade-offs between the tradable and non-tradable sectors of national economies (Jayasuriya 2001), the implications of this apparent change in thinking and the embrace of more universal policy ideas are profound. At this level, then, the long-term influence of the IFIs appears to be encouraging a major transformation of domestic relations and influencing the outcome of hitherto domestic economic and political contests (Stubbs 2000).

While this sort of long-term, subtle IFI influence may, ultimately, prove to be the most important, there is no shortage of more overt, short-term constraints on the ambitions of the region's political elites. Malaysia (US$48.6 billion), Thailand (US$59.2 billion), and, especially, Indonesia (US$132.2 billion) have high levels of external debt (*BBC News Online* 2005). In Indonesia's case in particular, this leaves it dependent on inflows of aid from institutions such as the World Bank to keep the economy afloat; it remains susceptible to reformist pressures as a consequence (Greenlees 2003). However, the World Bank and the IMF are not the only IFIs operating in the region, nor are they the only sources of policy advice and innovation. On the contrary, like the rest of the world, South-East Asia is steadily being drawn into an expanded web of transnational institutional relationships, some indigenous, some more externally driven. Whatever their origins, they look likely to be permanent features of the evolving international landscape through which South-East Asian states must navigate.

There is no doubt that, hitherto, the developed world has been the principal beneficiary of the institutional architecture it helped create, as the operation of the notoriously inequitable international trading system reminds us. Indeed, prominent South-East Asian activists such as Martin Khor (2001) have drawn attention to the negative impact the existing trading system has on the developing world. Yet it is not obvious that South-East Asia will be noticeably better off if the old IFI-dominated order erodes and the move toward bilateralism gathers pace. In such a world, the strong will be able to exert direct leverage over the weak, unconstrained even by the fig leaf of the rule-based reciprocity that underpinned the old Bretton Woods order. True, this order may have reflected the interests of the US and the rest of the developed world, but it may prove better than the emerging alternative. The challenge, of course, has always been to ensure that the rules of the international system of governance reflect a more equitable distribution of power and a wider array of stakeholders than they currently do. The failure to achieve meaningful reform of the established IFIs, so that they reflect a broader array of interests and perspectives, undercuts the legitimacy of the neoliberal agenda they champion and the stability of the global governance system of which they are such key parts (Chua 2003).

CONCLUSION

South-East Asia has been a victim and, to some extent, at least, a beneficiary of historical circumstance. The colonial legacy that so distorted the region's economic and political structures has proven a major handicap and has effectively delayed the more general development process. Yet the postwar period associated with US hegemony offered opportunities within certain constraints. For some countries in South-East Asia, the Cold War era was associated with rapid economic development. Although the IFIs have generally been enthusiastic and effective promoters of an economic agenda that was broadly in keeping with US preferences, there were limits to how far this process could go: not only were they constrained by wider geopolitical circumstances, but the political elites of South-East Asia have also always had some capacity to resist, deflect, or amend external influences. Indeed, it is arguable that the likes of Soeharto and Marcos owe their political longevity in part to their ability to take advantage of the IFIs and their willingness to prop up Cold War allies.

But things have changed in the post-Cold War period. The US is no longer as prepared as it once was to ignore political and economic practices of which it does not approve; neither are the IFIs. Yet the IFIs themselves have been subjected to greater criticism and scrutiny, which has made them more sensitive about their own actions, and revealing important policy differences within key institutions. This is, perhaps, less surprising than it may seem at first glance: the less ideologically charged and strategically fraught post-Cold War environment, especially when coupled with some egregious policy failures on the part of the IFIs, always had the potential to open up a space within which a more genuine policy debate could occur. It is significant that, within the wider East Asian region, there is widespread interest in attempting to establish indigenous institutions that might reflect local contributions to such debates and, ultimately, provide the institutional infrastructure to underpin greater regional independence.

There are formidable obstacles to such projects, not the least of which is the continuing importance of the US as the key external actor (Lincoln 2004). As Jim Glassman's chapter in this volume reminds us, even a possibly diminished US will continue to exert a major influence over the course of development in South-East Asia and the role of the IFIs. As far as South-East Asia is concerned, the nature and extent of the influence of the US and the IFIs will largely depend on a specific set of geopolitical circumstances. The reprioritising of strategic concerns in the wake of the war on terror suggests that South-East Asia's room to manoeuvre may be more constrained than it was during the Cold War as there is no credible strategic rival to the US—the rise of China notwithstanding. In such circumstances, and despite the existence of plausible alternatives (Held 2004), the influence of some form of augmented Washington Consensus looks likely to continue.

NOTES

1 I would like to thank the editors for their extensive feedback and commentary on this chapter. That said, I take full responsibility for the end result.

2 Significantly, financed capital was tightly regulated during the early postwar period when the US's strategic priorities privileged stability. See Helleiner (1993).

3 There is a good deal of debate in the theoretical literature about whether it actually makes sense any longer to talk about 'national' economies given the way the logic of production transcends national boundaries and financial flows are increasingly stateless; see Bryan (1995).

4 'Hegemony' is a contested concept and employed differently within various theoretical paradigms. Broadly speaking, however, there is agreement that it refers to the dominance of one country over the international system, its material and ideological ascendancy, and its capacity to shape the rules and norms that govern the conduct of inter-state relations. See Agnew and Corbridge (1995).

5 South-East Asia has suffered and benefited from the fact that North-East Asia industrialised first. On the one hand, it has access to capital and has been integrated into an established, increasingly regional production structure. On the other hand, South-East Asia occupies a less valuable niche in the region and must attempt to compete with the established giants of Japan, Korea, and 'greater China'; see Felker (2004).

6 There is a good deal of sensitivity about quite what to call the parts of the world variously known as 'the Third World', 'the South', 'the developing world', or even 'emerging markets'; see Berger (2004).

7 Interestingly, the World Bank acknowledged the importance and potential value of state intervention in a major report released just prior to the East Asia crisis; see World Bank (1997) and chapter 1 of this volume.

8 Policies aimed at protecting economic autonomy risk triggering capital flight or investor strikes if they are deemed unattractive by the controllers of mobile financial capital, an especially important consideration for South-East Asian countries, given their reliance on foreign capital.

REFERENCES

Agnew, Jonathan and Corbridge, Stuart (1995) *Mastering Space: Hegemony, Territory and International Political Economy*, London: Routledge.

BBC News (2005) 'Indonesia "declines debt freeze"', 25 January.

Beeson, Mark (1998) 'Indonesia, the East Asian crisis, and the commodification of the nation-state', *New Political Economy*, 3 (3):357–74.

——(2000) 'Mahathir and the markets: Globalisation and the pursuit of economic autonomy in Malaysia', *Pacific Affairs*, 73 (3):335–51.

——(2001) 'Globalisation, governance, and the political-economy of public policy reform in East Asia', *Governance: An International Journal of Policy, Administration and Institutions*, 14 (4):481–502.

——(2003a) 'East Asia, the international financial institutions and regional regulatory reform: A review of the issues', *Journal of the Asia Pacific Economy*, 8 (3):305–26.

——(2003b) 'Sovereignty under siege: Globalisation and the state in Southeast Asia', *Third World Quarterly*, 24 (2):357–74.

——(2004) 'US hegemony and Southeast Asia: The impact of, and limits to, American power and influence', *Critical Asian Studies*, 36 (3):323–54.

——and Yan Islam (2005) 'Neoliberalism and East Asia: Resisting the Washington Consensus', *Journal of Development Studies*, 41 (2):197–219.

Berger, Mark T. (2004) 'After the Third World? History, destiny and the fate of Third Worldism', *Third World Quarterly*, 25:9–39

Bhagwati, Jagdish (1998) 'The capital myth', *Foreign Affairs*, 77 (3):7–12.

Braithwaite, John and Peter Drahos (2000) *Global Business Regulation*, Cambridge: Cambridge University Press, 2000.

Brauchli, Marcus W. and Jay Solomon (1998) 'Was the World Bank part of Indonesia's problem?', *Asian Wall Street Journal*, July 15:1 and 5.

Bryan, Dick (1995) *The Chase Across the Globe: International Accumulation and the Contradictions for the Nation State*, Boulder: Westview Press.

Case, William (2002) *Politics in Southeast Asia: Democracy or Less*, London: Routledge-Curzon.

Caufield, Catherine (1996) *Masters of Illusion: The World Bank and the Poverty of Nations*, New York: Henry Holt.

Cerny, Philip (1995) 'Globalization and the changing logic of collective action', *International Organization*, 49 (4):595–625.

Chua, Amy (2003) *World on Fire: How Exporting Free Market Democracy Breeds Ethnic Hatred and Global Instability*, New York: Anchor Books.

Cox, Robert (1992) *'Global Perestroika', The Socialist Register*, London: The Merlin Press, pp. 26–43.

Felker, Greg (2004) 'Southeast Asian development in regional and historical perspective', in Mark Beeson (ed.) *Contemporary Southeast Asia: Regional Dynamics, National Differences*, London: Palgrave, pp. 50–74.

Foot, Rosemary, MacFarlane, S. Neil and Michael Mastanduno (2003) 'Introduction', in Rosemary Foot et al. (eds) *US Hegemony and International Organizations*, Oxford: Oxford University Press, pp. 265–72.

Gomez, Edmund Terence (ed.) (2002) *Political Business in East Asia*, London: Routledge.

——and Jomo, K. S. (1997) *Malaysia's Political Economy: Politics, Patronage and Profits*, Cambridge: Cambridge University Press.

Gowa, Joanne (1983) *Closing the Gold Window: Domestic Politics and the End of Bretton Woods*, Ithaca: Cornell University Press.

Greenlees, Don (2003) 'Lenders press a reluctant Jakarta for reform', *The Australian*, 21 January:8.

Held, David (2004) *Global Covenant: The Social Democratic Alternative to the Washington Consensus*, Cambridge: Polity.

Helleiner, Eric (1993) 'When finance was servant: International capital movements in the Bretton Woods order', in Phillip G. Cerny (ed.) *Finance and World Politics: Markets, Regimes, and States in the Post-Hegemonic Era*, Aldershot: Edward Elgar, pp. 20–48.

Higgott, Richard (2000) 'Contested globalization: The changing context and normative challenges', *Review of International Studies*, 26:131–53.

Hutchcroft, Paul D. (1998) *Booty Capitalism: The Politics of Banking in the Philippines*, Ithaca: Cornell University Press.

Ikenberry, G. John (1998) 'Institutions, strategic restraint, and the persistence of the American postwar order', *International Security*, 23 (3):43–78.

Jayasuriya, Kanishka (2001) 'Southeast Asia's embedded mercantilism in crisis: International strategies and domestic coalitions', in Tan, Andrew T. and Kenneth J. Boutin (eds) *Non-Traditional Security Issues in Southeast Asia*, Singapore: Select Publishing, pp. 26–53.

Jomo, K. S. (2001a) 'Rethinking the role of government policy in Southeast Asia', in Joseph E. Stiglitz and Shahid Yusuf (eds) *Rethinking the East Asia Miracle*, Washington, DC: World Bank, pp. 461–508.

——(2001b) 'International financial liberalization and the crisis of East Asian development', in K. S. Jomo and S. Nagaraj (eds) *Globalization versus Development*, London: Palgrave, pp. 188–216.

Kahler, Miles (ed.) (1998) *Capital Flows and Financial Crises*, Ithaca: Cornell University Press.

Kazmin, Amy (2002) 'The PM pledges to repay IMF debt earlier', <www.*FT*.com>.

Khor, Martin (2001) 'The World Trade Organization and the South: Implications of the emerging global economic governance for development', in K. S. Jomo and Shumala Nagaraj (eds) *Globalization versus Development*, London: Palgrave, pp. 59–84.

Latham, Robert (1997) *The Liberal Moment: Modernity, Security, and the Making of Postwar International Order*, New York: Columbia University Press.

Leftwich, Adrian (2000) *States of Development: On the Primacy of Politics in Development*, Oxford: Polity Press.

Lincoln, Edward J. (2004) *East Asian Economic Regionalism*, Washington, DC: Brookings Institution.

Mahathir Mohamad (1999) 'Asia's Road to Recovery: The challenge of pragmatism', speech to the World Economic Forum, Singapore, 18 October.

Marglin, Stephen A. and Juliet B. Schor (eds) (1990) *The Golden Age of Capitalism: Reinterpreting the Postwar Experience*, London: Clarendon Press.

McMahon, Robert J. (1999) *The Limits of Empire: The United States and Southeast Asia Since World War II*, New York: Columbia University Press.

O'Brien, Robert, Anne Marie Goetz, Jan Aart Scholte and Marc Williams (2000) *Contesting Global Governance: Multilateral Economic Institutions and Global Social Movement*, Cambridge: Cambridge University Press.

Pauly, Louis P. (1997) *Who Elected the Bankers? Surveillance and Control in the World Economy*, Ithaca: Cornell University Press.

Powell, Sian (2003) 'Indonesia to cut IMF cord', *The Australian*, July 30:30.

Rapkin, David P. and Jonathon R. Strand (2003) 'Is East Asia under-represented in the International Monetary Fund?', *International Relations of the Asia–Pacific*, 3:1–28.

Ravenhill, John 'US economic relations with East Asia: From hegemony to complex interdependence', in Mark Beeson (ed.) *Bush and Asia: America's Evolving Relations with East Asia*, London: Routledge (forthcoming).

Robison, Richard and Vedi Hadiz, (2004) *Reorganising Power in Indonesia: The Politics of Oligarchy in an Age of Markets*, London: RoutledgeCurzon.

Rosenau, James (1997) *Along the Domestic-Foreign Frontier: Exploring Governance in a Turbulent World*, Cambridge: Cambridge University Press.

Stiglitz, Joseph E. (2002) *Globalization and Its Discontents*, New York: W. W. Norton.

Stubbs, Richard (2000) 'Signing on to liberalisation: AFTA and the politics of regional economic cooperation', *Pacific Review*, 13 (2):297–318.

Trubowitz, Peter (1998) *Defining the National Interest: Conflict and Change in American Foreign Policy*, Chicago: University of Chicago Press.

Wade, Robert (2001) 'The US role in the long Asian crisis of 1990–2000', in Arvid Lukanskas and F. Rivera-Batiz (eds) *The Political Economy of the East Asian Crisis and its Aftermath: Tigers in Distress*, Cheltenham: Edward Elgar, pp. 195–226.

——(2002) 'US hegemony and the World Bank: the fight over people and ideas', *Review of International Political Economy*, 9 (2):215–43.

Williamson, John (1990) 'What Washington means by policy reform', in John Williamson (ed.) *Latin American Adjustment: How Much Has Changed?*, Washington: Institute for International Economics.

——(2005) 'The strange history of the Washington Consensus', *Journal of Post Keynesian Economics*, 27 (2):195–206.

Winters, Jeffrey A. (1996) *Power in Motion: Capital Mobility and the Indonesian State*, Ithaca: Cornell University Press.

Woods, Ngarie (2003) 'The United States and the intentional financial institutions: Power and influence within the World Bank and the IMF', in Rosemary Foot et al. (eds) *US Hegemony and International Organizations*, Oxford: Oxford University Press, pp. 92–114.

World Bank (1994) *Governance: The World Bank's Experience*, Washington, DC: World Bank.

——(1997) *World Development Report: The State in a Changing World*, New York: Oxford University Press.

10 Pathways from the Crisis: Politics and Reform in South-East Asia since 1997

Kanishka Jayasuriya and Andrew Rosser

KEY TOPICS

INTRODUCTION

IN the wake of the Asian economic crisis, scholars have been quick to declare the end of the Asian economic model (AEM), in both its developmental and oligarchic or crony capitalist forms. Neoliberal economists, for instance, have argued that the crisis has exposed the inherent weakness of the AEM and, as such, provided 'a historic opportunity' for the region to shift towards more market-based systems of economic organisation (Frankel 1998:11; see also Cathie 1997; Fukuyama 1999; and comments by Michel Camdessus in *AWSJ 13 November* 1997). Theorists have also suggested that the crisis has strengthened the position of the 'Wall Street–IMF–Treasury complex' and thus made it politically impossible for regional governments to continue with dirigiste policies (Jomo 1998; Winters 1999).

In this chapter, it is argued that predictions of the end of the AEM and the victory of liberal markets are premature. By increasing the need of countries within East and South-East Asia to attract internationally mobile capital, the Asian crisis has clearly generated strong structural pressures for liberal market reform within the region. Yet this has not made such reform inevitable. The reason for this is that these structural pressures have been refracted through domestic political and social systems that have varied in terms of the extent to which they have been conducive to reform and, hence, in the extent to which they have been vulnerable to these pressures. The result has been an uneven pattern of reform: economic liberalisation has gone further in those countries where domestic political and social systems have been relatively conducive to reform than it has in those countries where domestic political systems have not been so conducive to reform. This argument clearly fits in with the social conflict theory outlined in chapter 1 of this volume.

To illustrate these points, the dynamics of economic liberalisation in four South-East Asian countries—Singapore, Malaysia, Thailand, and Indonesia—since the onset of the Asian economic crisis are examined. In essence, the argument of this chapter is that the extent of economic liberalisation in these countries has been a function of three domestic political and social variables:

1 the extent to which liberal market ideas are accepted within society
2 the extent to which the institutional environment is capable of supporting liberal markets
3 the extent to which the crisis has shifted the balance of power within society away from coalitions that are opposed to reform and towards those that support it.

In each case we have chosen to focus on these variables, rather than on many alternative variables, because there are strong intuitive and theoretical reasons for believing that they are related to reform outcomes.

UNDERSTANDING REFORM OUTCOMES

In explaining reform outcomes in developing countries, neoclassical political economists have emphasised the political nature of the reform process (Krueger 1993; Williamson 1994). Economic policy-making, they have argued, is not simply a technical matter involving rational deliberations over the merits of alternative policy positions, but a political process in which there are winners and losers. They have also tended to emphasise the economic rationality of political elites who advocate economic reform and construe the role of politics in negative terms; that is, they have tended to view struggles over economic reform as essentially struggles between economic rationality as represented by liberal technocrats on the one hand, and, on the other, vested political and social interests (Rosser 1999a, 2002; Schamis 1999). As such, they have presented a highly voluntarist account of the dynamics of economic reform: in their view, reform outcomes depend not on the extent to which material interests get behind reformist strategies, but, rather, on the extent to which economic policy-makers are able to rise above behaviour that serves vested political and social interests (see chapter 1, this volume).

In contrast to this approach, it is argued in this chapter that reform outcomes are best understood in terms of three variables, all of which find expression in conflicts and struggles within the state.

The first of these is ideas. As a number of scholars have pointed out, responses to economic crises are shaped at least in part 'by the intellectual lenses through which economic advisors and political leaders perceive the crisis and the available options' (Nelson 1990:29; see also Haggard & Kaufman 1992:13–14). As such, extensive reform is most likely where orthodox ideas have gained widespread acceptance among a country's policy elite. By contrast, reform is much less likely to occur in societies where nationalist and radical populist economic agendas are dominant and liberal economic ideas have become tainted by an association with colonial rule, neocolonial domination, or past economic crises. In these societies, as Chaudhry (1994), among others, has pointed out, the ideological resources needed for governments to create more liberal economies simply do not exist.

In this chapter, ideas are brought into the analysis by distinguishing between internationalist ideological influences within the technocracy and nationalist influences. It needs to be pointed out that, although these ideas will reflect broadly the material interests of various political coalitions, ideological influences are located within institutional structures (such as the technocracy) that have their own specific history. It is important to recognise that these ideational factors are expressed in, and through, their embodiments in various state institutions and apparatuses. Indeed, different state institutions, the central bank for example, may come to express different ideological currents, and the conflict within the state may reflect the interplay of complex social and ideological conflicts. As Poulantzas (1978a:32) notes, 'The state does not produce a unified discourse, but several discourses that are adapted to the various classes and differentially incarnated in its apparatuses according to their class destinations'. Ideas, then, have a material expression within various state apparatuses and these, in turn, interact with the play of social interests in complex ways.

The second variable that plays a role in shaping reform outcomes is institutional capacity. As the World Bank (1997:1) has argued, markets cannot exist unless they are supported by effective states: 'An effective state is vital for the provision of the goods and services—and the rules and institutions—that allow markets to flourish and people to lead healthier, happier lives' (see also Evans 1992; Polanyi 1944). A key characteristic of an 'effective state' is that it is coherent and coordinated in organisational terms—that is, that it has a high degree of administrative capacity (MacIntyre 1994:4). The importance of this is not that it makes a country more likely to introduce economic reforms. As Haggard and Kaufman (1992:11–12) have pointed out, the evidence in this area is mixed. Rather, it is important because it affects a country's ability to implement reforms properly and to ensure that regulatory functions are adequately performed. In other words, it affects a country's ability to consolidate programs of reform once they have been initiated. Here, we bring institutional factors into the analysis by distinguishing between states with high and low levels of capacity.

It is important to point out that our approach here is different from that of those political economists who have emphasised the importance of state autonomy in promoting economic reform. Although we agree with their view that coherence and coordination are important determinants of whether reforms are successfully implemented, we are sceptical of the claim that state autonomy is a necessary prerequisite for economic reform. The point is that markets are not natural phenomena that exist independently of their political and social context. As with any other sort of economic systems, they embody the interests of specific elements within society and require the continued support of these elements to survive (Chaudhry 1993; Evans 1995; Robison & Rosser 1999). Market creation thus requires not an autonomous state, but one that is closely aligned with political and social coalitions that support market-oriented reform (see chapter 1, this volume).

More importantly, state capacity is not some technical attribute of state or governmental apparatus, but reflects deeper social and political conflict. So, for example, the erosion of institutional capacity is seen by institutionalists as one of the major causes of the Asian economic crisis (Wade & Veneroso 1998). Other institutionalists have identified the erosion of policy capacity in the emergence of a multiplicity of different institutional players within the polity (Macintyre 2003), while yet others, such as Weiss, identify the erosion with the decline of the transformative capacity of the state (Weiss 1998). The point is this: even as society is brought back in to the developmental literature through such notions as embedded autonomy, the implicit assumption is that the state itself becomes an autonomous actor that intervenes in or acts on society to produce certain desired outcomes. Indeed, some scholars working within institutionalist frameworks seem to reify institutions so much that their reification turns into a form of institutional fetishism. Where this institutional fetishism falls down is in occluding the deeper social relations that underpin those kinds of institutional capabilities seen to be so central to the developmental state; institutions are accentuated and social relations are attenuated. We suggest instead that institutional capacity is not a set of institutional attributes, but rather an artefact of broader relational properties within the state. Macintyre's work is insightful in noting the importance of the increasing weight of competing centres of power—veto players—within South-East Asia, but where we would differ is in explaining the emergence of these veto players in terms of the rise of new social and economic interests now located in various institutional sites within the state apparatus. The rise of electoralism and the growth of legislative institutions, for example, enabled domestic businesses to penetrate state institutions. It is important to realise that this is not a leakage of power from state elites to groups outside of the state but a relocation of power within the state. As evidence of this process, Jayasuriya (1995) notes the important role of electoral politics ('money politics' in Thailand and Malaysia) and in the role of legislative institutions (Korea). Rather than looking at state power as a quantum that rises and falls with the erosion of institutional capabilities, it is necessary to examine more clearly the way state power is produced and how the state itself is transformed in response to changes in social relations.

This leads to the third variable. Reform outcomes are also a function of the extent to which economic crises shift power and influence away from anti-reform coalitions of interest and towards pro-reform coalitions of interest. In neoclassical and rational-choice institutionalist accounts of economic reform, economic crises are important because they 'have the effect of shocking countries out of traditional policy patterns, disorganising the interest groups that typically veto policy reform, and generating pressure for politicians to change policies that can be seen to have failed' (Williamson & Haggard 1994:562–4; see also World Bank 1997)—that is, they are important because they weaken the position of anti-reform coalitions and make apparent the inherent economic rationality of market-oriented policies. However, this view obscures the way in which political and social interests are embedded in market-oriented policies, and hence, the way in which these interests underpin the process of reform. The point here is that economic crises not only weaken anti-reform coalitions, but also strengthen pro-reform coalitions. It is thus more reasonable to argue that reform outcomes depend not on the extent to which economic crises weaken anti-reform coalitions and cause policy elites to realise the mistakes of the past, but, as noted above, on the extent to which they shift power away from anti-reform coalitions and towards pro-reform ones (Rosser 1999a). This chapter brings these factors into the analysis by distinguishing between those cases where

- economic crises have weakened anti-reform coalitions and strengthened pro-reform coalitions
- they have had little or no impact on the coalitional structure of society, effectively leaving dominant anti-reform coalitions in a position of continued dominance
- they have weakened dominant anti-reform coalitions where pro-reform coalitions have been too weak to assume power.

Our analysis thus far is similar to that of Pempel (1998) who, in an insightful analysis of the political changes wrought by economic restructuring, has suggested that political outcomes need to be understood within the context of a specific regime, which he defines as a set of dominant socioeconomic coalitions, a set of institutional arrangements, and a stable set of policy strategies. Our analysis is different in that the role of political and social coalitions is more central to our analysis than it is to Pempel's. Pempel likens the relationship among the three elements on which he focuses to the relationship among the legs of tripod: each reinforces the other, and when one is removed the whole edifice collapses. Our framework, by contrast, is best characterised as being similar to a pyramid, with coalitions at the base, institutions in the centre, and ideas at the apex. The reason for this difference is that, in our view, although appropriate ideas, institutions, and coalitional structures are all essential for the emergence of markets, it is the coalitional structure of society that exercises the greatest influence on reform outcomes. This is because, above all else, markets are allocative mechanisms for determining who gets what, why they get it, and how they get it. As such, they can exist only if some sort of compromise, forced or otherwise, is reached among competing interests about how society's resources are to be allocated.

More importantly, we want to argue that these competing social coalitions do not exist outside of the state but find expression within the state apparatus.

> The [capitalist] state should not be regarded as an intrinsic entity: like capital, it is rather a relationship of forces or more precisely the material condensation of such a relationship among classes and class fractions, such as this is expressed within the state in a necessarily specific form.
>
> Poulantzas 1978a: 129

Our argument does not simply sum up reform outcomes—as is often done in the institutionalist literature—as the sum of interaction between coalitions, ideas, and capacities; rather, the broader conflicts between social interests and class fractions are played out in terms of competing political and ideological projects anchored within various institutional arenas within the state. This framework yields a total of six broad reform trajectories (and twelve overall reform outcomes), depending on the particular configuration of the three variables. These are summarised in table 10.1 on page 263.

In summary, the analysis presented here suggests that it is problematic to analyse a set of economic reform strategies as a rational set of economic policies that arise in response to the imperatives of market forces. Rather, economic reform is an intrinsically political process because any given set of economic strategies needs to be underpinned by a coherent dominant coalition of interests, a set of institutional structures, and a set of dominant ideas. We discuss these elements in more detail below in relation to South-East Asia, but the point that needs to be underlined here is that economic reform implies a dramatic change in the previously dominant or influential configuration of interests, institutions, and ideas and that, for this reason, any shift in economic strategies will bring forth serious resistance from political and social interests.

THE POLITICAL ECONOMY OF ECONOMIC LIBERALISATION IN POST-CRISIS SOUTH-EAST ASIA: FOUR CASES

Thailand

Until 2001, Thailand appeared to fit the profile of model 6(a) in table 10.1 (below). At the ideological level, international ideas have been dominant for much of Thailand's recent history. Nationalist and, more specifically, populist economic ideas were very influential during the two and a half decades following the overthrow of the Thai monarchy in 1932. At this time, figures within the populist People's Party and, later, the military government under Field Marshal Phibun, argued that the Thai state needed to intervene in the economy to reduce foreign control over the economy (which had increased with the opening of the country to foreign trade in the mid nineteenth century) and to promote the employment and investment of ethnic Thais, particularly in non-agricultural sectors (Hewison 1997:100–1). Since that time, however, internationalist ideas have been more influential. Although the country adopted an import-substitution industrial strategy during the 1960s, this was not done in the name of autonomous economic development, rather, in the name of reviving the Thai economy with the help of foreign aid and investment. Furthermore, the country has not produced any influential champions of inward-looking, high-tech, industrial projects along the lines of Indonesia's Habibie or Malaysia's Mahathir. Nor has there been a strong concern to restrain the economic role of ethnic Chinese and to promote that of indigenous peoples as there has been elsewhere in the region, largely because ethnic Chinese have been much better integrated into Thai society than they have been into some other societies.

Also in accordance with model 6(a) in table 10.1 (below), the state has had a relatively low degree of institutional capacity. In contrast to its counterparts in the East Asian newly industrialised countries (NICs)—that is, South Korea, Singapore, Hong Kong, and Taiwan—the Thai government has been characterised by high levels of inefficiency and corruption. Personal connections have been a far stronger determinant of business and political success than has genuine ability, and there has not been a clear separation between bureaucratic incumbents and their offices (Girling 1981; Riggs 1966). At the same time, as MacIntyre (1999) has pointed out, the fractured multi-party character of the country's parliamentary system has made economic decision-making extremely difficult. With so many parties in parliament and parliamentary coalitions so unstable, gridlock in relation to important economic issues has been common. Finally, the Thai judiciary has been inefficient and corrupt, meaning that a proper enforcement mechanism for economic rules has not been in place (Pasuk & Baker 1998:302).

TABLE 10.1 Expected reform outcomes

Model No.	Impact of the crisis on coalition structure	Ideological character of society	Broad reform trajectory	Institutional capacity	Expected reform outcome
1	Dominant anti-reform coalition remains strong	Nationalist	Very little reform	(a) Low	1(a) Very little reform and poor implementation
				(b) High	1(b) Very little reform with good implementation
2	Dominant anti-reform coalition remains strong	Internationalist	Limited reform	(a) Low	2(a) Limited reform with poor implementation
				(b) High	2(b) Limited reform with good implementation
3	Dominant anti-reform coalition weakened but pro-reform coalition too weak to assume power	Nationalist	Partial reform	(a) Low	3(a) Partial reform with poor implementation
				(b) High	3(b) Partial reform with good implementation
4	Dominant anti-reform coalition weakened but pro-reform coalition too weak to assume power	Internationalist	Substantial reform	(a) Low	4(a) Substantial reform with poor implementation
				(b) High	4(b) Substantial reform with good implementation
5	Anti-reform coalition weakened and pro-reform coalition strengthened	Nationalist	Widespread reform	(a) Low	5(a) Widespread reform with poor implementation
				(b) High	5(b) Widespread reform with good implementation
6	Anti-reform coalition weakened and pro-reform coalition strengthened	Internationalist	Thoroughgoing reform	(a) Low	6(a) Thoroughgoing reform with poor implementation
				(b) High	6(b) Thoroughgoing reform with good implementation

The impact of the Asian economic crisis on Thailand's coalitional structure was also, initially, consistent with model 6(a) in table 10.1 (above). The crisis dramatically strengthened the structural leverage of mobile capitalists and, in particular, their supporters at the IMF, which was called in by the Thai government during 1997 to bail out the economy. With the country desperately needing the IMF's aid, the Thai government had little option but to agree to a series of IMF-sponsored reform agreements. The crisis also led to a shift in the balance of power and influence within Thailand itself, away from well-connected provincial business groups and bureaucratic mandarins and towards metropolitan capitalists. The crisis made it apparent that the system of patronage and corruption in which the interests of provincial business groups and mandarins were embedded was no longer functional for capitalist development. This contradiction was clearest in the financial sector, where senior members of Chart Pattana, a political party with strong connections to provincial business groups, had substantial interests in ailing finance companies. Despite the fact that these companies were haemorrhaging severely, Chart Pattana figures were able to arrange for the central bank to provide them with generous financial support, which, in turn, contributed to a substantial blowout in the money supply and an increase in inflation (MacIntyre 1999:146–7). In this context, the position of metropolitan capitalists, who, as Pasuk and Baker (1997:25) have pointed out, have in recent years developed an interest in technocratic economic management and efficient business development, was to strengthen considerably. This shift in coalitional structure was to be consolidated by the fall of the Chavalit government, which had been based on a parliamentary coalition dominated by parties with strong connections to provincial business groups and the military, and the formation of a new government under Chuan Leekpai. In contrast to these parties, Chuan's Democrat Party, which constituted the dominant element in the new governing parliamentary coalition, was considered to be relatively free of corruption and to have a strong commitment to deregulation, privatisation, and regulatory reform.

However, the failure of the Chuan government's neoliberal reforms to revive the Thai economy during the initial stages of the crisis led to the unravelling of the coalition of interests that had underpinned it. As Hewison (2005:315) has argued, domestic capitalists, including many sections of metropolitan capital, found the economic medicine administered by the Chuan government and the IMF too bitter to swallow:

> In struggling to survive, domestic business complained about high interest rates, a lack of liquidity and about the 'fire sale' of local assets to foreign interests. More broadly, business groups and some economists argued for more domestic initiatives to save an economy that was spiralling into negative territory.

At the same time, there emerged widespread popular opposition to the IMF's reforms. The result was a dramatic shift in support among domestic capitalists and the broader voting public away from the Chuan government and towards Thaksin Shinawatra and his Thai Rak Thai (TRT) party. In contrast to the Democrats, Thaksin and TRT expressed a strong commitment to a nationalist and populist economic agenda aimed at protecting domestic capital from the ravages of neoliberalism. This did not mean an outright rejection of neoliberal policies, but a commitment to subordinate neoliberal reform to the interests of big metropolitan capitalists. Where neoliberal policies were in the interests of metropolitan capital, they would be pursued; where they were not, they would be abandoned or wound back. In terms of table 10.1, Thailand has shifted from resembling model 6(a) to more closely resembling model 4(a).

In accordance with our framework, the pattern of reform in Thailand since the onset of the Asian crisis thus needs to be seen as falling into two periods. In the immediate post-crisis period when the Democrats were in power, Thailand underwent a period of thoroughgoing neoliberal reform, albeit one characterised by serious implementation problems. Since 2001, however, as nationalist and populist agendas have become stronger, it has experienced a gradual winding back of the reform program.

This basic pattern of economic reform can be seen, for instance, in the area of insolvency law. Before the Asian economic crisis, Thailand's regulatory and institutional framework for dealing with corporate insolvency was extremely weak by international standards. The country's bankruptcy law, which was originally enacted in 1940, had not been amended since 1983 and was becoming increasingly out of date. Most importantly, it did not allow for the establishment of a special court to deal with insolvency-related matters, nor provide a mechanism by which corporate debt could be rescheduled and corporate debtors reorganised (*Asian Business* [*AB*] September 1997; *Far Eastern Economic Review* [*FEER*] 15 November 1997; Gibbons 1996). The receivership process was also widely considered to be cumbersome, expensive, and time-consuming. According to one source, it usually took three to five years for creditors to claim the assets of bad debtors, and could take as long ten years (*AB* September 1997). The result, as one commentator pointed out, was that 'the entire bankruptcy process in Thailand [was] very rarely used and inadequate to address the type of complex, multinational, cross-border insolvency situations that are becoming increasingly common in this day and age' (Gibbons 1996).

When the baht collapsed in mid 1997, the Thai government came under increasing pressure to revamp its insolvency framework. The collapse of the baht left most of the corporate sector insolvent and led to the closure of a large number of finance companies. With further lending to Thai companies to some extent contingent upon successful debt rescheduling and the reorganisation or liquidation of insolvent local companies, it was necessary for the government to develop a more effective mechanism by which creditors and debtors could reschedule debts, debtors could be reorganised, and creditors could seize control over debtors' assets. The closure of forty-six finance companies in late 1997 alone left an estimated US$18 billion worth of corporate assets up for grabs. The crisis also dramatically strengthened the position of the IMF, which made it clear that it expected significant reform in this area in return for its financial assistance. With the IMF effectively drawing a line in the sand, the Thai government had little choice but to agree to a wide variety of insolvency law reform measures as part of the various letters of intent it negotiated with that organisation (*FEER* 5 March1998; *Nation* 25 February 1998). In any case, although there was significant opposition to insolvency law reform from some members of the Thai senate who had financial interests in heavily indebted local companies, the dominant reformist elements within the Democrat-led coalition government appeared genuinely to support insolvency reform; given their numerical superiority within parliament, they were in a position to push reform bills through.

The result was the introduction of an extensive range of reforms in the insolvency area. In June 1998, the Thai Central Bank established the Corporate Debt Restructuring Advisory Committee (CDRAC) to promote and administer negotiation of debt restructuring between debtors and creditors. This was followed in early 1998 and early 1999 by amendments to the country's bankruptcy laws that made it possible for insolvent companies to be reorganised and provided for the establishment of a special bankruptcy court. In early 1999, the parliament also passed a new foreclosure law that was intended to speed up the receivership process. So extensive were the reforms that the usually critical World Bank, although still concerned about the possibility for delays in the receivership process, declared that the Thai bankruptcy court was 'clearly off to an excellent start' (World Bank 2000:19). By 2001, however, it had become clear that there were significant problems with the implementation of the new laws and the operation of the new court. As the World Bank (2000: 19) pointed out, concerns about judicial corruption and the workability of the new insolvency system had discouraged debtors and creditors from making use of this system, resulting in a low number of corporate bankruptcies being filed with the bankruptcy court or pursued through the CDRAC.

Since Thaksin's rise to power, the government has backtracked on the process of insolvency reform, most notably moving to limit the role that foreign consultants play in corporate restructuring exercises. It has also moved much corporate debt restructuring work to the state-run Thailand Asset Management Company, effectively placing it out of the reach of the bankruptcy court (Crispin 2003).

Indonesia

Indonesia fits the profile of model 3(a) in table 10.1 above. In contrast to Thailand, the dominant economic ideas in Indonesia have been nationalist rather than internationalist. Ever since Indonesia achieved independence in 1949, important sections of the country's political and bureaucratic elite have argued that extensive state intervention in the economy is necessary to promote national economic development and, in particular, to develop an autonomous industrial sector capable of producing not only low value-added products, but also complex capital and intermediate goods. They have also argued that state intervention is necessary to overcome foreign economic domination and to promote the development of indigenous business enterprise. At the same time, the indigenous petty bourgeoisie and other marginalised elements within society have supported radical populist agendas that have had strong parallels with nationalist economic ideas. Liberal economic ideas, by contrast, have had relatively little influence. It has been only when the dominant anti-reform groups have been weakened at times of economic crisis—such as the mid 1960s, the mid 1980s, and the period since the onset of the Asian economic crisis in 1997—that these ideas have had more than a minimal impact on policy (Chalmers & Hadiz 1997; Robison 1997:29–31; Rosser 1999a).

Also, as in model 3(a) in table 10.1, the state's institutional capacity has been low. Like the Thai government, the Indonesian government has been characterised by high levels of inefficiency and corruption—indeed, if the regular transparency and corruption ratings from organisations such as Transparency International are to be believed, Indonesia has been even more corrupt and inefficient than Thailand. Senior political and bureaucratic figures have sold access to state facilities—such as export and import licences, forestry concessions, and state bank loans—in exchange for material rewards. They have also used state enterprises to provide business opportunities for well-connected business groups and to generate extrabudgetary revenues for organisations such as the military (Crouch 1988; Robison 1986, 1997). Regulatory agencies, such as Bank Indonesia (the central bank) and Bapepam (the Capital Market Supervisory Agency), have been staffed by poorly qualified personnel (except at the most senior levels) and have had insufficient resources at their disposal to be adequate watchdogs (Rosser 1999a:81–200). As in Thailand, the judiciary has been inefficient and corrupt, meaning that Indonesia has also lacked a proper enforcement mechanism for economic rules (Thoolen 1987, World Bank 1993).

The coalitional consequences of the Asian economic crisis for Indonesia have also been consistent with model 3(a) in table 10.1. As in the Thai case, the crisis severely weakened anti-reform elements within the country, most notably the politico-bureaucrats who controlled access to state facilities and the major domestic conglomerates, most of which had benefited considerably from privileged access to these facilities. The collapse of the rupiah multiplied the domestic currency cost of the conglomerates' (generally substantial) foreign debt obligations, forcing most of them to default on their loans and making it almost impossible for them to raise new credit. In addition, the political instability produced by the crisis and, in particular, the growing violence towards ethnic Chinese businesspeople, forced many conglomerate owners to flee the country. The crisis also provided an opportunity for opposition figures, such as Amien Rais, Megawati Soekarnoputri, Abdurrahman Wahid, and various student groups, to challenge the authority of the New Order regime that had sustained and rewarded the conglomerates and their politico-bureaucratic patrons. Massive student demonstrations occurred, culminating in the capture of the Indonesian parliament and the forced resignation of President Soeharto in late May 1998.

However, reform-oriented coalitions were too weak to take full advantage of this situation. The crisis increased the structural leverage of mobile capitalists and, most notably, their representative organisations, the IMF and the World Bank. At several key points during the crisis, the IMF and the World Bank withheld their financial support in an attempt to force the government to move ahead with the various IMF reform agreements it had signed, in each case with significant effect. But mobile capitalists could not translate their structural power into direct political power because most of them were foreign and therefore unable to hold government office. The country's liberal technocrats were too weak to assume direct political power because of their lack of a strong domestic power base. Although their policies had the support of mobile capitalists, their domestic support base did not extend beyond some local economists and media commentators, and some downstream producers (Robison 1988:69; Rosser 1999a:62). They were, consequently, to remain important (but not dominant) players in the policy-making process. During the Habibie interregnum, the technocrats had a continued presence in the cabinet and the main economic policy-making bodies, but not a dominant one. Indeed, for the entire Habibie period, it seemed that the most influential members of Habibie's economic team were not the technocrats but figures associated with the previous government, such as Chief Economics Minister Ginandjar Kartasasmita and the populist forces aligned with Minister for Cooperatives Adi Sasono. The fall of Habibie and the formation of subsequent governments under Abdurrahman Wahid, Megawati Soekarnoputri, and then, Susilo Bambang Yudhoyono have done little to improve the technocrats' position. Few key economic cabinet postings have gone to technocrats. With the shift to a political system in which power is spread among a variety of political parties, Indonesia's recent presidents have been forced to allocate ministerial positions on the basis of party affiliation rather than qualifications and expertise to ensure their election and, once elected, continued support for their respective governments.

In accordance with model 3(a) in table 10.1, Indonesia appears, in the wake of the crisis, to be undergoing a partial program of neoliberal reform in which there are serious problems of implementation. The case of accounting policy illustrates this well.

Like Thailand's insolvency system, Indonesia's regulatory and institutional framework for accounting was relatively weak before the crisis. The collapse of international oil prices in the mid 1980s had made it necessary for the government to improve the quality of financial reporting within the country to promote the development of the capital market as a mechanism for attracting new sources of investment funds. But resistance to accounting reform on the part of the conglomerates and the politico-bureaucrats, both of whom were concerned that it would force them to be more transparent and accountable, made it difficult for the technocrats, the World Bank, and other groups that supported reform to make much progress. In the wake of a series of highly publicised financial reporting scandals (Rosser 1999a:162–9), the technocrats were able to push through the introduction of a new set of accounting standards that was based largely on international accountancy standards (IAS), and were able to ensure the inclusion of provisions in the new Companies Code and Capital Markets Law that gave this set of standards legal backing. The technocrats were also able to ensure the inclusion of provisions that made company directors and commissioners personally liable for any losses incurred by investors as a result of untrue or misleading information in company reports, specified the general format of financial reports, and imposed fines on company directors, commissioners, and major shareholders who did not report material events to the public (Cole & Slade 1999; *Info Finansial* [*IF*] October 1995; *Jakarta Post* [*JP*] 18 January 1996).

But the technocrats were to make very little progress in the area of enforcement. In the mid 1980s, the government had officially prohibited foreign accountants from practising in the country, forcing international auditing firms to operate through domestic affiliates rather than set up their own offices. This situation suited the conglomerates because it meant that they could have their books audited by firms that, although operating under the names of major international firms, were not (in most cases) directly controlled by these international firms, and consequently, did not always apply the same standards. In early 1997, following calls from the World Bank for Indonesian auditors to be more independent, the technocrats were able to push through regulations permitting foreign accountants to practise within the country on an individual basis. They were not, however, able to push through regulations giving foreign accountants permission to set up their own firms (*Media Akuntansi* [*MA*] June 1998). Nor were the technocrats able to promote reform of the country's court system, the institution that was ultimately responsible for enforcing accounting regulations. Indonesia's judiciary was widely regarded as inefficient, poorly trained, and corrupt; it was widely known that court decisions, in many cases, were for sale. But despite the problems caused by the collapse of oil prices, the politico-bureaucrats and the conglomerates remained strong enough to stave off attempts for judicial reform.

The collapse of the rupiah in 1997–98 was to provide an opportunity for the technocrats and the World Bank to push the process of accounting reform a step further. Much public analysis of the crisis argued that poor accounting practices, although not solely responsible for the crisis, had contributed to its severity (*AWSJ* 20 October 1998; Rahman 1998). Some commentators, such as the head of the US Federal Reserve, Alan Greenspan, argued that recovery would not occur until countries within the region adopted better and clearer accounting rules (*AWSJ* 3 May 1999). In addition, as noted earlier, the crisis strengthened the position of elements that supported accounting reform, most notably the controllers of mobile capital and their representative organisations, the IMF and the World Bank. In this context, the government was to push ahead with the process of accounting reform, introducing a requirement for all limited companies above a certain size to publish audited financial reports (through the Jakarta Stock Exchange), a set of corporate governance regulations for publicly listed companies, and a variety of new accounting standards (*JP* 23 February 1998; Rosser 1999b:15, 2005).

Importantly, however, it did not go much further than this. In particular, it did little to try to improve the quality of auditing within the country. It was only following the Enron scandal in 2002, and the consequent global moves towards tougher regulation of auditing, that the government introduced new regulations aimed at improving auditor independence. At the same time, it made little effort to investigate or prosecute auditors who breached accounting regulations (Rosser 2005). In this connection, a useful comparison can be drawn with Thailand where, as we have seen, the political and social preconditions for reform have been much stronger, at least under Chuan's prime ministership. In that country, the government responded to criticisms concerning the quality of financial reporting from local companies by not only improving its accounting regulations (World Bank 2000:21–2), but also by launching an assault on several international auditing firms. In August 1998, for instance, the Securities and Exchange Commission suspended two auditors, one at SGV-Na Thalang and Co. Ltd and the other at Deloitte Touche Tohmatsu Jaiyos Ltd, for failing to comply with standards when auditing the financial reports of finance companies that subsequently failed (*Nation* 13 August 1998). Around the same time, the commission also launched an investigation into the local affiliate of PeatMarwick over accounting irregularities at Alphatec Electronics that were reported to amount to more than AUS$40 billion (*Australian* 15 September 1998; see also MacDonald 1998). In short, then, the different political and social environments within the two countries produced different reform outcomes: whereas the Indonesian government's program of accounting reform was only partial in nature—being focused on the production of new accounting regulations, but not on improving auditing practice—the Thai government's program was much more comprehensive. As in Thailand, however, implementation of the new accounting regulations has been compromised by weak enforcement capacity, reflecting continued problems of corruption and inefficiency in the judicial system, despite limited efforts on the part of donors and others to promote judicial reform over recent years.

Singapore

Singapore's political economy has two distinct elements: first, a tradeable sector largely controlled by foreign capital and, second, a powerful domestic sector composed of government-led companies (GLCs) that effectively dominate the domestic economy and are strongly linked to the ruling People's Action Party (PAP). The effective political and policy segmentation of the economy between the external and the domestic sectors reduces (although it does not eliminate) potential conflicts between the two sectors. However, the powerful domestic enterprises are the core component of Singapore's dominant coalition. Therefore, any analysis of the policy reform in Singapore over the past decade or so needs to take into account the pivotal economic and political role of GLCs in Singapore's dominant coalitions. Indeed, even as privatisation and deregulation have proceeded apace, the government used key holding companies—Temasek, Singapore Technology, and Health Corporation Holdings—to retain control over some of the biggest corporate entities in Singapore (Rodan 1997; see also Vennewald 1994).

A significant facet of Singapore's liberalisation over the last decade has been its ability to separate ownership and control. Even as state enterprises were privatised, those controlling this powerful sector of the economy have had close links with the PAP. In this context, Rodan (1997:160) points out that 'this virtual "class" of public entrepreneurs is closely connected to the ruling political party, the upper echelons of the civil service having been the main recruiting for the PAP for some time'. Indeed, in this respect, Singapore's political economy differs significantly from that of other Tigers (South Korea, Taiwan, and Hong Kong) in relying on state-led companies rather than predominantly on private capital.

In fact, one of the distinctive features of the Singaporean political economy over the past fifteen years has been the gradual movement of state enterprises into the private sector without a concomitant shift in control of these enterprises. Singapore has, in effect, created a powerful group of what could be termed 'nomenklatura capitalists' who exercise immense control over the enterprises they manage but are yet dependent on the PAP for their position. This close linkage between the GLCs and the ruling party accounts for the failure of an alternative reform coalition to emerge. Even if there were powerful economic interests pushing for reform, such interests would have to operate outside the politically entrenched PAP—a difficult task in Singapore. Further, the growing significance of these groups has moved the organising centres of power within the state towards key holding companies such as Tamasek away from both the formal executive processes and party structures. Arguably, this shift within the state—reflecting the emergence of these state capitalists—is the most important transformation of the Singapore state during the Goh prime ministership.

Three further factors condition the nature of policy reform. First, the Singaporean state has exceptional fiscal resources that have not only moderated structural pressure from the global economy, but also have enabled the state to intervene to prop up ailing economic sectors (Velloor 1998). Second, the Singaporean state has considerable institutional capacity. In fact, as much of the developmental state literature suggests (see Weiss & Hobson 1995), its economic development has relied on the coordination capacity of the state. Finally, the Singaporean technocracy is strongly internationalist in orientation. Of all the economies in South-East Asia, the Singaporean state is the most deeply permeated by an internationalist ethos.

This unique combination of an entrenched status quo coalition with a high degree of institutional capacity and internationalist orientation in the bureaucracy produces limited reform with good implementation (see model 2b, table 10.1). Alternatively, this type of reform can be conceived of as offensive adjustment to structural pressure. The essence of offensive adjustment is the protection of companies within the dominant coalition by a process of gradual and selective liberalisation. It seeks to make GLCs and other parts of the dominant coalition more competitive by subjecting them to more international competition, but in a manner that will not threaten the economic and political position of the dominant coalition. Rather, it seeks to use this gradual liberalisation to further entrench its dominance within the Singaporean political economy. A good example of this process is economic policy-making in Singapore's telecommunications industry.

Singapore has made significant moves to liberalise and deregulate its telecommunications market. In part, this is due to the dramatic global technical change that transformed telecommunications markets. In parallel with these global changes, there has been significant international pressure on the Singaporean government to liberalise its telecommunications market. The impetus for these changes can also be located in the continuing effort by the Singaporean government to develop its information technology industries through the vehicle of its own GLCs. Given these potentially contradictory imperatives, the telecommunications reform provides an important window into the management of policy reform.

Three distinctive features of reform stand out.

First, there has been a policy of gradual liberalisation in segmented markets—such as mobile telephones—within the telecommunications sector. In 1995, the government issued a licence for a second mobile provider to commence services from 1997. In 1998, the market was further liberalised in a range of areas (Singh 1999) and, in January 2000, the government brought forward its liberalisation program and lifted limits on foreign equity. However, a significant aspect of these reforms is the fact that most new licensees are in partnership and alliance with government-led companies (Singh 1999). As a result, although the market has been liberalised, the government has ensured that strategic domestic corporate entities have become players within the newly liberalised market

One of the key advantages of the strategy of guided liberalisation is that it allows the state to focus on competition (rather than on ownership) in the deregulated market, and this dovetails with the Singaporean government's privatisation strategy, which separates the marketisation of government-owned assets from their ownership and control. It is a strategy that provides a significant advantage to powerful GLCs, which benefit from liberalisation without ceding managerial control over their corporations.

Second, the size and financial strength of SingTel, a GLC, gives it a significant competitive advantage over the rest of the market. But the gradual liberalisation of the market exposes SingTel to international market forces without threatening its fundamental economic strength. Hence, the policy of guided liberalisation in a range of markets from telecommunication to finance dovetails with the corporate and strategic interest of SingTel (Singh 1999). However, as Rodan points out (chapter 5, this volume), these strategies might well be increasingly problematic when government-led corporations attempt to compete in international markets.

Third, the telecommunication regulator, the Infocom Development Authority (IDA), is not independent of the executive. Given SingTel's influence and power within the government, the IDA's limited regulatory autonomy casts doubt on its ability to reign in entrenched dominant market players. Moreover, the IDA's mandate is not only to develop competition, but also to develop strategic industry policies for the Singapore information industry.

One of the crucial dimensions of Singapore's recent economic policy is the development of new institutional frameworks of economic governance. In the telecommunication sector, the IDA regulates and monitors the operation of the telecommunication authority but it has little real regulatory autonomy (Sivalingam 2005). SingTel, the dominant player in the telecommunication market, has, so far, little to fear from an assertive regulator, but in a few instances SingTel has lost out to its competitors. Sivalingam (2005:186), for example, points out that

> The IDA role as regulator has come under the spotlight due to a proposal by the IDA to force SingTel to provide access to its local leased circuits (LLCs) to its rivals at a fixed price for a two to three year period. The IDA's role has been questioned as it appears to be creating an adversarial situation between SingTel and its competitors.

Of course, these instances of direct conflict between the regulator and SingTel are rare, but what is important here is to note that the GLCs, like SingTel, now have to operate within a new framework of public authority or regulation. As Singapore faces more pressure to liberalise its markets, conflicts between transnational companies and local GLCs are likely to find expression in tensions and contradictions within these new frameworks of regulatory authority. Similarly, these new regulatory frameworks may embody ideas about transparency and competition that conflict with the way the GLCs operate, creating new tensions and conflicts with state capitalist actors (Rodan 2004). These conflicts are likely to become much more prominent in the next decade. The key point is that these conflicts find material expression within the state apparatus.

To summarise, the distinctive feature of the program of economic liberalisation pursued by the Singapore government is the introduction of guided or limited liberalisation that does not threaten key links between the GLCs and the state. One of the lessons of the Singapore liberalisation experience is that we need to focus not only on the structure of the playing field, but also on the players themselves; markets are embedded in systems of power and interests, and these, in turn, are reflected in tension and contradictions within and between various state apparatuses.

Malaysia

In Malaysia, as with Singapore, the economy is divided into two sectors: a tradeable sector largely owned by foreign capital and a domestic sector composed of enterprises with strong links to a ruling party. Central to the Malaysian political economy was the adoption, beginning in 1971, of the New Economic Policy (NEP) designed to promote greater Malay entrepreneurship in the domestic economy, which was previously largely in the hands of Chinese capital. It is beyond the brief of this chapter to document the working of the NEP (see Khoo, chapter 6, this volume), but two significant effects need to be noted.

First, the NEP created strong incentives for powerful Chinese capitalists to enter into alliances and relationships with Malay politicians. This nexus, which became increasingly important during the 1990s, blurred the distinction between Chinese and Malay capital, and formed the basis for a broadly-based dominant coalition (Gomez & Jomo 1997).

Second, the NEP initially rested on an ambitious state-driven industrialisation policy led by large state enterprises. These enterprises were controlled by powerful bureaucrats with close ties to the dominant political apparatus. However, after the economic recession of the late 1980s, Malaysia embarked on a program of quite extensive privatisation and deregulation. As with Singapore, this privatisation resulted in a shift of ownership from the public to the private sector, but control over the newly privatised assets was still dependent on links to the dominant political party—in Singapore, the PAP, in Malaysia, the United Malays National Organization (UMNO). In Malaysia, this was achieved through the creation of private companies that were controlled by UMNO. In short, ownership of key strategic enterprises shifted from state to party. As Bowie (1994:182) points out, these developments have led to the 'erection of corporate empires blessed with unrestricted access to state-issued licences and Malay preferences…used to raise funds for constituent and electoral purposes'. As with Singapore, Malaysia created its own brand of nomenklatura capitalists that remain a key component of the dominant coalition.

Although the crisis has severely undermined the viability of these enterprises, it is clear that the links between UMNO and key sectors of the domestic economy are so strong that any attempt to introduce market-oriented reform will be strongly resisted. The brutal treatment of Anwar Ibrahim is ample testimony to the strength of this domestic coalition. As with Singapore, the creation of a kind of nomenklatura capitalism allows very little political space for the emergence of an alternative reform-oriented coalition. Unlike Singapore, though, there are significant pockets of domestic capital that might form the basis of a future reform coalition. The recent electoral setbacks for the ruling party suggest that this might well be a plausible scenario.

In terms of institutional capacity, the Malaysian state is highly constrained fiscally; there are significant limits to the extent to which it can bail out strategically connected enterprises. Nevertheless, the state does have a relatively greater capacity to implement economic programs than is the case in either Indonesia or Thailand. More strikingly, Malaysian economic policies have a strongly nationalist orientation. As Khoo (1995:329) has pointed out:

> But it aspires to find its fulfilment in an equally committed Malaysian nationalist goal of competing equally with the advanced nations of the world. Mahathir himself has alluded to all this before.

The strength of the dominant coalition and the weakness of any putative reform coalition, combined with the strongly nationalistic orientation of Malaysian economic policy-making, suggests that the prospects for neoliberal reform programs are weak. But, unlike in Singapore, the Asian economic crisis greatly weakened the economic viability of key enterprises that would preclude the kind of offensive adjustment to the crisis that was evident in Singapore. Malaysia's response to the crisis was much more defensive and led to a temporary withdrawal from the international financial system (Nesadurai 2000).

Malaysia's response to the Asian crisis was dramatic. It imposed capital controls and turned its back on the kind of reforms being pursued in countries such as Thailand and Indonesia. Apart from the imposition of capital controls by Bank Negara, the Malaysian government instituted a range of policies in the financial and corporate sectors to protect politically linked firms and banks. It established an asset managing company to purchase non-performing loans from the financial sector to protect the banks from unmanageable debts, and also established a special-purpose vehicle to recapitalise banks (Nesadurai 2000). Given the fact that these agencies lack any real independence, it is clear that the underlying imperative for these moves has been to salvage the politically connected financial institutions and conglomerates.

It is clear that these reforms in the financial sector imposed by the Malaysian government represent a defensive adjustment to the structural pressures imposed by the global economy. It is defensive in the sense that the Malaysian response to the crisis exemplifies a series of moves to protect the economic and political interests of an entrenched dominant coalition that had become significantly vulnerable (see model 1b, table 10.1). Indeed, it is instructive to compare the Malaysian strategy with the Singaporean policies that have moved to gradually liberalise Singapore's financial sector, for example, by lifting the restriction on foreign entry to its banking sector (Rodan, chapter 5, this volume). Although both states have dominant coalitions that are deeply entrenched, the difference in the two strategies lies in the degree to which these coalitions have been exposed to the structural pressures of the global market.

The key, then, to understanding the Malaysian defensive reform strategy is the extent to which it has reflected the close connections among the dominant political apparatus and key financial and corporate entities.

In essence, the policy response to the crisis has been dictated by the fact that the privatisation of state enterprises that took place in the 1990s created a new group of nomenklatura—Malay capitalists who, acting in alliance with significant sections of non-Malay capital, controlled the commanding heights of the Malaysian economy. In Malaysia, as in Singapore, the emergence of these new groups of state capitalists found expression in the new sites of power within the state, particularly in the new informal networks of power around the former Prime Minister Mahathir. This was a noticeable shift away from the structures of the dominant party, UMNO. Yet, much more so than in Singapore, contradictions between these sites of power and more technocratic agencies were intense and, in part, underpinned the conflict between Mahathir and Anwar, leading to the latter's eventual imprisonment on trumped up charges. While most of the capital controls imposed in the aftermath of the Asian crisis have been dismantled, the key party-linked conglomerates dominate the commanding sites of state power. The advent of the new Prime Minister, Badawi, has not altered these basic tensions, and over the next decade the ongoing tensions over economic reform are likely to become much more salient.

CONCLUSION

The overriding issue to emerge from this analysis is the extent to which the enacting of liberal economic reform is enmeshed in the political process. Liberalisation strikes at the heart of deeply entrenched political and economic interests. To be successful, therefore, an economic liberalisation program must galvanise its own political support. From this perspective, economic liberalisation is not merely a technical exercise to implement the right policies, but a political project undertaken by the putative winners of liberalisation. For this reason, economic liberalisation is likely to be a deeply contested and a prolonged process. Our analysis of liberalisation serves to underscore the fact that markets are not neutral abstract entities; they are deeply embedded in a constellation of power and interests.

In this respect, our analysis differs from orthodox accounts that regard reform as a mere exercise in getting the policies right. Of course, many studies of economic reform, in explaining the widespread inability of governments to pursue active programs of economic reform in post-crisis Asia, have given great emphasis to issues of institutional failure. In these accounts, politics is conceived of as external to the market and the failure to get the policies right is often attributed to rent-seeking or irrational politics. Politics is not extrinsic to, but constitutive of, markets. A constitutive theory of markets being advocated in this chapter suggests a different understanding of politics from that which informs neoclassical political economy (see chapter 1, this volume).

In this context, it seems far too early to declare the victory of liberal markets in South-East Asia. Although the crisis has almost certainly brought an end to oligarchic–crony capitalism in Indonesia—or at least that brand of oligarchic–crony capitalism centred around the interests of the Soeharto family—and has given great impetus to economic liberalisation in Thailand, it does not appear to have had similar effects in Singapore and Malaysia. Indeed, the political and economic systems that existed in those countries before the crisis appear to have survived more or less intact. The more general point is that these pressures of globalisation are located within the institutions of the state itself (Povlantzas 1978b). Hence, the process of state transformation is the key to understanding the broader dynamics of economic liberalisation in East Asia. What is required is a more constitutive conception of the state and policy capacity that recognises the state not as an entity, but as a complex and constituted set of relationships between frameworks of political authority and the international political economy, domestic social forces, and the broader ideational notions of authority or stateness.

REFERENCES

Bowie, Alasdair (1994) 'The Dynamics of Business–Government Relations in Industrialising Malaysia', in Andrew Macintyre (ed.) *Business and Government in Industrialising Asia*, Sydney: Allen & Unwin, pp. 167–94.

Cathie, John (1997) 'Financial Contagion in East Asia and the Origins of the Economic and Financial Crisis in Korea', *Asia Pacific Business Review*, Winter 1997/Spring 1998, 4(2/3): 18–28.

Chalmers Ian and Vedi Hadiz (eds) (1997) *The Politics of Economic Development in Indonesia: Contending Perspectives*, London: Routledge.

Chaudhry, Kiren (1993) 'The Myths of the Market and the Common History of Late Developers', *Politics and Society*, 21(3):245–74.

——(1994) 'Economic Liberalization and the Lineages of the Rentier State', *Comparative Politics*, 27 (October):1–25.

Cole David and Betty Slade (1999) 'The Crisis and Financial Sector Reform', in H. Arndt and H. Hill (eds) *Southeast Asia's Economic Crisis: Origins, Lessons and the Way Forward*, Sydney: Allen & Unwin, pp. 107–18.

Crispin, Shaun W. (2003) 'Cat and Mouse', *Far Eastern Economic Review*, 8 May, p. 47.

Crouch, Harold (1988) *The Army and Politics in Indonesia*, Ithaca: Cornell University Press.

Evans, Peter (1992) 'The State as Problem and Solution: Predation, Embedded Autonomy, and Structural Change', in Stephan Haggard and Robert Kaufman (eds) *The Politics of Economic Adjustment*, Princeton: Princeton University Press, pp. 139–81.

——(1995) *Embedded Autonomy: States and Industrial Transformation*, Princeton: Princeton University Press.

Frankel, Jeffrey (1998) 'The Asian Model, the Miracle, the Crisis', paper delivered at US International Trade Commission, April, <www.stern.nyu.edu/~nroubini/asia/Asia Homepage.html>.

Fukuyama, Francis (1999) 'Asian Values and the Current Crisis', <wbln0018.worldbank.org/eap/eap.nsf/6ab4a4/3f71de9e0d22cc_4285256811 0078670>.

Gibbons, David (1996) 'Bankruptcy in Thailand', *Commercial Law Bulletin*, 11(4):50–4.

Girling, John (1981) *The Bureaucratic Polity in Modernizing Societies: Similarities, Differences and Prospects in the ASEAN Region*, Singapore: Institute of Southeast Asian Studies.

Gomez, Edmund T. and K. S. Jomo (1997) *Malaysia's Political Economy: Politics, Patronage and Profits*, Cambridge: Cambridge University Press.

Haggard, Stephan and Robert Kaufman (1992) 'Institutions and Economic Adjustment', in Stephan Haggard and R. Kaufman (eds) *The Politics of Economic Adjustment*, Princeton: Princeton University Press, pp. 3–37.

Hewison, Kevin (1997) 'Thailand: Capitalist Development and the State', in Garry Rodan et al. (eds) *The Political Economy of South-East Asia: An Introduction*, Melbourne: Oxford University Press, pp. 93–120.

——(2005) 'Neo-liberalism and Domestic Capital: The Political Outcomes of the Economic Crisis in Thailand', *Journal of Development Studies*, 41 (2):310–30.

Jayasuriya, Kanishka (1995) 'Political Economy of Democratisation in East Asia', *Asian Perspective*, Fall–Winter 18 (2):141–80.

——(2001) 'Globalization and the changing architecture of the state: regulatory state and the politics of negative coordination', *Journal of European Public Policy* 8(1):101–23.

Jomo, K. S. (ed.) (1998) *Tigers in Trouble: Financial Governance, Liberalisation and Crises in East Asia*, London: Zed Books.

Khoo Boo Teik (1995) *Paradoxes of Mahathirism*, Oxford: Oxford University Press.

Krueger, Anne (1993) *Political Economy of Policy Reform in Developing Countries*, Cambridge, Mass.: MIT Press.

MacDonald, Scott B. (1998) 'Transparency Transparency in Thailand's 1997 Economic Crisis: the Significance of Disclosure', *Asian Survey*, 38(7):688–703.

MacIntyre, Andrew (1994) 'Business, Government and Development: Northeast and Southeast Asian Comparisons', in Andrew MacIntyre (ed.) *Business and Government in Industrialising Asia*, Sydney: Allen & Unwin, pp. 1–28.

——(1999) 'Political Institutions and the Economic Crisis in Thailand and Indonesia', in Heinz Arndt and Hal Hill (eds) *Southeast Asia's Economic Crisis: Origins, Lessons, and the Way Forward*, Singapore: Institute of Southeast Asian Studies, pp. 142–57.

——(2003) *The Power of Institutions: Political Architecture and Governance*, New York: Cornell University Press.

Nelson, Joan (1990) 'Introduction: The Politics of Economic Adjustment in Developing Nations', in Joan Nelson (ed.) *Economic Crisis and Policy Choice: The Politics of Adjustment in the Third World*, Princeton: Princeton University Press, pp. 3–32.

Nesadurai, Helen E. S. (2000) 'In Defence of National Autonomy? Malaysia's Response to the Financial Crisis', *Pacific Review*, 13(1):73–113.

Pasuk Phongpaichit and Chris Baker (1997) 'Power in Transition: Thailand in the 1990s', in K. Hewison (ed.) *Political Change in Thailand: Democracy and Participation*, London: Routledge, pp. 21–41.

——(1998) *Thailand's Boom and Bust*, Chiang Mai: Silkworm Books.

Pempel T. J. (1998) *Regime Shift: Comparative Dynamics of the Japanese Political Economy*, Ithaca and London: Cornell University Press.

Polanyi, Karl (1944) *The Great Transformation*, New York: Octagon Books.

Poulantzas, Nicos (1978a) *State, Power and Socialism*. London: New Left Books

——(1978b) *Classes in Contemporary Capitalism*, London: New Left Books
Rahman, M. (1998) *The Role of Accounting Disclosure in the East Asian Financial Crisis: Lessons Learned?*, Geneva: UNCTAD.
Riggs, Fred (1966) *Thailand: The Modernization of a Bureaucratic Polity*, Honolulu: East–West Center Press.
Robison, Richard (1986) *Indonesia: The Rise of Capital*, Sydney: Allen & Unwin.
——(1988) 'Authoritarian States, Capital-Owning Classes and the Politics of Newly Industrializing Countries', *World Politics*, 41(1):52–74.
——(1997) 'Politics and Markets in Indonesia's Post-oil Era', in Garry Rodan, Kevin Hewison and Richard Robison (eds) *The Political Economy of South-East Asia: An Introduction*, Melbourne: Oxford University Press, pp. 29–63.
——and Andrew Rosser (1999) 'Surviving the Meltdown: Liberal Reform and Political Oligarchy in Indonesia', in Richard Robison et al. (eds) *Politics and Markets in the Wake of the Asian Crisis*, London: Routledge, pp. 171–91.
Rodan, Garry (1997) 'Singapore: Economic Diversification and Social Divisions', in Garry Rodan, Kevin Hewison and Richard Robison (eds) *The Political Economy of South-East Asia*, Melbourne: Oxford University Press, pp. 148–78.
——(2004) *Transparency and Authoritarian Rule in Southeast Asia : Singapore and Malaysia*, London: RoutledgeCurzon.
Rosser, Andrew (1999a) 'Creating Markets: The Politics of Economic Liberalisation in Indonesia Since the Mid-1980s', unpublished PhD, Murdoch University.
——(1999b) 'The Political Economy of Accounting Reform in Developing Countries: The Case of Indonesia', *Asia Research Centre Working Paper No. 93*, Perth: Murdoch University Asia Research Centre.
——(2002) *The Politics of Economic Liberalisation in Indonesia*, Richmond: Curzon.
——(2005) 'The Political Economy of Corporate Governance in Indonesia', in Ho Khai Leong (ed.) *Reforming Corporate Governance in Southeast Asia: Economics, Politics, and Regulations*, Singapore: ISEAS.
Schamis, Hector (1999) 'Distributional Coalitions and the Politics of Economic Reform in Latin America', *World Politics*, 51:236–68.
Singh, Kulwant (1999) 'Guided Competition in Singapore's Telecommunications Industry', *Industrial and Corporate Change*, 7(4):585–99.
Sivalingam G. (2005) *Competition Policy in the ASEAN Countries*, Singapore: Thompson.
Thoolen, Huns (1987) *Indonesia: The Rule of Law*, The Hague: International Commission of Jurists.
Velloor, Ravi (1998) '$2b Boost for Economy', *Straits Times*, 30 June.
Vennewald, Werner (1994) 'Technocrats in the State Enterprise System in Singapore', *Asia Research Centre Working Paper*, No. *32*, Perth: Murdoch University.
Wade, Robert and Frank Veneroso (1998) 'The Asian Crisis: The High Debt Model Versus the Wall Street–Treasury–IMF Complex', *New Left Review* March/April: 1–24.
Weiss, Linda (1998) *The Myth of the Powerless State: Governing the Economy in a Global Era*, Cambridge: Polity Press.
——and John Hobson (1995) *States and Economic Development: A Comparative Historical Analysis*, Oxford: Polity Press.
Williamson, John (1994) 'In Search of a Manual for Technopols', in John Williamson (ed.) *The Political Economy of Policy Reform*, Washington, DC: Institute for International Economists.
——and Stephen Haggard (1994) 'The Political Conditions for Economic Reform', in John Williamson (ed.) *The Political Economy of Policy Reform*, Washington, DC: Institute for International Economics, pp. 527–96.
Winters, Jeffrey (1999) 'The Financial Crisis in Southeast Asia', in Richard Robison et al. (eds) *Politics and Markets in the Wake of the Asian Crisis*, London: Routledge, pp. 34–52.

World Bank (1993) *Indonesia: Sustaining Development*, Washington, DC: World Bank.
——(1997) *World Development Report 1997: The State in a Changing World*, Oxford: Oxford University Press.
——(2000) *Thailand Economic Monitor*, Washington, DC: World Bank.

Newspapers and journals

Asian Business (*AB*)
Asian Wall Street Journal (*AWSJ*)
Australian
East Asian Executive Reports
Far Eastern Economic Review (*FEER*)
Info Finansial (*IF*)
Jakarta Post (*JP*)
Media Akuntansi (*MA*)
Nation

11 South-East Asian Industrial Labour: Structural Demobilisation and Political Transformation

Frederic C. Deyo

KEY TOPICS

INTRODUCTION

ECONOMIC development involves a broadly-based transformation of economic and social institutions, one outcome of which is sustained economic growth. The sociopolitical process through which this transformation occurs normally produces winners and losers as it alters patterns of economic claims and income flows. For this reason, economic development is, typically, a contested process, one in which shifting and emergent groups and coalitions contend for favourable economic positions in a changing and uncertain social order, and in which the very nature and extent of development is an outcome of social and class contention.

A political-economy view of economic development can usefully be applied to an understanding of the role of organised labour in the rapid industrialisation of South-East Asia during recent years. Of particular importance are changes in the labour systems through which labour is socially reproduced, mobilised for economic ends, utilised in production, and controlled and motivated in support of economic goals. These changes are joint products of the politically and economically driven labour strategies of government and business elites, global political and economic pressures and constraints, the process of industrialisation itself, and, variably, of the individual and collective responses of workers to elite strategies and industrial pressures.

This chapter explores the labour implications of recent economic development in the capitalist countries of South-East Asia, a region where rapid industrial development is being powerfully shaped and conditioned by two global transformations in economic ideology and policy. The first of these is the growing world influence of neoliberalism, a broad economic approach emphasising increased reliance on market forces to direct international and national economic processes. The second involves the adoption of more flexible production systems as a condition for success under intensified global economic competition. Neoliberalism and the need for increased production flexibility have powerfully influenced the nature of industrial change in the region and, consequently, the emergent characteristics of labour systems as well. Thus, the global context in which industrialisation is occurring during the process of economic development is closely related to major issues of contestation between workers and trade unions on the one hand, and government and business elites on the other.

The chapter begins with a brief overview of labour and development in capitalist South-East Asia during past years. It explores the way in which changing economic strategies of governments and firms have been reflected in corresponding labour policies, and the response of workers to those policies. It is seen that, with some exceptions, labour has been unable to challenge elite strategies effectively and that labour's weakness derives only in part from political constraint, rooted in the imperatives of regime survival and geopolitical challenges, and in the economic strategies of dominant firms and governments. Equally important for an understanding of weak regional labour movements has been the labour impact of economic structural change itself, the temporal sequencing of political and economic change, the world system timing of industrial deepening, market reform, and the economic crisis of the late 1990s.

LABOUR AND DEVELOPMENT IN SOUTH-EAST ASIA

Until relatively recently, the economies of South-East Asia were based largely on agriculture and service industries. As late as 1970, services alone accounted for two-thirds of GDP in Singapore and 46 per cent in Malaysia. Services and agriculture together accounted for 75 per cent of GDP in Thailand and Malaysia, 67 per cent in Indonesia, and 69 per cent in the Philippines. These two sectors together accounted for even larger shares of the workforce, ranging from 73 per cent in Singapore to 95 per cent in Thailand (World Bank 1995).

Much of the large service sector consisted at that time of small commercial establishments, government services, and a heterogeneous grouping of informal-sector jobs, self-employment, and unpaid family labour. In agriculture, the overwhelming majority of the workforce owned or worked on small family farms, the remainder serving as plantation workers.

Trade unions and other types of labour organisations in these countries were confined largely to plantation workers (especially in Malaysia, Indonesia, and the Philippines), dockworkers, miners, workers in large manufacturing companies, transportation workers, mill workers and, where legal, state enterprise employees (especially public-utility workers) and civil servants. Despite low levels of unionisation and confinement of unionism to these few occupational sectors, organised labour played a significant role in national politics until the mid twentieth century. In Malaysia and the Philippines, labour militancy during the economic crisis of the 1930s strengthened calls for a realignment of development policy away from reliance on exports of primary products and toward protection and encouragement of domestic industry. In Indonesia, the Philippines, and Malaysia, labour actively participated in anti-colonial independence struggles, especially after the Second World War (Arudsothy & Littler 1993; Ingleson 1981; Wurfel 1959). During the 1950s, militant labour groups in the Philippines successfully pushed for enactment of what was, by regional standards, highly progressive labour legislation (Ofreneo 1995), and, in Singapore in the early 1960s, leftist labour mobilisation came close to creating a socialist government and clearly shaped the social agenda of the government that was established after the defeat of the Left (Deyo 1989).

By the late 1960s, however, restrictive state controls over trade unionism and labour activism had substantially tamed and depoliticised organised labour. In Malaysia, ethnic and communal conflict that threatened state structures and conservative ruling groups was met by tight controls over organised labour. More generally across the region, a political assault on the independence and power of organised labour, associated with Western-supported efforts to contain communism, initiated a downward spiral of union influence (Hewison & Rodan 1994). In Singapore, Chinese communalism precipitated a violent confrontation with anglicised moderates in the ruling People's Action Party (PAP), which led to decimation of the Chinese Left, consolidation of moderate PAP leadership, and the institution of tight preemptive controls over organised labour through the government-dominated National Trades Union Congress (NTUC). Although labour organisation and agitation in the Philippines initially elicited a response of political accommodation and the establishment of a liberal, US-modelled labour-relations system, it was met in later years by ever-harsher restrictions, culminating in 1972 in martial law repression, justified in part by the need to contain Left radicalism and popular sector insurgency (Hutchison 1993).

Similarly, organised labour in Thailand was effectively suppressed under intermittent anti-communist military rule over much of the 1940s–1960s period, especially after the 1957 coup (Hewison & Brown 1994). In Indonesia, following the 1965 military coup that sought to eliminate growing Leftist influence in national politics, the powerful, communist-aligned, national labour federation (Sentral Organisasi Buruh Seluruh Indonesia, SOBSI) was banned and later replaced by a government-sponsored federation (Hadiz 1994).

But this was not to be the end of labour influence in the region. Even under tight political controls, labour continued, in some countries, to wield moderate influence, in many cases through community-based political mobilisation linked only loosely to trade unionism. Labour's oppositional potential became especially evident during interludes of political crisis and government transition. Following the collapse of military rule in Thailand in 1973, for example, labour militancy frequently paralysed business in Bangkok and elsewhere. During the subsequent three years of open politics, labour pressed successfully for the enactment of new legislation that provided for union recognition and collective bargaining rights, established a minimum wage, and required employers to provide a number of new benefits, including worker's compensation. These labour victories were to provide a foundation for the re-establishment of worker rights under subsequent democratic governments in the late 1980s and in the 1990s. Similarly, it will be seen below that, in the context of a growing debt and economic crisis in the Philippines in the 1980s, a seemingly moribund labour movement mounted strong opposition to structural reforms, as well as to the Marcos regime itself. In Singapore and Malaysia, a greater degree of political continuity precluded such periods of dramatic labour mobilisation. But even there, workers and unions continued to press employers and government for improved wages and benefits during the 1960s and into the 1970s.

If, by the late 1960s, South-East Asian labour movements had already been partially tamed by restrictive political regimes, subsequent decades were to see a further diminution in labour influence at enterprise and national levels. This continuing decline was reflected in changes in union density, collective bargaining, and the political role of trade unions. By the late 1990s, regional union densities were quite low (Asia Monitor Resource Center 2003). Malaysia, with its official encouragement of Japanese-style company unions was a bit higher, at 10 per cent, as was Singapore at 15 per cent; here, even stronger encouragement is given to membership in the government-linked NTUC. Kuruvilla notes that these union densities had, in some cases, noticeably declined during the late 1980s and early 1990s, despite continuing industrial development (see Kuruvilla 1995). Only the Philippines showed an increase in union density over this period.

The weakness of organised labour in the region is further reflected in the restriction of collective bargaining agreements to a very small percentage of employed workers (5 per cent or less in Thailand, the Philippines, and Malaysia) (Arudsothy & Littler 1993; Brown & Frenkel 1993; Kuruvilla 1995; Quintos 2003). At national levels, the weak political position of organised labour was similarly evident across the region. In Singapore and Indonesia, the dominant national trade union federations, the NTUC and Serikat Pekerja Seluruh Indonesia (SPSI) respectively, were so tightly integrated into ruling party structures in the mid 1990s that they could not provide an independent channel of representation for workers (Deyo 1989; MacIntyre 1994). In Malaysia, the largest national federation, the Malaysian Trades Union Congress, was weakened in its mobilisation and coordination role by restrictions on its status as a union federation (Somahsundaram 2003). Although Thai state enterprise workers achieved some limited political goals in the 1980—including, most notably, the passage of the comprehensive Social Security Act of 1990—the trade union movement has, more generally, been marked by divisiveness and factionalism, seen most dramatically in the existence of several competing union federations, each supported by high-level military and/or bureaucratic elites. Labour movements in the Philippines and Malaysia suffer from similar problems of disunity and internal competition (Arudsothy & Littler 1993; Crouch 1993; Hutchison 1993).

The weak political position of labour is perhaps most dramatically seen in the relative inability of workers to seize new opportunities flowing from democratic reforms in Thailand, the Philippines, and, most recently, Indonesia. In the first two cases, workers joined with middle-class groups in opposing military rule and instituting more open electoral regimes. But in neither case has the organisational strength or collective bargaining position of trade unions been subsequently enhanced. To the contrary, labour movements under the new democratic regimes have remained divided and stagnant.

In this context, it is not surprising that elite developmental and labour policies are rarely challenged significantly by organised labour. Where labour opposition has been more consequential, it has taken other forms, typically, in concert with larger community groups protesting against government policies or inaction.

It is noteworthy that stagnation in South-East Asian labour movements has occurred in the context of social transformations that, elsewhere, have been historically associated with the empowerment of labour and other popular sector groups. At the base of these transformations is the continuing course of industrial development itself. Singapore, Malaysia, the Philippines, Indonesia, and Thailand all have substantial manufacturing and industrial sectors and provide industrial employment for a sizeable portion of their workforces.

TABLE 11.1 Industrial and social indicators

Industry as a percentage of GDP, 2003

Singapore	Malaysia	Thailand	Philippines	Indonesia
35	49	41 (2000)	32	44

Source: World Bank 2005:260–61, table 3

Percentage of industrial employment

Singapore	Malaysia	Thailand	Philippines	Indonesia
30 (1997)	38 (1997)	20 (1997)	17 (1997)	19 (1997)
25 (2001)	32 (2000)	19 (2001)	16 (2001)	19 (2002)

Sources: United Nations 1998; *ILO Yearbook of Labour Statistics* 2003

Adult literacy rate (% of people 15 years and above), 2003

Singapore	Malaysia	Thailand	Philippines	Indonesia
96 male	91 male	97 male	95 male	92 male
88 female	83 female	94 female	95 female	82 female

Source: World Bank (2003:276–7, table 2)

Percentage of urban population for recent years

Singapore	Malaysia	Thailand	Philippines	Indonesia
100	58 (2001)	20 (2001)	58 (1999)	39 (1999)

Source: World Bank (2004:152–5)

Unemployment rates (%)

	1997	1998	1999	2000	2001	2002	2003	2004
Singapore	2.5	3.2	4.6	4.4	3.3	4.4	4.5	4.1
Malaysia	2.4	3.2	3.4	3.1	3.6	3.5	3.4	3.1
Thailand	1.5	4.4	4.2	3.6	3.3	2.4	–	–
Philippines	7.9	9.6	9.4	10.1	9.8	11.4	10.0	10.0
Indonesia	4.7	5.5	6.4	6.1	8.1	9.1	–	–

Asia Development Bank: *Outlook* 2003, table A6

In addition, these countries boast high levels of literacy and education, usually considered useful predictors of social awareness and political participation. Industrial development in Singapore, Malaysia, and Thailand has been associated with industrial deepening into more sophisticated, technology-intensive and capital-intensive production. Important, too, is the emergence across the region of an increasingly settled and thus organisable urban proletariat (see Hadiz 1994), an important basis for early unionisation in Western countries.

But despite these seemingly propitious socioeconomic changes, rapid industrialisation has not spawned effective trade unionism or sustained capacity on the part of labour to participate seriously in political or economic arenas. Instead, labour's engagement, especially in political affairs, has been largely episodic, emerging during periodic political and economic crises, only to falter during subsequent reconsolidations of dominant elite coalitions (see Brown & Hewison 2004).

In part, the marginalisation of South-East Asian labour during recent years derives from a continuation of earlier forms of political constraint, even in those countries (for example, Thailand, the Philippines, Indonesia) that have experienced recent democratic reforms—an ironic conjuncture given that labour militancy contributed importantly to those very reforms. In Thailand, exclusion of state enterprise workers from union coverage continues to undermine the national labour movement insofar as the state-enterprise unions have traditionally played the lead union role in that country. In the Philippines, the new Aquino regime took a hardline stance on strikes defined as illegal under existing Marcos-era labour legislation (Ofreneo 1994). There are also indications that the post-September 11, US-led anti-terrorism campaign has encouraged reversals of political reforms in favour of authoritarian responses to threats of political violence, although it is unclear how these reversals may affect workers (chapter 1, this volume). More generally, even to the extent that labour legislation is supportive of good working conditions and effective trade unions, lack of enforcement, excessive legalism, and a host of legal restrictions and exceptions throw workers largely on the mercy of their employers.

Where restrictive government controls remain important, they have been oriented less to the political imperatives of regime stability than to the requirements of economic competitiveness and foreign investment. Because of this increasingly close relationship between labour regimes on the one hand, and economic strategies on the other (see Deyo 1989; Kuruvilla 1994), these factors are considered together in the discussion that follows, emphasising throughout the ways in which the successful implementation of economic strategies has been rooted in, while subsequently reinforcing, the weakness of South-East Asian labour movements. The strategies of particular regional interest during recent years include the shift to light export-oriented industrialisation (EOI), economic liberalisation, industrial deepening under second-stage EOI, and, most recently, the adoption of flexible production systems in manufacturing.

LABOUR UNDER EARLY EXPORT-ORIENTED INDUSTRIALISATION

Light industry-based EOI in Singapore and the Philippines in the 1970s, and in Malaysia, Thailand, and Indonesia in the 1980s, was premised on the successful mobilisation of low-cost, semi-skilled labour for the assembly and manufacture of products for world markets. In Singapore, Thailand, and Malaysia, and in the export-processing zones of the Philippines and Indonesia, light EOI relied heavily on direct foreign investment.

In Singapore, the twin pressures of cost containment and the need to attract foreign investment elicited new labour legislation in 1968 that reduced permissible retrenchment benefits, overtime work, bonuses, maternity leave, and fringe benefits. Thenceforth, unions could not demand, nor could managers offer, benefits greater than those stipulated under law. In addition, the National Wages Council, a tripartite body, established wage guidelines that held industrial wages down through the 1970s. A second statute gave management full discretionary power in matters of promotion, transfer, recruitment, dismissal, reinstatement, assignment or allocation of duties, and termination, issues that were now removed by law from the range of legal negotiations. This array of legislation, along with a parallel set of new investment incentives, was followed by a wave of foreign investment that continued until the mid 1970s recession (Begin 1995; Deyo 1989).

In Malaysia, where legislation similar to that in Singapore also removed a broad range of personnel issues from collective bargaining, union organisation and collective bargaining were, throughout the early 1980s, banned in electronics, the single most important manufacturing export industry. Union militancy was repressed in the export-processing zones of the Philippines and, in the wake of declining oil prices in the early 1980s, the Indonesian government intensified labour controls under a more centralised national labour federation, giving special encouragement to light, export-oriented manufacturing to replace declining oil export earnings (Hadiz 1994:195). The association between early EOI and cost-containment labour regimes has been noted frequently in the literature on East Asian industrialisation (Kuruvilla 1994). An International Labor Organization (ILO) study of world employment trends explicitly links the globalisation of capital, production, and markets with reduced labour protection in developing countries, arguing that global integration has adversely affected the ability of governments to enact and enforce labour legislation. Globalisation, the ILO (1995:72–3) notes, gives 'governments an incentive to dilute, or fail to enact, measures intended to protect the welfare of workers, or to turn a blind eye to infringements of legislation with this in mind'. This same report also notes an increasing erosion of the quality of formal-sector employment through reduced job security, the diminished significance of local or national-level collective bargaining, new policies of 'firm-centric cooperation', union-avoidance strategies, promotion of company unions, reduced access to information, and diminished bargaining leverage on the part of local unions.

Less well documented has been the extent of labour opposition to such practices and the cost-focused labour systems they have created. Throughout the region, groups of young women, newly hired in export-manufacturing industries, have protested against low wages and benefits, harsh working conditions, and the lack of enforcement of labour standards legislation. Such protest was especially pronounced in the export-processing zones of the Philippines and Indonesia (Lambert 1993). That said, it remains the case that such protests have rarely brought enduring gains for workers. This follows, in part, from the characteristics of employment in light-export sectors, with their relatively transitory labourforce comprised of large numbers of young women in unstable, low-skill jobs that provide them with few career opportunities. The difficulties of organising such a workforce into effective unions, along with the associated difficulty of mounting well-organised pressure on employers, continue to undermine labour movements in the large export-manufacturing sectors of South-East Asia (Deyo 1989).

INDUSTRIAL DEEPENING: THE IMPACT OF DEVELOPMENTAL SEQUENCING

Despite the political and economic constraints facing organised labour, there have been cases of dramatic labour activation. The 1980s resistance to structural reforms in the Philippines provides the most striking exception to the broader pattern of decline among organised labour. To understand this exception, as well as the more general pattern of union weakness and decline, it is necessary to consider the temporal context of economic structural changes in the region. In particular, how has the domestic developmental sequencing of political and industrial change and the historical timing of regional industrialisation influenced the consequences of development for labour? In this section, the impact of developmental sequencing is explored; a later section examines the effects of historical timing across the region more generally.

The Philippines differs from the other countries in this discussion in its continuing economic and industrial stagnation and relatively higher levels of unemployment (see table 11.1), which are impediments to strong labour movements. In such an inhospitable setting, it is not surprising to find low and declining overall union densities, negligible unionism in many industries, and collective agreement coverage for only a small proportion of wage workers. It is important to recognise, though, that the growing economic crisis of the 1980s precipitated a 'rise in militant unionism whose depth and breadth has no parallels in the country's history' (Ofreneo 1995:3; see also Hutchison 1993). In part, this militancy, which preceded and contributed to the democratic coup of 1986, can be attributed to a sustained and successful process of industrialisation oriented to the domestic market, a process that sets the Philippines apart from other countries in the region and that parallels more closely the experience of several Latin American countries that pursued similar development strategies during the 1950s and 1960s. The Philippine exception underscores the importance for labour movements of differences in developmental sequencing.

It is often noted that early Latin American industrialisation in the 1940s and 1950s was based on import substitution, whereas that occurring during subsequent decades in Asia was more strongly rooted in export manufacturing. Latin American import-substituting industrialisation (ISI) sought, initially, to defuse a growing political crisis—occasioned by the collapse of primary export-based development—by fostering industrial growth, employment, and labour peace under policies of economic nationalism and the building of corporatist–political coalitions that encompassed strong, if government-dependent, trade union federations. Protection of local companies from foreign competition permitted sustained industrial development along with ever-higher wages and social benefits for politically supported trade unions in key economic sectors. Indeed, rising industrial wages were seen as supportive of continued industrial growth by increasing consumer demand for local products.

The Philippines, like these Latin American countries, entered a sustained ISI phase during the 1940s and 1950s, during which successful import substitution was combined with labour regimes (in this case, more liberal than corporatist) that encouraged unionisation and collective bargaining. In response to a balance-of-payments crisis associated with the collapse of the primary-commodity export strategy of early decades of the twentieth century, protective tariffs and foreign exchange controls marked a shift towards ISI-led development. This shift was, in turn, associated with the enactment of new labour legislation that greatly enhanced worker welfare and union security in the formal sector of manufacturing. Especially important was new minimum wage legislation in 1951 and the 1953 Industrial Peace Act, subsequently dubbed the 'Magna Carta of Labour', which was patterned after the US National Labor Relations Act of 1935 in providing protection for trade unions and encouraging effective collective bargaining at the enterprise level (Ofreneo 1995). This 'misplaced' Latin American experience, stemming in part from US political influence, led to the emergence of strong local unions that, under subsequent years of martial law and state repression (1972–86), sustained a latent, community-based opposition movement. This movement provided the essential foundation for labour mobilisation and militancy during the economic and political crisis of the mid 1980s.

The Philippines case contrasts strongly with the developmental sequencing of political and economic change elsewhere in the region. Early industrialisation in most countries of the region was accompanied by authoritarian state controls that sought either to repress or co-opt organised labour. It was noted that these political controls, encouraged and supported by Western governments, comprised part of a larger global strategy of communist containment. Preemptively demobilised or co-opted at the outset of sustained industrialisation, most Asian labour movements lacked the political capacity to shape new labour relations institutions in the early years of industrial development. The developmental labour systems subsequently created were to ensure continued labour subordination during later years of industrial deepening.

ECONOMIC LIBERALISATION

Compounding the EOI-linked structural demobilisation of labour, the 1980s and 1990s saw growing international pressures, associated with ongoing regional and global trade agreements, to open domestic markets further to imports. Trade liberalisation, increasingly reflected in the economic agendas of the governments in these trade-dependent countries, has subjected firms to ever-greater competition in both domestic and international markets. In many cost-sensitive sectors, managers have sought to meet these new competitive pressures through cost-cutting measures directed especially at the reduction of labour costs. These measures, including increased the use of temporary and contract labour and greater outsourcing of production, have themselves reduced the organisational capacity of labour. In addition, competitive pressures have created a credible threat of shutdowns, retrenchments, and relocation of production to cheaper labour sites, a threat given special salience by the explosive expansion of Chinese export manufacturing.

Economic reform has included a broader set of structural adjustments, as well including privatisation of state enterprises and services, reduced state regulation of the economy, and reduced public expenditures. Privatisation, most prevalent in Thailand, Malaysia, and the Philippines, in turn subjects large firms in public transport, communications, and other sectors to heightened competition, and thus to the possibility of workforce retrenchment and wage and benefit reduction.

These and other neoliberal economic reforms were often met by labour opposition and public demonstrations. In Malaysia, Thailand, and the Philippines, trade unions fought vigorously for legislation to restrict the use of temporary workers. In Thailand, public-sector unions successfully slowed privatisation during the late 1980s through mass demonstrations in central Bangkok, and, in the Philippines, a wave of strikes and public demonstrations opposing structural adjustment measures during the early 1980s contributed to the political crisis that ultimately brought down the Marcos regime.

Labour campaigns against economic liberalisation slowed—but did not stop—ongoing economic reforms. In Thailand, the use of temporary workers continued to expand despite legislation restricting the practice. Efforts to stop privatisation met with somewhat greater success, particularly in Thailand. There, as elsewhere, effective opposition drew strength from a cross-class defensive coalition of labour and bureaucratic–military elites whose economic interests and power base were threatened by privatisation of the enterprises they controlled. In addition, state-enterprise workers were politically insulated from many of the competitive pressures that progressively undercut organised labour in the private sector. Thus, they continued to struggle from a position of relative strength. But, in the end, larger state interests dictated a silencing of opposition from this unrestructured Thai labour sector through a banning of all state-enterprise unions following the 1991 military coup.

A further, more general, outcome of external trade liberalisation was declining export competitiveness in the face of rapid growth among new low-cost exporters such as China and Vietnam. As a consequence, and with the exception of low-wage Indonesia, light export manufacturing and industrial employment more generally began a gradual retreat in favour of service sector employment (see table 11.1). Insofar as service sector employment, particularly that in the private sector, presents its own constraints on union organising, this shift did little to foster union growth.

PRODUCTION FLEXIBILITY, LABOUR, AND HISTORICAL TIMING

Economic liberalisation signals a larger transformation in the economic and technological context of market competition and production. In response to heightened market competition and uncertainty, firms in South-East Asia, as elsewhere, are seeking to enhance manufacturing flexibility and adaptability. Flexibility here refers to the ability to introduce changes in product and process quickly, efficiently, and continuously. Such flexibility yields a superior capacity to respond to the intensified pressures of liberalised trade, world market volatility, market fragmentation, heightened demand for just-in-time production and continuous improvements in productivity and quality, and rapid technological change.

A useful distinction is often made between static and dynamic forms of flexibility. Static flexibility, which focuses on short-term adaptability and cost cutting, is the predominant managerial approach in the labour-intensive export sectors that have figured so prominently in many of Asia's developing economies. There is evidence in this regard of increased use of subcontracting casualisation, and contract labour (numerical flexibility) in the large export sectors of the Phillipines (Ofreneo 1994) and Thailand (Deyo 1995). Guy Standing (1989) similarly documents increasing numerical flexibility and casualisation in electronics and other export sectors in Malaysia. Even in Singapore, James Begin (1995) reports on a static numerical flexibility. The reasons for this strategic choice are clear: intensified global competition under trade liberalisation places firms under extreme pressure to cut costs in the short term. Risky long-term investments in training, research, and organisational development are eschewed where they seem to place a firm at a short-term disadvantage vis-à-vis other firms that do not make these investments. In some countries, lack of adequate public investment in collective goods (for example, training, research and development, and physical infrastructure) further discourages such long-term investments, whereas lack of effective government support for minimal labour standards, adequate wages and benefits, and fair employment practices encourages firms to compete through union avoidance and labour cost reductions.

Static flexibility strategies have the known effects of creating an insecure, floating workforce and of encouraging dispersal of production to smaller, contracted firms and households. Recognising the obstacles such trends create for effective unionism, unions throughout the region have fought to institute legislative restrictions on the employment of temporary workers and on similar practices (Charoenloet 1993; Ofreneo 1994).

Dynamic flexibility strategies, although less prevalent, are pursued in product niches requiring high levels of quality, batch versus mass production, and continuing innovations and improvements in process and product technologies (Deyo & Doner 2001). Such strategies are encouraged where states underwrite a supportive social infrastructure of training, education, and R&D; enforce adequate labour standards; and provide incentives to firms to invest in training and organisational development. Finally, such strategies are most likely to be undertaken by large, resourceful firms that are able, in part, to create their own support infrastructure and operate in relatively protected or oligopolistic markets characterised by moderate, rather than extreme, competitive pressure. For these various reasons, dynamic flexibility strategies tend to occur in the upper-tier NICs with developmentally active states (for example, in Singapore, South Korea, and Taiwan) and among dominant firms in semi-protected industrial sectors across the region.

Most research on dynamic flexibility has focused on the experience of innovative industrial firms in Japan and North America, and in the developed countries of Europe. In these settings, dynamic flexibility has generally been associated with enhanced worker welfare and security, as well as with increased worker participation in organisational decision making as firms have sought to increase worker commitment and loyalty, and to encourage workers to assume increased responsibility for enterprise success. A distinction has been drawn in this regard between bargained forms of flexibility (which are associated with strong, independent unions and high levels of participation in instituting and operating new production systems) and participative flexibility (characterised by captive enterprise unions and more circumscribed forms of worker participation confined largely to shop-floor problem-solving) (see Turner, Lowell & Auer, Herzenberg, and other chapters in Deyo (1996)). This body of research seems generally to suggest that the instituting of dynamic flexibility, whether bargained or participative forms, should have a similarly salutary effect for workers and, perhaps, unions in developing Asia. In fact, it has not.

In the higher value-added market niches where technological and product quality requirements preclude continued reliance on low-skill temporary workers and static flexibility, Asian firms are pressed to make long-term investments in worker training, product development, organisational restructuring, and other programs supportive of enhanced dynamic flexibility. In addition, such firms sometimes institute suggestion systems, modified quality circles, labour–management councils, and other means of mobilising worker involvement in quality and productivity improvements (on Malaysia, see Rasiah

1994). But even such instances of dynamic flexibility, typically accompanied by improved wages and benefits and other measures to enhance the stability and commitment of workers, rarely permit the level of worker decision making found even under participative flexibility. Indeed, improvements in compensation levels and working conditions are as often introduced to avoid unions as to foster long-term organisational improvements (see, for example, Deyo 1995). In general, flexibility-enhancing organisational reforms are overwhelmingly attentive to managerial agendas driven by competitive economic pressures, to the exclusion of the social agendas of workers and unions. In many cases, such strategies, along with their relatively benign labour-welfare policies, are confined to a few critical production processes, thus fostering internal labour-market dualism between core, stable workers on the one hand, and casual or contract workers on the other (Deyo 1995).

The reasons for the more autocratic forms of dynamic flexibility found across the region are not hard to discern. First is the vicious circle defined by initially weak labour movements, the subsequent reorganisation of industry exclusively around managerial goals, and the resultant institutionalisation of autocratic forms of industrial flexibility. Here we see most clearly the way in which the political resources and effectiveness of labour determine institutional outcomes that reinforce existing power inequalities. In the cases of Singapore and Malaysia, as noted earlier, state labour regimes have further encouraged the instituting of autocratic flexibility by excluding from collective bargaining such matters as job assignment and work transfers, that are important elements of labour flexibility. Correspondingly, multinational corporations often insist on operating in a union-free environment (Kuruvilla 1994; Rasiah 1994).

Second, worker participation and empowerment may be less critical to the success of programs of dynamic flexibility in developing Asian countries than in industrially mature economies. Following Amsden (1989), we can distinguish between innovative and learning-based industrialisation. Innovative industrialisation relies on the development of a stream of new products and technologies for changing markets. Learning-based industrialisation, by contrast, relies on the local adoption of technologies and products developed elsewhere. Insofar as newly developing countries pursue technology-dependent, learning-based industrialisation, employers may seek to institute forms of flexibility that minimise worker participation in favour of unchallenged managerial control over production. This is so because learning-based industrialisation depends mainly on local adaptation and implementation of already debugged production processes and products, thus minimising the need for an extensive involvement of workers in dealing with shop-floor production problems. In such a context, engineers and production managers assume the primary role in reorganising production around imported technologies. Thus, more autocratic forms of flexibility are adequate for the demands of industrial upgrading. Given that multinational firms, whose investments provide a major conduit for technology transfer and diffusion to Asian firms, are reluctant to relocate major R&D functions to foreign subsidiaries in developing countries, the perpetuation of learning-based industrialisation into future years might imply a long-term stability of such autocratic forms of flexibility and a corresponding discouragement of union or worker empowerment at the workplace level. In such a context, human-resource mobilisation efforts will continue to confine collective forms of shop-floor participation to co-optive, officially sanctioned, and closely circumscribed deliberative forums (such as quality circles and labour–management councils) and, more generally, to eschew collective participation in favour of suggestion systems, informal consultation, merit-based incentives, job ladders, and other individualised modalities of worker participation and involvement in organisational development.

In this context, state labour regimes have been substantially transformed. As employers have increasingly gained the upper hand in their dealings with workers, labour-market deregulation—the counterpart of economic liberalisation and marketisation—has proven a more effective policy than continued repression. Such deregulation has not typically been accompanied by proactive labour-protection measures that might provide a level playing field for unions in their bilateral dealings with employees. With the important exception of Singapore, South-East Asian governments are generally lax in their enforcement of existing labour standards—thus effectively subjecting workers to capricious managerial domination, attacks on unions, and non-compliance with minimum wage, health, and safety legislation (Brown & Frenkel 1993). In Thailand, union organisers receive no legal protection during organisational drives up until the actual date of official union registration, thus impeding organisation drives. In Thailand and the Philippines, labour-market deregulation under democratic reforms, unaccompanied by corresponding measures to strengthen and institutionalise trade unionism, has resulted in increased employer domination at the enterprise level, along with heightened union factionalism and conflict (Brown & Frenkel 1993).

The implications of market reform for production regimes suggests that the historical timing of industrial change may be as important as developmental sequencing for Asian labour movements. Labour-intensive EOI under flexible, post-Fordist production regimes differs from earlier standardised-production EOI in shifting the locus of labour control from state to enterprise and in fragmenting and dispersing the workforce to a greater extent than in the earlier period. Further, the global–temporal context of industrial deepening into more capital-intensive and technology-intensive production has shifted appreciably. Despite unfavourable developmental sequencing, earlier standardised-production industrial deepening gave somewhat greater encouragement and scope to emergent labour movements in South Korea, Taiwan, and elsewhere under labour-homogenising standardised production technologies. Under flexible production regimes, by contrast, incipient deepening into high value-added industrial production in Thailand and Malaysia has encouraged preemptive enterprise participation structures that often displace or co-opt unions. In Thailand, such resourceful and market-dominating firms as Toyota, Siam Cement, and Yamaha, although discouraging independent or oppositional collective action, have instituted skill-based job ladders, suggestion systems, enterprise unions, carefully circumscribed quality circles, dualistic internal labour markets, and other measures that mobilise worker ideas and involvement. In Malaysia, state encouragement for Japanese-style enterprise unionism contributes further to such an effect. More advanced technology-deepening in Singapore has been associated with even greater official sponsorship and encouragement of labour–management councils, sponsored enterprise unions, and other preemptive participatory forums.

ECONOMIC CRISIS

The economic crisis of 1997–99 had a number of seemingly contradictory outcomes for labour: it further weakened workers and trade unions in their dealings with employers and the state. As workers were laid off, government surveillance of the labour practices of hard-hit firms was relaxed, and employers took advantage of new circumstances to contain and demobilise organised labour.

How severe were the adverse employment effects for workers? One indicator of the impact of the crisis is to be found in official unemployment statistics,[1] which show a very mixed picture across the region. In the Philippines and Malaysia, unemployment increased by roughly 8–10 per cent. In Singapore, unemployment roughly doubled between 1997 and 1999, while in Thailand, the ranks of the unemployed more than tripled.[2] As important, increased unemployment during early crisis years remained at elevated levels for several years thereafter. It is important to place these absolute figures in a larger perspective. Table 11.1 shows that unemployment as a percentage of the workforce, approached or exceeded only 10 per cent (as officially counted) in Indonesia and the Philippines. In the other countries, unemployment rates also rose, but far more modestly.

Increased unemployment, typically, has the dual and contradictory effects of activating labour protest and of rendering it more impotent, as labour confronts capital from a more disadvantaged position. In addition, because layoffs during Asia's crisis occurred, most importantly, among workers in small to medium-sized enterprises,[3] with their generally low union densities, the crisis had the primary effect of activating poorly organised, sporadic militancy among non-unionised workers, rather than of encouraging organised protest among unionised formal-sector workers. Such activation without empowerment goes some distance in explaining elite policy shifts in several countries of the region, shifts intended to address social issues of contention that emerged during the crisis, but on terms decidedly favouring the interests and economic agendas of elites rather than of workers (Hewison

2005). This somewhat paradoxical outcome, common across the region, was accompanied by an important transformation in the manner in which worker influence was expressed: from trade unionism to insertion into broader and more socially inclusive popular-sector social movements. This transformation, an outcome of labour activation alongside disempowerment, offered new channels of worker influence, even as more traditional modalities, especially trade unions, declined. These general observations may be illustrated by the experience of Thailand during and after the crisis.

THE FINANCIAL CRISIS IN THAILAND

Even as the crisis contributed yet another obstacle to effective Thai trade unionism, it precipitated broader political outcomes that restructured and reoriented workers' organisations. First, economic crisis was an important factor in the legislative passage of a new Constitution in October 1997 (Brown & Hewison 2004). This Constitution establishes a broad spectrum of human rights for civil society groups, creates a fully popularly elected senate, and permits citizens, including farmers' associations and trade unions, upon securing 50 000 signatures on a petition, the right to introduce parliamentary bills.

Relatedly, the crisis mobilised and activated a broad coalition of popular-sector groups, including small farmers and farm workers, the urban poor, workers in the state and private sectors, and small-business owners. During previous years of continuing economic growth, growing inequalities and reform-led economic dislocations and instability were largely masked by a rising material standard of living. Those groups most severely affected, such as state-enterprise workers, were largely left to fight their own battles. The crisis had the effect of widely politicising reform programs, which came to be seen as sources of economic vulnerability and uncertainty. United now by common antipathy to economic reform and the agencies (for example, the IMF) and the domestic politicians promoting them, regional and national associations of farmers, urban poor, and workers allied themselves within national social movements organised and led by NGOs and university intellectuals. It is in this context that trade unionism came to be transformed into a social movement that was integrated into broader popular-sector civil society groups and organisations (Deyo 2000; Deyo & Agartan 2003). The mutuality among these disparate groups flowed from increased unemployment, a growing perception of shared hardship under early crisis austerity budgets, a corresponding unity of focus on government agencies and polities rather than on employers, an increased consensus that the IMF and other multilateral institutions had imposed policies that only exacerbated the crisis, and a shared antipathy to foreign companies seen as taking advantage of the weakened position of domestic firms through acquisitions at bargain prices.[4] From the standpoint of organised labour, a traditional politics of production gave way to an emergent politics of collective consumption as various groups of workers converged on demands for expanded social protection by the state. Given these political, institutional, and mobilisational transformations, it is not surprising that the Democratic Party, which generally followed IMF and neoliberal precepts in dealing with the first year of crisis in 1997, was soundly defeated by an ostensibly more populist Thai Rak Thai party led by media communications mogul, Thaksin Shinawatra, in late-year elections. The new government, appealing to nationalist and popular-sector agitation, offered a broad panoply of social and small business assistance programs, including direct assistance to rural villages, public works programs, small and medium enterprise developmental promotion, and a national health program under which citizens would receive hospital care for a fee of only 30 baht.

From the standpoint of effective policy impact, the resurgent populist coalition of domestic business, nationalist intellectuals, farmers, workers, and urban poor was, in fact, largely dominated by the interests of domestic business (Brown & Hewison 2004), albeit within the constraints of continued economic dependency on foreign investment, increased crisis-induced public debt,[5] and the need to mobilise popular electoral support under democratic reforms.[6] While domestic business groups in Thailand, as elsewhere in the region, have sought with some success to modify, reject, or selectively adapt market reform in support of their strategic economic interests, major elements of reform policy relating to such key issues as trade and privatisation have themselves been institutionally insulated from political pressures from labour and other popular-sector groups through binding international trade agreements, the creation of independent (non-political) regulatory agencies, and a variety of legal provisions taking economic policy out of politics.[7] Such institutional ring-fencing of policy, alongside labour weakness, has eventuated in a deepened exclusion of labour from participation in policy-making, despite democratic reform. Thus, from the standpoint of labour, and apart from a few particular programs relating to health care, employment protection, and the like, the crisis probably brought little substantial gain to workers and none to organised labour per se. Of particular importance, the traditionally most powerful union segment, the state-owned enterprise sector, continues to operate under tight government restrictions (Brown & Hewison 2004).

CONCLUSION

To return to the central question guiding this chapter, it is clear that organised labour has not played a forceful role in the sociopolitical construction of the developmental labour systems through which enterprise and state elites have sought to further their economic strategies. In addition, organised labour's role has largely diminished over recent decades in response not only to political constraint, but also to economic structural changes associated with liberalising economic reforms and the introduction of new, more flexible production systems in manufacturing. Finally, the developmental sequencing and post-Fordist, world-system timing of development have further contributed to labour's continuing decline. Whether the politicisation of workers during Thailand's recent economic crisis will durably enhance labour's political role is still uncertain, although the likely scenario of heightened social mobilisation amid continued political exclusion foreshadows higher levels of class conflict than during pre-crisis years. Perhaps the most important outcome was the transformation of narrowly focused trade unionism among state enterprise and formal-sector workers into a more encompassing, politicised, social movement unionism.

Several political and developmental ramifications flow from the generally diminished role of South-East Asian labour. First, economic liberal reforms and recent industrial restructuring have been associated with a growing irrelevance and anachronism of state labour controls, increasingly supplanted by enterprise controls rooted in market discipline or co-optive participation, except in a few unrestructured sectors (for example, Thai state enterprises) where repressive controls[8] remain in place (Brown & Hewison 2004; Hutchison 1993:208). Second, the growing power of employers over workers at enterprise levels provides an opportunity for national governments to respond more fully to international demands for improved recognition of labour and human rights[9] without threatening economic growth or political stability. Third, it also provides a solution to the problem posed by the internal instability of authoritarian regimes under sustained economic development and the rapid expansion of a new middle class, in part by enhancing the prospects for democracy by reducing the likelihood that labour can exploit new political opportunities offered by parliamentary reforms. Alternatively stated, the structurally rooted exclusion of labour from democratic politics under regimes of exclusionary democracy has enhanced the usefulness to business of parliamentary institutions, thus creating a critical political base for those institutions.

But what are the implications of a labour-exclusionary path of development for the economic future of the region? In the short term, a relatively weak popular-sector role in economic policy processes (increasingly dominated by private firms) speeds development inasmuch as private firms and government agencies need attend but minimally to the social implications of their strategies. The longer term is less certain. Developmental sustainability requires, inter alia, a political base. Popular-sector exclusion fosters inequities and alienation among large segments of the population, thereby eroding this essential base and, in the long term, bringing increased resistance even to the democratic institutions increasingly favoured by elites.

Similar considerations apply to the sustainability of firm-level economic strategies as well. An absence of strong, politically protected unions, along with managerial human-resource policies that are oriented mainly towards cost cutting and static flexibility, have encouraged short-term opportunism at the expense of long-run organisational development. Where training and human-resource investments have been undertaken, they have not been accompanied by increased worker participation in production decisions, which is so essential to higher levels of organisational adaptability and innovation. Nor have they generally been accompanied by the commitment-enhancing labour policies that provide a motivational foundation for the success of such participation.

States can play an essential role in this regard by providing the collective goods that individual firms are unlikely to produce, and incentives and inducements for longer-term R&D, training, and organisational development on the part of firms. A good example of such an inducement is the use, in Singapore and Malaysia, of a skill development levy under which employers contribute to a general training fund, receiving back portions of that fund to be used only for approved employee training programs. Without such external pressures and support from unions (even if co-opted, as in Singapore) and governments, short-term cost cutting and static flexibility will characterise firm level strategies in much of the region, even as such strategies become ever more futile, given the rise of China and other lower cost exporters.

NOTES

1 Such data must, of course, be used with caution, given the unevenness of data collection and inconsistencies in definition.

2 International Labour Office, *Yearbook of Labour Statistics, 2003.*

3 This is a further reason for caution in that data on the small enterprise sector are especially prone to error.

4 Eva Bellin (2000) argues that economic reform, by undermining the bargaining position of labour, encourages unions to align themselves with the state, upon whom they must increasingly depend. This argument fails to recognise that economic reform is also generally associated with a distancing of the state from labour constituencies in favour of closer capital–state relations and a corresponding social reorientation of labour to broader popular sector movements and agendas.

5 Public debt, including IMF debt, is substantially greater in the Philippines and Indonesia than in Thailand or Malaysia (*Asianewsnet* 2005, based on the *CIA World Factbook*). This difference in part explains the greater policy independence of the latter two countries as they openly rejected or modified key elements of market-oriented policy reform sought by the international financial community during and after the economic crisis.

6 Thailand's new populist Constitution partly shields legislators from popular-sector groups through a controversial provision requiring a university education on the part of candidates for election to parliament

7 See Robison (2004:415) for discussion of similar outcomes in Indonesia.

8 The year 2000 State Enterprise Labour Relations Act now permits state-sector unions, but erects a number of restrictions on these unions (for example, forbidding strikes in essential services), prevents affiliation with private-sector unions, and offers no protections in case of privatisation (see Brown & Hewison 2004).

9 Recognising, again, the somewhat diminished importance of such pressures in the post-September 11 era.

REFERENCES

Amsden, Alice (1989) *Asia's New Giant: South Korea and Late Industrialisation*, New York: Oxford University Press.

Arudsothy, Ponniah and Craig R. Littler (1993) 'State Regulation and Union Fragmentation in Malaysia', in Stephen Frenkel (ed.) *Organised Labour in the Asia–Pacific Region*, Ithaca: ILR Press, pp. 107–32.

Asia Development Bank (2003) *Asian Development Outlook 2003*. Hong Kong: Oxford University Press.

Asia Monitor Resource Centre (2003) *Asia Pacific Labour Law Review: Workers Rights' for the New Century*, Hong Kong: Asia Monitor Resource Centre.

Asianewsnet (2005) <www.asianewsnet.net/countryprofile/table1_5.html>.

Begin, James P. (1995) 'Singapore's Industrial Relations System: Is It Congruent with Its Second Phase of Industrialisation?', in Stephen Frenkel and Jeffrey Harrod (eds) *Industrialisation and Labour Relations*, Ithaca: ILR Press, pp. 64–87.

Bellin, Eva (2000) 'Contingent Democrats: Industrialists, Labor, and Democratization in Late-Developing Countries', *World Politics* 52:175–205.

Brown, Andrew and Stephen Frenkel (1993) 'Union Unevenness and Insecurity in Thailand', in Stephen Frenkel (ed.) *Organised Labour in the Asia–Pacific Region*, Ithaca: ILR Press, pp. 82–106.

Brown, Andrew and Kevin Hewison (2004) 'Labour Politics in Thaksin's Thailand', *Working Papers Series,* No. *62,* Hong Kong: City University of Hong Kong.

Charoenloet, Voravidh (1993) 'Export-Oriented Industry in Thailand—Implications for Employment and Labour', in Arnold Wehmhoerner (ed.) *NIC's in Asia: A Challenge to Trade Unions*, Singapore: Friedrich-Ebert Stiftung Foundation, pp. 7–14.

Crouch, Harold (1993) 'Malaysia: Neither Authoritarian nor Democratic', in Kevin Hewison, Richard Robison and Garry Rodan (eds) *Southeast Asia in the 1990s*, Sydney: Allen & Unwin, pp. 133–58.

Deyo, Frederic (1989) *Beneath the Miracle: Labour Subordination in the New Asian Industrialism*, Berkeley: University of California Press.

——(1995) 'Human Resource Strategies and Industrial Restructuring in Thailand', in Stephen Frenkel and Jeffrey Harrod (eds) *Industrialisation and Labour Relations*, Ithaca: ILR Press, pp. 23–36.

——(ed.) (1996) *Social Reconstructions of the World Automobile Industry*, New York: St Martin's Press.

——(2000) 'Reform, Globalisation and Crisis: Reconstructing Thai Labour', *Journal of Industrial Relations*, 42 (2):258–74.

——and Richard Doner (2001) 'Dynamic Flexibility and Sectoral Governance in the Thai Auto Industry: The Enclave Problem', in Frederic Deyo, Richard Doner and Eric Hershberg (eds) *Economic Governance and the Challenge of Flexibility in East Asia*, New York: Rowman and Littlefield.

——and Agartan Kaan (2003) 'Markets, Workers and Economic Reform: Reconstructing East Asian Labor Systems', *Journal of International Affairs*, Fall: 55–80.

Hadiz, Vedi R. (1994) 'Challenging State Corporatism on the Labour Front: Working Class Politics in the 1990s', in David Bourchier and John Legge (eds) *Democracy in Indonesia, 1950s and 1990s*, Melbourne: Monash University, Monash papers on Southeast Asia no. 31, CSEAS, pp. 190–203.

Herzenberg, Stephen (1996) 'Regulatory Frameworks and Development in the North American Auto Industry', in Fredrick C. Deyo (ed.) *Social Reconstructions of the World Automobile Industry*, New York: St Martin's Press.

Hewison, Kevin (2005) 'Neo-liberalism and Domestic Capital: The Political Outcomes of the Economic Crisis in Thailand', *Journal of Development Studies* 41(2):310–30.

——and Andrew Brown (1994) 'Labour and Unions in an Industrialising Thailand: A Brief History', *Journal of Contemporary Asia*, 4:483–514.

——and Garry Rodan (1994) 'The Decline of the Left in Southeast Asia', in *The Socialist Register 1994*, London: Merlin Press, pp. 235–62.

Hutchison, Jane (1993) 'Class and State Power in the Philippines', in Kevin Hewison, Richard Robison and Garry Rodan (eds) *Southeast Asia in the 1990s*, Sydney: Allen & Unwin, pp. 191–212.

Ingleson, John (1981) 'Worker Consciousness and Labour Unions in Colonial Java', *Pacific Affairs*, 54(31):485–501.

International Labour Office (ILO) (1995) *World Employment 1995: An ILO Report*, Geneva: ILO.

——*Yearbook of Labour Statistics*, various issues, Geneva: ILO Press.

Kuruvilla, Sarosh (1994) 'Industrialisation Strategy and Industrial Relations Policy in Malaysia and the Philippines', Proceedings of the Forty-Sixth Annual Meeting of the Industrial Relations Research Association, Boston, 3–5 January.

——(1995) 'Industrialisation Strategy and Industrial Relations Policy in Malaysia', in Stephen Frenkel and Jeffrey Harrod (eds) *Industrialisation and Labour Relations*, Ithaca: ILR Press, pp. 37–63.

Lambert, Rob (1993) 'Authoritarian State Unionism in New Order Indonesia', *Asia Research Centre Working Paper Series,* No. 25, Perth: Murdoch University.

MacIntyre, Andrew (1994) 'Organising Interests: Corporatism in Indonesian Politics', *Asia Research Centre Working Paper Series,* No. 43, Perth: Murdoch University.

Ofreneo, Rene E. (1994) 'The Labour Market, Protective Labour Institutions, and Economic Growth in the Philippines', in Gerry Rodgers (ed.) *Workers, Institutions, and Economic Growth in Asia*, Geneva: International Institute for Labour Studies, pp. 255–301.

——(1995) 'The Changing Terrains for Trade Union Organising', unpublished manuscript, Quezon City: University of the Philippines, School of Labour and Industrial Relations.

Quintos, Paul (2003) 'A Century of Labour Rights and Wrongs in the Philippines', in *Asia Pacific Labour Law Review: Workers' Rights for the New Century*, Hong Kong: Asia Monitor Resource Centre, pp. 277–93.

Rasiah, Raja (1994) 'Flexible Production Systems and Local Machine Tool Subcontracting: The Case of Electronics Components Transnationals in Malaysia', *Cambridge Journal of Economics*, 18(3):279–98.

Robison, Richard (2004) 'Neoliberalism and the Future World: Markets and the End of Politics', *Critical Asian Studies* 36(3):405–32.

Somahsundaram (2003) 'Workers Rights in Malaysia' in Asia Monitor Resource Centre, *Asia Pacific Labour Law Review: Workers' Rights for the New Century*, Hong Kong: Asia Monitor Resource Centre, pp. 209–18.

Standing, Guy (1989) 'The Growth of External Labour Flexibility in a Nascent NIC: Malaysian Labour Flexibility Survey (MLFS)', *World Employment Programme, Research Working Paper* No. 35 (November) Geneva: ILO.

Turner, Lowell and Peter Auer (1996) 'A Diversity of New Work Organisation: Human-Centered, Lean and In-between', in Frederick C. Deyo (ed.) *Social Reconstructions of the World Automobile Industry*, New York: St Martin's Press, pp. 233–60.

United Nations (1998) *Statistical Yearbook 1997*, New York: United Nations.

World Bank (1995) *World Development Report 1995: Workers in an Integrating World*, Washington, DC: Oxford University Press.

——(2004) *World Development Report 2004*, Washington, DC: Oxford University Press.

——(2005) *World Development Report*, Oxford: Oxford University Press.

Wurfel, David (1959) 'Trade Union Development and Labour Relations Policy in the Philippines', *Industrial and Labour Relations Review*, 12 (4):582–608.

12 China and South-East Asia: The Political Economy of Production

Shaun Breslin

KEY TOPICS

INTRODUCTION

THERE has probably never been a time when relations with China have not been important for the nations of South-East Asia. Yet for much of the period since the establishment of the People's Republic of China (PRC) by the Chinese Communist Party (CCP) in 1949, students of the *political economy* of South-East Asia could more or less ignore China. It is true that perceptions of a potential Chinese challenge influenced the development strategies of individual regional states and played at least some role in fostering regional integration. However, security concerns dominated even these analyses—what was important were the consequences of China's potential security challenge, not economic relations with China itself.

Today, it is all but impossible to consider the political economy of either the individual states or the region as a whole without considering China, not only regional relations with China, but also what Chinese growth and China's position in the global economy means for the region. While some suggest a threat to regional development—and stability—and others point to the opportunities and benefits of a relationship with China, each shares an understanding that the region's future is inextricably linked with China's.

This chapter first briefly explains why security has been at the forefront of the majority of writings on regional relations with China. It also considers why ethnocultural interpretations gained credence in explaining how non-state actors established informal transnational economic relations between Chinese family businesses (CFBs). The chapter concludes by considering how changing attitudes towards multilateral regional cooperation have created a more conducive environment for establishing deeper economic integration between China and regional economies.

However, the main focus of this chapter is to consider the way in which regional economic relations with China are shaped by the way in which parts of the Chinese economy have been inserted into transnational 'commodity driven production networks' (Gereffi & Korzeniewicz 1993). Such a focus leads to an emphasis on relations with those sections of the Chinese economy in which foreign investment to produce exports dominates. To be sure, this is not all there is to the Chinese economy or to regional economic relations with China, but this focus allows us to move away from purely bilateral understandings of international economic relations and focus instead on how individual national economies, bilateral relations, and regional production structures are conditioned by global structures and processes.

EXPLAINING THE RELATIONSHIP

The security agenda

For most of the history of the PRC, analyses of relations with the region have been dominated by security studies—and with some good reason, given the security challenges that emanated from China. Events in Indochina might have presented the most immediate and sustained challenge to regional security, but the Taiwan Straits crisis of 1958,[1] the border war with India in 1962, and border conflicts with the Soviet Union in 1969 all had the potential to lead to wider regional, even global, conflict. Within the region, the CCP was at the very least an inspiration to Chin Peng's communists during the Malayan Emergency,[2] was accused of complicity in the failed 1965 coup in Indonesia, encouraged communists for a brief period during the Cultural Revolution (when radical Red Guards seized control of the foreign ministry's communications apparatus) across the region to rise up in revolution, and, in a brief and bloody war of 1979, invaded Vietnam to 'teach it a lesson'. The resulting tensions meant that normal diplomatic relations were not reestablished with Indonesia and Vietnam until as late as 1991, the same year that China and Brunei formally recognised each other, and a year after the first formal diplomatic relations were established with Singapore.

Even today, China remains at the heart of three of East Asia's most important security challenges. The days when China used military power to reinforce territorial claims in the Spratley and Paracel Islands may have been replaced by a more conciliatory diplomatic approach,[3] but the People's Liberation Army's (PLA) presence remains and many are convinced that China's ultimate aim is to control everything that happens in the South China Sea (Gertz 2005). The Chinese government also acts as a key mediator in disputes over North Korea's nuclear capabilities and ambitions. And, perhaps most important of all, China's promise to use military force to prevent the independence of Taiwan continues to provide the most credible potential cause of regional military conflict, which, should it come to pass, would have repercussions far beyond the Taiwan Straits.

Nor is it surprising that realist ontologies have dominated the study of China's international relations, however broadly defined.[4] China was never quite a wholly totalitarian state with all power concentrated in the hands of one person; while Mao's policy preferences often prevailed, the ideas and views of others in the party were important. Nevertheless, this was a system in which power was heavily concentrated in the hands of a relatively small number of party leaders who not only did a good job of convincing the rest of the world that power lay totally in Mao's hands for much of the 1950s, 1960s, and 1970s, but also controlled virtually every aspect of China's external affairs. When China's split with the Soviet Union resulted in closer cooperation with the US (and a subsequent realignment of China's relationships with all other states), any belief that Chinese foreign policy was driven by ideology was replaced by a new dominant understanding that pragmatic national interest lay at the heart of everything. With the post-Mao leadership abandoning even the pretence of an ideological foreign policy and instead emphasising the importance of protecting Chinese sovereignty in an ungoverned international system, the dominance of realist understandings has remained firm.

Culture and ethnicity

Despite the dominance of security as an issue and realism as an ontology in studying regional relations with China, there is also a relatively strong academic tradition that has looked beyond state-centred security approaches to consider the role of non-state actors in transnational economic relations in the region. Here, the emphasis is less on China as a country and more on the Chinese as an ethnic group. Indeed, initial analyses of the transnational economic relations of ethnic Chinese did not consider the PRC at all, but instead focused on the overseas Chinese—the *huaqiao*.

Cultural explanations became increasingly popular in the 1980s (Gong

& Jang 1998) as analysts sought to explain rapid economic growth across South-East Asia—or, perhaps more correctly, sought to explain how growth had been achieved despite the fact that the expected preconditions for growth in 'proper' capitalist states were not in place. The answer appears to be that there is something inherently different about the way that Chinese do business, with culture rather than capital providing the basis for growth.[5]

At the risk of oversimplification, the main argument is that Confucianism has instilled in the Chinese people the importance of 'working hard, respect for learning, harmony and family' (Cheung 2004:578). This is manifest in the creation of individual CFBs, which, despite being highly hierarchical, are characterised by consensus and a sense of working communally for the collective benefit.[6] The resulting business structure is usually characterised by flexibility and risk aversion where companies seek to maintain relatively high amounts of liquid capital and tend to diversify investments across a range of economic activities.

These individual businesses are tied to other CFBs to form networks of interconnected firms that are bound more by trust, personal loyalty, and shared principles than by legal structures. Indeed, for Hamilton (1991), it is often difficult to identify where individual firms in the network start and end as it is the individual and personal networks of relationships that matter, not formal and legal understandings of property rights and ownership. Even when it comes to finances, Chinese businesspeople favour 'kinship networks and communal affinities' based on trust rather than legally binding contracts and accredited financial institutions (Crawford 2000:76).

Cultural ties, so the argument goes, are more important than national political borders—what matters is the relationship, not the administrative jurisdiction. As such, transnational 'bamboo networks' (Huntington 1996:170; Weidenbaum & Hughes 1996) have emerged that span the region, creating a parallel form of economic integration. While some focus on the resulting integration of national economies (Peng 2000), others argue that these transnational ethnic ties undermine the significance of nation and state. Instead, there is a diasporic 'stateless economy' (Hamilton 1993), in which non-state transnational contacts are so important that they undermine the efficacy of using the nation as a unit of analysis and conceiving of states as the principle actors in international relations (Cheung 2004:674).

There is something of an emerging consensus in second generation studies of Chinese capitalism that is supported by sound empirical work that purely cultural approaches are far too simplistic. If this model of Confucian capitalism exists at all, it is in small, family-run convenience stores, not in large multinationals owned and/or run by ethnic Chinese (Yao 2002) where the organisation and governance of firms is structured by strong relationships with other non-Chinese companies, governments, and markets (Menkhoff & Sikorski 2002). In short, the structure of the domestic political economy is much more important than the ethnicity of the CEO (Jomo & Folk 2003).

Gomez and Hsiao (2003) even argue that, rather than cooperate, evidence suggests that Chinese firms tend to compete with each other and it is this competition, rather than collaboration, that has done so much to forge the success of CFBs.[7]

Yao (2002:3) argues that the concept of Confucian capitalism is a myth constructed to support specific political interests. At a rather esoteric level, it reinforces ideas about different forms of capitalism and development. At a more pragmatic and perhaps cynical level, regional states have deliberately equated ethnicity with class and constructed a notion that the Chinese are not only always economically successful (ignoring many examples of groups of very poor ethnic Chinese), but are also different and separate—a group that does not share its success with local people. In times of crisis, this has facilitated a displacement of hostility away from the regime onto the ethnic Chinese populations in Malaysia in 1969 and in Indonesia in 1998.

Chinese investment in China

While cultural approaches to understanding transnational economic relations have been questioned—to say the least—they have retained considerable purchase in some analyses of China's emergence as a major participant in the global economy. In particular, they have found a new audience in the search to explain why US and, to a lesser extent, European companies had fared relatively poorly in comparison to Asian companies in accessing the Chinese market. China was a difficult place to do business, but CFBs seemed to have little trouble in succeeding where non-Chinese failed. Quite apart from the advantage of speaking a common language, the emphasis is again on ties of loyalty, trust, and cultural understanding. Crucially, it is not just a matter of overseas Chinese businesses building relationships with counterpart businesses on the mainland, but, more importantly, establishing the type of contacts with government officials that non-Chinese cannot hope to emulate (Rauch & Trindade 2002). The CFBs, then, have extended their existing networks into China, gaining not only privileged access to the domestic Chinese economy, but through investing in China to produce exports to other markets, also profiting at the expense of Westerners from the huge growth of Chinese exports (Haley et al. 1998).

How convincing and useful are these cultural approaches for understanding the political economy of China's economic relations with South-East Asia? It would be churlish to deny the importance of connections or *guanxi* (relationships) for doing business in China—or doing business well—and to deny that ethnicity and language give the overseas Chinese an advantage in establishing these connections. It would also be churlish to deny that at least some overseas Chinese have invested in China to give something back to the motherland (and often their *laojia*—the place in China that the family originates from, no matter how long it is since they left). Furthermore, statistical evidence seems to lend considerable support to the importance of ethnicity. Eschewing the normal method of calculating statistics on a national basis and using ethnicity instead, Charles Wolf (2002:134) estimates that 'two-thirds [of all investment has] come from "overseas" Chinese'; Liu Huijun has a slightly higher figure of 70 per cent (Heartfield 2005:209).

Nevertheless, we need to exercise care in considering its importance in generating economic ties between South-East Asia and China for three main reasons. First, the majority of Chinese investment into China does not come from South-East Asia. In fact, a large part of it is not investment at all: it is money that is illicitly routed out of the PRC (primarily to Hong Kong) and then back in again to take advantage of the tax breaks and other incentives provided for foreign investment. Such round tripping accounts for at least one-quarter of all investment into China (Bhaskaran 2003), with Geng Xiao (2005:21) calculating that it might be as much as half of all foreign direct investment (FDI). Of the remaining Chinese investment, Taiwan and Hong Kong account for the overwhelming majority, with Singapore by far the largest provider of capital from South-East Asia.

Second, some of the literature gets close to creating the idea that it is precisely because of cultural affinity that economic relations develop. Quite simply, we should not overlook the profit motive. Hong Kong, for example, was the source of some of the earliest Chinese investment into China in the 1980s. In large part, this entailed businesses closing down factories in Hong Kong and opening new ones across the border in the special economic zones of Guangdong Province to take advantage of tax exemptions for investors, government help with start-up costs, and, most importantly, an oversupply of extremely cheap workers. Being able to speak the language and understanding Chinese business culture, as well as geographic proximity, might be important in easing the process, but making a profit—and a bigger profit than before—is still the bottom line. Third, as the following section suggests, we need to avoid taking too narrow a perspective of international economic relations and assuming that what comes from Asia starts in Asia.[8]

THE FALLACY OF BILATERALISM: THE POLITICAL ECONOMY OF PRODUCTION NETWORKS

In using economic statistics to build arguments relating to the political implications of economic relations, there is a tendency to concentrate on bilateral relationships. But the reality of global production does not fit into a neat, two-country framework of analysis. Production of a single good can be, and now often is, spread across a range of countries. The factories that were moved from Hong Kong to China were not just producing goods for Hong Kong companies, but often also for Hong Kong companies that were subcontracting for other companies based in Japan, Europe, and the US. The same was true for a large amount of the investment that subsequently came from

Taiwan, not least as Taiwanese companies relocated part of their production of hi-tech goods to China.

As these factories are relocated to China, trade patterns are also readjusted. Despite the increased use of Chinese inputs in foreign-funded exports in recent years, foreign investors still overwhelmingly use components and materials produced outside China in their Chinese factories. Although figures vary on a sector by sector basis, imported components typically account for over three-quarters of the value of goods exported from foreign investment factories in China, and can be much higher.[9]

Economic statistics designate a nationality and/or ethnicity to investment or trade that quite simply does not reflect the complexity of how goods are produced today. It might be that somebody who is ethnically Chinese signs the deal to open a factory in China, but this can represent the endpoint of a long chain of relationships that originate far from East Asia. As international economic statistics tend to show only one part of that chain—in this case the last part of the chain—they reveal only part of the set of dynamics at play. The figures show us a large amount of investment and exports from Chinese East Asia in particular and East Asia in general into China. As a result, there is a tendency to turn to either culture–ethnicity (Chinese capitalism) or geography (East Asian regionalisation) to explain what is going on.

These explanations are not irrelevant. One of the reasons that foreign businesses often work in China through intermediaries in places such as Hong Kong and Singapore is that these intermediaries in some ways market their cultural expertise. They sell themselves as having the contacts, experience, and knowledge that is needed to succeed in a complex and difficult Chinese business environment.[10] And, as shall be seen later, China's re-engagement with the global economy has created new economic relations in East Asia that have created new patterns of linkages between regional economies—economic regionalisation really is occurring. But while it is important to consider these issues, it should be remembered that they are largely local manifestations or consequences of wider global processes.

Let's take the production of personal computers as an example. In 2005, China became the world's biggest exporter of mobile phones, laptops, and printers, the overwhelming majority of which carry foreign brand names. Imported components are particularly important in hi-tech industries (which have been the biggest source of new investment since 2000) and, while there is considerable investment into China from Western companies, the majority of hi-tech related imports and investment comes from the region.[11] However, these regional economic relations are highly conditioned by extraregional relations.

On one level, the majority of Taiwanese brand name computer producers rely heavily on hardware and software that they license from US and Japanese companies. On another level, many leading companies have devolved the production of their computers to subcontractors in Asia. Dell, for example, now devotes its attentions to developing its brand name through marketing endeavours, leaving Flextronics in Singapore to take care of the production process.[12] If Flextronics builds a factory in China and then sources components from Malaysia, Thailand, or Taiwan, the investment and trade statistics will point to the importance of regional relations and perhaps even the role of Chineseness and cultural ties. But if we take a step back, we can see that the regional relationship is driven by Flextronics' relationship with a US-headquartered company and that company's decision to develop a new transnational production structure, a structure that is becoming increasingly common—and not only in high-tech industries.[13]

China and production networks: analytical implications

The first thing to note is that it is important to disaggregate what we mean by relations with China. This brief discussion of transnational production networks focuses on those internationalised sectors of the Chinese economy. But while the Chinese authorities have developed a remarkably liberal environment in order to encourage investment to produce exports, this has sat alongside a relatively closed and protected domestic market designed to protect existing producers from the potentially fatal challenge of international competition (Naughton 2000). Even though China's entry into the WTO has seen greater liberalisation of the domestic economy, producing in China to sell to China remains much more difficult than producing in China to sell exports in third markets.

Thus, any analysis of the economic relations with China should really be divided into two. When it comes to the domestic economy, including domestically funded Chinese enterprises that produce exports, then the state remains the primary focus of attention. To be sure, it is not just a case of assessing what the national government in Beijing says and does; on a practical, day-to-day level, it is often the relationship with local governments and with state-owned enterprises that is most important. But although there is not a single state interest, state actors (and the relationship between them) are still the major determinants of the relationship. At the very least, it is clear that the relationship is with China. But when it comes to internationalised sectors in which investment to produce exports dominates, not only does the conception of key actors become more complex, but also it is not even clear if the relationship is really with China.

In terms of actors, then, state actors clearly remain important. Had the post-Mao leadership not decided to place economic growth ahead of ideological conviction as the primary source of legitimacy for the CCP, then we would not be where we are today. Integrating China into the global economy has entailed the government creating the hard infrastructure (roads, ports, railways, buildings, telecommunications, etc.) and the soft infrastructure (changing fiscal policy, customs and excises, elements of monetary policy, ownership legislation, etc.) necessary to attract investment. State actors and overall government policy remain important—though in the internationalised economy, the significance of local government actors with devolved autonomy to conduct international economic relations is even more important than in the domestic economy. But while governments can create incentives to attract investment, it is non-state actors in the form of companies that make investment decisions.

Around 60 per cent of all Chinese exports are produced for foreign companies—they might carry the 'Made in China' stamp, but they also carry non-Chinese brand names. These goods are not only sold on foreign markets, but they are also produced with foreign finance and investment decisions informed by foreign demand, and contain high proportions of foreign materials and components. While a quick glance at the bilateral figures might suggest that most of this investment comes from Asia, this Asian investment is itself often predicated on subcontracting and network relations with non-regional companies. So, in many respects, regional economic relations with these internationalised sectors of the Chinese economy are not really relations with China at all—or, perhaps more correctly, they are not *just* relations with China.

China might run a trade surplus with the major world markets (the US, Japan and the EU), but, typically, runs a deficit with the region. Thus, it has been argued that the US trade deficit with China should really be considered as a deficit with those countries that supply China's export industries as well as with China alone—that is, a deficit with the region as a whole.[14] In other words, the trade deficits that the US previously ran with other economies in Asia have, as China has become a major production site, been aggregated into a single ballooning trade deficit with China (Ross 1997). Conversely, we can suggest that regional relations with China are, to some extent, at least a hidden relationship with other economies—or maybe we should ignore political boundaries and suggest that they are relations with a global capitalist division of production rather than with a national entity as such.

As will be discussed in detail in the next section, China's economic growth, not least the rapid growth of exports, has had a profound impact on the region. But care needs to be taken not simply to equate growth and importance with the oft-cited statement that China is the 'engine of economic growth'. From 1998 to 2003, domestic demand in China hardly grew at all; overall growth was maintained largely by continued high export growth.[15] As has been demonstrated, most of this export growth is doubly dependent on external economies—dependent on external supply of finances and imports that, in themselves, are dependent on continued external demand for finished goods. China appears to be not so much the engine of economic growth as the conduit through which other engines of the global economy are increasingly channelling production. If this is the case, suggestions that China is close to attaining the status of economic superpower might be a little premature.

China and production networks: practical implications

Through a combination of government policy and the evolution of transnational production networks, China's re-engagement with the global economy has led to the restructuring of individual economies in the region and in the wider regional economy as a whole. There has been considerable debate within and outside the region over whether China's rise is beneficial. For some, China provides a massive opportunity that will guarantee the economic future of the region. In the long term, China itself will provide a market for regional producers as the domestic economy expands. More immediately, the growth of China as an export economy provides opportunities for the region to act as a conduit between China and the global economy, and for regional producers to export components and raw materials.

The converse argument is that China's rise could damage local economies in three main, but interrelated, ways. First, cheap Chinese exports produced by Chinese companies could swamp not only the regional market, but also squeeze regional producers out of the US, Japanese, and European markets (Voon 1998). Second, domestic producers could move offshore to take advantage of an even lower-cost production site. Third, there is concern that foreign investment that might once have gone to Malaysia, Thailand, or Indonesia is instead going to China, diverting not just finances, but also jobs away from the region (Snitwongse 2003:38). In short, just as regional economies developed through investment-based investment, those 'same historical forces' are now threatening growth in the region as multinational corporations (MNCs) seek even more profitable production sites in China (Felker 2003:255).

So who is right? Fernald, Edison, and Loungani (1998:2–3) found no statistical evidence to support the claim that exports from the region as a whole have declined as Chinese exports increased. However, Holst and Weiss (2004) note that exports did fall to the two most important—and most lucrative—markets of the US and Japan as labour-intensive production moved to China. The Japan External Trade Organisation went even further in the process of disaggregation by considering the export of individual goods. These figures show that, in a wide range of sectors, the rise in exports from China to the US and Japan has coincided with a decline in exports of the same goods to the same markets from Malaysia, Thailand, Indonesia, and the Philippines (Hughes 1999). As Felker (2003:280) notes, while FDI into the region as a whole fell between 1996 and 2001, most of the reduction occurred in Indonesia alone—indeed, FDI actually increased in the rest of the region compared to 1990–95.

What this suggests is that it makes little sense to consider the impact of Chinese growth on the region as a whole. What matters is the position relative to China in the global division of production—in short, fulfilling different roles in transnational production means that Chinese growth can be beneficial, but competing at the same level as China is a problem. For Tongzon (2001) the clear lesson is that state elites need to adjust development policies and move out of areas where they are in direct competition with China and do it sooner rather than later. Indonesia and the Philippines have the closest export profile to China and are considered to be the most threatened by the transfer of production to an even later developer—or, more correctly, the livelihood of unskilled labourers competing with unskilled but even cheaper Chinese labourers are the most threatened (Ianchovichina et al. 2004).

The best strategy for those that can is to go for high-skill, higher value added stages of the production process. In Singapore, the emphasis has been on becoming a source of finance, not least by trying to attract MNCs to establish their regional headquarters in Singapore (Felker 2003). In this way, Singapore aims to act as a conduit between China and the global economy in much the same way—though on a smaller scale—that companies in Hong Kong play a bridging role between foreign investors and Chinese factories. In addition to finances and services, regional economies can also benefit through supplying China with higher-skilled, higher value added exports and/or raw materials to be used in processing assembly within China.

Both the nature and destination of Thai exports, for example, has changed. While the export of labour-intensive manufactured goods to the US, Europe, and Japan has stagnated and, in some sectors, fallen, exports of products, particularly technology intensive components, to China that are used in foreign-invested export industries have risen dramatically (World Bank 2003). Similarly, Malaysian exports to China have come to be dominated by electrical components, chemicals, machinery parts, and petroleum, and Indonesia's by raw materials such as processed oil, rubber, timber, and gas, all materials or components that are in high demand in China's export-oriented industries. China is, typically, now the third biggest export market for regional states after the US and Japan;[16] in the Malaysian case, exports to China have now exceeded exports to both Japan and the whole of industrial Europe.

For the least-developed states in the region (Vietnam, Cambodia, Laos, and Burma), the relationship with China is somewhat different. If they are participating in the global division of production at all, then these states are typically at lower levels than China itself, emphasising low—or no—skilled labour that is even cheaper than China's cheap labour. Just as production has moved from the region to China in recent years, scholars and officials in China have noted in interviews the danger that China might lose out if production moves again to Indochina in the future. Indeed, increasing amounts of investment are going from Taiwan to Vietnam, partly because the Taiwanese government has urged its businesses to 'Go South' rather than become totally embedded in China, but, more importantly, because labour and land costs in Vietnam mean to go south makes sound economic sense.

CHINESE OUTWARD INVESTMENT

There is another element to China's economic relationship with these and other regional states that—with only a few exceptions—has been largely overlooked in the academic literature.[17] While the majority of the literature on China and investment in the region focuses on China as the recipient of foreign capital, Chinese outward investment is becoming more significant. To be sure it is relatively small on a global scale, accounting for only 0.55 per cent of global FDI in 2005; it also remains dwarfed by the amount of investment that goes into China, but it is growing every year, nearly doubling in 2004 to reach US$5.5 billion,[18] making China the fifth biggest source of investment in Asia after Japan, Hong Kong, Taiwan, and Singapore.

Reconciling international trade and investment data is always a tricky process and there is almost always a gap between two countries' accounts of their bilateral relations. There are particular problems in the Chinese case, partly because China sometimes uses different accounting methods than its economic partners and partly because of disagreements over how to treat goods and money that transit through Hong Kong. We should also bear in mind that corruption and smuggling means that the Chinese authorities do not always know what is coming in and out of the country.[19] All this contributes to a situation in which other countries can—and do—claim that they are importing three times as much from China than China claims it is exporting to them.

But if anything, these trade discrepancies are minor statistical anomalies when compared to the problems of studying China's outward investment statistics. The United Nations Conference on Trade and Development's (UNCTAD's) figures for gross Chinese outward investment, for example, exceed those produced by the Chinese government by a factor of eight (Wu & Yeo 2002:117).[20] The discrepancy is, perhaps, partly explained by Chinese companies operating outside China (mainly in Hong Kong) investing overseas, and thus not appearing in the PRC figure. It might also be explained by the huge amounts of money that leave China illicitly each year. Quite simply, the full extent of this capital flight is unknown, but Gunter's (2004:74) estimate of US$923 billion from 1984–2004 (and half of the total from 1999–2004) is based on a sound methodology.[21]

Frost (2004) has done more than most to make sense of these conflicting statistics,[22] so, bearing in mind the constraints of statistical uncertainty, what general trends can be observed?[23] Over half of Chinese outward investment goes to Asia, with Hong Kong being by far the leading destination. This is followed by Thailand or Singapore (depending on which set of statistics are used), then, Malaysia and Indonesia. Investment in the Philippines, Vietnam, Cambodia, and Laos remains relatively low in the number and the value of projects, but in the last three cases is on the rise. Official statistics from both sides suggest that Chinese investment in Burma is insignificant; however, primary research by Oo uncovered significant Chinese economic interests in

Burma,[24] particularly, but not only, in real estate in the 1990s that did not appear to be showing up in official data. China has also been a key supplier of finances and arms to the Burmese army. As such, China's economic interests in, and impact on, Burma are probably much more significant than the official words of the Chinese and Burma governments suggest.

Notably, the exchanges with Burma that are recorded show the importance of subnational governments as actors in China's international economic relations. The desire to redress uneven development within China has provided an impulse to create new transnational economic relations across China's west and southwestern borders as part of the central government's 'Look West' strategy. But while this policy is sanctioned and facilitated by the government in Beijing, the provincial government of Yunnan Province has been a key actor in establishing trade and investment links with Burma. It has also played a key role in the much greater economic interests that China is building in the Greater Mekong Sub Region, with a particularly notable agglomeration of Yunnanese investment in Chiang Rai in Thailand (Frost 2004).

At the risk of oversimplification, four main types of overseas Chinese investment in the region can be identified. First, investment in Singapore in particular is largely based on attempts to buy into those higher levels of the production process that China currently lacks, particularly in business services. Second, since the late 1990s, investment in manufacturing capacity increased, particularly in Thailand and Cambodia, primarily in labour-intensive and low value-added projects. Third, investment in infrastructure projects has been an important part of supporting other priorities in the region by creating, for example, a land link between Yunnan and Thailand through investments in Laos (Storey 2005, p. 4).

Fourth, and perhaps in the long term most significant, China's investment policy (not just in the region) is, in large part, driven by resource requirements. Considerable international attention has been focused on the implications of increased Chinese demand for oil in particular. Returning to the discussion of the security agenda at the beginning of this chapter, it is not just that this could increase prices and distort distribution flows, but that there could be crucial political consequences. Bad-case scenarios see China increasing its influence and, ultimately, control over the South China Sea, and providing political and economic succour to dangerous authoritarian states. Worst-case scenarios point to the real danger of China's involvement in resource-based wars.[25]

The politics of oil already play a role in Chinese investment in the region and are likely to play a more significant role in the future. Quite apart from importing oil from Indonesia, if oil from the Middle East is not to go through US-dominated sea lanes, then they will have to go through South-East Asia. Chinese policy-makers have considered applying to build a canal in Thailand (to ensure that oil tankers do not have to pass through US-dominated sea lanes), but seem to favour an alternative that entails building a pipeline through Burma to Kunming in Yunnan Province (Lee 2005:286).

But there is much more to China's resource demands than just oil. According to official Chinese sources, one-third of all Chinese investment (not just in the region) is in extraction industries; it is even higher when refining is added. Indonesia has already become a key site of China's resource-based investment in oil, gas, and coal-based electricity generation (*China Daily* 30 July 2005); Vietnam, Laos, and the Philippines actively tout for Chinese investment in extraction and energy industries.

We should not get carried away. With the exception of Vietnam, China is still relatively low on the list of each country's table of leading investors and Chinese investment remains relatively minor. Nevertheless, in part at least because of China's position in global production networks, China's voracious appetite for resources suggests that outward investment in the region will become ever-more significant—and, hopefully, ever-more transparent and calculable—in the future.

BRINGING STATE ACTORS BACK IN

The example of China's increasing investment in resource-related industries brings a focus on the relationship between companies and the state. Although the non-state sector is now a major—some say the major—part of the Chinese economy,[26] large state-owned firms still dominate in resource and energy industries. While it is representatives of these industries who negotiate specific investment projects, they do not act independently of the state. Their actions have been prompted by government leaders, they need the state's financial help, and are often supported by government goodwill projects (cancelling debt, aid, trade agreements, and so on) (Zweig & Bi 2005:26).

Although this chapter has focused on how regional economic relations with China have been conditioned by wider global processes and the evolution of transnational production networks, it would be remiss not to finish by acknowledging that high politics and diplomacy are of great consequence. Even in an era of economic globalisation, what governments say and do remains important in shaping economic trajectories and what the Chinese government says and does remains more important than most.

Two key events have helped propel China into closer relations with the region as manifest by participation in the Chiang Mai Initiative, the ASEAN plus Three process, and the creation of the ASEAN China Free Trade Area. The first was the 1997 financial crises, which exposed to the Chinese leadership that China's own economic fortunes were increasingly influenced by what happens in the region. The crises generated new debates in China over the nature of economic security and how to guarantee it (Fewsmith 1999; Zha 1999), with increasingly working together at a regional level to head off potential crises being seen as serving China's own self-interest.

The second was the diplomatic consequences of September 11. While the rise of China remains a key concern for many in the region and within the US, almost overnight, China shed the unwanted position of the number one threat to the Pax Americana. In the following years, Chinese elites have done much to try to persuade those who matter in the region that they have nothing to fear from China—indeed, that closer relations with China are the best option for the future. At the 2003 Bo'ao Forum for Asia meeting, Zheng Bijian promoted the 'Peaceful Rise of China' thesis that has subsequently become a quasi-official ideology.[27] Rather than providing the threat to international security that some had predicted, instead, China's rise would not only be peaceful, but would actually act also as a positive force for peace. In addition, China's rise would provide the sort of economic benefits outlined in the above and be a positive force for development in the region (Ahn 2004).

Cheng (2004) and Hund (2003:402) explain this turn towards South-East Asia change in terms of pragmatic and practical national interest in the realist tradition. It is part of China's longstanding attempt to build a counterweight to US hegemony in the global political economy—to create a new pole, or at least to provide a bulwark against the power of the single hegemon in a unipolar world system and compete with both the US and Japan to become the dominant power in the region.

This is not to say that regional elites have somehow swooned at China's advances and been lured into a relationship based on false promises. Ramo (2004) argues that China's leaders do not really need to try to persuade—China's sheer size and rapid growth simply means that others have no choice but to fall into line with their policy preferences. Others suggest a more positive and proactive approach. Heartfield (2005:197) argues that China's rise has been widely welcomed because it has at least taken the sting out of the regional impact of recession in Japan, while Shambaugh (2004–05:76) claims that the best way of dealing with China 'is to entangle the dragon in as many ways as possible'. But even if there is disagreement over why the relationship is developing, there is a growing consensus that a closer relationship with China is all but an inevitable component of ASEAN's future.

CONCLUSION

China's closer relationship with ASEAN reminds us of the multilevel nature of the political economy of regional relations with China. Government dialogue and negotiations at the regional and bilateral levels clearly remain important components of the relationship. Nor is it just national governments that are important; the role of local government has been a significant component in the evolution of China's international economic relations.

Dealing with the Chinese government is also an important feature of the relationship between regional non-state economic actors and China. While it is getting easier for outsiders to produce and sell in China, it is still not easy. Getting the necessary formal approval can still be a long and arduous process, and even when all the right papers are stamped in the right places, a good relationship with the relevant local government is still essential to ensure that other, less formal processes and procedures do not get in the way of making a profit. Assuming that the Chinese authorities continue to liberalise the domestic economy, the potentials and pitfalls of accessing the Chinese market are likely to become increasingly important. But even with liberalisation, it is likely that central and local governments will continue to play a crucial role in regulating the domestic economy for the foreseeable future.

Bilateral relations are important; so, too, are academic analyses that focus on how two countries and/or economies interact; however, considerations of bilateral relations should not be blinkered and should not ignore how that specific relationship fits into, and, indeed, is shaped by, wider global processes. Part of the reason that this chapter has focused on regional relations with China's foreign invested export industries is because it remains the most important driver of the relationship. It is also because this focus illuminates the extent to which the bilateral relationship is just a part of a much longer chain of relationships.

We might, for example, look at a specific bilateral relationship, let's say a Malaysian export to China. If we just look at the bilateral, we might consider the way that intergovernmental dialogue over trade makes it easier and cheaper to get the good into China, or perhaps the implications for Malaysian workers of rising exports to China—and quite rightly so. But this bilateral relationship can be part of and also conditioned by a contracting deal between a US and Taiwanese company, the Taiwanese contractor's sourcing of other components and raw materials from Japan, Thailand, India, Australia, or elsewhere, the use of a Hong Kong intermediary to invest the money in a Chinese factory on behalf of the contractor, and, ultimately, consumer demand in the US, Japan, and the EU. In some respect, the Malaysian export to China is a hidden export to Taiwan (the home of the subcontractor), or perhaps to the US (the home of the company that initiated the production process in the first place). Given that production does not work on a neat, two-country basis, it is important to develop frameworks of analysis that recognise the complexities of the global political economy.

The language of international relations typically refers to the state as the unit of analysis—'China thinks', 'China says', 'China wants'. This language is frequently echoed in analyses of international economic relations—'China dominates in the production of', 'China leads the way in exports of', 'China is the leading producer of'—which feeds into understandings of China's rising economic power. But, as we have seen, assigning a nationality to an export based on the place that it was finally put together tells us nothing about who or what actually produced it, or who or what gained most from its production. The world is not static; the position of Chinese industries in global production will change. Nevertheless, for the time being, Chinese economic power is often overstated, as dominant frameworks of analysis attempt to assign a nationality to power instead of focusing on the role of transnational networks of companies (typically, with their headquarters in the US, Europe, and Japan) that play the leading role in deciding not only what is produced, but also how it's produced and where it's produced.

NOTES

1 China continued to shell offshore islands that were under Taiwanese–Kuomintang (KMT) control on and off (with care not to provoke a war) until 1979.
2 Though there is considerable conflict over the extent to which the Malayan Communist Party (MCP) really followed Maoist principles of guerrilla warfare within the MCP itself and between the MCP and the CCP.
3 China signed the Declaration on the Conduct of Parties in the South China Sea in 2002 and joined the ASEAN Treaty of Amity and Co-operation in South-East Asia the following year.
4 Realism assumes that international relations are conducted solely by rational state actors seeking to maximise the national interest; there is no role for non-state actors such as multinational companies. Realist theorists are not particularly interested in domestic politics; their focus is on politics between states, rather than within states. In addition, the search for security and power maximisation rather than domestic ideologies and/or power configurations drives state actors' actions. States may claim to be acting for other reasons (for example, the promotion of human rights or the advancement of revolutionary ideology), but will only really act if in doing so promotes the national interest and ensures national security. For an accessible introduction to realism and other international relations theories, see Brown with Ainley (2005).
5 While the idea of Confucian capitalism has become relatively widespread, it is probably still most associated with the work of Redding (1990, 1991).
6 Some also suggest that Confucianism leads to an acceptance of authoritarianism that has also had a beneficial impact on development; see Gong and Jang (1998: 84–6).
7 Bardsley (2003) and Buckley (2004) argue that, while networks of CFBs do exist, they are a consequence of ethnic Chinese being discriminated against by colonial and post-colonial governments in the region. Denied access to finances, contracts, and markets, the CFBs were forced to depend on each other out of necessity rather than simply out of cultural affinity.
8 I have discussed this in more detail in Breslin (2004a, b, 2005a, b, c).
9 Figures provided by the China Association of Enterprises with Foreign Investment.
10 Although at least two US-based firms use intermediaries to create a degree of separation between themselves and low-wage sweatshop production.
11 Nokia, for example, dominates the domestic Chinese mobile phone market; it also uses China as a production base for exports to other markets.
12 Flextronics has its origins in the US, but has its headquarters in Singapore.
13 For more details on the creation of transnational production networks, particularly in high-tech industries, see Borrus and Zysman (1997), Chen (2002), Felker (2003), Gereffi and Korzeniewicz (1993), Luthje (2002), and Sturgeon (1997).
14 According to Chinese sources, if you trace all the chains back to their origins, over half of Chinese exports to the US are actually produced by US-based companies. As such, the US trade deficit with China is, in some ways, a deficit with itself.
15 With the key exception of demand for automobiles.
16 Including re-exports to Hong Kong and then into China.
17 In addition to the work cited below, see also Frost, Hewison and Pandita (2001), Wu and Chen (2001), and Wong and Chan (2003).
18 Compared to inward investment of US$60.63 billion, a 13 per cent increase on 2003 *People's Daily* 2005.

19 The central government in Beijing does not always trust its own data, suspecting that local officials who collect and report statistics manipulate what they tell Beijing for their own interests.

20 As Frost (2004:10) points out, nor does it help when a single Chinese source seems to indicate that investment from Yunnan Province is actually higher than investment from all of China in Thailand.

21 Yang and Tyers (2000:5) suggest that, despite the massive amount of FDI into China, there was actually a net outflow of capital between 1996 and 1998 in the order of US$30 billion.

22 Including Frost's web resource, *Asian Labour News*, <www.asianlabour.org/>, where he archives relevant news stories.

23 This section also draws on Ping Deng (2004), research conducted by the Singapore Ministry of Trade (Wu and Yeo 2002), and various news briefs from the official *People's Daily*.

24 Sadly, Koko Oo died before the completion of his PhD on China's impact on Burma's development.

25 For a good accessible overview of the possible implications of China's demand for resources in general, see Zweig and Bi (2005). For the specific implications of China's oil diplomacy, see Lee (2005).

26 Interpretations of the size and importance of the non-state sector vary, depending on whether township and village enterprises (TVEs) are considered to be state-owned. In addition, the legal status of an enterprise can be somewhat different from the reality of its relationship with the state. But most analysts would now suggest that the non-state sectors, including TVEs, now generate the majority of Chinese output.

27 Zheng is chairman of the China Reform Group, an independent (or, as independent as can be in China) think tank based in Beijing. He has had a long career as an official CCP theoretician in the Central Party School and the Ministry of Propaganda. For a more academic explanation of his ideas, see Zheng (2005).

REFERENCES

Ahn, Byung-Joon (2004) 'The Rise of China and the Future of East Asian Integration', *Asia Pacific Review*, 11(2):18–35.

Bardsley, Alex (2003) 'The Politics of "Seeing Chinese" and the Evolution of a Chinese Idiom of Business', in K. S. Jomo and Brian Folk (eds) *Ethnic Business: Chinese Capitalism in South-East Asia*, London: Routledge, pp. 25–61.

Bhaskaran, M. (2003) *China as Potential Superpower: Regional Responses*, Berlin: Deutsche Bank.

Borrus, Michael and John Zysman (1997) 'Wintelism and the Changing Terms of Global Competition: Prototype of the Future?', *Berkeley Roundtable on International Economy Working Paper no. 96b*, Berkeley: Berkeley Roundtable on the International Economy.

Breslin, Shaun (2004a) 'Greater China and the Political Economy of Regionalisation', *East Asia: An International Journal*, 21(1):7–23.

——(2004b) 'China in the Asian Economy, in Barry Buzan and Rosemary Foot (eds), *Does China Matter? A Reassessment*, London: Routledge, pp. 107–23.

——(2005a) 'Power and Production: Rethinking China's Global Economic Role', *Review of International Studies*, vol. 31(4):735–53.

——(2005b) 'China and the Political Economy of Global Engagement', in Richard Stubbs and Geoffrey Underhill (eds) *Political Economy And The Changing Global Order*, 3rd edn, Ontario: Oxford University Press, pp. 465–77.

——(2005c) 'China's Trade Policy', in Dominic Kelly and Wyn Grant (eds) *The Politics of International Trade in the 21st Century: Actors, Issues and Regional Dynamics*, Basingstoke: Palgrave, pp. 346–66.

Brown, Chris, with Kirsten Ainley (2005) *Understanding International Relations*, 3rd edn, Basingstoke: Palgrave.

Buckley, Peter (2004) 'Asian Network Firms: An Analytical Framework', *Asia Pacific Business Review*, 10(3/4):254–71.

Chen Shin-Hong (2002) 'Global production networks and information technology: The case of Taiwan', *Industry and Innovation*, 9(3):249–65.

Cheng, Joseph (2004) 'The ASEAN–China Free Trade Area: Genesis and Implications', *Australian Journal of International Affairs*, 58(2):257–77.

Cheung, Gordon (2004) 'Chinese Diaspora as a Virtual Nation: Interactive Roles between Economic and Social Capital', *Political Studies*, 52(4):664–84

China Daily (2005) 'Sino–Indonesian Deals Inked', *China Daily*, 30 July.

Crawford, Darryl (2000) 'Chinese Capitalism: Cultures, the South-East Asian Region and Economic Globalisation', *Third World Quarterly*, 21(1):69– 86.

Felker, Greg (2003) 'South-East Asian industrialisation and the changing global production system', *Third World Quarterly*, 24(2):255–82.

Fernald, John, Hali Edison, and Prakash Loungani, (1998) 'Was China the First Domino? Assessing Links between China and the Rest of Emerging Asia', *Board of Governors of the Federal Reserve System International Finance Discussion Paper, No. 604*, Washington, DC: US Federal Reserve.

Fewsmith, Joseph (1999) 'China in 1998: Tacking to Stay the Course', *Asian Survey*, 39(1): 99–113.

Frost, Steven (2004) 'Chinese outward direct investment in Southeast Asia: How big are the flows and what does it mean for the region?', *Pacific Review*, 17 (3): 323–340.

Frost, Steven, Kevin Hewison, and S. Pandita, (2002) 'The Implications for Labour of China's Direct Investment in Cambodia', *Asian Perspectives*, 26(4):201–26.

Geng Xiao (2005) 'Round-Tripping Foreign Direct Investment in the People's Republic of China: Scale, Causes and Implications', *ADB Institute Research Paper*, No. 58, Tokyo: Asian Development Bank Institute.

Gereffi, Gary, and Miguel Korzeniewicz (eds) (1993) *Commodity Chains and Global Capitalism*, Westport: Praeger.

Gertz, Bill (2005) 'China Builds up Strategic Sea Lanes', *Washington Times*, 18 January.

Gomez, Terence, and Hsin-Huang Michael Hsiao (eds) (2003) *Chinese Enterprise, Transnationalism and Identity*, London: Routledge.

Gong Yooshik and Jang Wonho (1998) 'Culture and Development: Reassessing Cultural Explanations on Asian Economic Development', *Development and Society*, 27(1): 77–97.

Gunter, Frank (2004) 'Capital flight from China: 1984–2001', *China Economic Review*, 15(1):63–85.

Haley, George, Tan Chin Tiong and Haley Usher (1998) *The New Asian Emperors: The Overseas Chinese, Their Strategies and Competitive Advantages*, Burlington: Butterworth–Heinemann.

Hamilton, Gary (1991) 'The organizational foundations of Western and Chinese commerce: a historical and comparative analysis', in Gary Hamilton (ed) *Business Networks and Economic Development in East and Southeast Asia*, Hong Kong: University of Hong Kong, Centre for Asian Studies, pp. 43–57.

——(1993) 'Stateless Economies: The Case of Overseas Chinese Capitalism', *The 1990 Institute Issue Paper nos 7–2*, Burlingame: The 1990 Institute.

Heartfield, James (2005) 'China's Comprador Capitalism Is Coming Home', *Review of Radical Political Economics*, 37(2):196–214.

Holst, David and Weiss, John (2004) 'ASEAN and China: Export Rivals or Partners in Regional Growth?', *World Economy*, 27(8):1255–74.

Hughes, Christopher W. (1999) 'Japanese Policy and the East Asian Currency Crisis: Abject

Defeat or Quiet Victory?', *Centre for the Study of Globalisation and Regionalisation Working Paper*, No. 24, Coventry: Warwick University.

Hund, Markus (2003) 'ASEAN Plus Three: towards a new age of pan-East Asian regionalism? A skeptic's appraisal', *Pacific Review*, 16(3):383–417.

Huntington, Samuel (1996) *The Clash of Civilizations and the Remaking of World Order*, New York: Simon and Schuster.

Ianchovichina, Elena, Sethaput Suthiwart-Nevueput and Min Zhao (2004) 'Regional Impact of China's WTO Accession', in Kathie Krumm and Homi Kharas (eds) *East Asia Integrates: A Trade Policy Agenda for Shared Growth*, Washington: World Bank, pp. 57–78.

Jomo, K. S. and Brian Folk (eds) (2003) *Ethnic Business: Chinese Capitalism in South-East Asia*, London: Routledge.

Lee, Pak (2005) 'China's quest for oil security: oil (wars) in the pipeline?', *Pacific Review*, 18(2):265–301.

Luthje, Boy (2002) 'Electronics Contract Manufacturing: Global Production and the International Division of Labor in the Age of the Internet', *Industry and Innovation*, 9(3): 227–47.

Menkhoff, Thomas and Douglas Sikorski (2002) 'Asia's Chinese Entrepreneurs, Between Myth Making and Regeneration' in Thomas Menkhoff and Solvay Gerke (eds), *Chinese Entrepreneurship and Asian Business Networks*, London: Routledge, pp. 23–42.

Naughton, Barry (2000) 'China's Trade Regime at the end of the 1990s', in Ted Carpenter and James A. Dorn (eds) *China's Future: Constructive Partner or Emerging Threat?* Washington, DC: Cato Institute, pp. 235–60

Peng Dajin (2000) 'Ethnic Chinese Business Networks and the Asia–Pacific Economic Integration', *African and Asian Studies*, 35(2):229–50.

People's Daily (2005) 'China's overseas investment totals 5.5 billion US dollars in 2004', 2 September.

Ping Deng (2004) 'Outward investment by Chinese MNCs: Motivations and implications', *Business Horizons*, 47(3):8–16.

Ramo, Joshua Cooper (2004) *The Beijing Consensus: Notes on the New Physics of Chinese Power*, London: The Foreign Policy Centre.

Rauch, James and Victor Trindade (2002) 'Ethnic Chinese Networks in International Trade', *Review of Economics and Statistics*, 84(1):116–130.

Redding, S. Gordon (1991) 'Weak Organizations and Strong Linkages. Managerial Ideology and Chinese Family Business Networks', in Gary Hamilton (ed.) *Business Networks and Economic Development in East and Southeast Asia*, Hong Kong: Centre for Asian Studies, University of Hong Kong.

——(1990) *The Spirit of Chinese Capitalism*, Berlin: Walter de Gruyter.

Ross, Robert S. (1997) 'Why Our Hard-liners are Wrong', *The National Interest*, 49:42–51.

Shambaugh, David (2004–05) 'China Engages Asia: Reshaping the Regional Order', *International Security*, 29(3):64–99

Snitwongse, Kusuma (2003) 'A New World Order in East Asia?', *Asia–Pacific Review*, 10(2): 36–51.

Storey, Ian (2005) 'China and Vietnam's Tug of War Over Laos', *Jamestown Foundation China Brief*, 5(13):3–5.

Sturgeon, Timothy (1997) 'Does Manufacturing Still Matter? The Organizational Delinking of Production from Innovation', *Berkeley Roundtable on International Economy Working Paper*, No. 92b, Berkeley: Berkeley Roundtable on the International Economy.

Tongzon, J. (2001) 'China's Membership of the World Trade Organization (WTO) and the Exports of Developing Economies of East Asia: A Computable General Equilibrium Approach', *Applied Economics*, 33(15):143–59.

Voon, Jay P. (1998) 'Export Competitiveness of China and ASEAN in the US Market', *ASEAN Economic Bulletin*, 14(3):273–91.

Weidenbaum, Murray and Samuel Hughes (1996) *The Bamboo Network: How Expatriate Chinese Entrepreneurs Are Creating a New Economic Superpower in Asia*, New York: Simon and Schuster.

Wolf, Charles (2002) *Straddling Economics and Politics: Cross-Cutting Issues in Asia, the United States, and the Global Economy*, Santa Monica: Rand.

Wong, John and Sarah Chan (2003) 'China's Outward Direct Investment: Expanding World-wide', *China: An International Journal*, 1(2):273–301.

World Bank (2003) *Thailand Economic Monitor*, <www.worldbank.or.th/monitor/economic/2003may.shtml>.

Wu, Friedrich and Han Sia Yeo (2002) *China's Rising Investment in South-East Asia: How ASEAN and Singapore Can Benefit?*, Singapore: Ministry of Trade and Industry.

Wu Hsiu-Ling and Chen Chien-Hsu (2001) 'An Assessment of Outward Foreign Direct Investment from China's Transitional Economy', *Europe–Asia Studies*, 53(8):1235–54.

Yang Yongzheng and Rod Tyers (2000) 'Weathering the Asian Crisis: The Role of China', ANU Asia Pacific School of Economics and Management Working Paper, No. 00-1, <http://ncdsnet.anu.edu.au/pdf/china/cp00-1.pdf>

Yao Souchou (2002) *Confucian Capitalism: Discourse, Practice and the Myth of Chinese Enterprise*, London: Routledge.

Zha Daojiong (1999) 'Chinese Considerations of "Economic Security"', *Journal of Chinese Political Science*, 5(1):69–87.

Zheng Bijian (2005) 'China's "Peaceful Rise" to Great-Power Status', *Foreign Affairs*, 84(5): 18–24.

Zweig David and Jianhai Bi (2005) 'China's Global Hunt for Energy', *Foreign Affairs*, 84(5): 25–38.

INDEX